H. Goering Co
Confederates

City Costs Up Sharply Furlong Says

Budget Director Finds Department Estimates Higher

Costs of Waterbury's governmental operations for 1947 will increase sharply, paralleling the current general cost-of-living increases, City Budget Director Arnold E. Furlong today told The Democrat.

Mr. Furlong will submit the first of the individual deparmental budgets to the Finance Board for review at the meeting scheduled for 4 P. M. tomorrow. The city's 1946 estimated Grand List will also be submitted at that time.

Salary increases for all city employes will comprise the bulk of the overall budgetary increases, with costs of materials and maintenance the next highest contributory factor, Mr. Furlong said.

Inflationary Cycle

"While we regret the necessity for such rising costs, conditions make it imperative that we meet such orderly demands as salary increases for employes," the budget director said.

"City employes, after all, must trade in the same markets and purchase the same goods as do industrial workers to maintain a standard of living," he added.

Tax authorities have predicted a potential doubling of governmental costs such as followed the post-war period of World War I when costs, during the years 1918-24 went from $30 to $60 per capita.

Because of increased salaries, particularly the $300 cost-of-living increase, now a permanent part of salaries of city employes, the city's share of the employes pension fund will increase approximately $50,000. This year the city allotted $380,000 as its share of maintaining the pension fund.

"That is clear example of the cycle of inflationary costs," Mr. Furlong said.

Materials Increase

"Cost of materials for new structures, maintenance of facilities and replacement of equipment is our

Plastic Mobile Boosts 'Red Feather' Drive

Mrs. Ruth Canfield, director of publicity for the Community Chest campaign, supervises the installation of photographs and posters describing the services offered by the 27 Red Feather agencies in a trailer located in front of City Hall this morning. The 26-foot plastic mobile freight trailer was donated to the Community Chest by the Trailm bile Company of Meriden Road. It will be kept front of City Hall for two days. In addition to t photographs, neon signs will be installed in t trailer to attract public attention.

Slaughtering at Municipa
Abattoir Reported Highe

Byrnes Says Yugoslavia To Sign Italian Treaty

100 Cattle, 30 Lambs Killed, Readied for Sa

Nearly 100 slaughtered cattle 300 lambs were waiting at

...y Democrat

City
Edition

...aterbury, Conn. Under the Act of March 3, 1879)

...CONN., WEDNESDAY, OCTOBER 16, 1946 ★ SIXTEEN PAGES PRICE 4 CENTS

...mmits Suicide;
...Die on Gallows

...Where Did Goering Get Cyanide?

Answer Sought By Authorities At Nuernberg

...Nuernberg, Oct. 16—UP) —A three-man U. S. Army ...ard opened an investiga- ...on today of how Hermann ...oering managed to cheat ...e hangman by gulping poi- ...n just before 10 fellow ...azis marched to the gallows ...the parade he was sup- ...sed to lead.

There were indications ...at unidentified persons who ...ight know where and when ...oering got his vial of potas- ...um cyanide were being ...lled in for questioning by ...e Army board.

...A spokesman for the Nuernb...r ...en commandant's office wh...n ...k...d if Frau Emmy Goering w...re ...spected of giving Goering the ...ison when she visited him last ... "As far as I am concerned, Mrs. ...ering is in the clear."

Bodies Spirited Secretly

Through the secrecy which the ...my maintained over the hanging ...the Nazi chieftains, signs were ...en that soon after they died in ...e dark hours after midnight, their ...dies were spirited secretly to ...atever disposal the Allies plan- ...d to avoid establishing any ...rines" for fanatics.

Just before dawn two closed and ...vered trucks sped away from a ...ck gate of the prison. Lacking ...ficial confirmation, the possibility ...as seen that they carried the ...dies.

Maj. Frederick Teich, operations ...ficer for the commandant's office ...uld say only that he was "not ...a position to say" whether bodies ...d been taken from Nuernberg. None of the bodies not even

Dramatic to End

HERMANN GOERING

Jackson Says Goering
Missed Martyr's Role

Washington, Oct. 16. (UP)— Supreme Court Justice Robert H. Jackson said today that Hermann Goering's suicide was ...ness of his whole life—cunning and crafty, always outwitting somebody, bullying and coward- ly—

No. 2 Nazi Takes Vial Of Poison

Escapes Hanging Less Than Two Hours Before Walk

Nuernberg Prison, Oct. 16 —(UP)—Ten surviving lead- ers of Adolf Hitler's Third Reich died on the gallows in the chill, dark hours after midnight today, but Hermann Goering, the eleventh Nazi condemned to pay with his life for crimes against the world cheated the noose by taking poison.

Shortly before dawn, at ...:40 A. M. (11:00 P. M. EST, T...sday) two closed and c...vered tr...ks were seen speeding from a rear ...e of the Nuernb...g Prison. It was ...s...ble that they were transporting the ...ven dead Nazis to secr...b...ial places but no of- ficial announcement was made on disposition of the bodies.

Less than two hours before Goer- ing was scheduled to lead the band of surviving Nazi leaders to the im- provised gallows erected in the Nuernberg Prison gymnasium a se- curity guard heard the prisoner make "a strange noise".

Investigation Under Way

The cell was instantly opened and Goering was found dead, a crushed vial of potassium cyanide between his teeth. The hour was 10:45 P. M. (4:45 P. M. EST Tuesday). Imme- diate investigation was started to determine how Goering had ob- tained the poison vial and placed it between his teeth under the scru- tiny of a guard charged with never taking his eyes off the prisoner.

How Goering had succeeded in what prison officials believed was a million to one chance of taking his life was not clear. He had gone to bed early.

GOERING'S SUICIDE:
'They Will Not Hang Me!'

GOERING'S SUICIDE:
'They Will Not Hang Me!'

Paul Hooley MBE

FRONTLINE BOOKS

First published in Great Britain in 2026 by
Frontline Books
An imprint of Pen & Sword Books Limited
Yorkshire – Philadelphia

A CIP catalogue record for this book is
available from the British Library.

Typeset by Mac Style
Printed in the UK by CPI Group (UK) Ltd, Croydon, CR0 4YY.

The Publisher's authorised representative in the EU for
product safety is Authorised Rep Compliance Ltd., Ground
Floor, 71 Lower Baggot Street, Dublin D02 P593, Ireland.
www.arccompliance.com

For a complete list of Pen & Sword titles please contact:

PEN & SWORD BOOKS LIMITED
47 Church Street, Barnsley, South Yorkshire, S70 2AS, England
E-mail: enquiries@pen-and-sword.co.uk
Website: www.pen-and-sword.co.uk
or
PEN AND SWORD BOOKS
1950 Lawrence Road, Havertown, PA 19083, USA
E-mail: uspen-and-sword@casematepublishers.com
Website: www.penandswordbooks.com

DEDICATED TO THE MEMORY OF
MY BELOVED WIFE HELEN

Also by Paul Hooley

Nuremberg's Voice of Doom

The Undercover Nazi Hunter

From Lockington to Gillingham

One Foot In The Grave

The Warrens and the Foots

CONTENTS

LIST OF ILLUSTRATIONS

Lives Remembered (Section Nine)

SELECTED QUOTATIONS

'A No. 2 man who knew nothing of the excesses of the Gestapo which he created, and never suspected the Jewish extermination program although he was the signer of over a score of decrees which instituted the persecutions of that race.'

Robert H. Jackson, U. S. Chief of Counsel, International Military Tribunal, describing Hermann Goering in his Closing Argument for the Conviction of Nazi War Criminals – 26 July 1946

'There was no way Goering could escape death … But he could "die like a man" after a full confession.'

General William 'Wild Bill' Donovan, in a 'private' meeting with Goering on 6 November 1945

'If Goering had his own teeth, why was he talking like a toothless person? My God, I thought because he was concealing something in his mouth.'

Captain Wolfe Frank, Nuremberg's Voice of Doom, Paul Hooley, Frontline/ Pen & Sword Books 2018

'They all speak with a Nazi double talk with which to deceive the unwary. In the Nazi dictionary of sardonic euphemisms "Final solution" of the Jewish problem was a phrase which meant extermination; "Special treatment" of prisoners of war meant killing; "Protective custody" meant concentration camp; "Duty labor" meant slave labor; and an order to "take a firm attitude" or "take positive measures" meant to act with unrestrained savagery.'

The Closing Arguments for Conviction of Nazi War Criminals, Robert H. Jackson, U. S. Chief of Counsel, IMT (Robert H. Jackson Centre December 26, 1946, Temple Law Quarterly 85)

'Goering called me to the prisoner's dock. Smirking and rubbing his hands … "Doctor, you were wonderful. I am so glad you quoted the old German proverb to these people – "The Nuernbergers hang no one before they really have them"... Only a person who had a secret or a surprise in store could have made this remark in such a situation.'

Dr Frederrich Bergold, Defence Solicitor to Martin Bormann (convicted in abstentia) referring to a conversation of 22 July he had had in court with Goering – 16 October 1946

' ... a dead man came in – a grotesque, self-destroyed remnant of a man who had once been destined to rule Nazi Germany. It was Hermann Wilhelm Goering ... the body of what was once the great marshal of the Reich, chief of the Luftwaffe and bearer of a dozen other titles. He had succeeded in wrecking plans of the Allied Control Council to have him lead the parade of condemned chieftains to death on the gallows ... The face of this 20th Century freebooting political racketeer was still contorted with the pain of his last agonising moments and his final gesture of defiance.'

Kingsbury Smith, Representing the Combined American Press, The Washington Evening Star, 16 October 1946

'No half-century ever witnessed slaughter on such a scale, such cruelties and inhumanities, such wholesale deportations of peoples into slavery, such annihilations of minorities ... The large and varied role of Goering was half militarist and half gangster. He stuck a pudgy finger in every pie ... He was, next to Hitler, the man who tied the activities of all the defendants together in a common effort.'

Closing speech of Justice Robert Jackson, US Chief Prosecutor at the IMT – 26 July 1946

'General Donovan was the sort of guy who thought nothing about parachuting into France, blowing up a bridge, pissing into Luftwaffe gas tanks, then dancing with a German spy on the roof of the St. Regis Hotel.'

Film Director Captain John Ford, referring to his commanding officer, General William 'Wild Bill' Donovan, first and only Director of the Office of Strategic Services (OSS) – forerunner of the CIA 'the D-day offensive would not have been successful without the Office of Strategic Services, nor would millions of Jews be alive today were it not for the countless acts of heroism by OSS agents that will doubtless go untold.'

Hon. Jack H. McDonald of Michigan, speaking in the House of Representatives, US Senate Congressional Record, *8 June 1971*

'Would that I might be shot! However, executing the German Reichsmarschall by hanging cannot be countenanced. I cannot permit this for Germany's sake. Besides, I have no more obligation to subject myself to punishment from my enemies. Therefore I elect to die as the great Hannibal did.'

Hermann Goering, in a suicide letter he left to the Allied Control Council – 15 October 1946

'I could scarcely repress a laugh. The old rascal had got away with it.'

Major Airey Neave, on hearing the news of Goering's suicide in October 1946 – Nuremberg – A Personal Record of the Trial of the Major Nazi War Criminals in 1945–6

The old Teutonic drums were beating strong in the sunlight. There were no German tears, no German regrets or shame. On the contrary, the Germans now had the feeling of triumph which they had lacked so long. Goering's one sharp, breath-taking act wiped away ten months of painstaking work.

John Stanton, Time *Magazine 28 October 1946*

INTRODUCTION

'I did not go looking for this narrative – it found me!'
PAUL HOOLEY

THE INFORMATION REVEALED AND PUBLISHED within this book will, I hope, be seen to be of historical importance. I also hope it will be accepted as being the conclusive answer to a conundrum that has, in equal measures, intrigued and frustrated historians, commentators and the public at large for the past eighty years.

Revolving, as it does, around a moment of great significance at the end of the Second World War, *GOERING'S SUICIDE: 'They Will Not Hang Me!'* chronicles events that occurred in Nuremberg during the crucial eight week period in the autumn of 1945 that immediately preceded the start of the International Military Tribunal (IMT)[1] – the trial of twenty-four leaders of Nazi Germany who had planned, carried out, or otherwise participated in the Holocaust[2] and other war crimes. I believe this narrative provides the definitive explanation of how Reichsmarschall[3] Hermann Goering, Adolf Hitler's deputy and the most senior Nazi on trial, obtained the capsule of potassium cyanide poison that allowed him, at the eleventh hour: to cheat the hangman; die a martyr; and humiliate the Allies.[4]

The question of how Goering obtained the poison has been: a recurring subject of conjecture; an official investigation; several reviews; intense debates; several theories; many books and articles; and several dramatisations and documentaries. The majority of these could only come up with 'possible' scenarios, or with conclusions that have not satisfied a large number of historians who have studied this subject – including Ann and John Tusa who, in their highly regarded book *The Nuremberg Trial*, echo the thoughts of many with their comment 'No explanation is very convincing; none is backed by any proof.'[5]

The answer was in fact unfathomable without knowledge of key information contained within statements made by two military personnel who, late in their lives, revealed they had been present during that history-defining moment of 1945. These hugely important utterances – one of which is now being divulged for the first time – when brought together, and in conjunction with established as well as more recently published records and the results of my investigations, provide crucial details and explanations that had been unavailable to, or had been overlooked by, previous investigators. These long-withheld revelations only came to light during casual meetings that had taken place in 2003 and 2019 respectively.

The disclosures made by the first of the two former war-time officers, during an interview he gave in 2003, are as astounding as they are unequivocal – yet it seems they have never been fully scrutinised until now and, as with the man who made them, they have not been afforded the levels of investigation, respect and credibility they deserve.

The revelations of the second officer have never been published before, or even discussed beyond a small group of close and trusted friends with whom he had shared a secret during his final days. That knowledge was passed on to me by the last surviving member of the group during a chance meeting we had in 2019. What was divulged astonished me and proved to be the catalyst for this book.

Once I had established a strong link between the two men, the streams of information that emerged needed to be investigated, analysed and, where possible, verified – both separately and in parallel. They then needed to be considered alongside, and as part of, the vast amount of existing evidence regarding this matter that is already widely acknowledged. Piecing together the separate and conjoined involvements of the former officers as part of an accepted wider scenario proved to be the key that unlocked the mystery surrounding the epic event.

GOERING'S SUICIDE: 'They Will Not Hang Me!' aims to show that no more than six US/British officers knew what took place on the day Germany's Reichsmarschall received the cyanide capsule that later allowed him to exit this world, in the eyes of his legions of followers, a martyr and a hero who lifted the spirits of a defeated nation in its darkest hours – the very departure the Allies were so desperate to avoid.

Four of those men took any secrets they possessed with them to their graves, while the other two only revealed their involvements during the final periods of their lives.

The Road to Discovery

As had happened on a previous occasion, my coming into possession of crucial unpublished information provided a unique and unexpected opportunity to take on a task I consider to be of considerable importance and value. It has ultimately brought me satisfaction and a feeling of achievement. Encouraged by an equally enthusiastic publisher (Frontline/Pen & Sword Books) it is therefore with a mixture of pleasure and trepidation that I present this work. Pleasure, in the final result of all my searching and in being able to bring details of historic importance to the attention of a wider audience; and trepidation, in view of the scrutiny that will be given to this work and because my findings suggest a different conclusion to one that may have previously been accepted, albeit with reservations, by others who have studied and written about these matters.

My journey had started a few years earlier when a friend, retired panel beater and paint sprayer Mike Dilliway, in the course of moving home, rediscovered six to eight cardboard boxes, a number of files and two briefcases crammed full of assorted documents and photographs that he had squirrelled away and had not thought about for over a quarter of a century.

Mike had inherited this cache (in 1988) from Wolfe Frank, a man he had befriended in the Wiltshire village of Mere – where Wolfe lived and Mike worked. Not realising quite what he had or what to do with the documents, Mike had placed them in his attic for safe keeping.

During the course of some of the conversations the friends had over the years, Wolfe had mentioned that prior to the Second World War he had been involved in an underground resistance movement in Germany before escaping to England in 1937. He had also indicated he had been an interpreter and interrogator at the Nuremberg trials of Nazi war criminals and that he had once been a successful journalist and businessman. Illness and some unfortunate incidents in both his professional and his personal life had, however, by 1988, reduced Wolfe's life to a low ebb – both physically and financially – and this had led to him taking his own life.

In 2015, needing to make a decision on what to do with Wolfe's collection of papers, Mike asked me (as a writer he knew who had an interest in historical and military matters) if I would take a look at the material to see if there was anything there that might be of importance.

After two years of sorting, re-sorting, cataloguing, assessing, researching, sequencing, checking and editing several thousand pages of data, and then obtaining many confirmations, I had a comprehensive picture of the life of Wolfe Frank who had, in fact, been Chief Interpreter at the Nuremberg Trials prior to becoming an intrepid investigative journalist for the *New York Herald Tribune* (*NYHT*). So important were my discoveries I knew by the end of my research, that I had to share the knowledge I had acquired – not only with military historians but also with a much wider audience. This led to the publication of firstly *Nuremberg's Voice of Doom*[6] and secondly *The Undercover Nazi Hunter*.[7]

It was following the launch of these books that I came into possession of the further knowledge contained within this book – knowledge that I am not alone in thinking should also be recorded for posterity.

Standing on the Shoulders of Respected Historians

I am acutely aware of the months, and in some cases years, of painstaking research and skilful analysis and writing contributed by many respected journalists, authors and historians who have, over the past eighty years, studied these matters and published their own thoughts and conclusions – that include highly relevant and important evidence and information – much of which remains valid and forms an essential part of this now extended narrative.

With admiration and respect I have read (or watched) their work – none of which is in anyway wasted, discarded or changed – other than the conclusions that might have been reached or reluctantly accepted – and there is room for some of the theories and suspects previously identified to have played a, albeit less prominent, role in Goering's suicide.

I especially praise the work of: Mark Felton, who has examined and written extensively on this matter and who has produced an excellent documentary that is available on YouTube[8]; biographer and historian Joseph E. Persico in his book *Nuremberg;* and the late Ben E. Swearingen, who dedicated so much of his life to studying and writing about this subject. I only wish I could have shared my discoveries with Ben during his lifetime and thanked him for all the valuable evidence he uncovered and published. The best I can do is to acknowledge his contributions, salute his memory and recommend his superbly researched book *The Mystery of Hermann Goering's Suicide*[9] – which Persico refers to as being 'an admirable work of historical detection invaluable to anyone writing on this subject' – I can vouch for that.

In the Acknowledgements (Section Twelve), I record my sincere thanks to others who have helped make this book possible. There are however two authors to whom I am particularly indebted and to whom I draw your attention. They are: Douglas Waller, who has given me permission to reproduce extracts from his best-selling, meticulously researched biography of General William Donovan – *Wild Bill Donovan* (FreePress); and Petronella Wyatt who has allowed me to include, in its entirety, an article she wrote that was published in the 1 February 2003 edition of *The Spectator*, of which Ms Wyatt was at that time the deputy editor. Both these works contain crucial evidence that is essential to this narrative and confirms some of my own beliefs and/or findings. I am therefore most grateful to both authors and their publishers. (For bibliographic information regarding Mr Waller, Ms Wyatt and their publishers please see Chapter Forty One).

To Assist the Reader

At the end of each chapter, I have added notes and references to clarify certain matters and to add further and better particulars that I feel are essential pieces of evidence that need to be shown – to explain my findings or to confirm any assumptions I might have reached. There are also some notes included to assist the reader to better understand certain situations. Unless they appear as part of official documents or titles the anglicised versions of 'Nuremberg', 'Goering' and 'Fuehrer' (instead of Nürnberg, Göring and Führer) have been used.

I hope and believe historians, students, linguists and those interested in military matters will find *GOERING'S SUICIDE: 'They Will Not Hang Me!'* to be an important addition to what is already known about the demise of Germany's Reichsmarschall. However, I feel this book will also appeal to a much wider audience that is not so well versed in the trials and/or the terminology used. If I seem therefore at times to be 'teaching grandmothers to suck eggs' it is only to assist those who may be less familiar with some of the historical events, references and jargon used, or to more clearly explain or expand upon the context being described. For these reasons, I hope the well-informed will appreciate why certain information, such as that presented in Chapter Four, has been included.

For the same reason I have included several pages (Plates 1 to 8), first used in *Nuremberg's Voice of Doom*, that I believe will be of further assistance to readers. These pages show: a plan of the courtroom at the Palace of Justice in Nuremberg; the names and positions of the principals involved in the IMT; brief details and a photographic image of each of the defendants; who sat where; and a short-form chart recording the counts, verdicts and sentences of the court. (I have also included, at Appendix H, details of *Courtroom 600* – an excellent on-line, free to use, easy to follow, learning resource for those who would like to learn more about the Nazis and the trials of the war criminals).

There are, at crucial points in the narrative, certain passages, or evidence, that are repeated. I have done this intentionally – for continuity and to save readers time in looking back, or breaking their concentration – I hope this will be found to be helpful.

Having uncovered the hidden solution to one of the 20th century's great unsolved mysteries, I feel duty bound to share my findings with as wide an audience as possible – hence this book. By the same order, in *GOERING'S SUICIDE: 'They Will Not Hang Me!'* my prime intention is to provide, not only a definitive record of what I firmly believe really happened in this ultimate case of assisted suicide, but also sufficient evidence to dispel doubts that might linger in the mind of anyone who may start out as being a sceptic needing to be convinced.

In writing this book, I put myself in the position of such a person and acted as my own 'Devil's Advocate.' I asked myself every question I felt a sceptic might ask. Every piece of evidence I uncovered, every twist and turn I came across and every fact I felt needed substantiating I poured over again and again, before checking with other sources. Eventually I was satisfied I had found enough evidence, verifications and corroborations to advance my belief in the integrity of admissions made by two brave and honourable men who had revealed, during the last phases of their lives, a secret they did not wish to take with them to their graves.

INTRODUCTION – NOTES & REFERENCES

1. The International Military Tribunal was the first and most high profile of The Nuremberg Trials – see Chapter Five.

2. Holocaust – The systematic state-sponsored killing of six million Jewish men, women and children and millions of others by Nazi Germany and its collaborators during the Second World War.

3. Reichsmarschall – Marshal of the Reich (Empire or Realm) – was the highest rank in the Wehrmacht (the unified armed forces of Nazi Germany). Hermann Goering was the only man promoted to the position by Adolf Hitler (in July 1940). This made Goering senior to all other Wehrmacht commanders and confirmed his position as Hitler's designated successor.

4. The Allies were those countries led, during the Second World War, by Britain, USA, France, Australia and Russia who were opposed to the Axis Powers – the coalition headed by Germany, Italy and Japan.

5. *The Nuremberg Trial*, Ann Tusa and John Tusa, p.484.

6. *Nuremberg's Voice of Doom* – see Appendix G.

7. *The Undercover Nazi Hunter* – see Appendix G.

8. *Hermann Göring's Mysterious Death*, Mark Felton – https://www.youtube.com/watch?v=2IMhFW7539s

9. *The Mystery of Hermann Goering's Suicide*, Ben E. Swearingen.

SECTION ONE

SETTING THE SCENE

MORE GRIPPING THAN FICTION

A real life 'Inverted Detective Story'
RICHARD AUSTIN FREEMAN[1]

WHEN COMPILING BOOKS SUCH AS *Nuremberg's Voice of Doom* (NVOD) and *The Undercover Nazi Hunter* (UNH) – as with all works referred to within this volume – we authors draw together all available new and established evidence which we then thoroughly test, and where possible have tested by others, against known facts, respected opinions and presumptions. When satisfied with the accuracy and integrity of our discoveries we then commit to paper what we believe to be the most accurate and honest record or theory based upon all our findings and any established and accepted views and general conclusions.

Some conclusions of course cannot always become final facts as previously unknown evidence can come to light that may change heretofore held beliefs and explanations, or may challenge historians to at least ponder other possibilities that may emerge.

This book, based on newly discovered information that emerged following the publication of the first editions of *NVOD* and *UNH*, falls into that category and, in view of what I am now about to disclose, I invite other writers and historians to seriously consider the following narrative which presents a new perspective, on one of the 20th century's most enduring and frustrating unsolved mysteries. These revelations also provide, I believe, a more cogent conclusion to a conundrum that stunned the world in 1946 and has vexed historians ever since – how did Hermann Goering, Adolf Hitler's deputy and the most senior Nazi on trial at the international war crimes trials in Nuremberg, obtain the poison that, literally at the eleventh hour, allowed him to take his own life?

Uncovering the evidence and revealing those who: commissioned; were directly or indirectly involved in; carried out; or bore witnesses to; an event that shocked the world, has been like: playing the role of a detective; solving a real life drama; and uncovering or eliminating suspects and evidence; in the fashion of an 'inverted detective story.'

Invented in 1912 by author R. Austin Freeman[1] and popularised by the television series *Columbo*[2], the structure of an inverted detective story starts by showing a crime being committed before describing the detective's attempts to solve the mystery, revealing the identities of the perpetrators and clearing up subsidiary puzzles, such as any backstories and why the crime was committed.

In his 1924 essay *The Art of the Detective Story*, Freeman described the genre and his intentions perfectly:

> The reader had seen the crime committed, knew all about the criminal, and was in possession of all the facts. It would have seemed that there was nothing left to tell, but I calculated that the reader would be so occupied with the crime that he would overlook the evidence. And so it turned out. The second part, which described the investigation of the crime, had to most readers the effect of new matter.[3]

All that follows is the real life inverted detective story of how Hermann Goering – Head of the Luftwaffe, founder of the Gestapo and Hitler's designated deputy – obtained the cyanide capsule that allowed him to cheat the hangman and turn the humiliating 'death by the rope' showpiece finale the Allies had planned for him into a final triumph for the 'Architect of the Holocaust.'

CHAPTER ONE – NOTES & REFERENCES

1. Dr. Richard Austin Freeman MRCS LSA (11 April 1862 – 28 September 1943) was a British writer of detective stories featuring the medico-legal forensic investigator Dr. Thorndyke.

2. *Columbo* is an American crime drama television series, written by Richard Levinson and William Link and starring Peter Falk, that popularised the 'inverted detective story' format.

3. *The Art of the Detective Story*, R. Austin Freeman: http://gaslight-lit.s3-website. ca-central-1.amazonaws.com/gaslight/detcritF.htm

THE CATALYST

'A journey of a thousand miles begins with a single step'
CHINESE PROVERB

SINCE THE LAUNCH OF *NVOD* AND *UNH,* I have given a series of lectures, interviews and broadcasts and have carried out a number of book signing assignments. These brought me into contact with several people who had known Wolfe Frank. They furnished me with further anecdotes about the man many believe should be counted amongst the most interesting, courageous, romantic and charismatic figures of the 20th century.

Chief amongst the providers of new information was a lady of standing and impeccable character who on several occasions was happy to talk to me about Wolfe and to sign, as true records, transcripts of the notes I had taken at our meetings. Because of earlier unwanted intrusions in her life (touched upon below) and her advancing years, this very private person prefers to have her identity protected. I shall therefore refer to her as 'Charlotte.'[1]

Having said that, like me and Mike Dilliway (Wolfe's close friend and the man who inherited his archive) Charlotte believes it is important to record all the known details about Frank and his involvements at Nuremberg – including and especially those which until now she, perhaps alone, possessed.

Charlotte knew Wolfe extremely well in his later years, to the extent that he had asked her to become the sixth Mrs Frank – a proposal she felt obliged to decline. However, they remained good friends and Charlotte was able to help Frank in a number of practical ways, increasingly so as his illnesses became progressively debilitating.

Following Frank's suicide, Charlotte was visited by a man (late at night and in her own home) who informed her he was a police officer. He insisted upon an immediate and lengthy interview. Soon after, she was approached by newspaper and television journalists seeking information. Charlotte also learned that Wolfe's home had been broken into and searched. It is not known if anything was taken, and Wiltshire Police have no record of the intrusion or of any of their officers carrying out interviews or investigations concerning Frank. This raises the possibility that Charlotte's late-night visitor was from a police force outside Wiltshire or from one of the intelligence agencies.

Major Humphrey Sykes

In another incident, having learned of Frank's demise, a retired army Major, Humphrey Sykes[2], travelled down from Scotland with the sole intention of searching through Wolfe's papers – and here it is necessary to briefly deviate from Charlotte's narrative to explain a linked incident and to ask the question: had Frank and Sykes been involved with one or other of the British intelligence agencies? (see Appendix A for a separate discussion on this possibility).

As is recorded in his memoirs, Frank had first met Major Sykes and his wife in February 1937, while he was on holiday in Italy with his fiancé Baroness Maditta von Skrbensky[3]. Because of his ancestry (his father and grandparents were Jewish), Frank was prohibited from marrying an Aryan lady, particularly one of noble descent, in Germany or in any other Axis-aligned country.

Despite having only just met, Major Sykes arranged for Frank and Maditta to: travel to England – by separate routes; stay at his home on the Army base at Tidworth in Wiltshire; and be married at Andover Registry Office (on 12th April 1937).

Four days later Frank returned to Germany to be told by a friend in the Gestapo that the authorities were aware of his activities as a resistance worker and that he was to be interviewed in Dachau concentration camp the following morning.

Frank managed to escape in the nick of time, just before less friendly members of the Gestapo arrived to arrest him. He fled to Switzerland where Sykes sent money for his passage to England. Sykes then allowed Frank to live with him at his home in Tidworth.

After a short period of integration, during which he learned English, Sykes appointed Frank to be the CEO of several of his companies and he introduced him to: many acquaintances in society and the theatre; friends at Scotland Yard; and members of both houses of Parliament. Sykes also arranged for Frank to work with a development scheme in Cape Canaveral and advised him how to completely disassociate himself from his former homeland to become 'a stateless person.'

During Frank's period of internment as an 'enemy alien' (along with all other former German and Austrian citizens), he and Sykes engaged with a number of parliamentary members and camp officials. This eventually led to Frank's release and to him joining the British Army where he gained a commission and rose to the rank of captain.

Sykes may of course have just taken a fraternal or comradely interest in Frank or he may simply have acted as a Good Samaritan. However following Frank's death Sykes, by then retired, made his journey down from Scotland in search of Frank's papers – some of which were sensitive documents that Frank should not have had. Mike Dilliway, the beneficiary of Wolfe's estate, was careful not to let Sykes see Frank's memoirs, however, the former army major did leave with a number of other files, at least some of which, no doubt, pertained to the army, Nuremberg and Frank's undercover operation in 'Cold-War Germany,' for the *New York Herald Tribune* (see Appendix G).

Among all the many documents in Frank's archives, and apart from what he had written in his manuscript and a single photograph, there is not one record of his service in the British Army – no discharge papers; identification, medical or grade cards; service record; pay book; certificate of transfer to reserve; or any other document connecting him to his years of service, or to Humphrey Sykes with whom he was particularly close.

(To add to this intrigue, Charlotte, who acted as Frank's PA, undertook manuscript and other typing duties, and she was instructed by Frank to destroy many documents and photographs relating to his past).

Returning to Charlotte's Testimony …

Of great importance to matters concerning Goering's suicide, Charlotte recalls lengthy conversations Wolfe had in her presence with various trusted mutual friends – some of whom had a military background[4]. The group often talked late into the night with guests questioning Frank about his resistance work, his escape to England and his role as 'The Voice of Doom'. Of particular interest to these gatherings were his encounters with Goering who, on the fateful day of judgement (1 October 1946), had heard directly from Frank that his sentence was to be 'death by the rope'. It was also decreed by the IMT that the Reichsmarschall would be the first of the eleven war criminals so sentenced to walk to the gallows at midnight on 16 October. Less than two hours before his execution was due to take place however, Goering took his own life by ingesting poison – one of the guards designated to constantly watch him saw Goering beginning to choke. By the time a medic arrived he was dead. Glass shards and traces of cyanide were found in his mouth. The capsule had been concealed in a modified brass cartridge case that was retrieved at the scene (see Plate 23).

Charlotte is very clear that, following Frank's death in 1988, she was present on further occasions when those who had taken part in the late night discussion groups openly opined they believed, from what they had heard from him, that Frank had been a witness to the passing of the cyanide capsule to Goering[4].

I was intrigued by the possibility that, late in his life, Frank had made such an admission, and the revelation, from a lady of Charlotte's standing, needed to be taken seriously. I had stored the information away and thought little more about the matter until I came across an interview, also given a few months before his death, by Edwin Putzell, the former Executive Officer of the Office of Strategic Services (OSS) – the Second World War's largest and most powerful intelligence agency – in which he openly admitted he had: at the behest of his commanding officer; with the support of the 'British contingent'; and in the presence of a witness; passed the cyanide to Goering.

Immediately an alert started ringing. Was it possible, I wondered, that the confessions of two men with no apparent connections in two different countries at two different times were referring to the same incident? Could they have known each other? Could they have worked together? Were they interrogating Goering during the same period prior to the start of the IMT, and was it possible for Frank to have been the witness to whom Putzell was referring?

The answer to all these questions was an emphatic 'yes'. It was more than possible – and so, figuratively speaking, began my 'journey of a thousand miles.'

CHAPTER TWO – NOTES & REFERENCES

1. During our discussions 'Charlotte' and I realised our paths had crossed before – during the time she had, for many years, held a position of considerable trust and importance within the City of London. I, as one of the Corporation's preferred suppliers, printed documents that Charlotte had personally prepared. Her role within the Corporation demanded high levels of diplomacy and attention to detail. I saw that at first hand when developing work she had originated. This had to be exact, especially on those projects she undertook to ensure the smooth running of state occasions such as banquets. Charlotte's reliability, tact, organisational skills, knowledge and integrity were major factors in the success of those events.

2. Humphrey Hugh Sykes was born in Shrewsbury, Shropshire in 1907. He was the son of Major Herbert Rushton Sykes and Hon. Constance Harriet Georgina Skeffington. He married, firstly, Grizel Sophie, daughter of Air Vice-Marshal Sir Norman Duckworth Kerr MacEwen, in 1936 – from whom he was divorced in 1948. He married, secondly, Muriel Hooper, daughter of Colonel John Charles

Hermann Goering (above) spent twelve hours in the witness box at the International Military Tribunal. Wolfe Frank (below, centre) spent nine of those hours interpreting what was being said.

Plate 1

COURTROOM LAYOUT AT NUREMBERG
For the IMT of Nazi War Criminals (Goering et al.)
35 (a)
35 (b)
35 (c)
35 (d)
36
38
37
33
23
8
32
22
7
47
31
21
34
34
34
30
20
6
29
19
40
39
1
42
18
28
17
2
27
16
3
47
26
15
31
31
25
14
4
24
13
41
5
9
10
11
12
13
46
PRESS
45
44
GALLERY

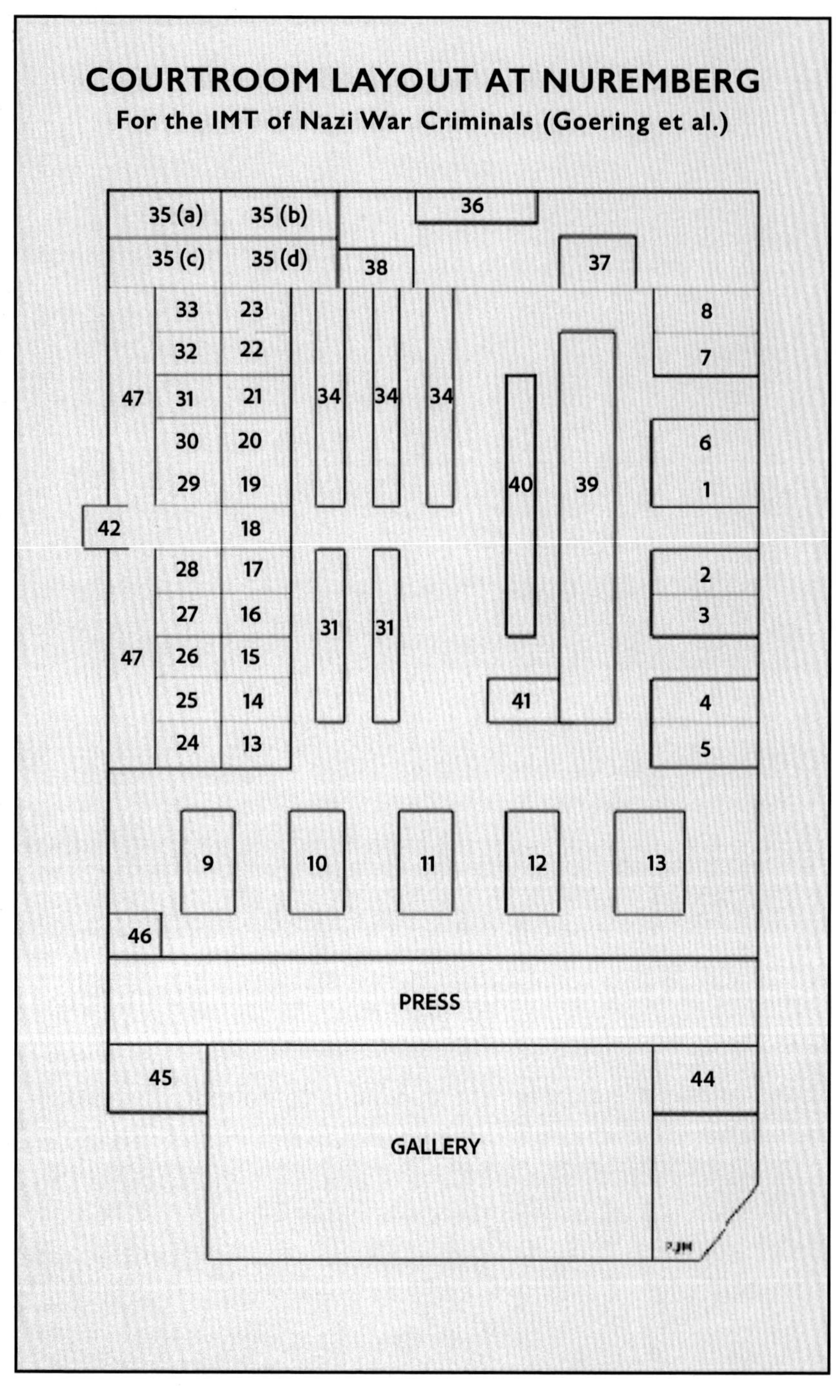

Plate 2

KEY TO THE COURTROOM

THE TRIBUNAL

1. Lord Justice Lawrence, *British Member, President*
2. Mr. Francis Biddle, *United States Member*
3. Judge John J. Parker, *United States Alternate Member*
4. Professor Donnedieu de Vabres, *French Member*
5. M. Robert Falco, *French Alternative Member*
6. Mr. Justice Birkett, *British Alternate Member*
7. Major General Iola T. Nikitchenko, *Russian Member*
8. Lt.-Col. Alexander F. Volchkov, *Russian Alternate Member*

PROSECUTORS

9. France – *Led by:* M. Francois de Menthon
10. Russia – *Led by:* Lieutenant-General Roman A. Rudenko
11. United States – *Led by:* Mr. Justice Robert H. Jackson
12. British – *Led by:* Sir Hartley Shawcross, KC

DEFENDANTS

13. Hermann Goering
14. Rudolf Hess
15. Joachim von Ribbentrop
16. Wilhelm Keitel
17. Ernst Kaltenbrunner
18. Alfred Rosenberg
19. Hans Frank
20. Wilhelm Frick
21. Julius Streicher
22. Walter Funk
23. Hjalmar Schacht
24. Karl Doenitz
25. Erich Raeder
26. Baldur von Schirach
27. Fritz Sauckel
28. Alfred Jodl
29. Franz Von Papen
30. Arthur Seyss-Inquart
31. Albert Speer
32. Constantin von Neurath
33. Hans Fritzsche

MISCELLANEOUS

34. Defence Lawyers
35. Inerpreters
    (a) German Desk
    (b) French Desk
    (c) Russian Desk
    (d) British Desk
36. Film Screen
37. Witness Box
38. Marshall of the Court
39. Secretaries of the Court
40. Court Recorders
41. Prosecutors Stand
42. Lift from Prison
43. Secretary of the IMT
44. Official Sound Film
45. IBM Apparatus Control
46. US Army Doctor
47. Military Police

Goering, bottom left (head in hands), and the other defendants hear the verdicts of the IMT from Wolfe Frank (top right) – 30 September 1946, sentences pronounced 1 October.

Plate 4

In the dock, front row l. to r., Goering, Hess, Ribbentrop, Keitel, Kaltenbrunner, Rosenberg, Frank, Frick, Streicher, Funk, Schacht. Behind them, l. to r., Doenitz, Raeder, Schirach, Sauckel, Jodl, Papen, Seyss-Inquart, Speer, Neurath, Fritzsche. The condemned were allowed four days in which to lodge appeals against the hanging to be carried out at Nuremberg on October 16, 1946. Those sentenced to imprisonment would go to a Berlin prison to be chosen by the four Allied Powers. 433

Plate 5

THOSE ON TRIAL AT THE IMT

Hermann Wilhelm Goering (or Göring) (1893-1946): Reichsmarschall, Commander-in-Chief of the Luftwaffe and Hitler's designated deputy. Stole artwork and property from Jews. He was found guilty on all four counts and sentenced to death, however he committed suicide by ingesting cyanide.

Rudolf Hess (1894-1987): Deputy Fuhrer until 1941 and third most powerful man in Germany was found guilty on two counts and sentenced to life imprisonment. He committed suicide at the age of 92.

Joachim von Ribbentrop (1893-1946): Foreign Minister 1938-45 was convicted for his role in starting the Second world war and enabling the Holocaust. He was sentenced to death and was the first to be hanged.

Wilhelm Keitel (1882-1946): Field Marshal and Chief of The OKW. Found guilty on all counts. He was denied a request to be shot and was hanged.

Ernst Kaltenbrunner (1903-1946): Obergruppenfuhrer and Chief of Security Police. He was the highest-ranked member of the SS to be tried at the IMT. He was found guilty on two counts and executed.

Alfred Rosenberg (1893-1946): Minister of the Occupied Territories and ideologist of Nazism. He was found guilty on all four counts and executed.

Hans Frank (1900-1946): Governor-General of Poland where he instigated a reign of terror against the civilian population and was directly involved in the mass murder of Jews. Found guilty on two counts and executed.

Wilhelm Frick (1877-1946): Former Reich Minister of the Interior in Hitler's Cabinet. He was found guilty on three counts and executed.

Julius Streicher (1885-1946): Known as the 'The Jew Baiter' he founded and published the anti-Semetic newspaper *Der Sturmer* – a central element of Nazi propaganda. Found guilty of War Crimes against Humanity and was hanged.

Walter Funk (1889-1960): Minister of Economic Affairs and President of the Reichsbank he was found guily on three counts. Sentenced to life imprisonment he was released in 1957 because of ill health.

Hjalmar Schacht (1877-1970): As Minister of Economics he played a key role in implementing Hitler's policies. He was put on trial for conspiracy and crimes against peace but was acquitted.

Karl Doenitz (1891-1980): Commander-in-Chief of the German Navy he succeeded Hitler as Head of State and ordered Jodl to sign the instruments of surrender. He was convicted of War Crimes and sentenced to ten years imprisonment.

Erich Raeder (1876-1960): Commander-in-Chief of the German Navy 1928-43. He was sentenced to life imprisonment but was released early due to ill health.

Baldur von Schirach (1907-1974): Leader of Hitler Youth movement. He was found guilty of Crimes against Humanity and for his role in deporting Jews to concentration camps in Poland. He was imprisoned for twenty years.

Fritz Sauckel (1894-1946): Plenipotentiary General for Manpower. He was found guilty and executed for War Crimes and Crimes against Humanity by deliberately working people to death.

Alfred Jodl (1890-1946): Chief of Operations Staff of OKW. He was found guilty on all four counts and of ordering prisoners of war to be executed on capture. He was executed.

Martin Bormann (1900-1945): Deputy Leader after Hess he was found guilty *in absentia* of War Crimes and Crimes against Humanity and sentenced to death by hanging. However it was later established that he had died trying to flee the Allies after Hitler's suicide in May 1945.

Franz von Papen (1879-1969): A former Chancellor of Germany von Papen stood trial on two Counts but was acquitted.

Arthur Seyss-Inquart (1892-1946): Austrian Minister and Reich Commissioner for Occupied Netherlands was found guilty on three Counts and of crimes against the Jews. Sentenced to death by hanging he was the last to mount the scaffolding.

Berthold Albert Speer (1905-1981): Minister of Armament and War Production, was also Hitler's Chief Architect. He was found guilty on two counts but was the only one of the accused to accept responsibility for the crimes and to say sorry. After much debate his life was spared and he was sentenced to twenty years imprisonment.

Constantin von Neurath (1873-1956): A former Minister of Foreign Affairs. Whilst he was found guilty on all four counts he was considered to be a minor adherent to the atrocities and was sentenced to fifteen years in Spandau Prison.

Hans Fritzsche (1900-1953): Head of Propaganda was charged on three counts and acquitted. However he was later charged by a deNazification Court and sentenced to 9 years imprisonment. He died soon after release.

COUNTS, VERDICTS & SENTENCES

INDICTMENTS: **Count 1: Conspiracy to Commit Crimes**

Count 2: Crimes Against Peace

Count 3: War Crimes

Count 4: Crimes against Humanity

Defendant	Count 1	Count 2	Count 3	Count 4	Sentence
Hermann Goering	G	G	G	G	Hanging
Rudolf Hess	G	G	I	I	Life
Joachim von Ribbentrop	G	G	G	G	Hanging
Wilhelm Keitel	G	G	G	G	Hanging
Ernst Kaltenbrunner	I	–	G	G	Hanging
Alfred Rosenberg	G	G	G	G	Hanging
Hans Frank	I	–	G	G	Hanging
Wilhelm Frick	I	G	G	G	Hanging
Julius Streicher	I	–	–	G	Hanging
Walter Funk	I	G	G	G	Life
Hjalmar Schacht	I	I	–	–	Acquitted
Karl Doenitz	I	G	G	–	10 years
Erich Raeder	G	G	G	–	Life
Baldur von Schirach	I	–	–	G	20 years
Fritz Sauckel	I	I	G	G	Hanging
Alfred Jodl	G	G	G	G	Hanging
Martin Bormann*	I	–	G	G	Hanging
Franz von Papen	I	I	–	–	Acquitted
Arthur Seyss-Inquart	I	G	G	G	Hanging
Albert Speer	I	I	G	G	20 years
Constantin von Neurath	G	G	G	G	15 years
Hans Fritzsche	I	–	I	I	Acquitted
Robert Ley*					
Gustav Krupp*					

Key: G: guilty; I: innocent; – (dash) defendant was not charged.

* Martin Bormann was tried and sentenced *in absentia*; Robert Ley committed suicide before the trial commenced; and the trial of Gustav Krupp was postponed indefinitely due to the onset of senile decay.

Hooper, in 1958. He was educated at Rugby School and gained the rank of major in the service of the 9th Lancers. He died in Dumfries, Scotland in 1991. (Sources: *The Peerage* – Person page 64880 and various on-line family trees).

3. Baroness Maditta von Skrbensky was the first of Wolfe Frank's five wives. He married her at Andover Registry Office on 12 April 1937. Four days later, having returned to Germany, Frank fled for his life and did not see Maditta again for almost ten years. On 8 January 1938, in London, Frank received a divorce decree. The marriage had been dissolved, it stated, because 'a German woman of the standing of the plaintiff could not be expected to remain married to a man of the defendant's type and character'. Frank, the son of a Jewish industrialist, had not known divorce proceedings were in progress. *NVOD* p.38.

4. Charlotte particularly recalls Captain Bonner Roberts, CBE (who served with the Royal Fleet Auxiliary in the Atlantic and Pacific Fleets during the Second World War and was later appointed Chief Marine Superintendent of the RFA) discussing the subject with Wolfe during his lifetime, and with others following his death, and that he, Roberts, was convinced Frank had been a witness to the event that saw the passing of the cyanide to Goering (Biographical Sources: Dorset Echo Memorial 02/09/2015 and The Royal Fleet Auxiliary Association Obituary 14/08/2015).

THE OBJECTIVES OF THIS BOOK

*'It is impossible in summation to do more than outline with bold strokes
the vitals of this trial's mad and melancholy record, which will live as the
historical text of the Twentieth Century's shame and depravity'*[1].

ROBERT H. JACKSON

CHRONICLED WITHIN THIS 'LIFE AND DEATH' account are the
intertwined involvements of the main characters in this history
defining chain of events, they are: the most notorious of all Nazi war
criminals; America's top spymaster; the prodigy he taught 'the dark
arts of espionage'; the Chief Prosecutor at 'history's greatest trial'; the
first escapee from Colditz Castle prisoner-of-war camp; and the man
the world's media dubbed 'The Voice of Doom.'

The information and cross-references disclosed in my findings also
expose the intrigue, skullduggery and power struggles that went on
behind the scenes at Nuremberg between the US military, intelligence
and judicial hierarchy during the two-month period immediately prior
to the start of the trials. They highlight too, a cocktail of wounded
pride, honour, rivalry, stubbornness and duplicity that threatened
to undermine the integrity of the trials but concluded, against the
Prosecution's wishes and the Tribunal's intentions, with the showing of
an extraordinary act of mercy towards one of history's most evil men.

The following is an outline of the intent of *GOERING'S SUICIDE:
'They Will Not Hang Me!'* as well as being a script that: (i) pinpoints the
time, place and setting of the history-defining incident that enabled
the suicide; and (ii) introduces the group of extraordinarily brave men
whose roles, actions and entanglements, to a greater or lesser extent,
links them with an event that, even after six years of the bloodiest war
in history, was still able to shock the world.

The Objectives: To establish: (a) that following an instruction given
to him by General William Donovan, US Army,
and with the agreement of the 'British contingent'
at Nuremberg, Lieutenant Edwin J. Putzell, Jr., US
Navy, passed to Reichsmarschall Hermann Goering
the cyanide that killed him shortly before midnight
on 15 October 1946; and (b) whether Captain Wolfe

Frank, British Army, acting as interpreter, was a witness to the event.

The Setting: The Prison cells and interrogation rooms at Nuremberg's Palace of Justice.

The Period: 3 October – 20 November 1945: the two-month period prior to the start of the International Military Tribunal – the first and most important of the Nuremberg Trials.

The Revelations: Details of the events leading up to and surrounding Goering's suicide and the involvements and admissions of those directly or indirectly implicated in, or connected to, this event.

The Principals Involved: Reichsmarschall Hermann Goering
Mr Justice Robert Jackson, Chief US Prosecutor at the IMT
General William 'Wild Bill' Donovan, US Army
Lieutenant Edwin J. 'Ned' Putzell, Jr., US Navy
Major Airey Neave, British Army
Captain Wolfe Frank, British Army

Others Involved: Colonel Burton Andrus, Commandant of Nuremberg Prison
General Telford Taylor, Assistant US Prosecutor
Lieutenant Jack Wheelis, US Army Guard
Sergeant Harry Shotwell, US Army Guard
General Erich von dem Bach-Zelewski, German SS Officer
Rudolf Diels, First Chief of the Gestapo

This work is not intended to be a text book that explains, opines upon and references every aspect or fact about the Second World War, its battles, its politics or its rights or wrongs. Also, other than is directly associated with or pertinent to the events and subjects hereunder scrutiny, it does not seek to dissect or comment upon the conclusions, conduct, decisions, verdicts or sentences of the war crimes tribunal. Neither does it record or explore every detail of the backstories of the personalities involved. An authoritative answer to almost any point raised about these wider issues already exists and can be found within the plethora of books, papers, articles and documentaries produced by eminent historians and writers, or is available, readily and instantly via the thousands of sites and references that are available on the internet. Too much peripheral information, if included here, would detract from the main matters and would, I believe, unnecessarily divert the reader's attention away from the substantive issues.

Instead the essence of this narrative – while including some general information to explain certain settings, contexts and underlying sub-issues and tensions – concentrates exclusively upon: (i) the events surrounding a single critical incident that occurred during the equally critical few weeks leadings up to the start of the IMT; and (ii) the involvements, in and surrounding that incident, of a group of men who found themselves bound together by a secret that could not be revealed until the final days of the last survivor. For a reason that will become obvious later, I refer to this period as being THE PREPARATIONS and the group of personalities as being THE PRINCIPALS and THE OTHERS involved.

CHAPTER THREE – NOTES & REFERENCES

1. *The Closing Arguments for Conviction of Nazi War Criminals*, Robert H. Jackson, U. S. Chief of Counsel, IMT (Robert H. Jackson Centre, December 26, 1946, *Temple Law Quarterly* p.85).

THE RISE AND FALL OF THE THIRD REICH

'Whoever in the future raises a hand against a representative of the National Socialist movement or of the State, must know that he will lose his life in a very short while.'[1]
HERMANN GOERING

THE INTERTWINED STORIES OF THE TWELVE MEN, (The Principals and The Others) brought together by happenstance for a few weeks and a history defining event in the autumn of 1945, began much earlier and were entirely shaped by the two world wars. One of those men, Justice Robert Jackson, described the period prior to Nuremberg through which they had lived in the following terms:

These two-score years in this Twentieth Century will be recorded in the book of years as one of the most bloody in all annals. Two World Wars have left a legacy of dead which number more than all the armies engaged in any war that made ancient or medieval history. No half-century ever witnessed slaughter on such a scale, such cruelties and inhumanities, such wholesale deportations of peoples into slavery, such annihilations of minorities. The Terror of Torquemada pales before the Nazi Inquisition. These deeds are the overshadowing historical facts by which generations to come will remember this decade.[2]

By the early 1930s Britain and Germany, among most of the world's nations, were still struggling to cope with the effects of the Great Depression[3] and the crippling financial legacy of the First World War.

Known also as 'The Great War', the First World War was the global conflict fought between two coalitions: The Allies – led by Britain, USA, France, Russia, Italy and Japan – and the Central Powers of Germany, Austria-Hungary, the Ottoman Empire and Bulgaria. US analysts have estimated that ten million servicemen died worldwide and that the cost of the war exceeded $200 billion. Between 1914–1918 over 947,000 British and Commonwealth soldiers were killed, the vast majority died on the Western Front and over 720,000 of them are buried there (including my grandfather and great uncle)[4].

The origins of the Second World War stemmed from the settlements of the 'Treaty of Versailles'[5] that were imposed on Germany at the end of the First World War. Blaming Germany for starting the Great War the Allies demanded Germany withdraw from all illegally occupied territories, pay vast war damages and restrict the size of her future armed forces.

An unprecedented slump in the world economy ensued followed by massive unemployment, rampant inflation and civil unrest throughout Germany. On 31 August 1932 Hermann Goering became President of the Reichstag (the national parliament of Nazi Germany)[6] and began to use his position to manipulate events. On 30 January 1933 Adolf Hitler[7] one of the leading members of the Nationalsozialistische Deutsche Arbeiterpartei (NSDAP – National Socialist Workers' Party) was appointed Chancellor. He soon had a considerable following among those who blamed their former leaders for 'dishonouring Germany' by signing the Versailles treaty.

The Significance of 5 March 1933

30 January 1933 is sometimes suggested as being the date the Third Reich came into existence, however the Nazis did not hold a majority in parliament at that time. That changed following a forced General Election that took place on 5 March when the NSDAP secured 43.9 percent of the vote. Backed by the Deutschnationale Volkspartei (DNVP) – the German National People's Party – who had gained 8 percent of the vote, Hitler was able to seize absolute power that day and he was elected Chancellor – later adopting the title Der Fuehrer (The Leader) – on the promise that he would avenge his country's humiliations.

5 March 1933 is therefore the date that many historians and writers accept as being the first day of the Third Reich – certainly it was a day of significance for the whole world and for Hermann Goering and Wolfe Frank in particular as will be revealed later in this book.

(On 5 March 1933 in the USA: William Donovan, already a national hero, was splitting his time between heading up a successful law practice in New York and gaining a reputation on the political scene within the Republican Party; Robert Jackson was a leading New York lawyer and an active worker within the upper echelons of the Democratic Party; Edwin Putzell was studying for his law degree at Harvard Law School; Telford Taylor had recently graduated, also from

Harvard Law School, and was working for the US government; Burton Andrus was an Air Corps Instructor at the US Army Cavalry School; Jack Wheelis was serving with the US Marines; and Harry Shotwell was an eight year old schoolboy studying in Carrollton, Texas).

On that same day in Germany: Hermann Goering, Rudolf Diels and Erich von dem Bach-Zelewski were celebrating: the Nazi Party's triumph; the first day of the Third Reich; and their soon to be respective positions as Reichsmarschall, Head of the Gestapo and SS Commander; for Wolfe Frank it was the day he 'discarded the attitude of the twenty-year-old irresponsible youth' as he witnessed what was, perhaps, the first atrocity committed by the Third Reich; and Airey Neave was a seventeen-year-old pupil at Eton preparing himself for a period of studying in Berlin to where he was being sent to 'brush up on his German').

Ignoring the conditions of the Versailles Agreement, Hitler immediately began building a large army and reoccupied the Rhineland, Austria and Czechoslovakia.

In 1938, Britain, through Prime Minister Neville Chamberlain, and France accepted these acquisitions provided no further invasions took place. At the same time the two countries also signed a pact with Poland pledging support in the event of any German aggression against that country. Hitler however, whose allies now included Italy and Japan (known collectively as the Axis Powers), had no intention of keeping to this agreement and made a separate deal with the Union of Soviet Socialist Republics (USSR – led by Russia) to invade and share out Poland. That invasion took place on 1 September 1939 and two days later, Chamberlain's withdrawal ultimatum having been ignored, Britain and Germany were at war.

Poland was overrun in weeks and, with Germany being so much better prepared, there was nothing Britain and France could do to help. In the Spring of 1940, the Nazis (the shortened name of the National Socialist Workers' Party) conquered Norway, Denmark, France and the Low Countries. The Allied forces, who were by then fighting in France were surrounded, apparently doomed, at Dunkirk. However, in a magnificent response to the Government's cry for help, hundreds of British fishing vessels, yachts, launches and other craft, supported by essential air cover from RAF Fighter Command, backed the Royal Navy and returned time and again to the beaches of Dunkirk to heroically rescue over 80,000 thousand of the 338,226 men ferried to safety.

Chamberlain resigned as Prime Minister in 1940, to be succeeded by Winston Churchill, and in July the Battle of Britain began – a six month barrage of London, the south east and other cities by the Luftwaffe (German Air Force)[8] as a prelude to Germany's planned invasion of the British Isles. The sustained campaign killed more civilians than had up until then died on active service and it was intended to crush the fight out of Britain. Instead, it inspired a new 'Spirit of the Blitz' (short for blitzkrieg – lightning war) and the enemy was repelled by the magnificent achievements of the men of RAF Fighter Command of whose heroic actions Churchill was to say 'Never in the field of human conflict was so much owed by so many to so few[9].

By August 1941 most of continental Europe was controlled by the Nazis or governments friendly to Hitler, and the war had truly become world wide. Hitler however was about to make a fatal mistake. Disregarding the pact of convenience he had made with Joseph Stalin, leader of the USSR, he ordered his troops to invade Russia. Creating a new war, with a new enemy, on a new front, in the middle of a Russian winter, proved too much for the German army which was halted short of Moscow and Leningrad.

Up until this time the United States, while being sympathetic to the British cause, had stayed out of the war. All that changed on 7 December 1941 when they were forced into the conflict by Japan who, backed by Hitler's promise of support, without warning attacked the American Pacific Fleet at Pearl Harbor in Hawaii.

Hitler in Retreat

By the autumn of 1942 the tide was turning, and the fight back had begun in earnest. The Allies (now forty-nine in number) had great victories at El Alamein in North Africa and Stalingrad, and Hitler began to retreat on all fronts, pursued by the Allies. Sicily and Italy were taken in September 1943, followed by more overwhelming Soviet victories in Russia and Poland. The Normandy landings of 1944 then saw British and American troops charge through Europe. By August Paris was back in Allied hands and British, Canadian and American troops quickly took Dunkirk, Antwerp, Liege and Luxembourg. Further progress was temporarily halted by long, drawn-out battles in the Low Countries with both sides suffering from the severe weather conditions and shortages of supplies. In the Spring of 1945, however, the Allies crossed the Rhine and occupied West Germany. At the same time, having forced the enemy out of the Soviet Union and Poland, the Red army advanced on Berlin via East Germany.

On 30 April 1945 Hitler, rather than be taken alive, committed suicide in his Berlin bunker together with his mistress Eva Braun, whom he had married just a few hours earlier. Germany's unconditional surrender came into effect on 8 May – Victory in Europe (VE) Day. The war continued in the Pacific theatre however until America dropped atomic bombs on Hiroshima and Nagasaki causing the Japanese to capitulate on 15 August – Victory in Japan (VJ) Day.

The war Hitler had started and maintained became the deadliest conflict in history with tens of millions dying due to massacres, starvation, disease and genocide. Under his dictatorship, the Nazi regime executed six million Jews and many millions more who they deemed to be inferior or undesirables including, Slavs, homosexuals, and Jehovah's Witnesses — 'life unworthy of life' Hitler's posters had proclaimed.

The IMT followed soon after – the conclusion of which marked the end of the Third Reich.

CHAPTER FOUR – NOTES & REFERENCES

1. Statement made by Hermann Goering in 1933. Source: *The Closing Arguments for Conviction of Nazi War Criminals*, Robert H. Jackson, U. S. Chief of Counsel, IMT (Robert H. Jackson Centre, December 26, 1946, *Temple Law Quarterly* p. 86).

2. Opening statement of Justice Robert Jackson's closing argument at the IMT on 26 July 1946. Source: *The Closing Arguments for Conviction of Nazi War Criminals*, Robert H. Jackson, U. S. Chief of Counsel, IMT (Robert H. Jackson Centre, December 26, 1946, *Temple Law Quarterly* p. 85). Thomas of Torquemada, was a Castilian Dominican friar and first Grand Inquisitor of the Tribunal of the Holy Office (otherwise known as the Spanish Inquisition). His name has become synonymous with the Inquisition's horror, religious bigotry, and cruel fanaticism.

3. The Great Depression was a world-wide economic downturn that began in 1929 and lasted until the late 1930s. It was the longest and most severe depression of the 20th century.

4. Privates 54981 Richard Robert Powell Foot and 54980 Roland Philamon Foot (grandfather and great uncle respectively of the author of this book), machine gunners of the 193rd Machine Gun Corps serving in the 56th (1st London) Division of the British Expeditionary Force's Third Army, were killed respectively on the 3rd and 8th of May 1917 whilst manning their guns near Arras during the Third Battle of the Scarpe. *One Foot in the Grave: In Search of My Grandfather*, Paul Hooley 2006 p. 28.

5. The Treaty of Versailles was signed by Germany and the Allied Nations on 28 June 1919, formally ending the First World War. The terms of the treaty required that Germany pay financial reparations, disarm, lose territory, and give up all its overseas colonies.

6. From 1919 the Reichstag was the lower house of Germany's parliament. Following Hitler's seizure of power in 1933 it became the national parliament of Nazi Germany.

7. There are many millions of web sites that refer to Adolf Hitler and he is the subject of hundreds of books – Wikipedia has drawn many of these titles together in a *Bibliography of Adolf Hitler:* https://en.wikipedia.org/wiki/Bibliography_of_Adolf_Hitler. These and other sources cover every known aspect of Hitler's life, times and atrocities. With that in mind the following is all that needs to be said for the purposes of this chapter: Adolf Hitler is one of the most reviled of all historical figures. Born in Austria in 1889 he was a First World War soldier turned politician who became the dictator of Nazi Germany from 1933 until his suicide in 1945.

8. Luftwaffe – German Air Force – was the largest and most formidable air force in Europe. In 1935 Hermann Goering became its Commander-in-Chief, a position he retained until the final days of the Second World War.

9. *Hansard* – 20 August 1940.

THE INTERNATIONAL MILITARY TRIBUNAL

'The Greatest Trial in History'[1]
SIR NORMAN BIRKETT

THE INTERNATIONAL MILITARY TRIBUNAL (IMT) was the first and the highest profile of the Nuremberg Trials – the military tribunals put in place after the Second World War to prosecute those members of the political, military, judicial and economic leadership of Nazi Germany responsible for the Holocaust[2] and other war crimes. It had been convened following the collapse of the Third Reich[3] and demands from the Allies for immediate retribution for the crimes committed by the Nazis.

In August 1945, the four Allied Powers of Britain, USA, France and the Soviet Union, signed the London Agreement, paving the way for the prosecution of the war criminals. Article 6 of the IMT's Charter listed three broad categories of crimes: (a) Crimes against peace; (b) War crimes; (c) Crimes against humanity; to which a fourth was added – (d) Conspiracy to Commit Crimes (see Chapter Twenty for full details).

(Following the conclusion of the IMT, other Germans including politicians, industrialists, high ranking military personnel, physicians and jurists were arrested and brought before the courts to face war crimes charges in a series of twelve further hearings conducted by the US. Officially entitled, 'The Trials of War Criminals before the Nuremberg Military Tribunals', these trials are more usually referred to as being the 'Subsequent Proceedings.')[4]

Held within the Palace of Justice at Nuremberg between 20 November 1945 and 1 October 1946, the IMT tried twenty-four of the most important political and military leaders of the Third Reich including Reichsmarschall Hermann Goering.

Mr Justice Robert H. Jackson, assisted by General Telford Taylor, led the US prosecution team and Sir Hartley Shawcross, assisted by Sir David Maxwell Fyfe, led the British team of prosecutors.

In his 'Closing Arguments for Conviction of Nazi War Criminals'[5] Justice Jackson summed up the Nazi regime and the roles the defendants had played in it by stating:

They all speak with a Nazi double talk with which to deceive the unwary. In the Nazi dictionary of sardonic euphemisms 'Final solution' of the Jewish problem was a phrase which meant extermination; 'Special treatment' of prisoners of war meant killing; 'Protective custody' meant concentration camp; 'Duty labor' meant slave labor; and an order to 'take a firm attitude' or 'take positive measures' meant to act with unrestrained savagery.

The US Chief Prosecutor said of Goering, in particular:

The large and varied role of Goering was half militarist and half gangster. He stuck a pudgy finger in every pie. He used his SA muscle-men to help bring the gang into power. In order to entrench that power he contrived to have the Reichstag burned, established the Gestapo, and created the concentration camps. He was equally adept at massacring opponents and at framing scandals to get rid of stubborn generals. He built up the Luftwaffe and hurled it at his defenseless neighbors. He was among the foremost in harrying the Jews out of the land.

Jackson also made it clear that while Hitler had created the Nazi monster and had made it possible for all the atrocities to be carried out, he could not have done it alone:

A glance over the dock [see Plate 4/5] will show that, despite quarrels among themselves, each defendant played a part which fitted in with every other, and that all advanced the common plan.

On behalf of the Allies and all who had directly or indirectly suffered under the Nazis, Jackson needed convictions and death penalties to be imposed and examples to be made that would show the world: justice had been done; the ultimate price would be paid: and the leaders, of perhaps the most evil regime that has ever existed, would be executed – not as war heroes, but in the manner reserved for the commonest of criminals.

It was also clear from Jackson's closing remarks, that while he blamed all the defendants for the war crimes as charged, symbolically he needed to be able to hold one man ultimately responsible for the war crimes of individuals, collectives, regimes and a nation – one man who would walk to the gallows and be seen to die as a common criminal with a rope around his neck. With Hitler dead only one other man matched that profile and that man was Hermann Goering, as Jackson emphasised.

No one lives who, at least until the very last moments of the war, outranked Goering in position, power, and influence … By mobilizing the total economic resources of Germany he made possible the waging of the war which he had taken a large part in planning. He was, next to Hitler, the man who tied the activities of all the defendants together in a common effort.

Ultimately, nineteen of the defendants tried at the IMT were found guilty, three were acquitted, one committed suicide whilst awaiting proceedings and one was found to be unfit to stand trial. Of the nineteen found guilty twelve, including Hermann Goering, were sentenced to death by hanging (see Plates 6–8 for full details of the defendants, charges, verdicts and sentences).

The Third Reich that Hitler had predicted would 'last for a thousand years' had risen and fallen in thirteen. All that remained was for the sentences to be carried out on 16 October 1946 with Germany's Reichsmarschall leading the group of condemned war criminals to the gallows.

CHAPTER FIVE – NOTES & REFERENCES

1. Sir William Norman Birkett, later Baron Birkett, PC was the Alternate British Member (judge) of the International Military Tribunal which he described as being the 'greatest trial in history' – Robert H. Jackson Centre, recording events that had taken place at the IMT on November 21, 1945.

2. The Germans referred to the Holocaust as being 'the final solution to the Jewish question' – a phrase first used by Hermann Goering in an official order he sent to Reinhard Heydrich, the head of the security branch of the SS, on 31 July 1941 (see Plate 12).

3. The Third Reich (Realm) is the name given to that period of German history under the dictatorship of Adolf Hitler through the Nazi Party (1933–1945). The First Reich was the period known as the Holy Roman Empire (962–1806) and the Second Reich the German Empire (1871–1918).

4. The Subsequent Proceedings were also held in the Palace of Justice at Nuremberg – between December 1946 and April 1949. General Telford Taylor, one of the US assistant prosecutors under Mr Justice Jackson at the IMT, was appointed Chief Prosecutor and Wolfe Frank was appointed Chief Interpreter. In total almost 500 cases were tried at the SP involving over 1,600 defendants of which 1,400 were found guilty. Less than 200 were executed and only 279 were sent to prison.

5. *The Closing Arguments for Conviction of Nazi War Criminals*, Robert H. Jackson, U. S. Chief of Counsel, IMT (Robert H. Jackson Centre, December 26, 1946, *Temple Law Quarterly* p. 96).

SECTION TWO

THE PRINCIPALS &
THE OTHERS
AND
THE REVELATIONS OF
EDWIN PUTZELL

REICHSMARSCHALL HERMANN GOERING

'The large and varied role of Goering was half militarist and half gangster.
He stuck a pudgy finger in every pie'.[1]
JUSTICE ROBERT JACKSON

FORMER HEAD OF THE LUFTWAFFE, founder of the Gestapo, Hitler's designated deputy, Architect of the Holocaust and the most senior Nazi to be put on trial at Nuremberg, Reichsmarschall Hermann Goering (German Göring) was found guilty on all four indictments: Conspiracy to Commit Crimes; Crimes Against Peace; War Crimes; and Crimes Against Humanity. He was sentenced to death by hanging but requested he be shot as a soldier – to Goering 'death by the rope' was the ultimate disgrace that he was never going to allow to happen. His repeated requests were refused.

Goering was born on 12 January 1893 in Rosenheim, Bavaria to Heinrich Goering, a judge, and his wife Franziska. His godfather was Hermann Epenstein, a wealthy Jewish businessman, who provided a home for Goering and his mother (who became Epenstein's mistress) at his castle in Mauterndorf near Nuremberg. Interested in the German army from an early age, Goering attended a military academy from 1905 (see Plate 9) until 1911 before joining the Prince Wilhelm Regiment of the Prussian Army in 1912.

At the beginning of the First World War, he saw service as an infantry lieutenant but, following a period in hospital with rheumatism, he transferred to the air corps where he became a national hero racking up twenty-two aerial kills and earning the coveted *Pour le Mérite* (Blue Max) – the highest Prussian order of bravery. In 1918 he was promoted to commanding officer of Jagdgeschwader I – Manfred von Richthofen's 'Flying Circus'[2]. Wounded on several occasions Goering was awarded Iron Crosses (1st and 2nd Class) and several other coveted honours.

In the summer of 1921 Goering began university courses in history and political studies. The following year he met Adolf Hitler at a Nazi party rally and soon became a member –who Hitler immediately put in charge of an SA[3] unit. The same year he met his first wife Carin and he married her soon after. In 1923, together with Hitler, he took part in the Beer Hall Putsch[4] – a protest against the German government – and he was badly wounded. The treatment for the injury included morphine to which Goering developed a lifelong addiction. Hitler was arrested and jailed, but Carin Goering smuggled her husband out of Germany, firstly to Italy and then to Sweden. Goering returned to Germany four years later.

In 1928 Goering was one of only twelve Nazis to be elected to the Reichstag (the Party secured just 2.6 percent of the vote) but in the 1932 election the Nazis' growing influence became apparent when they won 230 seats, following which Goering was elected President of the Reichstag, a position he retained until 23 April 1945.

In 1931 Goering's wife Carin, to whom he was devoted, died suddenly of heart failure. Two years later he built a hunting lodge which became his home and he named it Carinhall in her honour.

5 March 1933

Four weeks after Hitler was sworn in as Chancellor there was an arson attack on the Reichstag building. Blaming Communists, Hitler used this to cement his and the Nazi Party's positions – although others were blamed (and lost their lives), some accused Goering of having started the Reichstag fire and whipping up hostilities to further the Party's standing and support. This incident, and an emergency law that was imposed, allowed the Nazis to arrest over 4,000 Communists and to call for a further general election. This took place on 5 March 1933 and resulted in the Nazis, with the support of the DNVP, securing a majority. From that moment Hitler took absolute control of Germany, and the Third Reich was established with Goering becoming a minister in the new government.

One of Goering's first acts was to create the Geheime Staatspolizei, the much-feared Gestapo, and he appointed Rudolf Diels (see Chapter Eighteen and Plate 11), to whom he was related by marriage, to be its first head. Having become the second most powerful man in Germany, Goering assumed further power when Hitler appointed him to be commander-in-chief of the Luftwaffe, a position he also held until the final days of the war.

Four weeks after the elections, in Berlin, Goering married his second wife Emmy Sonnemann, an actress from Hamburg. A large reception was held the night before the wedding at the Berlin Opera House. Hitler was best man and fighter aircraft flew overhead both on the night of the reception and after the ceremony the following day. Goering's daughter, Edda, was born on 2 June 1938.

In September 1939, Hitler gave a speech to the Reichstag designating Goering as his successor. After the Fall of France in 1940, he was bestowed the specially created rank of Reichsmarschall, which gave him seniority over all officers in Germany's armed forces.

On 31 July 1941, Goering sent his infamous letter to Reinhard Heydrich, head of the security branch of the SS, authorising a 'Final Solution to the Jewish Question' (meaning the annihilation of Jews).

After the Luftwaffe proved incapable of preventing the Allied bombing of German cities in 1942/3 Goering's standing with Hitler declined and he began to withdraw from military and political affairs to devote his attention to collecting property and artwork, much of which was stolen from Jewish victims of the Holocaust.

Informed on 22 April 1945 that Hitler intended to commit suicide, Goering sent a telegram to the Fuehrer requesting his permission to assume leadership of the Reich. Considering his request to be an act of treason, Hitler removed Goering from all his positions, expelled him from the Party, and ordered his arrest.

Goering withdrew to his castle at Mauterndorf (which Epenstein's widow had bequeathed to him) and on 5 May he made his way to nearby Bruck where he surrendered to the advancing US forces rather than be captured by the fast approaching Russian Army. The following day he was taken into custody at Radstadt by elements of the 36th Infantry Division of the US Army which led to his arrest and ultimately to his appearance at the IMT where he was convicted on all counts. He was sentenced to death by hanging but committed suicide by ingesting cyanide hours before the sentence could be carried out.

Goering left several suicide notes in his cell, the following is part of one addressed to the Allied Control Council:

Would that I might be shot! However, executing the German Reichsmarschall by hanging cannot be countenanced. I cannot permit this for Germany's sake. Besides, I have no more obligation to subject myself to punishment from my enemies. Therefore I elect to die as the great Hannibal did.

Goering had earlier told Prison Psychologist Dr Gilbert that he would be 'taking some secrets to the grave' and that he was planning a 'secret revenge on the Allies'. He also told his wife Emmy, at their last meeting on 7 October 1946, that 'They will not hang me!'[5]

CHAPTER SIX – NOTES & REFERENCES

1. *The Closing Arguments for Conviction of Nazi War Criminals*, Robert H. Jackson, U. S. Chief of Counsel, IMT (Robert H. Jackson Centre, December 26, 1946, *Temple Law Quarterly* p. 96)

2. Jagdgeschwader I was a fighter wing of the German air force during the First World War, with Manfred von Richthofen, the 'Red Baron,' as its first commanding officer. The squadron became known as "The Flying Circus' because of the bright colours of the aircraft and because, like a circus, it moved from area to area, setting up its own tents for accommodation wherever it went.

3. SA, is an abbreviation of Sturmabteilung (Assault Division). It is the name given to Nazi Storm Troopers or Brownshirts whose methods of violent intimidation played a key role in Adolf Hitler's rise to power.

4. The Beer Hall Putsch, also known as the Munich Putsch, was a failed coup attempt by the Nazi Party leader Adolf Hitler, in November 1923, to seize power in Munich. The Putsch (meaning a secretly plotted and suddenly executed attempt to overthrow a government) brought Hitler, who was arrested and charged with treason, to the attention of the wider German public.

5. *Nuremberg – Infamy on Trial*, p.408.

CHIEF JUSTICE ROBERT H. JACKSON

'There would be no Nuremberg without Robert Jackson.'[1]
HENRY T. KING, JR

ROBERT HOUGHWOUT JACKSON was the United States' Chief Prosecutor at the IMT. He was born on 13 February 1892 in Spring Creek Township, Pennsylvania to William Jackson, a farmer and Angelina Houghwout. At the age of eighteen he began to study law under the tutelage of an uncle who introduced him to Franklyn Delano Roosevelt – then Senator for New York State but who was destined to become President of the USA. Jackson qualified as a lawyer and was admitted to the bar in 1913. Three years later he married Alice Gerhardt in Albany and over the next fifteen years he built up a successful law practice and became one of New York's leading attorneys.

Jackson was appointed to many prominent legal positions in the years that followed. He continued his association with Roosevelt and in 1934 he joined the president's administration team, becoming Assistant Attorney General in 1936 and US Solicitor General two years later. By 1940 Roosevelt saw Jackson as a possible future President of the USA and he appointed him Attorney General. In 1941 Jackson was elected by the Senate to be an Associate Justice of the US Supreme Court.

On 2 May 1945, new US President Harry S. Truman appointed Jackson to be 'US Chief of Counsel for the Prosecution of Nazi War Criminals' and gave him complete authority to choose his own staff and to design, structure and implement the Nuremberg Trials. Between June and August 1945 Jackson helped to draft the London Charter of the IMT which created the legal basis for the trials. In accepting the job, he took on enormous responsibility, not just as the lead prosecutor, but also as the trial's administrator.

The IMT began on 20 November 1945, and Jackson was the first to make an opening statement. In exquisite language he stated the importance of making sure that each of the defendants, no matter how heinous the charges against them, received a fair trial:

The former high station of these defendants, the notoriety of their acts, and the adaptability of their conduct to provoke retaliation make it hard to distinguish between the demand for a just and measured retribution, and the unthinking cry for vengeance which arises from the anguish of war. It is our task, so far as humanly possible, to draw the line between the two. We must never forget that the record on which we judge these defendants today is the record on which history will judge us tomorrow. To pass these defendants a poisoned chalice is to put it to our own lips as well. We must summon such detachment and intellectual integrity to our task that this trial will commend itself to posterity as fulfilling humanity's aspirations to do justice.[2]

The Robert H. Jackson Center in Jamestown, New York exists: 'to be the preeminent, enduring source of knowledge on the life and guiding principles of Robert H. Jackson'. The center's leading statement encapsulates what Jackson's contribution was to the IMT and all similar cases that have followed:

It was through the energy, intelligence and leadership of Justice Jackson that the Nuremberg Trial was organized and carried out, standards of evidence developed, rights of defendants defined, and prosecutorial action commenced. Jackson was the driving force behind the conduct of the trials themselves. Jackson said the most important work of his life was at Nuremberg, where his diligence and vision set legal precedents that continue to affect the international law community today.[3]

Jackson's opening statement on 21 November 1945 (the second day of the IMT), also set out the prosecutions' intentions

The wrongs which we seek to condemn and punish have been so calculated, so malignant, and so devastating, that civilization cannot tolerate their being ignored, because it cannot survive their being repeated. That four great nations, flushed with victory and stung with injury, stay the hand of vengeance and voluntarily submit their captive enemies to the judgment of the law is one of the most significant tributes that Power has ever paid to Reason. … In the prisoners' dock sit twenty-odd broken men. Reproached by the humiliation of those they have led almost as bitterly as by the desolation of those they have attacked, their personal capacity for evil is forever past. It is hard now to perceive in these men as captives the power by which as Nazi leaders they once dominated much of the world and terrified most of it.'[2]

Jackson understandably regarded his participation in the Nuremberg Trials as the crowning achievement of his career. Telford Taylor (see Chapter Fourteen), his leading assistant prosecutor at Nuremberg, said of Jackson's performance 'More than any other man of that period, Jackson worked and wrote with deep passion and spoke in winged words. There was no one else who could have done that half as well as he.'

Despite that praise from his own team and Justice Jackson's outstanding contributions to the success of the Nuremberg Trials, there were many, including and especially General William Donovan (see Chapter Eight), who thought that, whilst his opening and closing speeches were of the highest order, Jackson's examination and cross-examination skills were at times extremely weak. Goering often got the better of him during the trial and repeatedly baited Jackson, who was rebuked by the judges for losing his temper.

At the time he was appointed, Jackson said this was:

The first case I have ever tried when I had first to persuade others that a court should be established, help negotiate its establishment, and when that was done, not only prepare my case but find myself a courtroom in which to try it.'[3]

It was General Donovan who eventually recommended the IMT should be conducted at the Palace of Justice, Nuremberg, and in the early days of the preparations he and Jackson seemed to be singing from the same hymn sheet. However, as the trial date grew nearer, it became clear that they were moving in two entirely different directions. A bitter rivalry built up between the two men and their respective camps that threatened to destabilise the whole of the prosecution's case – as will become apparent as this story unfolds.

CHAPTER SEVEN – NOTES & REFERENCES

1. Essay entitled: *Robert H Jackson and the Triumph of Justice at Nuremberg*, Henry T. King Jr., one of the US prosecutors at the IMT.

2. Second Day, Wednesday, 11/21/1945, Part 04, in *Trial of the Major War Criminals before the International Military Tribunal. Volume II*. Proceedings: 11/14/1945–11/30/1945. [Official text in the English language.] Nuremberg: IMT, 1947. pp. 98–102. – Robert Jackson Center.

3. Robert H. Jackson Center, 305 E. Fourth Street, Jamestown, New York – web site: https://www.roberthjackson.org/

GENERAL WILLIAM 'Wild Bill' DONOVAN

'Donovan's exploits … portray a brave, noble, headlong, gleeful, sometimes outrageous pursuit of action and skullduggery.'[1]
EVAN THOMAS

MAJOR GENERAL (GENERAL) WILLIAM JOSEPH 'WILD BILL' DONOVAN was an American soldier, lawyer, intelligence officer and diplomat, who became the first and only Head of the Office of Strategic Services (OSS), the famous US Second World War 'cloak-and-dagger' agency that later evolved into the Central Intelligence Agency (CIA) – of which Donovan is considered to be the founding father. A hero of two world wars, Donovan is the only person to have received all four of the United States' highest awards: the Medal of Honor; the Distinguished Service Cross; the Distinguished Service Medal; and the National Security Medal. He was also awarded the Silver Star and Purple Heart, and further decorations from other nations for his service during both world wars (see Appendix B for a list of Donovan's major honours).

William Donovan was born on 1 January 1883 in Buffalo, New York to Timothy and Anna Donovan. Whilst his parents were also born in the USA, all four of his grandparents were Irish immigrants. A handsome man of great charm and charisma, he studied at Niagara, a private NY Catholic university for pre-law studies, before transferring to Columbia University where he became a bachelor of arts. During his two years at Columbia Law School he was a classmate of future US President Franklin D. Roosevelt (FDR).[2]

Within four years of graduating he and another classmate, Bradley Goodyear, formed their own legal partnership and in 1912 he became a cavalry troop leader in the New York National Guard – a unit that was mobilised in 1916 to take part in the military operation known as the Pancho Villa Expedition[3]. In 1914 he married Ruth Rumsey, an heiress of Buffalo (the couple had two children – David born in 1915 and Patricia born in 1917).

Donovan's remarkable levels of endurance, which far exceeded that of much younger soldiers, led to those under him giving him the nickname 'Wild Bill', which stuck with him for the rest of his life.

Following further action on the Mexican Border, Donovan was promoted to the rank of major and he joined the 69th Infantry Regiment of the US Army[4] – known as the 'Fighting Irish'. During the First World War he led the 1st Battalion, 165th Infantry[4] of the 42nd Division, where he was considered to be a hero by his men who noted that, even when wounded, he refused to leave the battlefield until the US tanks started turning back.

Following the First World War, and having been promoted to the rank of colonel, Donovan stayed in service in Europe for a year before undertaking intelligence missions in Japan, China, Korea and Siberia. Eventually he returned to his law practice where he became known as a vigorous crime-fighter.

In 1924 President Calvin Coolidge[5] appointed Donovan to be an assistant attorney general and his skills as an advocate within the Supreme Court led to him being considered a suitable candidate for both Governor of New York and even Vice President of the USA. Instead, he formed a new law firm in New York – Donovan, Leisure, Newton & Irvine – and, despite the Great Depression, he proved himself to be hugely successful with both his legal court work and in handling mergers, acquisitions and bankruptcies.

Throughout the inter-war years Donovan travelled extensively in Europe, ostensibly on business, but also gathering intelligence. During this time, he made connections with the Nazis whilst protecting his Jewish European clients from the regime. He predicted a second world war was inevitable.

Donovan's profile rose even further in 1940, due in no small part to the film *The Fighting 69th*[6] in which the part of Donovan was played by George Brent.

His old friend President Roosevelt noting Donovan's popularity, as well as his skills as a lawyer and a leader of men, gave him a number of very important assignments, especially in conjunction with the UK.

Donovan greatly impressed key members of the British Government and he struck up a great friendship with Prime Minister Winston Churchill – who gave Donovan unlimited access to classified material. Donovan was also very close to Maxwell Knight, Britain's top spymaster, who ran his operation from apartments in the next and the same block of flats to Wolfe Frank's in Dolphin Square, Pimlico[7]. It was here that Knight recruited James Bond author Ian Fleming as an agent, and it was Fleming who advised Donovan on how best to set up the OSS.

Donovan's involvements with Britain's MI5 and MI6[8], led to the idea of the OSS and in 1941 Roosevelt appointed Donovan as its Head. US author and historian Evan Thomas (who was granted historical access to classified CIA files) in a 2011 *Vanity Fair* profile on Donovan entitled *Spymaster General* observed:[1]

> Donovan set up espionage and sabotage schools, established front companies, arranged clandestine collaborations with international corporations and the Vatican, and oversaw the invention of new, espionage-friendly guns, cameras, and bombs. Donovan also recruited agents, selecting individuals with a wide range of backgrounds – ranging from intellectuals and artists to people with criminal backgrounds.

Always actively involved in some of the great battles of the Second World War, Donovan was promoted to brigadier general in March 1943 and to major general in November 1944. Legendary film director and OSS agent John Ford, who headed up the OSS Field Photographic Branch (see Appendices C & D), said of his commanding officer: 'General Donovan was the sort of guy who thought nothing about parachuting into France, blowing up a bridge, pissing into Luftwaffe gas tanks, then dancing with a German spy on the roof of the St. Regis Hotel.'[13]

By the time of the preparations for the Nuremberg trials Donovan had over '13,000 agents, analysts and operatives under his command' – his Alumni puts the number at up to 16,000[11], and the US Government's official National Park Service website[12] indicates that between 1941 and 1945 up to 24,000 people may have served with the OSS. The true number will never be known as many never appeared on official records and were never paid, including multi-millionaires, politicians and film stars and directors – true patriots who were won over by Donovan's charm and the urge 'to do whatever they could for their country.' Donovan once famously said 'I'd put Stalin on the payroll if I thought it would help us defeat Hitler.' What is known, according to National Park Service, is that by the Spring of 1945 the OSS consisted of 13,000 personnel of whom some 9,000 were uniformed members of the armed forces. It is also known that Donovan brought 172 of his intelligence officers onto the prosecution team at Nuremberg, where he had been appointed special assistant to Justice Jackson.

Douglas Waller[9], author of *Wild Bill Donovan*[10], records that, initially, there was a reluctance to deal with the war criminals via an international military court and that it was Donovan who pressed for this route to be taken. The following is a precise of Mr Waller's narrative.

British authorities and the US military and State Department were relatively indifferent to the question of trying war criminals after the war, but Donovan was lobbying Roosevelt as early as October 1943 to arrange for such prosecutions. FDR tasked Donovan with looking into the legalities and technicalities, and in the months that followed Donovan collected testimonies about war criminals and related information from a wide range of sources. In addition to seeking justice, Donovan wanted to exact retribution for the torture and killing of OSS agents. When FDR's successor, Harry S. Truman became president, he named Supreme Court Justice Robert H. Jackson to serve as chief U.S. counsel in the prosecution of Nazi war criminals. Jackson, discovering that the OSS was the only agency that had seriously explored the issue, invited Donovan to join his trial staff as special advisor[10].

(As, with his permission, I shall be referring to other passages within Douglas Waller's excellent book, I strongly recommend readers refer to Note 9 of this chapter and Chapter Forty-One to see the full extent of Mr Waller's painstaking research and the authority with which he writes).

On 17 May 1945, Donovan flew to Europe to prepare for the prosecutions, and eventually brought the aforementioned 172 OSS officers onto Jackson's team. They had been interviewing Auschwitz survivors, tracking down SS and Gestapo officers and documents, and uncovering other evidence. Donovan, whose idea it was to hold the trials in Nuremberg, also introduced Jackson to useful foreign officials and even released OSS funds to bankroll the prosecution effort. Eventually, Jackson, who had been a political rival of Donovan's in New York State, considered him a 'godsend'. In return, for Donovan's help, and because the OSS had proven 'vital for the prosecution team,' Jackson lobbied President Truman in person to approve Donovan's plans for a permanent postwar intelligence agency.

However, while the initial hopes and ambitions of Donovan and Jackson seemed to be heading in the same direction, that apparent air of cordiality and cooperation was soon to be irreparably damaged, and to a point where it could not be allowed to continue[10].

CHAPTER EIGHT – NOTES & REFERENCES

1. *Spymaster General: The Adventures of Wild Bill Donovan and the "Oh So Social"* O.S.S., written by historian Evan Thomas and published in *Vanity Fair* 3 March 2011.

2. Franklin Delano Roosevelt, commonly known by the initials FDR, was the 32nd President of the United States. He served from 4 March 1933 until his death on 12 April 1945.

3. The Pancho Villa Expedition was a military operation conducted by the United States Army against the paramilitary forces of Mexican revolutionary Francisco 'Pancho' Villa from March 14, 1916, to February 7, 1917, during the Mexican Revolution of 1910–1920.

4. The 69th Infantry Regiment is a regiment of the United States Army. It is part of the New York Army National Guard. It is known as the 'Fighting Sixty-Ninth', a name said to have been given by Robert E. Lee during the Civil War. Between 1917 and 1992 it was also designated the 165th Infantry Regiment.

5. Calvin Coolidge was the 30th President of the United States. He served from 2 August 1923 until 4 March 1929.

6. *The Fighting 69th* is a 1940 American war film starring James Cagney, Pat O'Brien, and George Brent. The plot is based upon the actual exploits of New York City's 69th Infantry Regiment during the First World War.

7. *Scandal at Dolphin Square*, Simon Danczuk and Daniel Smith (The History Press, 2022).

8. MI5 (Military Intelligence, Section 5), is the United Kingdom's domestic counter-intelligence and security agency and is part of its intelligence machinery alongside the Secret Intelligence Service MI6.

9. Douglas Waller was a former correspondent for *Newsweek* and *Time* and reported on the CIA for six years. He also served for eight years on the staffs of Rep. Edward Markey and Sen. William Proxmire. He is the author of a number of bestselling books on these involvements and the critically acclaimed biographies of Donovan and General Billy Mitchell – see Chapter Forty One for an extended description of Mr Waller, his sources and his works.

10. *Wild Bill Donovan*, pp. 325–329 and 343–349.

11. Columbia College:
https://www.college.columbia.edu/cct/issue/summer20/article/
swashbuckling-lawyer-who-was-ultimate-spy

12. National Park Service:
https://www.nps.gov/articles/a-wartime-organization-for-unconventional-
warfare.htm

13. Defense Media Network: https://www.defensemedianetwork.com/stories/
the-oss-society-keepers-of-gen-donovans-flame/

THE REVELATIONS OF EDWIN PUTZELL

'Next to me is the man who killed Hermann Goering —
or rather helped him to kill himself'[1]
PETRONELLA WYATT

I HAVE DECIDED THIS TO BE an appropriate place to introduce the crucial evidence of Edwin Putzell that he revealed during an exclusive interview he gave to author and journalist Petronella Wyatt[1] – published in 1 February 2003 edition of *The Spectator*, of which Ms Wyatt was at that time the deputy editor. I hasten to add however that, at this stage, I do not comment upon, analyse or interpret anything Mr Putzell states or suggests – all that will come later.

The reason I have chosen this point for the inclusion of this vital information is that I feel it to be essential, at an early stage, to consider Mr Putzell's statements alongside his background and character – each, in my opinion, being dependent upon the other to be able to convey, judge and balance the reliance of what is being said against the integrity of the person who is saying it, and vice-versa. I feel therefore that publishing these two elements alongside each other in back-to-back chapters is the best way of achieving that objective at an early stage.

I will reintroduce this article again later, at the appropriate place in this narrative, together with full analysis, explanations and further evidence, where necessary, in support of the statements made by Mr Putzell.

All that follows in this chapter is the full interview Edwin Putzell gave earlier in the year of his death, at the age of ninety. I am most grateful to *The Spectator* and Ms Wyatt for giving me permission to include the article, in its entirety, as part of this book.

'THE QUALITY OF MERCY'
PETRONELLA WYATT

I am sitting on a cream sofa in the evening sunset of Florida. Next to me is the man who killed Hermann Goering — or rather helped him to kill himself. Some received wisdom says that Goering committed suicide without aid, but this is not the case, as I have just found out. When a young man of about thirty, this person beside me gave the Reichmarshall the cyanide pill that saved him from having to undergo the ordeal of the gallows.

The name of this extraordinary man is Ned Putzell. Now eighty-nine, he has retired to Naples on the Gulf coast. He is tanned, spare and has laser-bright brown-grey eyes. He is wearing a crisp, white shirt, chequered trousers and large spectacles.

It all began when my host mentioned to me casually that in the apartment upstairs lived the man who gave Goering a cyanide pill. At first, I thought he was joshing. But here I am, sipping a Diet Coke and listening to this fantastic tale.

Mr Putzell was born in Louisiana. He attended Harvard Law School and eventually ended up working for the law firm of a man called Donovan. This was no ordinary Donovan, but the great American hero of the First World War. Mr Putzell, leaning forward conspiratorially, told me that Donovan was a far greater soldier than MacArthur, the latter a name far better known to English ears.

During the 1914–18 war, Donovan was stationed in northern France, fighting in the trenches. MacArthur was leading the regiment next to him, geographically. When the Germans attacked, it is a little-known fact that MacArthur turned on his heels. Donovan, however, stood his ground, won and was awarded the Congressional Medal of Honor. Americans, it seems, do not appear to know of MacArthur's behaviour on this occasion.

'Through Donovan, I came to examine Goering during the preparations for the Nuremberg trials,' Putzell told me. 'A lot of high-ranking Americans believed his heart had not really been in the Nazi cause. Before Hitler killed himself, Goering was already giving vital information to us which I passed on to the president.'

Roosevelt had decided a while before that the United States required a proper espionage system. This was started by Donovan and became known as the OSS — the Office of Strategic Services. Donovan was chosen to be one of the co-prosecutors at Nuremberg and took Putzell with him as his aide. Other high-ranking Nazis on trial were Albert Speer, Ribbentrop, Alfred Rosenberg and Julius Streicher.

What was Goering like? I asked Putzell. 'Oh, he could be very charming indeed.' This was a view shared by Hartley Shawcross on the British side, who recollects that Goering repeatedly winked at him during examination. 'Then, again, he might have been acting,' Putzell continues.

'When I questioned Goering, the plan was to find out whether he had been a truly dedicated Nazi. I don't think he was, Hitler had suspected him of disloyalty and other Germans told us that Goering was not a strong supporter.'

But he was condemned, nonetheless. I retorted. Putzell nods, his glasses sliding towards the middle of his aquiline and rather handsome nose.

'Yes, but Donovan secretly decided, with the agreement of the British contingent, to let him die by cyanide. Goering had been very co-operative with us and he genuinely did seem deserving of some sort of mercy.'

How did they get hold of the cyanide? I was surprised by the answer. 'Everyone in active service in the OSS was given a cyanide pill in case they were captured by the Germans and tortured. So we had quite a few on us.'

Putzell and a colleague handed one tablet to Goering. How did he react? Putzell laughs gutturally. 'I think he was glad to have it. It was better than being hanged.' Much better as it turned out. Some of the hangings were botched horribly.

Putzell and his wife Dorothy, a pristine and smart blonde, now live in Naples permanently. Most English people believe that the west coast of Florida is quiet and uneventful, full of purblind retired bankers and brokers. Full of men and women whose reminiscences are solely about dosh. But this is not the case.

Consider my host: his division was one of the first into Hitler's house beneath the Eagle's Nest. Opposite me now sits the Führer's silver cigar box with the logo of the Third Reich on its lid. Then, in a drawer in the next room, there is an exquisite, lacquered box given to Hitler by the Emperor of Japan. These mementoes of the Second World War are unique. So is Mr Putzell.

CHAPTER NINE – NOTES & REFERENCES

1. Petronella Wyatt is a journalist, author, broadcaster, political commentator and streaming channel consultant. She is best known as a weekly columnist for the Sunday Telegraph and as a deputy editor of *The Spectator* magazine – see Chapter Forty-One for an extended description of Ms Wyatt and her works and information about *The Spectator*.

LIEUTENANT EDWIN J. 'NED' PUTZELL, Jr.

'We honor you. We salute you. We thank you for a job well done.'[1]
PRESIDENT RONALD REAGAN

IN THE BRIEF, BUT I HOPE ADEQUATE, biographical details I am including in this Section (more will be provided later) regarding each of 'The Principals and The Others' I am attempting to convey – up until the time of the Nuremberg trials and Goering's suicide – something of their identities and personalities, and to chronicle their lives, times, careers and activities in so far as they may be important to the theme of this book.

However with the admissions and revelations of Lieutenant Edwin Putzell being so crucial and so central to all matters, I feel it essential at this stage to go into more detail about the man, his involvements and his accomplishments – both before and after Nuremberg and up until his interviews with Ms Wyatt in February 2003 and, soon after, the US Library of Congress. I also draw on elements of a further interview he gave (in 1997) to the Oral History Project of Georgetown University. I include extracts of these records in order to more fully convey what I believe to be the character, integrity, achievements and standing of a man who, as the fruits of my researches will reveal, dedicated his life to serving his country, the US judicial system and the communities in which he lived – a man who was held in the highest regard at all levels of society, from humble citizens and voluntary organisations to the very top echelons of: the US military and judicial systems; heads of state; directors of federal agencies (such as the CIA); executives of US corporations; national and regional voluntary causes; foreign dignitaries; and several presidents of the USA. (At this point I only give brief details of these involvements, all of which will be developed and more fully referenced as this narrative unfolds).

Formative Years

Edwin J. 'Ned' Putzell was born in 1913 to Edwin and Celeste Putzell in Birmingham Alabama, but the family moved to New Orleans when

Portraits of Hermann Wilhelm Goering. Above left: In 1907, at age 14.
Above right: In 1932, wearing Pour le Mérite (Blue Max) medal.

Below: Partners in crimes against humanity – the Fuehrer and the Reichsmarschall.
'He [Goering] was, next to Hitler, the man who tied the activities of all the defendants together in a common effort.' – Justice Jackson, Closing Remarks at the IMT.

Major General William Donovan.

Captain Wolfe Frank.

Lieutenant Edwin J. Putzell, Jr. (in later life – *photo courtesy of Lila Zuck*).

Major Airey Neave.

Justice Robert Jackson (right) and Colonel Telford Taylor.

Erich von dem Bach-Zelewski.

Rudolf Diels.

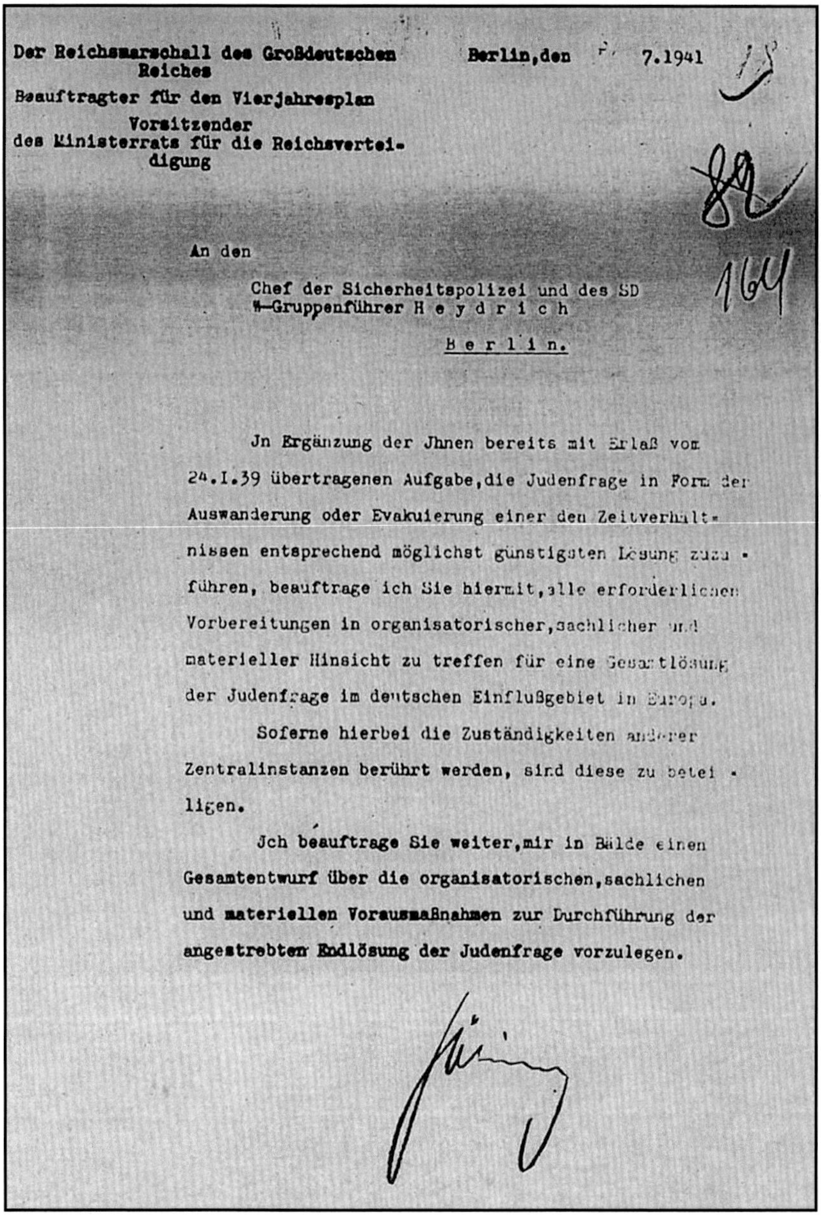

Der Reichsmarschall des Großdeutschen
Reiches   Berlin,den   7.1941

Beauftragter für den Vierjahresplan
            Vorsitzender
des Ministerrats für die Reichsvertei-
                digung

            An den

                Chef der Sicherheitspolizei und des SD
                #-Gruppenführer H e y d r i c h

                        B e r l i n.

            Jn Ergänzung der Jhnen bereits mit Erlaß vom
24.1.39 übertragenen Aufgabe,die Judenfrage in Form der
Auswanderung oder Evakuierung einer den Zeitverhält-
nissen entsprechend möglichst günstigsten Lösung zuzu-
führen, beauftrage ich Sie hiermit,alle erforderlichen
Vorbereitungen in organisatorischer,sachlicher und
materieller Hinsicht zu treffen für eine Gesamtlösung
der Judenfrage im deutschen Einflußgebiet in Europa.
            Soferne hierbei die Zuständigkeiten anderer
Zentralinstanzen berührt werden, sind diese zu betei-
ligen.
            Jch beauftrage Sie weiter,mir in Bälde einen
Gesamtentwurf über die organisatorischen,sachlichen
und materiellen Vorausmaßnahmen zur Durchführung der
angestrebten Endlösung der Judenfrage vorzulegen.

July 1941 letter from Reichsmarschall Hermann Goering to Reinhard Heydrich, Head of the Security Branch of the SS, concerning the 'Final Solution of the Jewish question' (a euphemism for extermination – here used for the first time). By the end of 1941, several hundred thousand Jews had been murdered. By the end of the war the number of Jews murdered by the Nazis and their collaborators had risen to over six million.

Plate 12

Above: The two sides of Nuremberg. (Left): Lieutenant Jack 'Tex' Wheelis on duty in Courtroom 600. (Right): Erich von dem Bach-Zelewski at his cell door.

Wolfe Frank (right) and Judge Michael Musmanno (centre) interrogating SS-Obergruppenfuehrer (General) Karl Wolff. The hand written inscription on the photograph reads: 'To Wolfe Frank – Ace Interpreter at Nuremberg International War Crimes Trials – and so far as I am concerned the whole world round. Most sincerely, M A Musmanno.'

General Donovan receiving a briefing in Xian, China in August 1945. The man looking over the General's left shoulder is, hands on hips, thought to be Lieutenant Putzell.

Because Goering was causing disruption, and influencing the other defendants at meal times, it was decided he should eat alone in his cell.

Airey Neave as a Prisoner of War (Oflag IX-A – Spangenberg), between May 1940 and May 1941.

Lt. Col. Donovan in 1918. He earned a Medal of Honor as a battalion commander in World War I.

Justice Robert Jackson prosecuting at the IMT. His opening and closing statements are considered to be amongst the finest examples of courtroom oratory.

The birth of simultaneous interpretation – Wolfe Frank and a colleague practicing the history defining technique in readiness for the start of the IMT.

The Press Gallery at Courtroom 600. General Donovan, who was very aware of the need to have a good relationship with the world's press, was instrumental in seeing reporters were provided with adequate and comfortable facilities (see plate 21).

Plate 16

Ned was only five months old. He was educated at Tulane University and Harvard Law School.

Even as an undergraduate, during the great depression, Putzell was seen to be an exceptional talent. While at Harvard, he expressed a desire to gain some experience with a Wall Street law practice. The university secretary, however, told him he was 'whistling in the wind because there were no law clerking jobs available, this being still part of the depression of the 30s.'[14]

Putzell saw these remarks as a challenge – as he explained in his Georgetown University interview:

I caught a sleeper into New York one Thursday night [in 1937] and found my way down to Wall Street and walked both sides of the pavement, all day Friday and all day Saturday at the end of which I had five job opportunities to my amazement. One of them being an opportunity to draft political speeches for a man who was going to run for, I believe, Lieutenant Governor of New York named William J. Donovan. He was a hero in my family's home in Louisiana since World War I and that was an opportunity that couldn't be missed so I took it instead of the law-clerking jobs ... I went back to New York at Donovan's invitation for a compensation of a hundred dollars a month, in September of 1938, and commenced a relationship with him which was like father-and-son for many, many years, a relationship which I will always treasure as one of the greatest and most exciting, most stimulating experiences a man could have.[14]

So began a life that led to Putzell becoming both a leading lawyer and a top spymaster. His office was situated next to Donovan's in the law practice and he lived with the general and his family for a while. When President Roosevelt picked Donovan to head up the OSS Donovan picked Putzell to be his right-hand man and pulled strings to get his protégé into the US Navy so he could remain at his side throughout the war and at Nuremberg – Putzell's own application having been rejected on health grounds. Of the setting up of the OSS, Putzell told the *Naples Daily News* in a 1990, 'We had to grow a government agency out of nothing.'[8]

Donovan appointed Putzell to be his Executive Officer (second in command) of the OSS,[2] initially to specifically 'manage Donovan's schedule and the paper flow to him'[3] but he became much more than that – he was the general's 'Gatekeeper'[4]. Donovan's biographer,

Douglas Waller, describes the relationship between the two men as follows:

> Putzell was more than the scheduler and paper flow manager for Donovan, a man he had known since joining the law firm in 1938. They had developed practically a father-son relationship. Putzell became Donovan's traveling companion, attending to the minutest details of his trips. Donovan's two most trusted assistants became Putzell on the road and Doering[5] in Washington. They watched his back, handled the dirty administrative chores of enforcing his orders and easing out poor performers.[6]

Throughout his long and distinguished life Putzell was ever considered a man of great integrity, and during the war he was highly regarded by Donovan, the OSS, the CIA, presidents of the USA and even Winston Churchill, with whom, amongst other world leaders, he dealt directly. Donovan and Putzell were involved in Allied advances through Sicily and Italy, then moved on to the China-Burma-India Theatre, devising ingenious ways to confuse the enemy and to learn of his plans (see Plate 14).

(Many of the following details, and any unreferenced comments, are taken from a transcript of the recorded interview Edwin Putzell gave on 12 March 2003 at his home in Naples, Florida to Mary Jane Robinson for the US Library of Congress Veterans History Project[7]. This interview, also recorded in Putzell's ninetieth year, further emphasises the qualities I refer to above, and demonstrates the sharpness of his mind and wit and his remarkable ability to assess current affairs as well as instantly recall and articulate, even at the age of eighty-nine, names, places, and events that had occurred fifty years or more earlier).

In his interview with Mary Jane Robinson, Putzell reaffirms the comments he made in his Georgetown recording: that he had graduated from Harvard Law School in 1938, during the Great Depression when jobs were hard to come by and that the year before, on his own initiative, he had travelled to New York and walked the length and breadth of Wall Street seeking a position.

> I got five job opportunities as a law clerk for the summer of '37 ... one of which was with General Donovan, Wild Bill Donovan, in his law firm at 2 Wall Street ... I chose to go there and he was nice enough to attach – let me attach myself to him ... he was an incredible guy. He is the only one in my limited experience who had both physical and intellectual daring in one person ... he

asked me to return when I graduated. And I did. And that began a 20-year relationship. He was a very warm and a very affectionate man. He was blue-eyed and had typical Irish personality and he wooed everybody.

In the years prior to the US entering the Second World War, Putzell often accompanied Donovan on his overseas fact finding trips where they met many heads of states including Italian Prime Minister Benito Mussolini. Of one such visit Putzell recalled in his Georgetown University interview:

I think it was '40. It was in there somewhere; and again, it was twofold. You know, he saw Mussolini first on that trip. First Donovan again was pursuing this goal he had of pulling together the influence of intelligence on world history, and secondly he was on a mission for the president to find out what was going on with the Italians in Africa … One went through two or three levels of security and what not. We got inside, it was a huge hall, totally black, except for a desk at the far end with a big spotlight down on Mussolini sitting behind it, bald head showing, no other human being in sight; and you walked down the marble hall and every footstep resounded, the full length of it, to this guy's desk. Talk about staged … as a result of his acquaintanceships he [Donovan] didn't have to break the ice with a lot of introductory conversation the way people often do when they go and see somebody they don't know.[15]

(On 25 April 1945, with the Allies advancing through Italy, the fascist dictator Benito Mussolini was captured trying to escape to Switzerland, where the OSS were waiting for him. He had been intercepted en route by Italian partisans, who summarily shot him and his mistress, Claretta Petacci, on 28 April. The following day Karl Wolff, Supreme SS and Police Leader in occupied Italy, after intense negotiations with Allen Dulles (head of the OSS in Switzerland and later Director of the CIA) surrendered all German forces in Italy, thereby ending the war in that theatre. Wolff was taken to Nuremberg, where he was interrogated by Wolfe Frank, but he escaped prosecution by giving evidence against other Nazis on trial – see Plate 13 and Note 8, Chapter Nineteen).

The Second World War

Donovan and Putzell watched very carefully as the war in Europe developed:

> Donovan was intimate with Churchill and some of the other key people there. And there was a lot of messaging back and forth. So his sympathy for Britain was building. And as the Germans took initiatives, hostility in one way or another, like the Coventry raid and all of that, Donovan's feeling increased … and he told the President [Roosevelt] this. Then the President suggested that he create, within the Executive Branch of the government, an office called The Coordinator of Information. And that became the OSS a little later on. About a year later.[7]

In her interview Mary Jane Robinson then asked Putzell 'So the story of you and the OSS began with Donovan?'

> Oh, yeah. At the very beginning of the COI [The Office of the Coordinator of Information], which is the forerunner of the OSS, and I was there until the night of September 30, 1945 [when the OSS ceased to exist] – at midnight Donovan and I locked the office up and walked to his home in Georgetown [after copying all the OSS' files and taking the microfilms with them].
>
> We were quite close, as I say. My office was next to his. I was privy to just about everything that went on.
>
> And he invited me to go down to Washington with him when the President offered him the job of Coordinator of Information. And we set up office in the basement of the White House. Then moved to 25th and E Streets, Northwest, to a public health service building that had been evacuated.

Mary Jane Robinson then asks Putzell if he had already applied to join any branch of the armed forces:

> I had before Pearl Harbor but my eyes had prevented it, nearsightedness. In those days they wouldn't take you. This was before the all out effort, before Pearl, he [Donovan] says, 'you still want to get in the Navy?' I said, yes! So behind him was a bank of phones. One to the President, one to the Secretary of the Navy. He picks it up and he called Frank Knox [US Secretary of the Navy].
>
> So Donovan wrote an address on a pad of paper, 16th Street, Northwest, to the Naval Officers' Recruiting Center, told me to get

in his car and to get his chauffeur to take me to it. So we arrived at this place and it was on the second floor above a drugstore.

Putzell was immediately drafted into the US Navy and given the rank of lieutenant. Mary Jane then asks Putzell about the setting up of the OSS:

A courier came from the White House and told Donovan that the President wanted him to get back immediately, which he did. And that's when he set up the COI.

The Office of Strategic Services was the first effort by this country at unorthodox warfare and strategic intelligence. Prior to that time the Army and Navy had what we call tactical intelligence. That had to do with battlefield operations and the like. But Donovan felt, and convinced the President, that we had to know what the capabilities and the intentions of other nations were from a strategic point of view called strategic intelligence.

COI started in '41, before Pearl Harbor. And the OSS was in early '42, as I recall it. I can't remember the exact dates, but I remember appearing before the – with Donovan, of course – appropriations committee led by a man named Clarence Cannon from Missouri. And we needed money, of course. Big money in those days. Donovan, being the kind of warm personality he was, got Cannon on his side very quickly and so we got what was called unvouchered funds both from the President, who had money he didn't account for, and then the funds from the House of Representatives, and that's what funded the initial parts of our operation. After – I can't recall how long now – but in 1942, by Executive Order, we moved from the aegis of the President, to reporting directly to the U.S. joint chiefs of staff and we did that for the rest of the war.

I admired Roosevelt. I was absolutely impressed by any number of these big-name people. Very much so. I admired them. I did not envy them. I have never envied anybody and I don't to this day. I admire a hell of a lot of people, but I have never envied anybody.

In a 1990 interview Putzell told the Naples Daily News[8]:

The OSS was responsible for collecting enemy intelligence and engaging in unorthodox warfare, which included sabotage.

The Naples Daily News then reported:

In late 1943, Putzell took part in a plot to capture Adolf Hitler while on a yacht out at sea. 'We were going to surface by submarine and board the damn thing and kidnap Hitler' Putzell told the Daily News.' It was well thought out. We'd even rehearsed the damn thing.' President FDR foiled the plan because he thought it might set a precedent for kidnapping future heads of state.

Putzell's career in the OSS included creating explosives, some disguised as camel dung, and bringing convicted counterfeiters from prison to help doctor passports and currency.

He travelled the world from the Soviet Union to Algiers to Great Britain.

He met Queen Elizabeth II, Lord Louis Mountbatten, knew William Casey, the former CIA Director, and Andrei Gromyko, former Soviet foreign Minister.

Putzell called his life a fabulous, fascinating life, but he kept his silence about his own missions – 'But I could tell you stories about being in a haystack scared to death, carrying a cyanide pill' [Putzell said in the interview].[8]

After Nuremberg

Putzell left Nuremberg and the US Navy at the end of November 1945. Still only thirty-two years of age, he travelled to Hollywood to assist and advise legendary film director and former OSS colleague John Ford (see Appendices C & D) produce films that were used at the IMT – evidence that helped to convict the Nazi war criminals.

On his way back from Hollywood he stopped off for a few days in St Louis at the home of the chairman of Monsanto, the petrochemical giant, who immediately offered Putzell a directorship. He went on to become general counsel, company secretary and vice president of Monsanto, before moving back into the legal profession as senior partner in Coburn, Croft & Putzell, a practice that displayed over seventy attorneys on its letter-heading. During his years in St Louis Putzell was also: vice chairman of the St. Louis County Board of Police Commissioners; president of the Social Planning Council; chairman of the St. Louis Public TV Commission;[19] a board member of the Manufacturers Bank & Trust Co and of St Luke's Hospital and had numerous other community involvements[9]. He was also invited to join the board of Westminster College, where he became vice chairman and played a leading part (in March 1946) in arranging the visit of Winston Churchill to deliver his 'Iron Curtain' speech – one of Churchill's most famous peacetime addresses (see Chapter Forty Six for further referenced details of this and other events surrounding Putzell's continuing extraordinary life post Nuremberg).

Upon retirement in 1979, Putzell moved to Naples in Florida where he became chairman of the Naples Airport Authority and was responsible for the building of the airport's passenger terminal. In 1986 he was appointed Mayor of Naples. The Naples Chamber of Commerce said his four-year term of office 'was marked by an environmental awareness that helped to make Naples the town it is today … Putzell helped form careers and created leaders around Collier County. He earned respect, garnering commitment and financial support for projects around Naples.' In the years following his mayoralty, 'he sat on the boards of Moorings Park Hospice, the Chamber of Commerce and the Community Foundation, and he was the recipient of both the *Naples Daily News* Outstanding Citizen Award'[10],[20] and the Greater Naples Leadership Award.

It appears that, from the time Donovan had invited him to join his law practice in 1938, and for the rest of his life, Edwin Putzell never put himself forward for any position, but was always 'persuaded' to take on the many roles he fulfilled with such distinction.

Recognised by the President

As with the CIA today, because of the sensitivity surrounding OSS officers and their work, few knew who they were or what they did, and they never received the credit nor the plaudits they deserved. However, in 1986, in a speech he gave at a 'Dinner for Former Members of the Office of Strategic Services', President Ronald Reagan, on behalf of a grateful nation, thanked those involved. Donovan of course was given the highest praise, but of the up to 24,000 personnel who had served in the OSS, the office's Executive Officer, Ned Putzell, was one of only six agents President Reagan personally named and held up as examples of 'dedication and heroism':

> None of America's intelligence agents have inspired and protected their nation more than the men and women of the OSS. I cannot attempt to recount tonight the individual deeds. Bill Donovan, for example, what a remarkable man … And then there was the dedication and heroism of so many other OSS officers, from guerrilla leaders like Jim Kellis, Joe Alsop, and Carl Eifler to the strategists and planners like Dick Helms, Ned Putzel [sic], and

Bill Casey [Helms and Casey both held the office of Director of the CIA].

So, tonight I join you to honor the memory of Bill Donovan and all the veterans of OSS, those who heard no bugles and received no medals, but who struggled and sacrificed so that freedom might endure. Let me say to each of you tonight what the American people would have said 40 years ago had they known your story. Let me say to each of you tonight what every living American would say if he or she had the chance: We honor you. We salute you. We thank you for a job well done.[1]

Opinions Often sought

OSS in general, and William Donovan in particular, were still being referred to in glowing terms in the House of Representatives in the 1970s, and Edwin Putzell was still advising congressmen, as the Congressional Record of 8 June 1971 records

Hon. Jack H. McDonald of Michigan. Mr Speaker ...Our Nation's leaders have long recognised that vigilance is a necessary component of national security. And certainly one of the finest examples of a modern American patriot is Gen. William J. Donovan. It was Donovan who succeeded, with the help of the highly trained, ethnically diverse, and dedicated cadre of the Office of Strategic Services, in mounting an intelligence effort during World War II to which much credit can go for our success in resisting Hitler's advance. Certainly, the D-day offensive would not have been successful without the Office of Strategic Services, nor would millions of Jews be alive today were it not for the countless acts of heroism by OSS agents that will doubtless go untold. It was the need for continuing our vigilance that led to the establishment of the Central Intelligence Agency after the OSS had been disbanded.

To the vision and restraint of Bill Donovan we owe the model of a war time intelligence agency which managed to pursue its goals in informing our military strategy without provoking those American foreign policy decisions which are historically and correctly reserved for Congress, a vision which we hope guides the historical successor to the OSS.

As General Donovan's executive assistant and former president of the OSS [Society], Edwin J. Putzell, Jr. has pointed out 'Much of the future safety and progress in peacekeeping for the 1970's will depend on the high calibre of young men and women who in the years to come will serve in the American intelligence service. These future O.S.S. [CIA] leaders can help our country at peace and expand the knowledge gathered by the present officers and members of the O.S.S.'[11]

Putzell also attended meetings of the Joint Committee on Atomic Energy – another area in which he had some knowledge from his days as Executive Officer of the OSS[12], when he was among those entrusted with details of the Manhattan Project – the research and development programme undertaken during the Second World War to produce the first nuclear weapons – as he explained in the audio interview he gave to Georgetown University: 'we got involved with Manhattan District and I knew about it. Whenever we started learning about our role in trying to find out what the Germans in developing their atom bombs were doing I got involved and had knowledge of it.'[13] Following the war, Putzell was often called upon to represent the atomic energy industry, and he presented lectures and wrote extensively on the subject, including articles that appeared in the *Bulletin of the Atomic Scientists*.[18] (See Chapter Forty Six for further details of Putzell's involvement in the nuclear industry).

From 1963 until 1977, Edwin Putzell served as a member of the United States' highly prestigious and influential Council on Foreign Relations (CFR)[16], a leading 'think tank' whose meetings 'convene government officials, global business leaders, and prominent members of the intelligence and foreign-policy communities to discuss international issues.' The CFR also runs the David Rockefeller Studies Program, which 'makes recommendations to presidential administrations and the diplomatic community, testifies before Congress, interacts with the media, and publishes research on foreign policy issues.'[17] Members of CFR have included US 'presidents, and senior politicians, secretaries of state, CIA directors, bankers, lawyers, professors, corporate directors, CEOs, and prominent media figures'. During Putzell's time, Henry Kissinger was also a member of CFR and chaired sessions on 'Nuclear Weapons and Foreign Policy'. He also served as US Secretary of State under presidents Nixon and Ford, both of whom were also CFR members. Other US presidents who were CFR members include: Dwight D. Eisenhower, George H.W. Bush, George W. Bush, Bill Clinton and Jimmy Carter.[16]

One further highly regarded position which Putzell held late in life was President of the Forum Club of South West Florida, an organisation nationally recognised in the USA for its outstanding speaker programme whose aim it is to 'Promote the highest civic, moral and ethical standards.'

Throughout his long and distinguished life Edwin Putzell met those standards in abundance: on the world stage; nationally; locally; and in his personal life. Every position he held was one of trust, and as a leading lawyer of sixty-five years' standing – making representations at every level within the US justice system up to and including Congress and the Supreme Court – it is also safe to say he had a natural, professional and ethical commitment to tell the truth.

This then was the standing and character of the man Petronella Wyatt interviewed and wrote about in her article *The Quality of Mercy* that appeared in the 1 February 2003 edition of *The Spectator*, the world's oldest general interest weekly publication.

CHAPTER TEN – NOTES & REFERENCES

1. *Remarks [made] at a Dinner for Former Members of the OSS*, President Ronald Reagan (The Reagan Presidential Library & Museum): https://www.reaganlibrary.gov/archives/speech/remarks-dinner-former-members-office-strategic-services

2. Currently, in the US Army, Executive Officer duties include acting as the commander's second-in-command to handle administrative and logistical details, which allows the commander to focus on tactical operations. Key responsibilities include managing staff and personnel, overseeing logistics and supply, and ensuring training readiness and property accountability. The Executive Officer also serves as the commander's representative, implementing policy, and advising on plans, acts as the commander's representative for daily operations, manages the commander's schedule, and often serves as the acting commander in their absence.

3. *Wild Bill Donovan*, p.97.

4. ibid, p.203.

5. Otto Doering, another lawyer from Donovan's law practice, became the General's chief of staff during the Second World War – *Wild Bill Donovan*, p.97.

6. *Wild Bill Donovan*, p.230.

7. Edwin Putzell Interview 12 March 2003 with Mary Jane Robinson (US Library of Congress): https://memory.loc.gov/diglib/vhp-stories/loc.natlib.afc2001001.08441/

8. *Naples Daily News*, 25 December 2003.

9. Harvard Law Today 'In Memorium' page: https://today.law.harvard.edu/in-memoriam-summer-2004-bulletin/

10. *Naples NP Business Comments – Business Currents –* Greater Naples Chamber of Commerce May 2007.

11. *US Senate Congressional Record,* 8 June 1971 p.18802.

12. *US Senate Congressional Record,* 16 June 1953 p.404.

13. Georgetown University, *OSS Oral History Project: Interview with Edwin Putzell,* 11 April 1997, transcript p.72.

14. ibid, pp.1 – 2.

15. ibid, pp.44 – 45.

16. https://tomjefferson1976.wordpress.com/2013/08/07/council-on-foreign-relations-membership-chart/

17. Council on Foreign Relations https://www.cfr.org/about

18. *Bulletin of the Atomic Scientists,* Volume 8, Number 8, November, 1952 pp.275–277

19. *Variety,* 7 September 1977, p.80.

20. Zuch, Lila, *He Wore Many Hats,* City of Naples: www.naplescentennial.com/untold-stories/he-wore-many-hats/

CAPTAIN WOLFE FRANK

'I had been involved in the writing of a chapter of human history that would be read, talked about and remembered forever.'[1]
WOLFE FRANK

VARIOUSLY DESCRIBED AS HAVING BEEN a refugee, resistance worker, soldier, playboy, Nazi hunter and wrongfully forgotten hero, Wolfe Frank was: Chief Interpreter at Nuremberg; *THE* leading pioneer of the simultaneous interpretation process; an intrepid undercover reporter for the *New York Herald Tribune;* and one of the most charismatic figures of the 20th century. He was dubbed 'The Voice of Doom' by the world's media following his announcing of the death sentences to the war criminals – the first of which was Hermann Goering. Apart from being the finest interpreter at Nuremberg, before the trials started (20 November 1945) Frank was, from early October, part of the interrogation team that gathered evidence against the war criminals and assisted them in choosing their legal representatives. During this time Frank drew much vital information out of the defendants which was later used as evidence – including Bruno Tesch's confession to manufacturing and distributing the gas used in the extermination chambers[2], and Otto Ohlendorf's admission to 'humanely' killing 90,000 Jews with his mobile gas chambers.[3]

Born on St Valentine's Day in 1913 the man who became known as Wolfe Frank[4] was the son of an industrialist, Ferdinand Frank, and his second wife Ida. Wolfe's father and grandfather were both Jewish, however Wolfe, like his mother, was a Protestant. He was brought up in the family home, Villa Frank in the village of Beierfeld, Saxony, and he went to the local elementary school before completing his education at the Grunewald Gymnasium in Berlin.[5]

Wolfe's childhood and formative years were generally happy and, as the son of a wealthy businessman, he enjoyed a comfortable and privileged lifestyle, clouded only by his father's strictness and infidelities – which eventually led to Wolfe running away from home and going 'underground' in Berlin, where he secured an apprenticeship with BMW. Later he joined the Adler Motor Works, then a local garage, where he managed over twenty staff before, at the age of twenty-two, going into partnership with a colleague to start a successful car sales and repair company – and a not so successful, short-lived, career as a rally driver.[6]

From his teenage years until his final days Wolfe, an exceptionally handsome and charming man, proved to be irresistible to the ladies and in his early adulthood (and indeed throughout his life) he took full advantage of the opportunities that presented themselves to him, while at the same time enjoying the lifestyle of the Bavarian 'playboy' he admits to having become.

5 March 1933

Two events in 1933 ended Wolfe's idyllic situation and brought home to him the harsh realities of the times. They also highlighted his own vulnerable position. Firstly, his father – who had by then lost his several factories and realised what, as a Jew, lay ahead of him – took his own life.

The second event occurred on the evening of 5 March. Frank was present in Munich – 'The Birth Place of the Nazi Movement' – watching the Nazis' triumphant parade through the city as they announced Hitler's coming to power. During the rally he witnessed what was almost certainly the Third Reich's first public beating of a Jew[7] – a middle-aged man standing in front of him was struck to the ground by a Brownshirt[8] simply for not giving the Nazi salute.

This incident led Wolfe to resolve that, from that moment onwards, he would never again give the Nazi salute himself, and he managed to avoid doing so for the next three years – even on the many occasions he was in the same rooms as the Fuehrer.[9]

Having seen what was happening to Jews – including the confiscation of their properties and goods; the beatings and humiliations; the internments in ghettos and then concentration camps; and the disappearance of friends and family – Wolfe became an active member of an underground resistance movement that was involved in smuggling large amounts of money and endangered Jewish citizens out of Germany.[10]

In 1936 Wolfe's life changed dramatically again. He met and fell in love with the woman who was to become his first wife – Baroness Maditta von Skrbensky. They were unable to marry in Germany (or in any other Axis-aligned country) because of Wolfe's non-Aryan ancestry. However, while on holiday in Italy the couple were befriended by a British Army officer, Major Humphrey Sykes (see Chapter One and Appendix A), who in April 1937 arranged for Wolfe and Maditta to:

travel to England; be married at Andover; and honeymoon at his home on the army base at Tidworth in Wiltshire.

Four days later, on his return to Germany, Frank was tipped off, by a friend in the Gestapo, that he was about to be arrested the following morning and interned in Dachau concentration camp. Branded 'An enemy of the State, to be shot on sight' he escaped to Switzerland and then (following a cash advance from Humphrey Sykes) to England, leaving behind his bride of six days whom, like his mother, he did not see again for almost ten years.[11]

Arriving in England without money and very few possessions, and unable to speak the language, Frank began to immediately and enthusiastically integrate himself into the British way of life. Within two years he had become: fluent in English; risen to the position of Managing Director of two of Sykes' companies; the producer of a West End musical; and an executive with a land corporation in Cape Canaveral, Florida.[12]

In 1938, with the growing tensions in Europe, Frank was advised to formerly disassociate himself from Germany. He did this by marching into the German Embassy in London and insulting Hitler 'with a list of unprintable adjectives' before spitting on a portrait of the Fuehrer. Shortly after he received notification that he had been deprived of his German citizenship as an individual who was 'Hostile to, and an enemy of, the National Socialist German Reich.'[13]

For a short while life could not have been sweeter for Frank. He was: officially 'Stateless;' fully established in England; an executive of several companies; had a new luxury apartment in London's exclusive Dolphin Square;[14] rented a large house on the Thames; and owned his own narrow boat. He had friends in the highest circles of society, government and the theatre and was also in a long-term relationship with a beautiful actress and dancer, Patricia Leonard,[15] who was destined to become one of the wealthiest women in the world.

Despite all this, his known heroism as an underground resistance worker and his having been officially declared an enemy of the Third Reich, at the outbreak of the Second World War Frank was arrested, along with all other former German and Austrian citizens, and interned as an 'enemy alien.'[16]

Having lost everything he had worked so hard for and furious at what the authorities had done to him Frank was determined to clear his name, gain his freedom and join the British Army. Within weeks of his detainment, he was appointed Camp Leader (of nearly 2,000 men) and for the next several months he applied pressure on those commanding the various camps he was moved to while enlisting the help of Humphrey Sykes, other influential friends and Members of Parliament. Amongst those officers directly involved in his detainment was Sir Timothy Eden, brother of the then War Minister Sir Anthony Eden (who later became Prime Minister).[17]

Frank's persistence eventually paid off and he was not only released, but he and a number of other internees were allowed to enlist in the British Army's Auxiliary Pioneer Corps.[18] Following twenty-three requests to be allowed to join a fighting unit he was transferred firstly to the Royal Armoured Corps and then, in December 1944, having gained a commission, to the Royal Northumberland Fusiliers where he passed out as a second lieutenant.[19]

During the remaining months of the war Frank distinguished himself in a number of roles and his linguistic skills came to the fore especially whilst training Belgian soldiers (in French) how to use the Vickers machine gun.[20]

Following the Allies' victory in Europe Frank was appointed staff captain and instructed to join the British War Crimes Executive (BWCE)[21] where he was informed: 'This unit will be engaged in collecting material for the prosecution of the major war criminals. That's Goering and others, you know. We leave on Sunday.'[22]

Frank was therefore involved with the BWCE from day one of its operations, and he was given the very first piece of evidence to translate – Hitler's infamous *Nacht und Nebel* (Night and Fog) decree,[23] which ordered the execution of political activists and resistance 'helpers'. Issued by the Fuehrer in 1941, the decree dealt with the elimination of persons in occupied territories. Victims of the decree were said to have disappeared into the night and fog without a trace.

The BWCE moved from London to Paris to Bad Oeynhausen near Hanover where Frank honed his skills as a translator, investigator and interrogator. This led to him being singled out as being an interpreter with exceptional skills and brought him to the attention of Colonel Leon Dostert, Head of the US Language Division, who, at their first meeting, immediately had Frank transferred from the BWCE onto the US team for the Nuremberg Trials. This eventually led to Frank being appointed Chief Interpreter.[24]

Frank was also the leading pioneer of simultaneous translation (now generally referred to as being 'conference interpreting'). First used at Nuremberg, the system proved to be more successful than anyone had ever hoped, and Frank's contributions at the IMT were considered to be major factors in seeing that justice was fairly and meticulously interpreted and translated to all parties in a way that, it is said, shortened proceedings at the IMT by an estimated three years.

CHAPTER ELEVEN – NOTES & REFERENCES

1. *Nuremberg's Voice of Doom,* p.172.

2. ibid, p.103. Dr Bruno Tesch was one of the two owners of a Company called Tesch & Stabenow in Hamburg. They were manufacturers of a gas called 'Zyklon B' (or Cyclone B) – used to exterminate the inmates of Nazi death camps. Tesch was tried and found guilty and he was executed on 16 May 1946.

3. ibid, pp.164–166. Otto Ohlendorf, Chief of the Special Action Group in the East, perpetrated mass murder in Moldova, South Ukraine, the Crimea and the North Caucasus. He was tried, found guilty, sentenced to death and executed by hanging in 1951.

4. Wolfe was originally named Johann Wolfgang Frank, and then Hans Wolfgang Frank. He later became Hugh Wolfe Frank – the name under which he was granted British passports and, in 1948, British citizenship – however he preferred to be known as Wolfe Hugh Frank or just plain Wolfe Frank.

5. Grunewald Gymnasium, founded in 1903, was, during Wolfe Frank's time there, a grammar and boarding school for boys. Until the Nazis came to power in 1933 approximately one third of the pupils and many of the teaching staff were Jewish.

6. Having purchased and prepared a hand built 'Tracta' racing car that he described as being 'twenty years ahead of its time' Wolfe entered it in an important race on the rally circuit (the Kochelberg Hill-climb) only to lose the vehicle in dramatic circumstances. Coming out of a bend at full throttle he was forced to swerve to avoid one of Germany's top drivers, Ernst von Delius, who had stalled. Frank's car skidded and 'disintegrated on the way down the mountainside'. Miraculously, Frank was thrown clear – *Nuremberg's Voice of Doom,* p.24.

7. ibid, p.9.

8. The Sturmabteilung (SA) – Storm Detachment – was the parliamentary wing of the Nazi Party. Its members were known as 'Brownshirts' because that was the colour of the uniform they wore.

9. *Nuremberg's Voice of Doom,* p.16.

10. ibid, pp.26–32.

11. ibid, pp.37–41.

12. ibid, pp.42–47 and 51–55.

13. ibid, pp.48–50.

14. Dolphin Square is a block of luxury flats, favoured by members of both Houses of Parliament and the gentry, which were built between 1935–1937 near the River Thames in Pimlico. Maxwell Knight, Britain's top spymaster, ran his operation from apartments in the next and the same block of flats to

Wolfe Frank's and it was here that Knight recruited James Bond author Ian Fleming as an agent.

15. Patricia Leonard was a starlet at 17 and became a leading lady in many West End productions in the 1930s and during the war years. Soon after the war she married the noted American philanthropist Francis Francis, heir to the Standard Oil fortune. The couple purchased Bird Cay, one of the Berry Islands, and transformed it into 'one of the most developed islands of the Bahamas'.

16. *Nuremberg's Voice of Doom*, pp.64–69.

17. ibid, pp.70–76.

18. Members of the Auxiliary Military Pioneer Corps performed a wide variety of tasks in all theatres of war ranging from handling all types of stores, laying prefabricated track on beaches and stretcher-bearing. They also worked on the construction of harbours, laid pipes under the ocean, constructed airfields and roads and erected bridges. (In 1940 the Corps' name was changed to the Pioneer Corps and, following the war, King George VI designated it to be the Royal Pioneer Corps).

19. *Nuremberg's Voice of Doom*, pp.76–86.

20. ibid, pp. 87–89.

21. The British delegation for the prosecution of Nazi war criminals was designated the British War Crimes Executive. Consisting of some 170 persons including: barristers; analysts; translators; secretaries; and typists; the BWCE was responsible for the British legal administration of the trials.

22. *Nuremberg's Voice of Doom*, p.94.

23. ibid, p.95.

24. ibid, pp.119–122.

MAJOR AIREY NEAVE

*'He was a public servant who never really stopped
being a secret agent.'*[1]
PAUL ROUTLEDGE

MAJOR AIREY NEAVE was a British soldier and lawyer (who later became a Member of Parliament). In 1942 he became the first British prisoner-of-war to successfully escape from the German prisoner-of-war camp, Oflag IV-C – better known as Colditz Castle.[2] Upon his return to England he joined MI9 (Military Intelligence Section 9), a secret department of the British Secret Service MI6 that was responsible for gaining intelligence from enemy prisoners-of-war and he was soon heading a section within MI9 known as Room 900 (named after its location within the War Office). Room 900's main objective was to rescue downed Allied airmen and escaping prisoners-of-war trapped behind enemy lines. After the war he served with the IMT at Nuremberg, firstly investigating the Krupp[3] empire and then, being a qualified lawyer, he was chosen to serve the indictments on the war criminals where he was assisted by Wolfe Frank.

Airey Middleton Sheffield Neave was born in Knightsbridge on 23 January 1916 to Sheffield Neave, a well known entomologist, and his wife Dorothy (née Middleton). The family later moved to Beaconsfield and Airey was sent to a boarding school in Worthing before moving on to Eton College, where he served in the school cadet corps. In 1935 he received a territorial commission as a second lieutenant in the Oxfordshire and Buckinghamshire Light Infantry.

Following Eton, Neave read Jurisprudence at Merton College, Oxford and was elected to the exclusive Myrmidon Club, 'a group of undergraduates, never more than a dozen in number, who dedicated themselves to the good things in life'[4].

During 1933

While at Eton in 1933, Neave wrote a prize winning essay that examined the likely consequences of Adolf Hitler's rise to supreme power and he predicted a world war would break out in Europe in the near future.[5] In the September of that year his parents sent him to

Germany to improve his knowledge of the country and its language. He stayed with a family near Berlin, attended school with members of the Hitler Youth movement and came to realise that Hitler was preparing these young men for war.

Upon graduating in 1938 Neave joined a firm of solicitors in the City of London and after learning the basics of law, moved on to become a pupil in a barrister's chambers. His territorial commission was transferred, firstly to the Royal Engineers and then, in August 1940, to the Royal Artillery.

Days before Britain declared war on Germany, Neave, anticipating what was about to happen, enlisted and was posted to an anti-aircraft searchlight regiment that was soon deep in action at Calais – a town that Churchill instructed 'had to be defended to the end'. Leading his men in battle Neave received a serious wound to his side and was hospitalised. This led to his capture by the advancing Nazis. He was put on a stretcher and, at the age of twenty-four, he became a prisoner-of-war.[6] For his bravery in this battle he was awarded the Military Cross.

Neave was taken firstly to Spangenburg near Kassel (see Plate 15) and then, in February 1941, on to another PoW camp – Stalag XX-A at Thorn (Torun) in Poland – from where he attempted to escape. After several days on the road, he was eventually recaptured and interrogated by the Gestapo and the SS, at which point he feared for his life. Eventually he was returned to Thorn only to be told he was being moved to the 'Bad Boys Camp' at Colditz. This impregnable castle was situated high on a hill and was surrounded on three sides by sheer rock precipices. It could only be approached by a narrow, cobbled causeway over a deep moat.'[7] Neave and four other 'bad boys' arrived on 14 May 1941 and after another failed attempt that August he made his successful escape on 5 January 1942. In a diary entry of that date the Chaplain recorded:

> Neave and a Dutch officer, second Lieutenant Lutyen, escaped ten minutes ago. It was a scheme requiring the boldest initiative and at least eight weeks' preparation. It was carried out with the utmost secrecy, and already they are outside the castle.[8]

Neave's successful and adventurous escape is well recorded by Paul Routledge in *Public Servant, Secret Agent*, but in brief: Neave and Lutyen made their escape via a quick exit from a theatrical production using the trap door beneath the stage. By train and on foot they travelled to Leipzig and then on to the border with Switzerland. Neave returned to England via France, Spain and Gibraltar – arriving in April, three and a half months after making his break for freedom. He was the first British officer to escape from Colditz Castle. Shortly after his return, he received his Military Cross.[9] (He was promoted to the rank of captain in April 1945 and, at the war's end, was made a temporary major. He was also awarded the Distinguished Service Order).[10]

Upon his return to London in 1942, Neave was immediately recruited as an intelligence officer by MI9 and he chose the codename 'Saturday'. Soon after he met and fell in love with Diana Giffard. On only their third date he asked her to be his wife, she accepted and they were married on 29 December. He gave his occupation as being a captain in the British Army, she as a secretary with the Red Cross – both were in fact working for different branches of the Secret Service with Neave 'commanding agents in the field' and Diana working on 'equally secret operations.'[11]

Neave remained with MI9 and Room 900 for the rest of the war and his main responsibilities included: supporting underground escape organizations in occupied Europe, with equipment, agents, and money; and assisting downed Allied airmen and other military personnel evade and escape capture by the Germans. In Western Europe, about 5,000 British and American military personnel were rescued by resistance-led escape organizations and repatriated to the United Kingdom. After D-Day (the Allied invasion of Normandy) Neave journeyed to France and Belgium and set up 'Operation Marathon' a scheme that helped rescue more than 300 allied airmen who had taken refuge in forest camps after being shot down.

During the Second World War, about 35,000 Allied military personnel, many helped by Room 900, escaped PoW camps or evaded capture and made their way to Allied or neutral countries after being trapped behind enemy lines. (In 1948 Neave was awarded the Bronze Star Medal [BSM] – a United States Armed Forces decoration awarded for either heroic achievement, heroic service, meritorious achievement, or meritorious service in a combat zone).

In 1945, like Wolfe Frank, Neave was posted firstly to the BWCE in London and Bad Oeynhausen and eventually Nuremberg, and he was instructed to gather evidence against the Krupp Empire.[3] This led to its head, Gustav Krupp, being charged and brought before the IMT, where he was found to be unfit to stand trial due to the onset of 'senile decay'. (At a later Subsequent Proceedings trial Krupp's son Alfried and ten other Krupp executives, largely on the evidence obtained by Neave, were charged and found guilty of crimes against humanity and crimes against peace).

As a well-known war hero and a qualified lawyer who spoke fluent German, Neave was honoured with the task of serving the indictments on the Nazi leaders. The irony of the role was not lost on the major – here were the hierarchy of the Third Reich reduced to the state of common criminals, deprived of their freedom and now suffering in the corners of enemy cells with him playing the role of the inquisitor – a reversal of the suffering he had endured in Colditz at the hands of the Gestapo and the SS.

CHAPTER TWELVE – NOTES & REFERENCES

1. *Public Servant, Secret Agent* p.10.

2. Oflag IV-C, was the name given to the Nazi prisoner-of-war camp based at the castle overlooking the town of Colditz in Saxony. Many captured Allied officers were imprisoned at Colditz, especially those who had attempted escapes from other camps. Oflag is short of Offizierslager, meaning 'officers' camp'.

3. The Krupp dynasty of Essen was prominent throughout both world wars in the manufacture of steel, artillery and other weapons ranging from small arms and ammunition up to and including battleships, U-boats and tanks. Many tens of thousands incarcerated by the Nazis were used as slave labourers by Krupp Industries under the most appalling of conditions.

4. *Public Servant, Secret Agent*, p.31

5. ibid, p.35.

6. ibid, pp.38–49.

7. ibid, pp.67–70.

8. ibid, p.93.

9. The Military Cross (MC) is awarded for an act or acts of exemplary gallantry during active operations against the enemy on land, to captains or officers of lower rank up to warrant officers (The Gazette).

10. The Distinguished Service Order is awarded for meritorious or distinguished service by officers of the armed forces during wartime, typically in actual combat, serving under fire, and usually awarded to those above the rank of captain. Until 1943, the recipient must have been mentioned in despatches by the commander-in-chief of the Army, or admiral of the Navy (*The Gazette*).

11. *Public Servant, Secret Agent*, pp.134–135.

COLONEL BURTON ANDRUS

'The non hero of the story'[1]
WOLFE FRANK

COLONEL BURTON ANDRUS was a military officer who served in the US Army from 1917 until 1952. Dwight D. Eisenhower, Supreme Allied Commander, General of the Army, (and later 34th President of the USA) appointed Andrus to be Commandant of the prison to house those high-ranking Nazi officers who were to be tried for war crimes. A strict disciplinarian, he spent many hours planning every detail of the prisoners' lives and felt cheated by Goering's action.

Burton Curtis Andrus was born in 1892 to Hermine and Major Frank B. Andrus. Burton attended the University at Buffalo in 1914 and, while there, he joined the Officer Reserve Corps. He married Katherine Elizabeth Stebbins on 12 April 1916, and the couple went on to have four children – two boys and two girls. Prior to his years of service in the Army Andrus worked for the Standard Oil Company of New York.

He was commissioned into the regular army in 1917 and made a 1st lieutenant and commander of the stockade at Fort Oglethorpe, Georgia, where he imposed strict rules and ordered his guards to shoot anyone trying to escape. He was promoted to captain in 1919 and was posted to California, Kansas and Kentucky and became involved in prison and intelligence work. From 1924 until the outbreak of the Second World War, Andrus saw service at various bases in the US and the Philippines during which time he became: an Air Corps instructor; liaison officer to the 16th Observation Squadron; commander of a Civilian Conservation Corps; and a training officer with the 13th Cavalry. He was promoted to the rank of major in 1935 and to lieutenant colonel in 1940.

From early 1940 Andrus served with the Pennsylvania National Guard before being posted to Washington as an instructor to the Armored Forces School. The following year he was sent to Britain to study air-ground operations, RAF manoeuvers, and installations. Following the US entry into the Second World War, Andrus was promoted to colonel (in 1942) and joined General George Patton's Third Army as an air-ground observer. (Andrus was a great admirer of General Patton and copied the general's style by carrying a riding crop and wearing pressed uniforms and a highly polished helmet.

Eisenhower selected Andrus to be prison Commandant because of his experience in security, and, on 6 May 1945, he opened an interrogation centre for senior Nazi leaders at Mondorf les Bains in Luxemburg – codenamed 'Ashcan'. On 12 August the prisoners were moved by air to Nuremberg. Andrus was recognised by both serving officers and prisoners alike as being a strict disciplinarian who made no distinction between those Nazi leaders who were military or civilian, treating them all as war criminals.

At Nuremberg, Andrus had guards maintain constant surveillance to prevent suicides, checking each cell every thirty seconds, and inmates were required to sleep with their hands outside their blankets. Even so, Dr. Leonardo Conti, German health officer responsible for the Nazis' euthanasia program, hanged himself in his cell on 6 October 1945, to be followed on 24 October by Robert Ley, Nazi labour leader. Having promised there would be no further similar incidents, he accepted full responsibility for failing to prevent Goering's suicide. This severely tarnished his reputation, and he was removed from his command in December 1946.

Andrus had not been popular with the press, and after the third suicide of a Nazi leader attacks on him grew. *Time* magazine, in its 28 October 1946 issue, called Andrus:

A pompous, unimaginative, and thoroughly unlikable officer who wasn't up to his job. Colonel Burton C. Andrus loved that job. Every morning his plump little figure, looking like an inflated pouter pigeon, moved majestically into the court, impeccably garbed in his uniform and highly shellacked helmet. His bow to the judges as they entered was one of the sights of Nürnberg. He loved to pen little notes: 'The American Colonel invites the distinguished French prosecutor and his staff to accompany him to a baseball game.'

He had spent long hours with his staff planning every last detail of the prisoners' life. He arranged anti-suicide cells in which even the tables were designed to collapse under a man's weight. He posted 24-hour guards before each cell and insisted that the prisoners sleep with hands outside the blankets. He required prisoners to take exercise periods during which their cells were searched. He had designed interview booths in which prisoners and visitors could converse with one another without being able to touch hands. All seemed well, but Andrus forgot that a pattern had been set, and with men like Göring, just to see the pattern was to see ways to break it.'[2]

In his memoirs Wolfe Frank says much the same, and he does not hold back in his opinion of Andrus and his lack of ability to prevent suicides:[3]

CHAPTER THIRTEEN – NOTES & REFERENCES

1. *Nuremberg's Voice of Doom*, pp.155–6.

2. *Time* magazine, 28 October 1946 – *'Down without Tears'*:
   https://time.com/archive/6606341/international-down-without-tears/

3. *Nuremberg's Voice of Doom*, pp.155–6.

COLONEL TELFORD TAYLOR

'One does not build a stupendous war machine in a fit of passion, nor an Auschwitz slave factory during a passing spasm of brutality.'[1]
TELFORD TAYLOR

COLONEL (LATER BRIGADIER GENERAL) TELFORD TAYLOR was a US lawyer, professor, historian and teacher. He was best known for his role as a lead counsel for the prosecution at the IMT, where he was assistant to Justice Robert H. Jackson, and then as Chief Counsel of the Subsequent Proceedings.

Taylor was born in Schenectady, New York on 23 May 1908. His parents were John Bellamy Taylor and Marcia Estabrook Jones. He attended Williams College and Harvard Law School, where he received a law degree in 1932. He was married twice: firstly, to Mary Ellen Walker in 1937, with whom he had three children; and secondly to Toby Golick in 1974, with whom he also had three children.

During the 1930s, Taylor worked for several government agencies within the Roosevelt administration, and he was a staff member in the United States Senate prior to the Second World War. In 1940 he became general counsel for the Federal Communications Commission.

Following the outbreak of war, Taylor joined Army Intelligence as a major on 5 October 1942, where he served under General Donovan at the OSS,[6] and he attained the rank of colonel. He led the American group at Bletchley Park and became the liaison between US and British intelligence and was responsible for the group's activities in analysing information obtained from intercepted German communications using ULTRA[2] encryption.

Taylor was promoted to lieutenant colonel in 1943 and returned to England, where he helped negotiate the BRUSA Agreement[3]. He attained the rank of full colonel in 1944, and in 1945 was assigned to the Robert H. Jackson team, which helped work out the London Charter of the International Military Tribunal.

By the end of the war Taylor had learned a great deal about the inner workings of the Nazi dictatorship and in the Spring of 1945 Justice Jackson asked him to serve as an American war crimes prosecutor at the IMT. Taylor accepted the job and emerged during the pre-trial debates as a voice of moderation who warned his superiors about the implications of their proposed actions.

When Jackson resigned his position as prosecutor after the first trial and returned to the US in October 1946, Taylor was promoted to brigadier general and became Chief Counsel for the remaining twelve trials. One of Taylor's first tasks as Chief Counsel was to appoint Wolfe Frank to be Chief Interpreter.

While Taylor was not wholly satisfied with the outcomes of the Nuremberg Trials, he considered them a success because they set a precedent and defined a legal base for crimes against peace and humanity. In 1950, the United Nations codified the most important statements from these trials in the seven Nuremberg Principles.

Taylor's contributions at the IMT were not only highly acclaimed, some of his arguments formed the basis of future legislation such as the precedent he set in the Justice Case of the Subsequent Proceedings, where he established: nine officials from the German Ministry of Justice and seven members of the Nazi-era People's and Special Courts had carried out 'judicial murder and other atrocities, which they committed by destroying law and justice in Germany, and then utilising the emptied forms of legal process for the persecution, enslavement and extermination on a large scale.' In his opening remarks Taylor described the nature of the crimes committed as follows:

> The crimes with which these men are charged were not committed in rage or under the stress of sudden temptation. They were not the slips or lapses of otherwise well-ordered men. One does not build a stupendous war machine in a fit of passion, nor an Auschwitz factory during a passing spasm of brutality.'

In praise of his work at the IMT, the website of Columbia University, where he taught for over thirty years, states:[4]

> Telford Taylor helped establish the guidelines for trying German war criminals after World War II, which became a model in future years for similar tribunals around the globe.'

Herbert Wechsler, a fellow law school professor who worked with Taylor at Nuremberg, added:

> If I was asked to name the person of my generation whom I most admired, I would promptly answer Telford Taylor … [W]ise counsellor, persuasive advocate, careful scholar, all the qualities that signify distinction … were his in high degree.[4]

While *Nation* magazine, in 1995, wrote:

> The human rights movement owes much of its legal foundation to the work of Gen. Telford Taylor … Nuremberg gave legitimacy to the concept that the world had something to say about how governments treat their own citizens. In 1950 the United Nations codified Nuremberg's most important statements into seven Nuremberg Principles, which have since been adopted by the legal systems of almost every major nation.

Taylor himself concluded that despite the difficulties, the trials were a success but suggested that any future war-crimes trial must look at the actions of the winners as well as the losers. 'The laws of war are not a one-way street,' he said.[5]

CHAPTER FOURTEEN – NOTES & REFERENCES

1. Film: *Telford Taylor During Justice Case*, United States Holocaust Museum.

2. ULTRA was the designation adopted by British military intelligence in June 1941 for wartime signals intelligence obtained by breaking high-level encrypted enemy communications at the Government Code and Cypher School at Bletchley Park.

3. The 1943 BRUSA Agreement (Britain–United States of America agreement) was an agreement between the British and US governments to facilitate co-operation between the US War Department and the British Government Code and Cypher School at Bletchley Park.

4. Columbia University Web Site.

5. *The Anatomy of the Nuremberg Trials: A Personal Memoir* Telford Taylor, p 641.

6. The US Naval Institute records: 'Churchill told Roosevelt about Ultra and the Enigma intercepts at Bletchley Park. In violation of American neutrality—an impeachable act if discovered—Roosevelt ordered General William J. (Wild Bill) Donovan to dispatch Army, Navy and civilian cryptanalysts to Bletchley months before Pearl Harbor … American cryptanalysts began arriving at BP in large numbers in 1942. Some would later advance from the obscurity of Bletchley to very public positions … Telford Taylor became chief counsel at the Nuremberg war crime trials and an author: https://www.usni.org/magazines/naval-history-magazine/1997/december/secret-bletchley-park Taylor's obituary in *The Independent states:* During the Second World War, he rose to the rank of Colonel in the Office of Strategic Services, and spent most of his time at Bletchley Park in England where he served as a liaison between American and British intelligence: https://www.independent.co.uk/news/obituaries/obituary-telford-taylor-1157311.html

LIEUTENANT JACK WHEELIS

'the perfect model for a Marlborough cigarette commercial.'[1]
GENERAL EUGENE PHILLIPS

LIEUTENANT (LATER CAPTAIN) JACK 'TEX' WHEELIS was a US army officer responsible for guarding high ranking Nazi prisoners during the Nuremberg trials.

He was born at Mart near Waco in Texas on 22 April 1913 to a farmer, Benjamin Wheelis, and his wife Dorothy. Wheelis attended the local high school before enrolling at Texas Tech in Lubbock, where he excelled at American football and in military training. This interest in the armed forces led to him enrolling in the US Marines before resuming his studies at Texas Tech in 1937. He graduated with a BSc degree in agriculture in 1941.

In 1943 he was drafted into the army and posted to Europe and promoted to second lieutenant. As a soldier of the First Infantry Division, he was selected for guard duty at Nuremberg and was further promoted during the trials to first lieutenant.

Wheelis befriended Hermann Goering and he accepted gifts from the Reichsmarschall, including a pen, watch, and postcards. (The *Jack Wheelis Papers* are held at the Dolph Briscoe Center for American History, University of Texas in Austin. They include the official record of the *Trial of the Major War Criminals Before the International Military Tribunal*, other U.S. military documents, Wheelis' personal correspondence and postcards he sent to Hermann Goering).

General Eugene Phillips, who had known Wheelis well at Nuremberg, said of the lieutenant: 'Tall, brawny, and muscular, with a rugged, chiseled face, Jack Wheelis would have been the perfect model for a Marlborough cigarette commercial. His appearance commanded attention, his friendly and outgoing manner drew people to him. Handsome in his army uniform, he was a striking figure.'[2]

In his book *Nuremberg – Infamy on Trial* Joseph Persico records the words of Rose Kobb, Colonel Andrus' secretary:

Colonel Andrus had plans for Wheelis. The colonel was having a deuce of a time with personnel. In his judgement, the security mission required superior people; yet the army kept sending him green second-raters ... this brawny Texan had a commanding presence and certainly looked like a leader. Andrus was going to appoint him assistant operations leader.[3]

Persico also records details of the friendship Goering had developed with Wheelis:

Riling his keepers was not a policy Hermann Goering could afford. He needed not antagonists but friends, like Tex Wheelis.[4]

Wheelis became property officer of the baggage room, and it has been suggested he helped Goering visit the room to retrieve a cyanide capsule hidden among Goering's personal effects that had been confiscated by the US Army. Although some historians and writers, including Ben Swearingen, have thought this possible, many others view this with scepticism – the prisoners were on twenty-four-hour suicide watch (see Plate 18) that would not have allowed for such a visit to have gone unnoticed, unrecorded or unconsidered by the Board of Officers that was immediately set up to investigate Goering's suicide (see Chapter Thirty Five).

The statement Wheelis gave to the Board of Officers was remarkably similar to the ones given by ten other guards – it read:

I have had in my possession the key to the baggage room of the prison during the period 10 October 1946 to 15 October 1946 and can state positively that Goering received nothing from, nor had access to the baggage room during this period.[5]

In an interview given to author Ben Swearingen, Jack Wheelis' son, Judge James Wheelis, indicated that his father never discussed matters concerning the war criminals, but he did recall seeing the fountain pen, watch and other memorabilia in a draw and a publication accusing his father of helping Goering kill himself. When the judge asked if there was any truth in what was being said, his father refused to answer.[6]

While Lieutenant Putzell's admissions make clear it was not Wheelis who handed Goering the cyanide capsule, there is room to believe that he could well have played a role in both the incident itself and a possible diversion that followed – as will be revealed a little later.

CHAPTER FIFTEEN – NOTES & REFERENCES

1. *The Mystery of Hermann Goering's Suicide*, p.160.

2. ibid.

3. *Nuremberg – Infamy on Trial*, p 139.

4. ibid, p 299.

5. *Report of Board of Proceedings in Case of Hermann Goering (Suicide) October 1946*

6. *The Mystery of Hermann Goering's Suicide*, p 174.

SERGEANT HARRY SHOTWELL

*'[General Donovan] stuck his finger right in my face and said
"by God I order you not to hear a single word uttered in this room –
is that clear soldier."'[1]*
HARRY SHOTWELL

DURING THE SECOND WORLD WAR, HARRY GLENNWOOD SHOTWELL was a machine gunner of the First Infantry Division of the US Army. He was born on 12 January 1925 in Carrollton, Texas and his parents were Ross and Emma Shotwell. He was educated at Carrollton High School from where he graduated in 1942.

At the age of eighteen Shotwell enlisted in the First Infantry Division and he was among the first men to land on Omaha Beach in Normandy during the D-Day landings of 6 June 1944[2] that began the liberation of France and ultimately victory on the Western Front.

General Donovan was also involved in the Normandy Landings. Alighting on Utah Beach and under heavy enemy fire the general told his aide, David Bruce, 'You understand of course, David, that neither of us must be captured. We know too much'. The pair realised at once that Bruce had left their poison pills behind. Donovan then took out his revolver and said to Bruce 'if we are about to be captured I'll shoot you first. After all I am your commanding officer.' Then Donovan said, he would shoot himself.[3]

Harry Shotwell was no less brave. For his service and actions during the Battle of the Bulge[4], he was awarded a Bronze Star (given for either heroic service or achievement, or meritorious service or achievement) and a Purple Heart (awarded in the name of the President to those wounded or killed in action). 'We weren't trying to win the war we were trying to survive' Harry told *The Alliance Review*, Minerva, shortly before he died.

At the war's end Shotwell became a guard at Nuremberg, initially serving under Colonel Andrus. However, in October 1945 'out of the blue' he and five other guards were ordered to go with two OSS 'Spooks'. 'I still do not know to this day why I was chosen but I was told I was to follow the orders of these two men from now on ... I remember during this time as a guard thinking that: for an old Carroll County farm boy, this isn't bad ... The only thing I did not really like was the fact that I was not allowed to convey what I was doing to my family.'[5]

Under a veil of secrecy Shotwell was assigned to be a personal guard to Goering where one of his duties was to escort the Reichsmarschall to and from interrogations – including at least one conducted by General Donovan that has a bearing on these matters. Shotwell had no idea, or was not prepared to say, why he thought he had been chosen for these special duties or why, to his great surprise, he was unceremoniously relieved of them on 17 November 1945 – just three days before the start of the IMT – but there are some clues, as we shall see later, as to why his services might have been dispensed with, as he explained in a recorded interviewer he gave to *The Canton Repository* that discussed a day he was ordered to take Goering to see General Donovan[6] (to be continued in Chapter Twenty Three).

CHAPTER SIXTEEN – NOTES & REFERENCES

1. Recorded interview: *Harry Shotwell Recalls a Day with Nazi Hermann Goering and "Wild Bill" Donovan.* https://omny.fm/shows/rep-audio-vault/harry-shotwell-recalls-a-day-with-nazi-hermann-goe

2. On 6 June 1944, the US Army's 1st and 29th Infantry Divisions landed on Omaha Beach as part of the Normandy Landings. Codenamed *Operation Neptune* and better known as 'D-Day'. It remains the largest seaborne invasion in history, in which 34,000 Allied troops landed and suffered 2,400 casualties.

3. *Wild Bill Donovan* pp.244–245.

4. The Battle of the Bulge, also called the Battle of the Ardennes, (December 16, 1944–January 16, 1945) was the last major German offensive on the Western Front during WWII which saw the Allies repel all German attempts to push them back. The name for the battle was taken from Winston Churchill's description of the 'bulge' being the wedge that the Germans had driven into the Allied lines.

5. Interview given to Thomas Clapper, *The Alliance Review*, Minerva.

6. Recorded interview: *Harry Shotwell Recalls a Day with Nazi Hermann Goering and "Wild Bill" Donovan:* https://omny.fm/shows/rep-audio-vault/harry-shotwell-recalls-a-day-with-nazi-hermann-goe

ERICH VON DEM BACH-ZELEWSKI

*'A traitor … bastard … and the bloodiest murderer in
this whole system.'*[1]
HERMANN GOERING

ERICH VON DEM BACH-ZELEWSKI was a high-ranking SS
commander who during the Second World War was in charge of
Nazi security in the occupied territories of Eastern Europe. Despite his
responsibility for numerous war crimes and crimes against humanity
he did not stand trial at Nuremberg and instead appeared as a witness
for the prosecution.

Born on 1 March 1899 in Lauenberg, Pomerania[2] (now Lebork,
Poland) as Erich Julius Zelewski, he was the son of Otto and Amalia
Zelewski. His father died when he was young. He grew up in relative
poverty and was taken in by a local landowner who saw that he
received an education in Strasburg and Konitz.

At the age of fifteen he enlisted in the Prussian Army and served
throughout the First World War. He was wounded in 1915 and suffered
a gas attack in 1918. He was awarded the Iron Cross 1st and 2nd Class
and was promoted to lieutenant. Following the end of the war, Zelewski
remained in the armed forces and fought against Polish uprisings. He
also joined an active anti-Semitic organisation and added 'von dem
Bach' to his name (it is said he manipulated his genealogy numerous
times during his career to impress his superiors). He joined the Nazi
Party in 1930, became a member of the Reichstag in 1932 and was a
Senior SS and Police Leader in Silesia by 1937. Following the outbreak
of the Second World War he was appointed 'Commissioner for the
Strengthening of Germandom' in East-Silesia which resulted in up to
20,000 being forced from their homes and Bach-Zelewski becoming
involved in the planning of the concentration camp at Auschwitz.

From 1941 he oversaw the murder of Jews in Riga and Minsk
and other areas and, having for a while dropped the second half of
his name, Von dem Bach was promoted to SS-Obergruppenführer
(General) and General of Police. In June 1943, Himmler issued the
Bandenbekämpfung (bandit fighting) order. Under Bach-Zelewski,
these formations were responsible for the mass murder of 35,000
civilians in Riga and more than 200,000 in Belarus and eastern Poland.

Following the Allies' victory in Europe, Bach-Zelewski went into hiding and tried to leave the country. US military police arrested him on 1 August 1945. In exchange for his testimony against his former superiors at the Nuremberg trials Bach-Zelewski never faced trial for any war crimes and avoided extradition to Poland or to the USSR.

During his testimony at Nuremberg, Bach-Zelewski stated that he disapproved of Himmler's aim to exterminate 30 million Slavs, but explained it thus: 'when, for years, for decades, the doctrine is preached that the Slav is a member of an inferior race and that the Jew is not even human, then such an explosion is inevitable'. In saying this, Bach-Zelewski effectively linked the facts of mass murder on the ground to Nazi ideology, and established the connection between the Wehrmacht[3] and the actions of the Einsatzgruppen[4] in the Soviet Union, which turned out to be of great value to interrogators and prosecutors at the Nuremberg Trials.

On 7 January 1946, General Telford Taylor called Bach-Zelewski to the stand. He testified that at the beginning of the war he was a Higher SS and Police Leader in the central section of the campaign against the Soviet Union stating:

At the end of 1942, he became the Chief of Anti-Partisan Combat Units for the entire Eastern Front. He confirmed that orders were issued by the highest authorities that German soldiers committing excesses were not to be punished in the military courts.'[5]

Later, at the Einsatzgruppen Trial – the 9th at the Subsequent Proceedings – the opening statement of the prosecution emphasised:

The judgement of the IMT declared 2 million Jews were murdered by the Einsatzgruppen and other units of the Security Police. The defendants in the dock were the cruel executioners, whose terror wrote the blackest page in human history. Death was their tool and life their toy. If these men be immune, then law has lost its meaning and man must live in fear.

Bach-Zelewski left prison in 1949, and in 1951 he claimed partial responsibility for getting the poison to Goering. As evidence, he produced cyanide capsules to the authorities with serial numbers not far removed from the one used by Goering. The authorities never verified Bach-Zelewski's claim and did not charge him with aiding Goering's death. He never satisfactorily explained how he had passed the capsule to Goering – who was no friend of Bach-Zelewski's and who openly described the general as being 'a traitor ... a bastard ... and the bloodiest murderer in this whole system.'[6]

Most modern historians dismiss Bach-Zelewski's claim that he passed the capsule to Goering in a bar of soap. However, in its issue 2/59 the German magazine *Der Spiegel* reported:

In April 1951 Erich von dem Bach-Zelewski appeared before the American District Attorney in Ansbach, William D. Canfield[7], and declared that Petermartin Bliebtreu [a previous claimant] was a swindler: 'The poison came from me'. The American was Skeptical. He took Bach to task for a day, but the chemotechnical examination in the Nuremberg-based laboratory gave the decisive factor for his judgment. Bach-Zelewski had brought a poison messenger from the same series from which he had served Hitler's first Paladin. The ampoule had the same glass structure as the splinters in Goering's oral cavity, which had been analyzed at the time. Canfield: 'I am inclined to believe that your story is true.'[6]

An Associated Press report that appeared on 2 April 1951 in *The Washington Evening Star* said much the same thing[8]:

General Tells How He Slipped Poison to Goering in Soap
Ansbach, Germany, April 2. – A new claimant to the distinction of having supplied Hermann Goering with his suicide poison was revealed today, A United States official said he was inclined to believe this one.

United States District Attorney William D. Canfield said former SS (Elite Guard) Gen. Erich von dem Bach Zelewski has admitted to American officials that he slipped the poison to Goering in a bar of soap. Goering later used it to escape the gallows in Nuernberg jail in 1946.

'I am inclined to believe his statement is rather credible', Mr Canfield said. A 29-year-old Austrian journalist, Peter Martin Bleibtreau, made a similar claim last week. Later he admitted his story was false.

Mr. Canfield said Bach Zelewski made his confession on Saturday in his office in the presence of American and German officials. He was a prisoner at the Nuernberg war crimes trials together with Goering. He said he gave the poison, potassium cyanide, which was concealed in a bar of soap, to Goering when they passed each other Mr Canfield stated.

'He had still another bar of soap containing a capsule of potassium cyanide which he surrendered to us' the prosecutor said.

Bach Zelewski was convicted as a major Nazi offender by a German denazification court last week and sentenced to 10 years special labor.

'We still are trying to make up our minds whether we should try him on this Goering affair or forget about it' Mr Canfield said. 'The maximum sentence would be one year.'

The charge would be helping a convicted killer prisoner escape punishment.

CHAPTER SEVENTEEN – NOTES & REFERENCES

1. *Deutsche Welle (DW)* – Germany's international broadcaster – https://www.dw.com/en/daddy-was-a-man-of-honor-daughter-of-nazi-ss-officer-insists/a-51853837

2. Pomerania is a historical region on the southern shore of the Baltic Sea that is split between Poland and Germany.

3. The unified armed forces of Nazi Germany.

4. The Einsatzgruppen (task forces) were Schutzstaffel (SS) paramilitary death squads of the Nazis. They were responsible for the murder of much of the intelligentsia, including members of the priesthood, and they played an integral role in the implementation of the so-called 'Final Solution to the Jewish Question'.

5. Robert H. Jackson Centre – Bach-Zelewski II, 7 January 1946.

6. *Der Spiegel* 2/59.

7. William D. Canfield was working as a US Prosecutor in Frankfurt and Passau as is evidenced by two cases that were reported in the *New York Times* on 23 May 1953 and 31 May 1954 respectively.

8. *Washington Evening Star*, 2nd April 1951, front page.

RUDOLF DIELS

'One of the most fascinating men I had ever encountered'[1]
WOLFE FRANK

RUDOLF DIELS WAS A GERMAN CIVIL SERVANT and the first head of the Gestapo. He obtained the rank of SS-Oberführer (senior leader)[2] and was a protégé of Hermann Goering.

Diels was born in Berghausen on 16 December 1900. He was the son of a farmer, and he went to school in Wiesbaden. He served in the German army towards the end of the First World War and was posted to Alsace as an intelligence officer. Following the war, he studied law at the University of Marburg where he had a reputation as a heavy drinker and philanderer.

Rudolf Diels proved to be of great value to Frank and General Donovan as the source of 'inexhaustible, infallible and completely accurate information.' Frank also suggests there was an ongoing, perhaps clandestine, connection between Diels and the general that had started prior to the Second World War.

Authors Note: The remainder of this chapter are the words of Wolfe Frank – as they appear in his memoirs[3]. I have included them in this way as they provide concise, first-hand descriptions of: Rudolf Diels; his background; his involvements with Goering and the Nazis; the 'special' arrangements under which he was detained and interrogated; and the unique relationship he had with Frank and Donovan. These extracts also reveal: Diels' reluctance to co-operate with other prosecutors; that tensions were beginning to emerge between Justice Jackson and General Donovan – whose opinions on how the trials should be conducted were moving in two entirely different directions; and that Donovan and Frank, not only wielded powers and influence beyond their respective ranks, they were two men totally committed to the cause but who possessed maverick tendencies that saw them prepared to break with convention and bend the rules, sometimes almost to breaking point, in the name of a greater good.

A Deal with Diels

On my way out of camp [at Bad Oeynhausen in early October 1945] I encountered the captain who was the official interpreter. He told me he had heard I would soon be going to Nuremberg. He then informed me that they had a man in camp who might be of interest, not only to me, but as a witness for the prosecution at Nuremberg. The captain knew this man to be a relative of Goering and that he had been a high-ranking officer in the Gestapo. He said he would send the man over, if I was interested.

That is how I came to meet Dr Rudolf Diels, one of the most fascinating men I had ever encountered. He was brought into an interrogation room by the Camp Interrogator who then left us alone. I took a look at my new customer. He was tall, very dark haired and had heavy duelling scars on his face[4]. He was extremely intelligent and spoke beautiful cultured German. He was also emaciated, dreadfully nervous whilst being sure of himself, and he was courteous without being servile or afraid. His face showed the weariness he expected from yet another interrogation.

I told him who I was and that I would be involved in the trial of Goering and the other top Nazis, and I asked whether he might have anything pertinent to contribute to the picture we would be developing of them. He said he did have. He wasn't suggesting that he would be of considerable value to us at Nuremberg. He merely, in a few sentences, gave an outline of his activities in the Third Reich, which were as follows:

He was married to a cousin of Goering and he had been Chief of the Prussian Gestapo at the time of van der Lubbe's burning down of the German Reichstag[5]. He had been Chief of the Shipping Division of the Hermann Goering Works (a national industrial unit engaged in a multitude of economic and production activities) and also Lieutenant Governor of the City of Hanover. He had been denounced as having been involved in the 20 July 1944 plot against Hitler[6] but had been spared execution following Goering's intervention. Instead he had been sent to the Russian Front as a private in a 'Strafkompagnie' (penal company) where he ought to have been killed. He had however escaped to the West and had been captured by the British.

This potted history was delivered in the briefest of terms and in less than five minutes. I could not detect any improbabilities or any attempt to promote my sympathy or compassion. I decided that I would hang on to Diels. The question was – how? I asked my friend the interpreter.

'Why that's easy', he said. 'Sign for him and take him with you [to Nuremberg].'

Diels was told to be ready the following morning but not where he was going. I signed a piece of paper stating my name and rank and that, 'I had received one prisoner, Rudolf Diels.'

I then took him back to my billet in the Oeynhausen compound. This was, of course, monumentally irregular and pleased me enormously since breaking rules was, and still is, one of my favourite pastimes.

We didn't talk much on the way, but I could see that his face twitched when the gate to the compound was flung open and we drove into yet another camp. His expression changed to incredulity, however, when I took him to a nicely furnished bedroom and told him to make himself comfortable.

'Come down for lunch,' I told him, and left him to it.

We were alone at lunch (my two colleagues were off on some assignment) and I noticed that Diels was totally tipsy after a small aperitif. He hadn't had a drop of alcohol in nearly two years and his stomach was, obviously, rather empty. It had also shrunk, and he ate very little for a day or so, after which he raised his intake by leaps and bounds.

Our conversation centred around the problem of how this unorthodox arrangement between him and me could be continued. I asked him to give me an undertaking not to run out on me. He did, and he kept to it scrupulously.

Then he came up with a list of names of those people who, he thought, would be involved in the administration of the trials at Nuremberg. This was the first time that I discovered his uncanny ability to remember names, situations and to assess people's characters.

There were, indeed, two names on his list who did eventually turn up at Nuremberg – Dr Robert Kempner, German-born Assistant Prosecutor for the USA, and General William 'Wild Bill' Donovan, former head of the Office of Strategic Services (OSS), the USA's famous cloak-and-dagger outfit. Donovan had been involved in some intelligence activities in Berlin where Diels had met him when he was in the Ministry of the Interior and before he became a Head of Gestapo.

I got hold of both Kempner and Donovan and found them entirely agreeable to my scheme of bringing Diels to Nuremberg. A request to the British in Bad Oeynhausen to have Diels transferred into US custody was approved and he was picked up from my villa.

The story Diels told me, during a long night, his tongue loosened by Rhine wine and *Steinhager* (German gin), ran as follows:

He had met Goering's cousin in Berlin shortly after Hitler had come to power and Goering, who had taken a liking to him, indicated that he would look favourably upon a marriage into the Goering family. The marriage did not last long.

Goering arranged Diels' nomination as first Chief of Gestapo in Berlin and the Reichstag Fire had happened whilst Diels held that position. However, as he was not a member of the 'inner circle' the investigation was taken out of his hands and fabricated charges were brought against van der Lubbe, a young Dutchman, in order to achieve the desired political objective.

As far as they go, Diels accounts of the events of those days may be considered correct and he later wrote a book about his life during the Third Reich, *Lucifer ante Portas*, which is remarkably analytical so far as these events and the leading figures amongst whom he lived are concerned, but it is almost schizophrenically un-analytical regarding Dr Diels. He did not however claim ignorance of the horrors of the time, only the impossibility for anyone to swim against the monstrous tide. Nor did he – and Kempner and Donovan made certain of this – commit any act of his own that would have made him a guilty contributor.

[Diels and Goering had then fallen out] … and so Diels departed from Goering's orbit and patronage.

Diels was first sent from the Goering Works into a non-political activity with no future, then he became Government President of Cologne, another job of little consequence, then down another step to Government President of Hanover and finally he was implicated in the attempt on Hitler's life on 20 July 1944 … Goering, as a last act of generosity for a man he once liked a great deal, had Diels' name taken off the list of death candidates and he had him sent, instead, to a penal company of the Waffen-SS (the fighting section of the SS) which was being decimated on the Eastern Front. Diels made his getaway from there and had been taken prisoner by the British Army.

CHAPTER EIGHTEEN – NOTES & REFERENCES

1. Wolfe Frank comment regarding the arrangements he put in place for the detainment of Rudolf Diels, *Nuremberg's Voice of Doom*, p.106.

2. Oberführer had no military equivalent but was regarded as being senior colonel rank.

3. *Nuremberg's Voice of Doom*, pp.106–112.

4. A duelling scar or 'bragging scar' was seen amongst upper-class Germans and Austrians, especially those involved in academic fencing, as being a 'badge of

honour' that emphasised one's class and status in society. German military laws permitted men to wage duels of honour until the First World War, and in 1933 the Nazis legalised the practice once more.

5. Marinus van der Lubbe (1909–1934), a Dutchman, was tried, convicted and executed for setting fire to the Reichstag building in Berlin on 27 February 1933, an event that became known as the Reichstag fire.

6. On 20 July 1944, Claus von Stauffenberg and others attempted to assassinate Adolf Hitler in his field headquarters near Rastenburg.

SECTION THREE

THE ROAD TO NUREMBERG

THE ROAD TO NUREMBERG
Part One: April – July 1945

'We did not even know whether a court-house that could house such a trial was still standing in Germany, or if so, where it was to be found'.[1]
JUSTICE ROBERT JACKSON

PLANS TO BRING THE NAZI WAR CRIMINALS before an international court of law were already underway as early as 1942. This eventually led to the setting up of the United Nations War Crimes Commission (UNWCC), which was based in London and first met in October 1943. On 1 November that year the UK, USA, China and USSR signed a series of declarations in Moscow warning Germany of the Allies intentions to bring before an international tribunal those Nazi perpetrators of war crimes whom they would 'pursue to the uttermost ends of the earth.'[2]

By early 1945 the UK had decided it wished to deal with the criminals by summary executions (death without trial) whilst the USSR favoured a Show Trial[3] with a predetermined outcome. President Roosevelt would perhaps have favoured either of these options, however his successor, Harry S. Truman,[4] was of a different mindset and decided the war criminals should face a court of law. This view was eventually adopted by the Allies, albeit with reservations from some.

APRIL 1945

General Donovan (accompanied by Lieutenant Putzell), with the end of the Second World War in sight, had by, early April 1945 turned his attention to preserving the OSS empire he had built up – which by that time employed over 13,000 analysts, covert operators and saboteurs. He had written a secret memo to President Roosevelt proposing the creation of a postwar intelligence agency with him as its head (this was to become the CIA). Although FDR was not entirely convinced, Donovan believed he could persuade the president it was a good idea, as he had done on previous occasions.

There were many within the US administration however who wanted to see a smaller post-war government and they were looking for cuts in expenditure. To compound the issue Donovan was seen by many to have assumed too much power and there were a number of detractors in Washington who were anxious to clip his wings. Their chance came when President Roosevelt suddenly died on 12 April.

The Washington Times-Herald published details of the secret memo Donovan had sent to FDR and compared his proposed agency to the Gestapo. With the death of FDR, Donovan's political position had been substantially weakened and although he continued to argue forcefully for the OSS' retention, and had the full backing of General Eisenhower,[5] he found his ideas were opposed by new president Truman.

Hermann Goering saw Hitler for the last time on 20 April. It was at a party held in the Fuehrer Bunker in Berlin to mark Hitler's birthday. The Russian Army were fast approaching and Goering, amongst others, had no wish to stay and greet them. He travelled to his estate at Obersalzberg, arriving on 22 April, to learn that Hitler had declared the war was lost and that he intended to commit suicide.

The following day Goering sent a carefully worded telegram to Hitler asking for his permission to take over as the leader of Germany, adding that, if Hitler did not reply by 22:00 that night (23 April), he would assume Hitler had lost his freedom of action and that he, Goering, would assume leadership of the Reich. It was Goering's belief at that time that he could negotiate a peace settlement with the Allies and that he would be invited to be chancellor.

Hitler sent a reply accusing Goering of being a traitor and rescinding the 1941 decree naming him as his designated deputy. He threatened him with execution for high treason unless he immediately resigned from all his offices. Goering duly resigned and Hitler ordered him to be put under house arrest. By 26 April, the Obersalzberg estate was under attack by the Allies, so Goering was moved by the SS to his castle at Mauterndorf.

In his last will and testament (signed on 29 April), Hitler expelled Goering from the party, formally rescinded the decree making him his successor, and accused him of 'illegally attempting to seize control of the state'. He then appointed Karl Dönitz[6], commander-in-chief of the Navy, to be his successor as president of the Reich and supreme commander of the armed forces. Hitler and his wife, Eva Braun, committed suicide on 30 April 1945, a day after they had married.

Robert Jackson was serving as an associate justice of the US Supreme Court and, on 13 April 1945, he delivered a keynote speech at the annual conference of the American Society of International Law (ASIL),[7] in which he expressed his views on how he thought an international trial for the captured German leaders should be undertaken.

Wolfe Frank, having been given a commission and achieved the rank of second lieutenant was, in April 1945, busy teaching Belgian soldiers (in French) how to operate the Vickers machine gun. These were huge achievements for a German refugee who had arrived in the UK in 1936 unable to speak English and who had – in spite of his known heroism as a resistance worker and his having been officially declared an enemy of the Third Reich – been interned at the outbreak of war as an 'enemy alien'.

Airey Neave was, during this period, heading up a department in MI9 known as Room 900. The role of this clandestine division was to carry out espionage and surveillance on German agents and spies and to organise escape routes for those agents and air crews stranded behind enemy lines.

The Surrenders Begin

On 29 April, SS-Obergruppenführer (senior group leader) Karl Wolff,[8] who had been negotiating with Donovan's OSS for some weeks, signed a written agreement at Caserta, Italy, that formalised the surrender of German and Italian Fascist forces in Italy. This ended the Italian Campaign of the Second World War. Known as 'Operation *Sunrise*,' General Donovan had appointed Allen Dulles (later Director of the CIA) as Swiss Director of the OSS and he handled the negotiations that led to the surrender. [In the photograph shown at Plate 13 Wolfe Frank (right) and Judge Michael Musmanno[9] (centre) can be seen interrogating Karl Wolff. The hand-written inscription on the photograph reads: 'To Wolfe Frank – Ace Interpreter at Nuremberg International War Crimes Trials – and so far as I am concerned the whole world round. Most sincerely, M A Musmanno'].

MAY 1945

On 2 May, in anticipation of victory in Europe, President Truman announced an International Military Tribunal would be formed to prosecute prominent leaders.

Truman, who had accepted responsibility for setting up and running the administration of the trials, and having been greatly impressed by his speech to ASIL, appointed **Robert Jackson** to be 'US Chief of Counsel for the Prosecution of Nazi War Criminals' and he gave him complete authority to choose his own staff and to design, structure and implement the trials. Of this event Jackson said:

I was designated to act as representative of the United States and as its chief counsel 'in preparing and prosecuting charges of atrocities and war crimes against such leaders of the European Axis ... as the United States may agree with any of the United Nations to bring to trial ...' I was to receive no additional compensation, but should receive my expenses.

I was given broad authority by the executive order. One reason probably was that the other authorities were willing to get rid of the problem by delegating responsibility to me. In the second place, it was a totally unploughed field.[10]

From the mandate the president had given him, Jackson's first challenge was to find a venue for the IMT. He initially expressed concern that 'a suitable courthouse might not even be standing in Germany'. Jackson, along with his team, faced the difficulty of locating such a facility within the war-torn German landscape. He also recorded 'the prosecution must be conducted in four languages by lawyers trained in four different legal systems' and 'very little real evidence was in our possession, the overwhelming mass of documents being still undiscovered and their existence largely unsuspected.'[11]

Hermann Goering was freed from the house arrest Hitler had imposed upon him at Mauterndorf on 5 May by a passing Luftwaffe unit, and he made his way to the US lines where he surrendered to the US rather than be taken by the Soviets who were fast approaching. He was greeted cordially and taken into custody near Radstadt on 6 May by a section of the 36th Infantry Division. At this point Goering still believed 'he was no mere prisoner of war but a plenipotentiary[12] acting on behalf of the German Reich in armistice discussions with the enemy' and he called for an immediate meeting with General Eisenhower.

Goering was taken the next day to Kitzbühel where he laughed and joked with US soldiers and members of the press before Eisenhower clamped down and ordered that Goering should be treated no differently than any other prison of war. He was flown to Augsburg and stripped of his medals, jewellery and the solid gold marshal's baton he carried to demonstrate his standing and authority. For the next two weeks he was interviewed by US interrogators who, having assessed him, on 19 May, sent a report to Army Headquarters stating:

[Goering] is by no means the comical figure he has been depicted so many times in newspaper reports. He is neither stupid nor a fool ... generally cool and calculating ... able to grasp the fundamental issues under discussion immediately ... not a man to be underrated ... he denied having had anything to do with the concentration camps, with the SS and the atrocities committed both in Germany and outside ... Goering is at all times an actor who does not disappoint his audience ... the canny Hermann, even now, thinks only of what he can do to salve some of his personal fortune and to create an advantageous position for himself. He condemns the once loved Führer without hesitation ... behind his spirited and often witty conversation, is a constant watchfulness for the opportunity to place himself in a favorable light.'[13]

Victory in Europe

On 7 May 1945, at his headquarters in the French city of Rheims, General Eisenhower, accepted the unconditional surrender of all German forces. The document of surrender was signed on behalf of Germany by General Alfred Jodl (one of the defendants at Nuremberg)[14] and came into effect the following day (VE Day) marking the official end of the war in Europe.

Goering, was flown to Mondorf les Bains in Luxembourg on 21 May, and was housed in sparsely furnished rooms at the Palace Hotel. With the codename 'Ashcan' it became the chief interrogation centre for Nazi war criminals.

Colonel Andrus was Commandant of the Ashcan and it was here that Goering was put on a strict diet and a programme was started to wean him off his addiction to morphine, about which Andrus later said: 'When Goering came to see me at Mondorf he was a simpering slob with two suitcases full of paracodeine. I thought he was a drug salesman. But we took him off his dope and made a man of him.'[15] Goering spent the next four months at Ashcan.

General Donovan and Lieutenant Putzell had been collecting evidence against suspected Nazi war criminals since December 1944 and Donovan had ordered his staff to put together 'a top flight staff on war crimes ... he wanted payback for the torture and murder of his agents.'[16]

Justice Jackson met up with Donovan on 15 May. The two men knew each other from their days as New York lawyers and although supporters of different political parties – Jackson was a Democrat, Donovan a Republican – this initial meeting appeared on the surface to be cordial and constructive, but Donovan had a hidden agenda – as Douglas Waller clearly explains in *Wild Bill Donovan:*

He [Donovan] offered the full resources of his spy agency. Jackson was grateful; he had only a handful of loyalists to call on, including his son who was a lawyer, and none was experienced in war crimes prosecutions. Donovan also said he knew Jackson would be 'the captain of the team' and he 'would play wherever' the Justice could use him. Donovan didn't really mean that. He intended to play a star role in the trial. He wanted to put Hermann Göring, who had surrendered to the Allies, on the stand for a dramatic cross-examination. Jackson was intrigued and told Donovan he should send agents to interview the Reichsmarschall.[17]

Donovan needed no second invitation. On 17 May he flew to Europe: in search of a suitable location to hold the trials; to gather more evidence against the war criminals; and to start assembling and briefing the team of OSS personnel he intended to take with him. At this stage Donovan was Jackson's most trusted ally.

Airey Neave had been ordered by MI6 not to return to occupied Europe until after D Day. The War Office had decided he knew too much, and it could not risk him being captured. After the Allied invasion, however, he had immediately returned and had followed the Allied troops in their victories throughout Europe, liberating the remaining aircrews and thanking all resistance 'helpers' who, in support of MI9's objectives had 'inspired by a sense of outrage, resisted tyranny and oppression'

Wolfe Frank, following his success at interpreting for Belgian soldiers, had badly broken his leg during a training session, and was given several months' sick leave.

JUNE 1945

By early June 1945, with its work of rescuing trapped aircrews completed, Room 900 was officially disbanded, but **Airey Neave** carried on with his work within an agency that 'continued in a discreet manner long after the war'. The number of Room 900's helpers who died – shot, tortured or starved in concentration camps – is estimated to have been 'in excess of the 500 recorded names.'[18]

General Donovan and Lieutenant Putzell, together with their ever-growing number of OSS staff involved at the IMT, were by early June involved in every aspect of Justice Jackson's arrangements and Donovan provided funds from his OSS budget to help out with the enormous costs.

By mid-June Donovan had presented his team captain [Jackson] a detailed plan for organising the prosecution staff with the spy chief acting as his deputy and his star attorney during the trial. Jackson, who thought Donovan and his OSS had been a godsend, agreed to practically all the suggestions.[19]

Justice Jackson returned the favour by suggesting to President Truman that it might be a good idea to allow Donovan and the OSS to continue. The three men met up in the Oval Office at the White House on 16 June for a very cordial meeting during which the president showed the other two the gold and diamond baton that had been confiscated from Goering, and Jackson again advanced Donovan's and the OSS' position by saying they were 'vital for the prosecution team'. The general was stunned 'Jackson was the best lobbyist he could have ever found.[20]

Others, however, were still agitating for the OSS to be disbanded, and this was playing on Donovan's mind as he and Jackson headed back to Europe on 22 June.

Four days later Jackson was present for the start of the conference known as 'The London Agreement and Charter' which was the advisory committee, made up of the leading representatives of the four major Allies, charged with drawing up rules and procedures for the prosecution and punishment of the major war criminals and defining the laws and procedures by which the trials were to be conducted. (It was signed on 8 August).

July 1945

Donovan and Jackson travelled to Nuremberg together in early July. Donovan had been urging that this is where the trials should be held. His reasoning was good: the Palace of Justice offered sufficient room for the numerous representatives of the four Allied nations; the adjacent prison simplified the problem of housing and protecting prisoners; it was located in the zone administered by the US; and, as Nuremberg had been a focal point for Nazi propaganda rallies in the years leading up to the Second World War, it would be seen to be a fitting symbol to mark the death of the Third Reich. On this vital issue Douglas Waller writes:

Donovan and Jackson flew to the Bavarian city of Nuremberg the cultural home for National Socialism, where Hitler staged his grandest propaganda rallies ... The Russians wanted the war crimes trials held in Berlin, which they controlled. Donovan pressed for Nuremberg, not just because of its symbolic importance to the Nazis, but also because it was in the American zone and had the spacious Palace of Justice, damaged but still intact, with a large prison near the courthouse. Jackson agreed.[21]

Donovan returned to Washington on 13 July and turned his attention to the war still going on in Japan, and later in the month he travelled to Asia and took command of a tug that towed ships and cleared mines in the Pacific.

Wolfe Frank, having recovered from his broken leg and keen to get back into the action, was promoted to staff captain and instructed to attend the inaugural meeting of the British War Crimes Executive (BWCE)[22] – the title given to the British delegation for the prosecution of Nazi war criminals.[23]

CHAPTER NINETEEN – NOTES & REFERENCES

1. *Nuremberg in Retrospect*, Robert Jackson: *American Bar Journal*, October 1949.

2. 'The Moscow Declarations' were four declarations signed, on 30 October 1943, during the Moscow Conference, one of which, *The Declaration on Atrocities*, was signed by U.S. President Franklin D. Roosevelt, British Prime Minister Winston Churchill and Soviet Premier Joseph Stalin.

3. A Show Trial is 'A judicial trial held in public with the intention of influencing or satisfying public opinion, rather than of ensuring justice' – *Oxford Dictionaries*.

4. Harry S. Truman (May 8, 1884 – December 26, 1972) served as the 33rd president of the United States, from 1945 to 1953.

5. Dwight David 'Ike' Eisenhower (1890–1969) was the 34th President of the USA (from 1953 until 1961). During The Second World War he was a five-star general and Supreme Commander of the Allied Expeditionary Forces in Europe.

6. Karl Dönitz (16 September 1891 – 24 December 1980) was supreme commander of the German Navy. He succeeded Hitler as head of state of Nazi Germany on 30 April 1945. He held the position until Germany's unconditional surrender to the Allies on 8 May. At Nuremberg he was found guilty of Crimes Against Peace and War Crimes and was sentenced to ten years imprisonment.

7. *The Anatomy of the Nuremberg Trials: A Personal Memoir*, pp.44–45.

8. Obergruppenfuehrer Karl Wolff was formerly Chief of Personal Staff Reichsfuehrer (Commander) and SS Liaison Officer to Hitler until sometime in 1943. At the end of WWII, he was the Supreme Commander of all SS forces in Italy and negotiated the surrender of all German forces in Italy, ending the war on that front in late April 1945. At Nuremberg, Wolff was allowed to

escape prosecution by providing evidence against his fellow Nazis and was then transferred (in January 1947) to the British prison facility in Minden.

9. Rear Admiral Michael Angelo Musmanno (1897–1968) was the Presiding Judge at the Einsatzgruppen Trial. He had served in the military justice system of the US Navy during the Second World War and then as a governor of an occupied district of Italy before becoming a trial judge at Nuremberg.

10. *Justice Jackson's Story*, transcript of tape recording taken by Harlan B. Phillips, Oral History Research Office, Columbia University, New York, N.Y., 1952–1953.

11. *Robert Jackson: Nuremberg in Retrospect,* (American Law Journal, October 1949).

12. A 'plenipotentiary' is a person, especially a diplomat, invested with the full power of independent action on behalf of their government, typically in a foreign country – *The Reich Marshal* p.387.

13. *The Reich Marshal*, p.390.

14. Alfred Josef Ferdinand Jodl (10 May 1890 – 16 October 1946) was Chief of Operations Staff of the Wehrmacht High Command who held a rank equal to a four-star general. He was found guilty on all Counts at Nuremberg and was hanged on 16 October 1946.

15. *The Reich Marshal*, p.394.

16. *Wild Bill Donovan*, p.324.

17. ibid, p.325.

18. *Public Servant, Secret Agent*, pp.155–157.

19. *Wild Bill Donovan*, p.326.

20. ibid, pp.328–330.

21. ibid, p.330–331.

22. *Nuremberg's Voice of Doom*, p.94.

23. The British delegation for the prosecution of Nazi war criminals was designated the British War Crimes Executive. Consisting of some 170 persons including: barristers; analysts; translators; secretaries; and typists; the BWCE was responsible for the British legal administration of the trials.

THE ROAD TO NUREMBERG
Part Two: August – September 1945

'I doubt whether a more novel or challenging task ever was set before members of the legal profession.'[1]
JUSICE ROBERT JACKSON

BY EARLY AUGUST 1945, preliminary preparations for the IMT were officially underway and involved the most extensive planning ever undertaken in legal proceedings, including: finding a suitable location with a courthouse and prison attached; creating an organizational structure capable of dealing with what would become 'history's greatest trial'; establishing a system for translating the proceedings into English, German, French and Russian; interrogating war criminals; arranging their legal representations; and gathering all the evidence.

The first major hurdle was overcome when the Allied Powers (UK, USA, France and USSR) accepted General Donovan's recommendation that the IMT should be held in the Palace of Justice at Nuremberg. The massive task of adapting the building began immediately and a wooden connecting passage was constructed between the adjacent prison and the East Building as a means of securely and safely transporting the prisoners from their prison cells to the courtroom (see Plates 17 – 21).

Adopting the IMT Charter

Justice Jackson was in London on 8 August 1945. His task was twofold: to negotiate the Charter of the world's first criminal tribunal, and to decide how best to try the Nazi war criminals. On that day, after two months of intense discussions, the Allied Powers agreed and signed 'The London Agreement'[2] which formerly adopted the Tribunal's Charter. Jackson's Notes record:

On August 8, 1945 we signed the agreement, as I was authorized to do on behalf of the United States, and it was announced to the world. Up to that time there had been some press rumors that we were having difficulties in arriving at it. We had frankly admitted we had, but there had been no exploitation of our differences.

I may say that the chief critics of it were a few international lawyers who simply could not adjust themselves to the idea that the world had moved since the time of the Hague Conventions and that the treaties outlawing war and renouncing it as an instrument of policy had made a change in the old doctrine that it always is legal for a country to go to war for aggressive ends if it pleased its interests to do so.[3]

Article 6 of the charter listed three broad categories of crimes that would be dealt with by the IMT:

(a) **Crimes against peace:** namely, planning, preparation, initiation or waging of a war of aggression, or a war in violation of international treaties, agreements or assurances, or participation in a common plan or conspiracy for the accomplishment of any of the foregoing;

(b) **War crimes:** namely, violations of the laws or customs of war. Such violations shall include, but not be limited to, murder, ill-treatment or deportation to slave labour or for any other purpose of civilian population of or in occupied territory, murder or ill-treatment of prisoners of war or persons on the seas, killing of hostages, plunder of public or private property, wanton destruction of cities, towns or villages, or devastation not justified by military necessity;

(c) **Crimes against humanity:** namely, murder, extermination, enslavement, deportation, and other inhumane acts committed against any civilian population, before or during the war, or persecutions on political, racial or religious grounds in execution of or in connection with any crime within the jurisdiction of the Tribunal, whether or not in violation of the domestic law of the country where perpetrated

To which a fourth was later added

(d) **Conspiracy to Commit Crimes:** namely a common plan or conspiracy to commit the criminal acts listed in the first three counts.

The Demise of the OSS

General Donovan was in Asia dealing with his Far East OSS team when he received the news that the US had dropped atomic bombs on Hiroshima and Nagasaki on 6 and 9 August respectively. He instructed his agents to gauge the Japanese government's reaction to the devastation.

He returned to Washington on 14 August where his budget had been almost halved. Desperate to secure a future for the OSS, Donovan released details of more than a hundred OSS success stories to the press.

This had an adverse reaction to the one he had intended and a smear campaign started against Donovan and his agency. His many critics were delighted when it was suggested in a report by Colonel Richard Park, an army officer who ran the White House map room, that the OSS was 'an arm of British intelligence' and that there were 'scores – over 120 – items accusing OSS or its personnel of incompetence, insecurity, corruption, "orgies," nepotism, black marketing, and almost anything else one could name.'[4]

In writing about these events in a 2011 edition of *Vanity Fair* author Evan Thomas commented: 'The report was a vicious act of score-settling by the many bureaucratic rivals of the OSS. (General Douglas MacArthur banned O.S.S. officers from even entering his theater of operations in the Pacific.')[4]

Following these developments President Truman, who had been looking for an opportunity to curtail the activities of Donovan and his agency, went much further than anyone expected and signed an executive order on 20 September abolishing the agency.

Donovan's beloved OSS ceased to exist ten days later. However, there was one more dramatic incident in this chain of events.

Donovan, believing Truman would not remain long in office, always thought he would be called back and asked to head up the CIA – especially if someone like General Eisenhower became president. With this in mind, and in the several days leading up to abolition day, Donovan together with Ned Putzell microfilmed all the OSS documents in their possession. These were retained – some in Donovan's law practice, others by Putzell (which he later destroyed) – not for malicious purposes, but so that Donovan would be in the best position possible to pick up from where he left off if a new president was appointed. (This monumental breach of security and protocol is equivalent to a vast number of current CIA files being copied and retained outside the Agency by a handful of lawyers in a private practice).

A document confirming this extraordinary event is included in an archive of OSS files released by the US Government that is now deposited with the US National Archives. Entitled *OSS Project: General Donovan's Files,*[5] the project was researched by fifty-three volunteers over a period of thirteen years. It includes and explains the significance of the OSS documents copied and highlights the breathtaking audacity of the two OSS executives in the final days of the office's existence – selected paragraphs of this document are as follows:

> On September 20, 1945, only weeks after V-J Day, President Truman announced that the Office of Strategic Services (OSS) would be terminated effective October 1. In the few days before the first American secret intelligence and special operations service went out of business, OSS director Major General William J. Donovan and his administrative assistant, Lieutenant Edwin J. Putzell, Jr., spent several nights at OSS headquarters microfilming Donovan's office files. So hastily did they work that their palm and finger prints appear on many of the frames.
>
> The OSS had been established under the Joint Chiefs of Staff in June 1942, in succession to the short lived (1941–42) Office of the Coordinator of Information (OCOI), to conduct intelligence activities for the benefit of appropriate Federal agencies, as well as clandestine operations in support of military operations against the Axis powers.
>
> The existence of the Donovan/Putzell microfilms did not become publicly known until 1980, when the widow of Otto Doering, one of Donovan's closest associates, turned them over in a number of Bloomingdale shopping bags to Donovan's biographer, [British journalist, author and historian] Anthony Cave Brown. As author Brown and other researchers have found, the files represent a trove of contemporaneous inside information on many of the critical events and personalities of World War II. Comprised of approximately 120 cubic feet of material, the records of General Donovan's office are among the most heavily referenced of World War II records.

(Otto Doering was an associate of Donovan's in his law practice who, like Putzell, the general had taken with him when he created the OSS. Donovan's biographer Dan Waller records: 'Donovan's two most trusted assistants became Putzell on the road and Doering in Washington.')[6]

To add to these problems Donovan's relationship with Justice Jackson was rapidly deteriorating, with each man entrenched in differing views on how the prosecutions and interrogations of defendants and witnesses should be undertaken.

The Ashcan

Hermann Goering had spent the months following his surrender on 5 May in a small suite of sparsely furnished rooms at the Palace Hotel in Mondorf, Luxembourg (Ashcan).

Colonel Burton Andrus was the Commandant at Mondorf. An impeccably dressed, strict disciplinarian, Andrus had nothing but contempt for the Nazi prisoners whom he referred to as being a 'bunch of Krauts'. Despite his personal feelings Andrus did, however, demand that the prisoners be treated with human dignity despite the actions for which they had been charged.

During this period Andrus, together with US army psychiatrist Douglas Kelley, were instrumental in weaning Goering off his drug dependency. They also put the Reichsmarshall on a strict diet to combat his obesity.[7]

Goering had been allowed to take with him to Mondorf his valet Robert Kropp, who had served him well since the early 1930s and of whom the Reichsmarshall was very fond. This arrangement ended in June when Kropp was moved to another prison facility. It was said that tears were seen in Goering's eyes at their final parting.

Following this incident Goering indicated he thought he was destined to face the gallows. In a session with Douglas Kelley, he told the psychiatrist: 'Yes I know I shall hang. You know I shall hang. I am ready'.[8] On 12 August Andrus moved his notorious prisoners, including Goering, by plane to Nuremberg.

To outsiders the choice of Andrus, a cavalry officer, to be a prison commandant might have seemed odd, but he did have some experience in prison and security work. Early in his thirty-five-year Army career he had served as a prison officer at Fort Oglethorpe, Georgia. For two years during the early part of the Second World War, he served in various security and intelligence positions around New York city, which included security for the New York Port of Embarkation. Drawing on his earlier experience at Oglethorpe, Andrus went about establishing a rigorous security protocol for the prison at Nuremberg.[9]

At Nuremberg the Reichsmarshall and the other war criminals destined to be tried at the IMT, were imprisoned in two rows of cells each measuring 13 feet long, 7 feet wide and 7.5 feet high (see Plate 19). Goering was allocated Cell 5. Leonard Mosley, in his book the Reich Marshall, describes the conditions perfectly:

Each cell contained a washbowl, a flushing toilet, one standard prison bunk with hair mattress, a chair, a mat and a table. To reduce the possibility of suicide, the cells had been modified by the removal of all metal projections from the walls, all electrical wiring, and the replacement of glass in the one window with clear plastic material. Everything was arranged so that, except during the act of defecation (when only the legs and possibly the head could be seen) the prisoner was completely visible at all times to the guard on the door, who was charged with keeping him under constant and remitting vigilance. At night the prisoner was not allowed to sleep with his arms inside the blanket, even when he was cold.

At unannounced times, there were spot checks and searches in addition to regular ones.

The door would open, in would rush burly troopers of the 1st division, and roughly order the prisoner to take off his clothes and stand naked while his room, clothes belongings and body were thoroughly searched. Colonel Andrus often came to Goering's cell on these occasions to see that the naked Reich Marshall received especially close attention.[10]

Wolfe Frank meanwhile, along with the BWCE, moved first to Paris where he worked as a translator at Justice Jackson's headquarters, then to Bad Oeynhausen near Hanover. After a period of honing his skills as an interpreter and an interrogator, Frank moved on to Nuremberg where his exceptional ability was recognised by the Americans – who arranged for his immediate transfer from the BWCE onto the US translating team.[11]

Lieutenant Jack 'Tex' Wheelis (see Chapter Fifteen) and **Sergeant Harry Shotwell** (see Chapter Sixteen) were both appointed to be prison guards with special duties at Nuremberg under Colonel Andus, although Shotwell (and possibly Wheelis) was soon to be told to take his instructions only from the OSS.

Airey Neave had joined the BWCE in August and his initial task was to gather evidence to incriminate Gustav Krupp (see Chapter Twelve).

CHAPTER TWENTY – NOTES & REFERENCES

1. *Nuremberg in Retrospect,* Robert Jackson: *American Bar Journal,* October 1949.

2. 'The London Agreement' created the IMT and its Charter. *The Charter of the International Military Tribunal – Annex to the Agreement for the prosecution and punishment of the major war criminals of the European Axis –* defined the laws and procedures by which the Nuremberg Trials were to be conducted.

3. *The Reminiscences of Robert H. Jackson* Columbia University Oral History Research Office, 1955.

4. *Vanity Fair* 3 March 2011 *Spymaster General: The adventures of Wild Bill Donovan and the "Oh So Social" O.S.S.* by Evan Thomas.

5. *OSS Project: General Donovan's Files US National Archives.*

6. *Wild Bill Donovan*, p.230.

7. *The Reich Marshal: A Biography of Hermann Goering*, p 394.

8. *ibid*, p.397–398.

9. US Army Official website.

10. *The Reich Marshal: A Biography of Hermann Goering*, p.398.

11. *Nuremberg's Voice of Doom*, pp.94–112.

SECTION FOUR

THE PREPARATIONS

THE ARRIVAL OF THE PRINCIPALS AND THE OTHERS

*'Donovan's last act at the OSS was his surreptitious
copying of his own files'*[1]
OSS PROJECT

THERE ARE THREE LEGAL TERMS that should be explained at this stage as they have great significance when considering substantive issues presented later. These terms are 'Preparation', 'Examination' and 'Evidence'. Typical definitions when using them in legal contexts are:

Preparation: 'refers to the proper preparation of any case by an attorney. It includes witness interviews, knowing the facts and laws applicable to the case and having consultation with the client' – *The Law Dictionary*.

Examination: 'examination, in law, the interrogation of a witness by attorneys or by a judge' – *Britannica*.

Evidence: 'in law, any of the material items or assertions of fact that may be submitted to a competent tribunal as a means of ascertaining the truth of any alleged matter of fact under investigation before it' – *Britannica*.

For the purposes of this narrative 'The Preparations' refers to the period 1 October – 20 November 1945.

1 October 1945

Not surprisingly, General Donovan never forgave those responsible for the ending of the world-wide intelligence network that he had so painstakingly and effectively built up during the US' involvement in the Second World War, although it did lead to the birth of the CIA of which Donovan is considered to be the 'founding father'.

(Contrary to Donovan's belief that he would not be president for long, Harry Truman remained in office for eight years. He appointed Sidney Souers as the CIA's first Director in 1946 and General Hoyt Vandenberg as its second in 1947. Truman did, however, set up the Agency in a way that was broadly in line with Donovan's recommendations and vision).

The *OSS Project* records the demise of the office – as well as indicating the lengths to which Donovan was prepared to go and the chances he was prepared to take:

> According to Lieutenant Putzell, who lives in Florida, Donovan got his marching orders from the President [Truman] verbally.
>
> Many records document Donovan's and other senior officials' views on the need for and the shape of the nations' post-war intelligence system. Donovan would have been pleased to have been given the authority to build that organization. But his proposal was leaked to unfriendly journalists (among them Drew Pearson[2] and Walter Trohan[3]), who characterized it as advocating an American Gestapo. In the end, Donovan's views did not prevail. Rather, as author Brown has described it, Donovan's last act at the OSS was his surreptitious copying of his own files.[1]

By early October, 'The Principals' – Goering, Jackson, Donovan, Putzell, Neave and Frank – as well as 'The Others' – Andrus, Taylor, Wheelis, Shotwell, Bach-Zelewski and Diels – had all arrived at Nuremberg. They took up the various positions that would define their involvement in the final explosive moments of the IMT.

CHAPTER TWENTY ONE – NOTES & REFERENCES

1. *OSS Project: General Donovan's Files* US National Archives

2. Andrew Russell Pearson was an American columnist, noted for his syndicated newspaper column *'Washington Merry-Go-Round'* which was the most widely circulated in the USA.

3. Walter J. Trohan was a reporter for the Chicago Tribune who specialised in covering national politics in Washington.

The Palace of Justice in Nuremberg, with its adjacent prison behind (within the semi-circle), was situated in the zone administered by the US.

The Prison Wing which housed the Nazi's on trial. The major war criminals, Goering, et. al., occupied the ground floor, which was connected to the Palace of Justice by a specially constructed wooden tunnel.

Plate 17

Above: Inside the prison wing at Nuremberg. Goering's cell is No. 5, extreme right. Below left: Guards were posted at each door and the prisoners were on 24 hour suicide watch. Below right: Colonel Andrus (left) in the connecting tunnel.

Plate 18

Inside one of the identical cells at Nuremberg, which were 13 feet long, 7 feet wide and 7.5 feet high. To prevent suicide attempts, the tables were designed to collapse under a prisoner's weight.

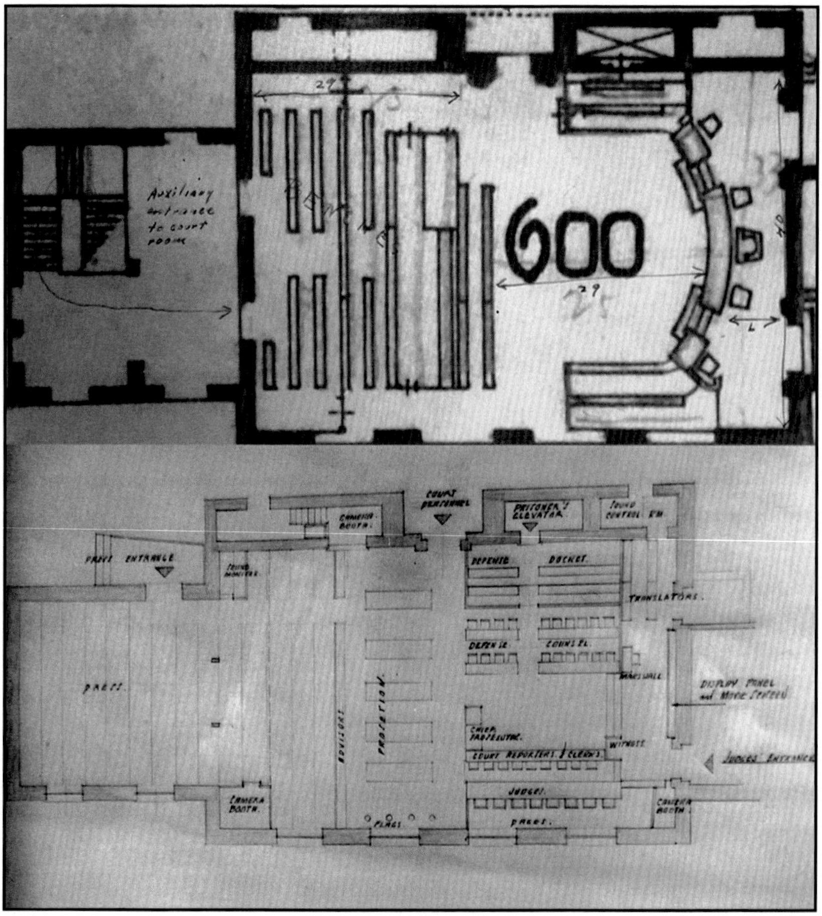

Above: Plans of Courtroom 600 – before and after conversion.

Right top: General Donovan's comments on the layout.

Left: Personal mementos of Goering on his cell table.

Right: The interpreters booths (top left German, top right French, bottom left Russian, bottom right English). Wolfe Frank was the only interpreter capable of occupying either English or German booths.

Plate 20

                                                        28 June 1945

MEMORANDUM

TO: Chief of Counsel

SUBJECT: Lt.Dean's Memorandum on the Site of the Trial

I have gone over Lt. Dean's memorandum to you on "Site of the Trial".
It contains one fundamental fallacy which, I believe, should be dealt with
at once. This is the idea that the Press should be separate from the
court. If the Press were to be placed behind a glass partition in a
separate balcony, I am afraid they would, in effect, feel themselves
separated from the court. If any limitation must be placed on the
audience, I do not believe it should be imposed on the Press, other than
to prevent an unreasonable number of representatives from any one country.
The Press should be given precedence over all visitors to the court inasmuch
as they are the medium through which information on the proceedings of the
trials will reach the general public.

It seems to me preferable to have the courtroom limited to a seating
capacity of approximately 500.

                                 William J. Donovan
                                 Major General, U.S.A.

Plate 21

Plate 22

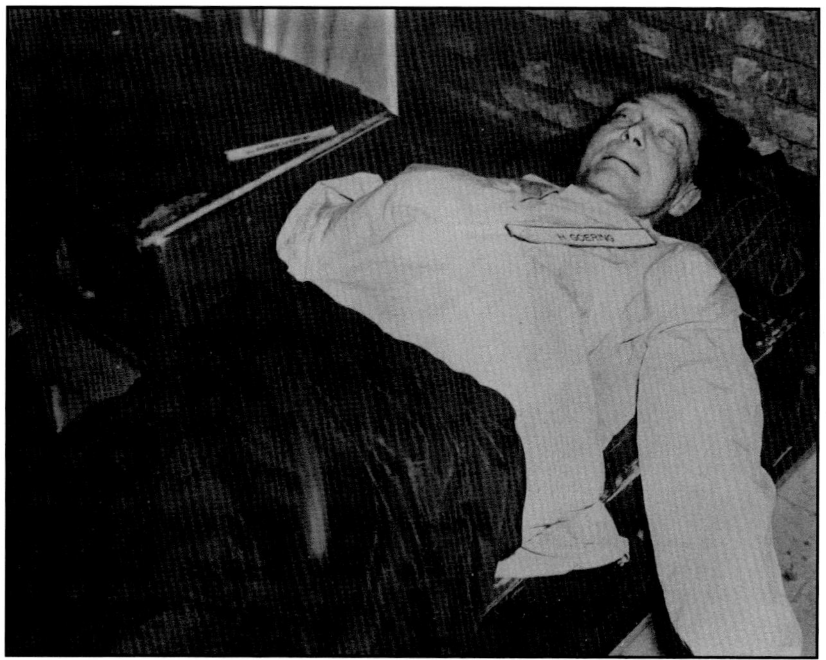

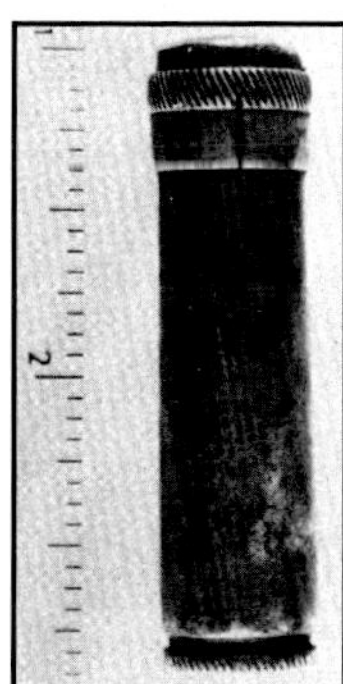

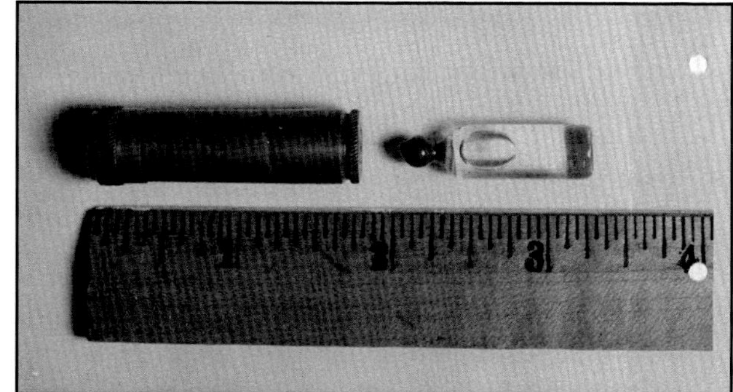

Above (top): The body of Hermann Goering was, along with the bodies of the other war criminals, photographed clothed and unclothed to dispell any doubts that all had been executed. Above (left): The cartridge case that had contained the capsule of poison that Goering ingested; (right). The complete device that had been found in a jar of Vaseline amongst Goering's belongings.

Opposite page (top): Clerical staff assembling the verdicts of the IMT. (Bottom far left): Burton C. Andrus, whom Goering referred to as the 'Fire Brigade Colonel.' (Left): Goering and Lieutenant Wheelis – the reverse of the original bears an inscription written by Goering that says 'the great hunter from Texas'.

Top: The author of this book, Paul Hooley, unveiling a plaque in honour of Wolfe Frank. Left and above: bronze statues of General William Donovan at Columbia University and CIA Headquarters in Langley, Virginia respectively (by kind permission of the University and the OSS Society) – see Chapter Forty Five for further details of these memorials.

THE EXAMINATIONS BEGIN

*'In the world of law, the path to success often hinges
on meticulous preparation'*[1].
DE NOVO LEGAL

ON 20 SEPTEMBER 1945 President Truman announced that 'the Office of Strategic Services (OSS) would be terminated effective October 1'. By that date it was clear to all, especially those involved in the IMT, that Donovan's power base had been severely curtailed. At the same time his relationship with Justice Jackson was showing signs of a deepening rift. As a former prosecutor himself, Donovan had openly and severely criticized Jackson's lack of skill and experience at putting together a strong case and at courtroom examination and cross-examination.

October 3 – Settling In

This was the backdrop to Donovan's and Putzell's return to Nuremberg on 3 October[2] following the dissolution of the OSS. They, and that section of the former OSS involved in the trials, continued to operate, but now as part of the Counter Intelligence Corps (CIC) of the Strategic Services Unit of the US War Department.

Hermann Goering, along with the other major war criminals, had been transferred from the Ashcan to the Palace of Justice at Nuremberg in August, where the prisoners were housed on the bottom floor of the prison wing (see Plates 17 – 19) in conditions described in Chapter Twenty. Other Nazi war criminals were held on the floors above, including General Erich von dem Bach-Zelewski, although it is doubtful he was ever in a position to come into contact with Goering.

Rudof Diels, the first head of the Gestapo, in a continuing arrangement sanctioned by General Donovan, remained under the supervision of Wolfe Frank. He was moved from Bad Oeynhausen to Nuremberg where Frank arranged for him to live with his former mistress. This astonishing state of affairs, first recorded in *Nuremberg's Voice of Doom*, is worth repeating here to: indicate the importance of Diels' input into the investigations and to the interrogations officers; show the level of authority Frank at times assumed; and as an indication of the extraordinary liberties Frank and Donovan seemed to be able to take – and get away with:

As our guest in Nuremberg and as a source of information Diels proved himself to be inexhaustible, infallible and completely accurate. He had a photographic memory as far as channels of command, responsibilities, positions, officeholders, terms of office and organisational charts were concerned. He did however refuse, from the very beginning to the end, to implicate any of his former friends, colleagues or enemies in the Nazi hierarchy. This so angered some of the American prosecutors [Judge Jackson and his team] that at one stage they had him re-arrested – although this was quickly corrected on Donovan's intervention.

The status Diels was occupying in Nuremberg was so far outside any of the known categories – he was not a witness, not a prisoner, not a potential defendant, not a free man – that we had some trouble keeping him close at hand. He was, for the moment, living in the building set aside for German witnesses for the prosecution, however as he wasn't one of those, the officer in charge wanted him out. He could not be let loose into the community because the Germans would have arrested him. I could not put him up in my house in Nuremberg, as I had in Bad Oeynhausen, because my CO, Colonel Hugh Turrell, was a stickler for the rules and kept sniffing around our billets. He would have had a heart attack if he had found Diels in a 'billet, British officers, for the use of'.

Diels came up with the solution himself but an account of it will require some degree of camouflage of identities. Many years earlier Diels had had a blistering love affair with a young lady, a gifted musician, who was hotly pursued by Dr Goebbels[3] (not in his capacity as patron of the arts). Diels had successfully protected the damsel, who was not German, from Goebbels' unwanted attention. This lady was now living somewhere outside Nuremberg, having married into a well-known Bavarian family. Diels felt that Marianne (as we shall call her) and her husband might put him up, as they had all been quite friendly in the past.

I made a call at the house where Marianne lived, some 25km from Nuremberg. She was indeed beautiful, charming and unusually intelligent. I had them investigated by the CIC before I called and found that the husband had had his problems with the Nazis and the Communists within his factory, who had denounced him to both the Americans and the German de-Nazification[4] office as well.

My friend at the CIC [Donovan and Putzell headed the CIC] and I cleaned up the mess and Marianne's husband, who looked quite terrified when I made my first call in British uniform, began to relax and, yes, of course, he would welcome Dr Diels as a guest to his house. Marianne had listened to it all with a Cheshire Cat's smile and refrained from making any comment … (During my long stay in Nuremberg I spent many a happy weekend in that house and it is regrettable that, for reasons of tact and discretion, no more than that can be told)'[5].

(In other notes within his manuscript Frank reveals that the house was the hunting lodge of Count Roland Faber-Castell and his wife Nina. Joseph Persico records meetings that took place there with both Wolfe Frank and Rudolf Diels present and confirms that Countess Nina admitted she had been pursued by Goebbels. Another interesting link is that the Count's Castle at Schloss Stein was being used as the Press Camp for the world's press – and the Count did not seem to mind).[12]

Family Reunions

Frank's journey to Nuremberg had not been without incident. On his arrival at the Palace of Justice he was severely reprimanded, and lucky not to be court martialed or even cashiered, for going AWOL for several days – and for taking his driver and a staff car with him! His reason for taking these chances was to (successfully) track down his former wife and his mother, neither of whom he had seen since he fled Germany almost ten years earlier[6]. As was often the case with Frank however, it seems his abilities were deemed to be of such value to the cause as to lead the establishment to simply rap his knuckles and look the other way. In fact, he was promoted and transferred to the US team, on a substantially higher grade of pay – much to the chagrin of his superior officer who had for some time been giving him a hard time. Frank recalls with some satisfaction: 'The CO was upset. Here was the worst officer he had, getting the best job. He even put up some resistance and got himself into everybody's bad books'[7].

From early October Frank was assigned to the Interrogations Team where he drew much vital evidence out of the war criminals which was later used at the trials, including the admissions of Otto Ohlendorf that he was personally responsible for 'humanely' killing 90,000 Jews with his mobile gas chambers. Of this event, and as an example of the horrors with which the interrogators were dealing, Frank records:

> The staggering aspect of this testimony was not so much the ghastly story, which had already become terribly familiar, but the manner in which Ohlendorf told it. He was, without doubt, proud of his work. He talked quietly – with expressive gestures of well-shaped hands, smoking our cigarettes – of the attacks on German occupation troops by Polish freedom fighters and the unreasonable time and effort required to dispose of the Jews at the same time. It was here, he felt, that his talents as an organiser and his ingenuity had served the Fatherland so well, and surely, he deserved everybody's recognition – including ours?
>
> None of us could ever have imagined, until that day, such utter total lack of moral, ethical or human standards as we had witnessed. The man was proud, self-satisfied and mentally at peace. Unlike all the other murderers, the henchmen, the executioners, the sadists, the monsters I had encountered, he was searching for no explanation, no excuse, no justification, because he saw it all in his outstanding services, rendered to the cause. He did so to the end of his trial quietly, accurately and steadfastly, and I am certain he remained thus as he was walking up the steps to the gallows.
>
> There were days, such as that, when after my day in court I could not eat and I had to drown myself in alcohol before I could sleep – days when my reactions to anything or anyone German were not normal.[8]

By the start of the trials, as an interpreter, Frank was peerless. He spoke and understood German better than most Germans did and he spoke English with the depth, clarity and diction of a highly educated British aristocrat. He was also the leading pioneer of simultaneous translation (conference interpreting). First used at Nuremberg, the system simultaneously translated all that was said in court into English, German, French and Russian and proved to be more successful than anyone had ever hoped – as R.W. Cooper, correspondent of *The Times* wrote in his book *The Nuremberg Trial*, and Ann and John Tusa repeated in their book of the same name:

> The unanimous judgement on the simultaneous translation system was that it was a miracle like Pentecost. No one was

ever unreasonable enough to expect all the translators to reach the standard of the ace of them all – Wolfe Frank … his use of German and English was noticeably better than that of most native speakers. His voice and manner, the nuances of his vocabulary, the ability to convey the character of the person for whom he was translating were all outstanding.[9]

(The trials and their administration were ultimately seen to be a landmark event in international law, and the meticulous preparations carried out in the period leading up to the start of the trials (20 November 1945) ensured that Justice Jackson's hope of 'fair and just conduct at the proceedings' was seen to be carried out. This was largely achieved to the satisfaction of all concerned, including the war criminals, as Wolfe Frank confirmed in a 1970 interview he gave to *The Oregonian* [a daily newspaper based in Portland, USA]: 'Even Goering thought the trials were fair. I talked to him many times off the record. As far as the principle went, he refused to recognise our right to try him, the victor trying the vanquished. But even he agreed the court was incredibly fair').[10]

Between the beginning of October and 15 November, the date he became fully involved in interpreting the proceedings, Frank helped interrogate all the war criminals including Hermann Goering, Rudolf Hess (former deputy Fuehrer), Joachim von Ribbentrop (Foreign Minister), Wilhelm Keitel (chief of the High Command of the Armed Forces), Ernst Kaltenbrunner (Chief of Security Police), Karl Doenitz (Commander in Chief of the German Navy) and Albert Spear Hitler's Minister of Armament and War Production – who Frank agreed to meet after he had served the twenty year jail sentence imposed by the IMT. Speer asked the court's permission, which was granted, for a private conversation with Frank, who records in his memoirs:

Albert Speer was the only one of all the guilty men I met before and during Nuremberg for whom I developed a liking; because here was an outstandingly intelligent man who conveyed, throughout our conversation, a very clear sense of guilt that he would carry with him for the rest of his life. There was none of the maudlin self-incrimination I had heard from the other Nazis – high ranking and low ranking – nor was an accusing finger pointed at the Führer, or polemics put forward against the trial and the right of the victor to try the vanquished. It was clear that Speer had come to terms with the past, the present and the future – and himself.

Can twenty years imprisonment be termed future? I asked him.

'The twenty years will pass,' he replied wistfully, 'survival is so much a question of one's inner attitude, of willpower. Yes, I will survive that sentence, I am sure. I will write, and I will paint – I haven't had time to paint. Now I will – landscapes. It will serve a double purpose. I will be occupied, and I will train my imagination to visualise the things I won't be able to see – mountains, trees, the countryside, colours. Physically, I will be in a cell, but my mind won't be.[11]

CHAPTER TWENTY-TWO – NOTES & REFERENCES

1. De Novo Law is one of the UK's leading legal costs practices.

2. *Wild Bill Donovan*, p.343.

3. Paul Joseph Goebbels (1897–1945) was Germany's Minister of Propaganda from 1933 to 1945 and one of Hitler's closest associates and most devoted followers. He advocated progressively harsher discrimination against the Jews, including extermination in the Holocaust. On 30 April 1945 Goebbels succeeded Hitler as Chancellor, the following day he and his wife committed suicide, after poisoning their six children with cyanide.

4. After the war the Allied Powers initiated a comprehensive 'de-Nazification' programme. Its purpose was to eradicate National Socialist thought from political, economic, intellectual and cultural life. Nazi laws were abolished and all signs and symbols of National Socialism were removed. The main focus of the programme was the systematic screening of all former members of the NSDAP – party membership was defined as the criteria for their dismissal from executive positions in industry and from public office.

5. *Nuremberg's Voice of Doom*, p.110.

6. ibid, pp.113–118.

7. ibid, p.122.

8. ibid, pp.165–166.

9. *The Nuremberg Trial*, R. W. Cooper; and *The Nuremberg Trial*, Ann and John Tusa, p.219.

10. *The Oregonian*, 23 September 1970.

11. *Nuremberg's Voice of Doom*, p.142.

12. *Nuremberg: Infamy on Trial*, Joseph Persico, p. 220–221 and 272–274.

A COURAGEOUS STAND

'I order you not to hear a single word uttered in this room.'[1]
GENERAL WILLIAM DONOVAN

ON A DAY BETWEEN 3 October and 17 November 1945, Sergeant Harry Shotwell, who was originally under the command of Colonel Burton Andrus at Nuremberg, was ordered to take his future instructions from OSS/ CIC 'spooks'. He then became part of a small group especially assigned to guard Goering.

During this period, and under a veil of secrecy, Shotwell was instructed to take Goering to an interview room where the Reichsmarschall was to be interrogated by General Donovan. Shortly before his death in 2018, aged 93, Shotwell gave an audio interview[1] and a magazine interview[2] detailing this occasion, which had clearly left a lasting impression upon him and is of importance in these matters.

In the audio Shotwell reveals that at that meeting General Donovan offered to open the interview room's French windows in order to allow Goering to commit suicide by jumping off the balcony. Shotwell also states that Donovan 'waved a finger in his face' and menacingly told the guard 'I order you not to hear a single word uttered in this room'.

Selected parts of that interview and another he gave to *The Alliance Review* a Minerva newspaper, are as follows:

The Alliance Review: In October 1945 'out of the blue' I and five other guards were ordered to go with two OSS 'Spooks'. I still do not know to this day why I was chosen but I was told I was to follow the orders of these two men from now on ... I remember during this time as a guard thinking that: for an old Carroll County farm boy, this isn't bad ... The only thing I did not really like was the fact that I was not allowed to convey what I was doing to my family'[2].

The Canton Repository: [I was] told General Donovan would make you leave the room. Our general order was to never be more than five paces from the prisoner at any time ... we were fully responsible for that prisoner under pain of court martial ... we went in the room and there stood General Donovan behind a big beautiful desk with a glass top that had all these trinkets on it

... he was head of OSS, at this time they'd changed it to the CIC – Counter Intelligence Corps ... he had a 45 strapped to the outside of his long black coat ... Donovan said 'Alright sergeant you can leave us now, I'll call you when I'm done.' I said: no sir, I can't leave my prisoner. He said: 'you what?'. I said: no sir, I can't leave my prisoner. He said 'you are telling me you can't leave this prisoner?' I said: yes sir, if I leave the room I take the prisoner with me. He said 'who told you that'. I said: Captain Miller, sir. He then said 'well you know I'm a general and that outranks a captain and I order you to leave the room – I'll call you'. I said: I have a general order from Captain Miller and he's the only one who can rescind it.

Shotwell then has a 'pretend' telephone conversation with Captain Miller who, having shown no interest whatsoever in his sergeant's plight, had hung up. Using his initiative Shotwell repeats that Captain Miller has instructed him not to leave Goering's side, at which point Donovan swept all the trinkets off the desk against the wall. Goering is looking at the floor, the (unnamed) interpreter is looking at the ceiling and Shotwell is looking at Goering – to make sure nothing has hit him. Donovan then comes in front of Shotwell who continues:

He [Donovan] said: 'alright then, by God, I order you, and he stuck his fingers right in my face, I order you to stand over there by the door and, by God, I order you not to hear a single word uttered in this room. Is that clear soldier? I said: yes sir, thank you sir, turned about face and stepped over about three or four paces to the door. Inside my pants my knees were quivering.

There then followed an exchange between Donovan and Goering about the art treasures the Nazi had stolen which ended with Goering admitting he had taken them but only to save them from being destroyed in the war. Shotwell's narrative then continues:

Donovan looked over at me and gave me a real dirty look, he certainly did. Sitting behind his desk, trinkets all over the floor. Right behind him is these big French doors/windows from floor to ceiling and outside is a little balcony which I can see. He told Goering: 'I see you eyeing them windows back there. Do you want to jump? Do you want to save me trouble, you trouble? I'll open them up for you. Come on'. Goering said: 'Nein, nein, nein'

> – like you crazy bastard … finally he [Donovan] said: 'now you
> can leave the room with him'. I took two steps over to Goering
> and we were out of there … I took him back to his cell … and I
> had to go to the bathroom.

Shotwell does not give the date of his steadfast refusal to leave Goering alone with Donovan, but on 17 November, three days before the start of the IMT, without being given a reason and to his great surprise, he was suddenly removed from the rota guarding Goering. Harry Shotwell's final remark regarding those matters was to say that the events during this encounter, 'might have been the reason we got kicked out of there!'

(On reflection Shotwell may have realised he was most probably relieved off these duties because, having been instructed to take his orders from the OSS, he then refused to comply with an order given to him directly by it's commanding officer – who also happened to be the most senior military officer at the IMT – a general who expected absolute loyalty and obedience. Other COs may have put an insubordinate sergeant on a charge, but not Donovan: partly because he could hardly reveal to any proceedings that might ensue, the nature and content of the 'private meetings' he was having with Goering; and partly because he would have admired Shotwell's courageous stand – as Charles Pinck, President of the OSS Society revealed, Donovan had once said he would 'rather have a young lieutenant with enough guts to disobey a direct order than a colonel too regimented to think and act for himself).'[3]

It seems that, like Edwin Putzell and Wolfe Frank, and perhaps feeling able to talk about what went on in the meeting between Goering and General Donovan for the first time, Shotwell only released this information very late in his life. His interview with *The Alliance Review* was conducted on his 93rd Birthday (12 January 2018) – less than three months before his death on 1 April – and the recorded interview he gave to *The Canton Repository* was not published until 1 May.

For the purposes of these matters however, there are several very important points to be noted from these interviews:

1. Sergeant Shotwell confirms General Donovan ordered guards out of the room when he interviewed Goering.
2. If a guard stood his ground and refused to leave, he was forcefully ordered 'not to hear a single word uttered in this room'.

3. If any guard did hear anything, they were bound by statutory acts and were sworn to secrecy by General Donovan – who was so senior that he was answerable only to the US President and the Joint Chiefs of Staff.
4. Most importantly Donovan indicated he was prepared to give Hermann Goering an opportunity to commit suicide.

CHAPTER TWENTY THREE – NOTES & REFERENCES

1. Recorded interview *The Canton Repository*: Harry Shotwell Recalls a Day with Nazi Hermann Goering and General Donovan: https://omny.fm/shows/rep-audio-vault/harry-shotwell-recalls-a-day-with-nazi-hermann-goe

2. Interview given to Thomas Clapper, *The Alliance Review*, Minerva. https://eu.the-review.com/story/news/2018/01/26/world-war-ii-veteran-harry/15364896007/

3. https://www.thecrimson.com/article/2011/4/21/war-oss-donovan-world/

SERVING THE INDICTMENTS

'Of course I want Counsel. But it is even more important to have a good interpreter.'[1]
REICHSMARSCHALL HERMANN GOERING

ON 18 OCTOBER 1945 the charges to be put to those Nazi war criminals who were to appear at the IMT were officially read out at the High Court in Berlin. The following day Major Airey Neave, accompanied by Captain Wolfe Frank acting as interpreter, began the tasks of: serving the defendants with customised copies of the indictments each were to face; and assisting them to choose a lawyer to represent them at the IMT (see Plates 6 – 8 for details of the full list of defendants, the charges put to each of them, and the verdicts and sentences of the Court).

Major Neave, who came to consider it a great honour to have been asked to undertake these duties, was not only highly regarded for his work with military intelligence agencies and for his famous escape from imprisonment, he was also a qualified lawyer who spoke good German. Of his totally unexpected appointment and the important role that was suddenly thrust upon him, he commented: 'This seemed to me the most dangerous situation I had faced since Colditz.'[2]

In its edition of 29 October, *Time* magazine published these events, as well as comments made by defendant on receiving their indictments (which are broadly in line with the records of Neave and Frank), as follows:[1]

In Berlin's high-ceilinged Kammergericht[3] last week the International Military Tribunal formally indicted 24 top Nazis as war criminals. For 50 solemn minutes the session proceeded in English, Russian, French and German. The presiding judge, Russian Major General I. T. Nikitchenko, quoted from the 25,000 word indictment: the U.S., France, Britain and Russia 'hereby accuse [the defendants] as guilty … of crimes against peace, war crimes and crimes against humanity and of a common plan or conspiracy to commit these crimes …

Next day Allied officers [Neave and Frank] handed copies of the indictment to each of the defendants in the lightless cells of

Nurnberg prison. Informed that they could choose their attorneys from prepared lists, the indicted reacted variously …

Reich Marshal Hermann Göring [said]: 'Of course, I want counsel. But it is even more important to have a good interpreter.'

In his memoirs Major Neave, no doubt recalling his days of incarceration as a prisoner-of-war, described his first impressions on arriving at Nuremberg as a city in ruins with six thousand civilians buried under rubble and 'a sickening smell of disinfectant'. Neave noted the Palace of Justice as being 'a solid municipal building with wide corridors' with rooms overlooking a grim patch of ground from where he observed Goering and his former colleagues. In horror he records: 'At first I shrank from the sight of these men … I was afraid to face them, as they awaited trial … I imagined them crouching in their cells like wounded beasts. I feared to approach them as a man backs away from a corpse.'[4]

But, beginning on 19 October, face them he did, recording that on that day:

I sat next to Wolfe Frank, a German from Munich, who had joined the British Army as a refugee from Hitler. He had acquired the most elegant English accent and became one of the best-known interpreters in the courtroom. He accompanied me on subsequent visits to the cells.[5]

Later that afternoon, the Indictment was served on Goering (in his cell) by Major Neave, accompanied by Colonel Andrus, two prison guards and an interpreter. (It was later discovered Goering had written on a copy of the indictment 'The victor will always be the judge and the vanquished the accused').

Neave's biographical sketch of the Reichsmarschall was damning:

The comfortable impression that Goering, the jovial military man, was more 'humane' than his Nazi colleagues has no basis in fact. His reputation outside Germany as a moderate was not justified. On July 31st, 1941 Goering sent an order to Heydrich, [see Plate 12] head of the Security Service, to set in motion the extermination of Jews. He charged Heydrich with organising the 'final solution of the Jewish question in the German sphere of influence in Europe'. This programme of genocide, which came to be associated at Nuremberg with the name Eichmann[6], was one of the most awful crimes in the history of the world. While the real author was Hitler, Goering played a major part.[7]

During this meeting Goering's choice of counsel was discussed. Neave recorded Goering's reply 'Lawyers' he said contemptuously 'They will be no use in this trial. What is required is a good interpreter. I want my own private interpreter'. On the same day Neave served indictments on the other top Nazis and describes their personalities and demeanours, which correspond to those Frank records in his memoirs.[8]

Of his first encounter with Goering Neave writes:[9]

The man was still an actor. He bowed to me and smiled ... When I first entered, his mouth had twitched nervously; he seemed unsteady. Now he was in possession of the stage again. There was a trace of geniality in those cruel eyes as he gestured towards the bed. It was as if to say, "I am afraid I cannot offer you a chair ... on my next visit to his cell, on the following day he used those very words in a fruity voice, as I called to discuss the choice of German Counsel [Neave's official record shows this was in fact two days later – Sunday 21 October].[10]

In his official report Neave also records:[11]

Goering, for the second time (he last drew my attention to this on Oct. 19) requested a special interpreter. He attached great importance to this.

Frank describes this meeting, his first with Goering, in similar terms, but with one additional comment that is of importance. This, and Neave's record above, are discussed and analysed in more detail in Chapter Twenty-Seven. During these visits, Dr Robert Ley, Hitler's labour leader, made an extraordinary request, recorded by both Neave and Frank, to be represented by a Jewish Lawyer – earlier he had declared 'We swear we are not going to abandon the struggle until the last Jew in Europe has been exterminated.' Ley committed suicide in his cell four days after this interview by strangling himself to death in his prison cell using a noose he had made by tearing a towel into strips and fastening it to the toilet pipe.

CHAPTER TWENTY FOUR – NOTES & REFERENCES

1. *Time* 29 October 1945. https://time.com/archive/6772741/germany-the-defendants/

2. *Nuremberg – A Personal Record of the Trial of Major Nazi War Criminals in 1945–6*, p.48.

3. The Kammergericht is the highest state court of Berlin. On 18 October 1945, the International Military Tribunal (IMT) of the Nuremberg trials held its constituent meeting here.

4. *Nuremberg – A Personal Record of the Trial of Major Nazi War Criminals in 1945–6*, pp.42–45.

5. ibid, p.61.

6. Otto Adolf Eichmann (1906–1962) was a German-Austrian officer of the Nazi Party and one of the major organisers of the Holocaust. After the end of the Second World War, he fled to Argentina, living under a pseudonym but was captured in 1960 and then tried, found guilty and hanged in Israel on 1 June 1962.

7. *Nuremberg – A Personal Record of the Trial of Major Nazi War Criminals in 1945–6*, pp.67–68.

8. *Nuremberg's Voice of Doom.*

9. *Nuremberg – A Personal Record of the Trial of Major Nazi War Criminals in 1945–6*, Airey Neave, p.70.

10. *Memorandum [written by Major Airey Neave] to the General Secretary of the International Military Tribunal*, 24th October 1945 (National Archives), p.1.

11. ibid, p2.

INTRANSIGENT DIFFERENCES OF OPINION

'Indicting the entire German High Command is unbecoming of our country.'[1]
GENERAL WILLIAM DONOVAN

IF FRANKLIN D. ROOSEVELT HAD NOT DIED SO SUDDENLY in April 1945, General Donovan's opinions would have been major considerations in how proceedings at the IMT should be conducted. Also, the continuation of the OSS, or some similarly constituted successor organisation, with Donovan as its head, would have been most likely. Robert Jackson may not even have been FDR's choice to be US Chief Prosecutor, and Donovan's reasoning, methods and motives regarding the interrogation of witnesses and how prosecutions should be conducted may have been adopted. How things can change overnight.

Vice President Harry S. Truman, who was already questioning the cost and value of the OSS, assumed the Presidency and within weeks he had appointed Justice Jackson to be Chief Prosecutor at the IMT with General Donovan, a highly qualified lawyer in his own right, to be Jackson's special assistant.

Truman gave Jackson complete authority to choose his own staff and to design and implement the trials. Initially Jackson was grateful for Donovan's involvement, and he had accepted the general's plans for organising the prosecution staff with the spy chief acting as his deputy and his lead attorney during the trial.

As the preparations progressed however the two men began to develop two entirely different strategies on how proceedings should be conducted in general and how the prosecution of defendants and witnesses should be handled in particular.

The biggest issue of all became Donovan's belief that a plea bargain with Goering was the best option, with the Reichsmarschall accepting full responsibility for the crimes with which he had been charged in return for being granted a more honourable execution. Donovan saw this as being the path to gathering the best evidence against the other defendants and of saving huge amounts of time, effort and money.

Jackson however was set against such an arrangement (although he did adopt this tactic with other defendants, notably Bach-Zelewski and Karl Wolff) and avowed to see Goering answer for all Nazi crimes and, following his conviction, be hung by the neck as a common criminal.

With the OSS having been closed down, and with Jackson asserting his authority at the IMT, Donovan saw, disappearing before his eyes, his dual roles as chief of the world's largest intelligence agency and star prosecutor at Nuremberg – where he had already told other attorneys he would be bringing 'big rabbits out of a hat.'

The following extracts from pages 341–348 of *Wild Bill Donovan*, Douglas Waller's excellent biography of General Donovan, are compelling and form a most important part of the continuing narrative that chronicles General Donovan's dealings with Goering during his eight-week period at Nuremberg (3 October – 30 November 1945) as well as his fall out with Justice Jackson:

Donovan [and Putzell] had flown to Nuremberg on 3 October, two days after the OSS closed down ...

Donovan expected to take up the star prosecution role he envisaged for himself ... Jackson's son, Bill [a member of the prosecution team] suspected from the first day Donovan returned that he wanted to take over his father's job as part of a scheme to revive the OSS. But Donovan had been away from Nuremberg for nearly four months. He was out of the loop and did not command the influence he once had over the Tribunal. Jackson no longer needed the spymaster or his organisation so much. Research material had already been assembled for the trial, the indictment had been drafted and the prosecution staff had grown to some 650, only a quarter of whom were former OSS members ... tension between Donovan and Jackson soon surfaced. It had much to do with different personalities and lawyering styles. Jackson found Donovan's behaviour often erratic, and temperamental when he didn't get his way. Donovan he feared was a manipulator trying to trap him in schemes for the trial that suited his personal agenda but not what was best for the prosecution. Donovan thought Jackson was a poor administrator (even the justice's loyalists admitted he was hopeless on that score) and weak in the courtroom. Jackson was skilled at preparing trial briefs and analyzing arguments lawyers presented to him in the High Court. But he had no experience handling witnesses and criminals before a jury and Donovan thought he should have paid more attention to someone who had actually prosecuted cases in Buffalo as a U.S. attorney.

Jackson thought the prosecution strategy should depend heavily on the thousands of documents he had accumulated to demonstrate Nazi guilt rather than on the flashy examinations and cross-examinations Donovan envisioned. Donovan argued intensely that the case needed live Germans and Holocaust victims to testify instead of Jackson spending days reading dreary records to judges. Sensitive to image, he feared the press would grow bored and the Nazi defendants would turn public opinion against the tribunal if a dramatic case were not presented against them. Other lawyers on the team agreed with Donovan; Germans on the stand would counter the impression among their countryman that Nuremberg was nothing more than 'victor's justice.'

The targets of the prosecution also divided the two men. Donovan believed Germany's top officers should be charged with the war crimes they actually committed. He was nervous about Jackson's intention to prosecute the entire German High Command collectively as members of a 'criminal organization', with simply proof of membership enough to convict an officer.

Convinced that Jackson's approach was wrong, Donovan went off reservation and began organizing his own prosecution strategy for the trial … Goering was the biggest prize, Donovan thought. He began private negotiations with the Reichsmarschall and his lawyer to have him testify for the prosecution. Donovan prepared a lengthy pretrial questionnaire for Goering and the Reichsmarschall promised he would give truthful written answers to the questions.

Robert Jackson was no fool. He knew what Donovan was up to and deeply resented the challenge to his authority. Jackson eventually was persuaded he would need some witnesses on the stand, but he moved to shut down Donovan's negotiations with Schacht[2] and Goering. The economist [Shacht] was one of the most guilty Nazis, Jackson argued, because he financed Hitler's war making. Striking a deal with the devious Reichsmarschall was fraught with danger, Jackson correctly worried. Neither would testify for the prosecution he ruled.

By early November, Jackson and Donovan were barely on speaking terms – their communication handled with testy memos back and forth – and Donovan was openly ridiculing the trial tactics in staff meetings, calling them utterly foolish.' Other lawyers on the team began taking sides and the feuding bogged down preparations for the trial. 'What this organization needs is about six tickets – one way – to New York' complained Thomas Dodd, a young attorney who had not worked for the OSS and one day would be senator from Connecticut. Jackson began to shrink Donovan's role in the tribunal which infuriated Donovan. Jackson, who had depended on him so much in the prosecution team's early days, now hoped the spymaster would take one of those tickets to New York.

As the trial opened the third week in November and Jackson began plodding through a reading of his documents, another clash with Donovan outside the courtroom erupted that caused the final breach in their relationship.

(Donovan had been discussing with a German PoW general and a lawyer, at a private dinner party, how best to handle the defendants. Donovan considered them to be valuable sources of information and had arranged for them to be put up in a guesthouse reserved for prosecution witnesses, an action that incensed Jackson).

On 15 November Dr Stahmer (Goering's lawyer) sent a memo[3] to General Donovan concerning matters that had been agreed at a meeting that had taken place between the general and Goering on 12 November at which he, Dr Stahmer, and Dr Robert Kempner (Jackson's Assistant Chief Council) had also been present. The memo confirmed Goering had promised to give 'truthful answers, in writing, to any questions which might be put to him by General Donovan' – this was to be the script of the performances Goering and Donovan would give at the IMT which would be, for both men, the highlight of the Nuremberg trials. The memo went on to say 'I made the further request that Goering not be interrogated by anyone else during the process of this work so that he might not be disturbed by such other interrogations. General Donovan has promised that he will attempt to comply with my wishes insofar as this may be possible.'

What Kempner heard at that meeting, perhaps for the first time, must have alarmed him and alerted him to the fact that Donovan and Jackson were planning two entirely different strategies on how the Nazi defendants in general and Goering in particular would be dealt with in the witness box at the IMT.

Following the altercation outside the courtroom, and Kempner's briefing of the 12 November meeting, Jackson denied Donovan any further access to Goering (and Schacht) and felt compelled to write to the general in the strongest possible terms, as Douglas Waller records:

Jackson finally sent a letter to Donovan on November 26[4], one of the most hostile he had ever put to paper. 'You and I appear to have developed certain fundamental differences' he wrote. 'Frankly, Bill, your views and mine appear to be so far apart that I do not consider it possible to assign to you examination and cross-examination of witnesses.' Jackson, in effect, was firing him.

Enraged, Donovan shot back a letter[5] just as pointed. Indicting the entire German High Command is 'unbecoming of 'our country' he bluntly wrote. Relying 'exclusively on documents' is a mistake. Getting Goering, 'the last sane leader of the gang,' to 'confess on the stand' was not intended as a 'stunt' or as a dramatic episode, but as a very practical means of bringing home to the German people the guilt of these men. The case Jackson has assembled sorely lacks 'central administrative control' or 'intellectual direction'. Donovan, in effect, accused him of being an incompetent lawyer.

What further exacerbated the already inflamed situation was a detailed memo sent to Donovan by Colonel Telford Taylor (Jackson's deputy) which was also dated 26 November. Clearly unaware of the extent of the fall-out between the two men and his boss' decision to dispense with Donovan's services, Taylor gave the general, who had previously been his commanding officer, a detailed update on the prosecution's intention to use Bach-Zelewski as a witness against the German High Command and he mentions Goering in particular[6]. This will have infuriated Donovan even more, for Jackson was indicating he was prepared to do a 'deal' with Bach-Zelewski in return for immunity against prosecution, but was not prepared to go along with the same arrangement Donovan had negotiated with Goering – and this on the very day Jackson had informed Donovan in writing:

In short, I do not think we can afford to negotiate with any of these defendants or their counsel for testimony ... To use one of them ourselves will create the impression that there was some kind of a bargain about his testimony, opening the door for that defendant to plead for leniency on the ground he was 'helpful' and may give a background for claims that promises were made to that effect. My view is, therefore, that we should prove our case against these defendants with no use of them as witnesses.[4]

In a few short months Donovan's expectations of being the star of the show at Nuremberg had disappeared. He had been sidelined. He told Jackson in his letter of 27 November that he was leaving Nuremberg – and he did a few days later.

CHAPTER TWENTY-FIVE – NOTES & REFERENCES

1. *Wild Bill Donovan*, Douglas Waller, p.347.

2. Hjalmar Schacht (1877–1970): As Minister of Economics he played a key role in implementing Hitler's policies. At Nuremberg he was put on trial for conspiracy and crimes against peace but was acquitted.

3. *Memo from Dr Stahmer [Goering's Lawyer]* 15 November 1945 (US National Archives).

4. *Letter from Robert Jackson to William Donovan, 26 November 1945* Harry S. Truman Library & Museum.

5. *Letter from William Donovan to Robert Jackson, 27 November 1945* Harry S. Truman Library & Museum.

6. *Memorandum from Colonel Telford Taylor to General Donovan and others 26 November 1945* Cornell University Library.

SECTION FIVE

THE TRANSFER

AN ACRIMONIOUS PARTING OF THE WAYS

'He [Jackson] didn't intend to get into a "pissing contest"
with the "skunk"'[1]
JUSTICE ROBERT JACKSON

GENERAL DONOVAN LEFT NUREMBERG on 30 November 1945, and had nothing further to do with the IMT. He had only been back in Nuremberg for eight weeks, but during that time a seismic rift had developed between him and Justice Jackson that threatened to undermine the integrity of both the trials and Jackson's reputation and authority. Douglas Waller writes[2]:

Dodd saw Mary [the General's daughter in law] and Donovan off at the airport, sad to see them leave. Donovan, he thought, was a skilled trial lawyer and Jackson should have paid more attention to his ideas. Donovan left Nuremberg as bitter as he had ever been. He packed up thousands of pages of court papers and classified documents he had collected there and put them on his plane, further angering Jackson, who believed he had stolen government documents. The justice thought Donovan was a shallow, social climbing headline grabber. He didn't intend to get into a 'pissing contest' with the 'skunk' he told Dodd, but he suspected Donovan was planting stories in the press to smear him. *The Washington Times-Herald* carried a piece complaining Jackson's 'inefficient and undramatic presentation of evidence' was 'boring everyone silly.' To preempt any damage the negative publicity might cause him with the White House, Jackson rushed a letter and thick file to Truman with an account ... and copies of Donovan's most pungent notes. Friends had warned him Donovan 'would not work in second place with anybody,' Jackson wrote Truman, and he had found that to be the case. The package further convinced Truman he was right to be rid of the bad apple.

While Jackson's embittered rival had removed himself from the trials, Donovan had already arranged for Goering to be provided with the means that would allow him to die the martyr's death he craved[3]. The plan of action the two men had agreed would also enable Goering to tell his story, his way.

Despite Justice Jackson's resistance to this strategy, Donovan had ploughed on regardless with his tactics of gaining Goering's respect and agreement. His objectives had been to obtain a full confession from the Reichsmarschall, and create what would be seen as a glorious achievement for himself and the OSS. This, he hoped, would lead to a resurrection of his beloved agency, or a similar successor organisation, with him as its head. Douglas Waller explains how that agreement between the Reichsmarschall and the general had been achieved during a series of 'off the record' discussions:[5]

> The Reichsmarschall insisted that no official reporter record their meetings. Donovan obliged. (After he left the room, however, he always promptly wrote down the conversation for the prosecution team.) Donovan had worked hard to cultivate the Reichsmarschall. He wore his uniform each time pinned with every medal he had received to impress Goering, who liked to drape himself with military decorations. Goering believed the spymaster was approachable and sent word he was open to cooperating. The two had a total of ten private meetings. Donovan, who had always been intensely curious about what made evil men like Goering and Hitler tick, found the sessions fascinating. The Reichsmarschall seemed to Donovan only too willing to regale him with inside stories, such as Hitler's early diplomatic bluffs to win European territory before the war's outbreak. Like a skilled intelligence operative, Donovan eventually convinced Goering they were both like-minded conspirators who could share secrets.

Waller goes on to say (citing all relevant evidence within his meticulously researched biography that included over 500 referenced sources):

> Donovan filed a report on Goering's sex stories, but he had a bolder gambit in mind. There was no way Goering could escape death, Donovan told him in one of their meetings. But he could 'die like a man' after a full confession, Donovan said. The egotistical Goering, who knew the only question remaining was how he met his end, was intrigued with the idea of copping a plea and ratting on his comrades – if the price was right. Donovan was after what could be the world's most sensational plea bargain. Goering would accept full responsibility for the war crimes, which would

dramatically shorten the trial, and would take the stand to sell out Doenitz[4] and the other top Nazis under indictment with testimony on their complicity. In return, the Reichsmarschall would be executed as a soldier before a firing squad instead of suffering the humiliation of hanging as a common criminal. The scene in the courtroom with Donovan as the star prosecutor and Goering on the witness stand could be dramatic, the spy chief knew, if he could pull it off, which on November 6 was far from certain.[5]

This was all Goering had asked for, and he began to co-operate immediately. It was during this series of meetings that Donovan 'secretly decided, with the agreement of the British contingent', to let Goering 'die by cyanide' if the authorities refused to allow him to 'die like a man' as Donovan had promised.[3] Clearly Donovan's motives for providing the cyanide were to: honour commitments he had made to Goering – as part of the plea-bargain 'deal' they had struck that would enable the Reichsmarschall to die other than by the rope; and prove points to those who had been involved in disbanding the OSS.

While being entirely in agreement with Donovan's intentions and believing the general to be an honourable man and the only prosecutor he could trust, Goering could not have afforded to rely purely upon a verbal agreement. The Reichsmarschall would have wanted insurance and would have insisted that, in return for his compliance, he be provided with a guaranteed alternative means of avoiding the rope.

By agreeing to provide a suicide capsule – as a back-up – Donovan also showed his total commitment to their agreement, and that he was a man of his word. This would have given Goering all the comfort he needed to be able to comply entirely with the agreed plan – in fact both men had everything to gain and nothing to lose by such an arrangement. If he pulled it off Donovan would be: seen to be the ace prosecutor at Nuremberg, thereby raising his standing and achievements; proving his and not Jackson's style of prosecution was the correct method; saving the Tribunal huge amounts of time and money; and demonstrating the value of the OSS – which he hoped would be seen as being indispensable. While Goering knew whether he met his end by firing squad or by poison, he would be given his moment in the witness box, in a carefully choreographed performance with Donovan asking the pre-agreed questions. Goering intended to justify his and the Nazis actions. He would then be allowed to depart this world as an honourable warrior who remained a hero in the eyes of the German people – which of course is what he achieved – and more – as Wolfe Frank commented sometime after the event:

During his trial at Nuremberg, in his thirteen hour speech in his own defence, he [Goering] had restated, without equivocation the whole Nazi philosophy which had been so widely accepted among the German people. The fact that he had not backed down and tried to change colours to save his skin and the fact that he had contrived to cheat Germany's conquerors of carrying out their sentence on him had made a tremendous impression on many Germans.[6]

Goering had pressed on regardless with the agreed plan,[7] but with his counsel, Stahmer, asking the questions instead of Donovan. With the cyanide capsule safely in his possession he could have taken the poison anytime from November 1945, but chose to use it after he had had his moment in court and at the most dramatic point in the final, final moments of the Third Reich, well knowing this would inflict maximum damage on the Allies and bring into question the whole of the Nuremberg proceedings.

CHAPTER TWENTY-SIX – NOTES & REFERENCES

1. *Wild Bill Donovan*, p.347.

2. ibid, pp.347–348.

3. Lieutenant Putzell's admissions to Petronella Wyatt in her article that appeared in the 1 February 2003 edition of *The Spectator* p 48 (see Chapters Nine and Forty-Two).

4. Karl Doenitz (1891–1980): Commander-in-Chief of the German Navy succeeded Hitler as Head of State and ordered the signing of the instruments of surrender. He was convicted of War Crimes and sentenced to ten years imprisonment.

5. *Wild Bill Donovan*, pp.342–343.

6. *New York Herald Tribune* 7 December 1949 and *The Undercover Nazi Hunter*, p.70.

7. *Wild Bill Donovan*, p.348.

THE WISH BECOMES THE DEED

'A thousand words will not leave so deep an impression as one deed.'
HENRIK IBSEN

TO FULFIL HIS PART OF THE AGREEMENT he had made
with Hermann Goering, General Donovan assigned the task
of dispensing the poison capsule to his protégé and most trusted
colleague, Ned Putzell – the man he could rely upon to 'handle the
dirty administrative chores of enforcing his orders.'[1]

How exactly the transfer was made is not known, but that would
not have been a problem for Donovan and Putzell – *THE* leading
practitioners of the 'dark arts of espionage' and acts requiring sleight
of hand.

Neither can the exact timing of the transfer be pinpointed, but it
had to have taken place between 3 October and 30 November (the
period Donovan and Putzell were in Nuremberg) and there are strong
indications that Goering's wish became the deed sometime during the
week following a crucial meeting the Reichsmarschall had on 'Tuesday
evening, November 6, with the American spy chief.'[2]

In *Wild Bill Donovan* (published 2011) Douglas Waller records:

A large military detail mingled outside the interrogation room
[on 6 November]. Rumors had circulated in Nuremberg that
Nazi diehards still at large were hatching a plot to spring Goering
from jail, he was under heavy guard. Inside the room only an
Army private sat with Donovan to translate – although both men
could have dispensed with the interpreter. Goering understood
English well and Donovan had been practicing his German for
the cross-examinations he planned at trial. The Reichsmarschall
insisted that no official reporter record their meetings. Donovan
obliged. (After he left the room, however, he always promptly
wrote down the conversation for the prosecution team).'[3]

Two important points to note from this extract are the prevailing
conditions and that no guards were present in the room to hear
what was said – presumably Donovan had ordered the guard detail

to wait outside – as Sergeant Harry Shotwell had indicated was the general's practice.

On 15 November Dr Stahmer sent the memo to General Donovan concerning matters agreed at a meeting that had taken place between the general and Goering on 12 November. The memo confirmed Goering had promised to give 'truthful answers, in writing, to any questions which might be put to him by General Donovan'. The memo went on to say 'I made the further request that Goering not be interrogated by anyone else during the process of this work so that he might not be disturbed by such other interrogations. General Donovan has promised that he will attempt to comply with my wishes insofar as this may be possible.'[4]

Wolfe Frank's Recollections

Donovan's description of the conditions that prevailed in Nuremberg on 6 November 1945, when he had that crucial meeting with Goering, was published by Douglas Waller in 2011. In his memoirs (written prior to 1988 but not published until 2018), Wolfe Frank describes the conditions on the occasion he later realised Goering was 'concealing something in his mouth' in almost identical terms to those Donovan had recorded.

However, while Frank is clear on detail, in this part of his narrative he has, in fact, unwittingly or perhaps deliberately, merged conversations that had taken place on separate occasions. Any confusion in Frank's mind might have been due to him trying to recall what had taken place forty years earlier, or there might have been another motive to why he brought together events that had taken place at different meetings. I will explain why I think this is a strong possibility in a subsequent chapter. In the meantime, however, I will reproduce Frank's record[5] interspersed with my comments and/or explanations, which are *printed in italics*.

[Frank]: Shortly after I had my first encounter with Hermann Goering. Intelligence reports had reached the security people in Nuremberg that all over Germany an unusual number of railway tickets were being purchased for Nuremberg. Unfounded rumours suggested that plans were afoot to kidnap Goering from jail. Security precautions in the courthouse had been dramatically increased and an order had been issued excluding him from the daily exercise period prisoners were allowed in the courtyard of the building.

This was not Frank's first meeting with Goering. The conditions he outlines are identical to those recorded at the time of the Goering-Donovan meeting which took place on the evening of 6 November. This strongly suggests that at least part of the meeting to which Frank is referring occurred on, or soon after, 6 November. Frank and Neave had first met with Goering, and on more than one occasion, between 19–21 October when the indictments and trial date papers were served upon the Reichsmarschall and when his choice of counsel was discussed with him.

[Frank]: Goering could not, I was told, be brought to an interrogation room, so I would be taken to his cell to discuss with him his choice of counsel.'

The date of the meeting where Frank and Neave discussed Goering's counsel, as recorded by Neave in both his official report[6] and his memoirs[7] was Sunday 21 October and it took place in an interrogation room, not in Goering's cell, on a sunny Sunday morning, not a rainy Sunday afternoon as Frank suggests below.

[Frank]: On that dark, rainy Sunday afternoon I came very close to making history – and I missed my chance! As the door of Goering's cell was noisily unlocked, the former Reichsmarshall rose from his cot where he had, obviously, been napping. Feeling rather nervous, I told him why I was there.'

Neave wrote in his memoirs: 'Next day was Sunday, October 21st, and I started a round of interviews of defendants about their choice of counsel ... Wartime still continued at Nuremberg. It was not therefore extraordinary to Fisher [a US attorney], Wolfe Frank and myself that we should find ourselves on the way to the prison on a Sunday morning. The sun shone in the exercise yard ... The accused Nazis were brought to us from their cells, dressed in their prison garb, as we sat in a bare little room adjoining the entrance. Each was accompanied by two sentries, who stood beside them vigorously chewing gum and occasionally swinging their blackjacks. The first on my list was Goering who made an impressive, hearty entrance.

[Frank]: 'Ah,' he said 'sehr schoen' (splendid). He offered me a seat on his cot and proceeded to apologise for the lack of hospitality. 'I have asked for some of my furniture from Carinhall[8] to be brought here,' he declared, poker-faced. 'It has still not arrived. I blame the management.'

Neave writes: '[on Friday 19 October] Goering rose unsteadily to his feet ... The man was still an actor. He bowed to me and smiled ... When I first entered, his mouth had twitched nervously; he seemed unsteady. Now he was in possession of the stage again. There was a trace of geniality in those cruel eyes as he gestured towards the bed. It was as if to say, 'I am afraid I cannot offer you a chair' ... on my next visit to his cell, on the following day [Saturday 20 October] he used those very words in a fruity voice, as I called to discuss the choice of German Counsel ... 'Lawyers!' he said contemptuously. 'They will be no use in this trial. What is required is a good interpreter. I want my own private interpreter.' You will have to apply to the tribunal. I shall be coming to see you tomorrow about your counsel.'[9]

[Frank]: Quite a sense of humour, I thought, looking at Goering for the first time, somewhat overawed by the occasion. I also noted that he was not using his dentures. He was lisping in the manner typical of the temporarily toothless. He had not bothered to put his trousers on either but had wrapped a blanket around his legs as he was sitting down next to me. He certainly looked very different from photographs I had seen. He was much slimmer and with a pasty complexion after several months in prison. He also had deep rings under his eyes, probably the effect of the drug withdrawal programme he had undergone, but his eyes themselves were very alert and his intelligence was obvious.

We turned to the matter at hand – the choice of a defence counsel. He looked at the list I presented to him and ran a well-kept finger down the forty-odd names. 'Thissh ish difficult,' he lisped. 'I don't know any of theesh people. In the past, when I had a legal problem, I changed the law.' But let me see ...' and he stopped at a name of Dr Otto Stahmer of Hamburg. 'Ah, that's a nice-sounding German name. I will have him' – and he did.

Stahmer arrived in Nuremberg a few days later, totally overawed by the thought of his client and the assignment. He needn't have been. Goering handled his own defence brilliantly as a strategist, tactician and performer par excellence. Stahmer was assigned his cues and, during Goering's performance in the witness box Stahmer's role was that of a prompter who asked hundreds of questions, all suitably arranged by his client in order to deliver a thirteen-hour speech in his, and the Third Reich's, defence. The questions had been dictated to a bewildered Stahmer whose own questions had been impatiently waved aside. He didn't really fathom the story line until he surfaced at the end of Goering's testimony.

The appointment of Dr Otto Stahmer as the counsel for Goering was announced on 31 October.[10]

Some time after Goering's suicide, I was relating the story of my Sunday visit to his cell to a friend, Tom Ready [sic, should be Reedy] of Associated Press. Tom stared at me in amazement for a long time and then exploded 'You stupid ****,' he screamed. 'Didn't you know Goering had perfect teeth?' It took some time to sink in. If Goering had his own teeth, why was he talking like a toothless person? My God, I thought, because he was concealing something in his mouth … but more about that later.'

There are extremely important sequels and a continuing narrative to these events, to which I will return in Chapter Thirty-Three, but it was important at this stage to establish that Donovan and Frank were both describing events that occurred on and after 6 November 1945 and to note Frank's comments about Goering concealing something in his mouth.

CHAPTER TWENTY-SEVEN – NOTES & REFERENCES

1. *Wild Bill Donovan*, p.230.

2. ibid, p.341.

3. ibid, p.342.

4. *Memorandum of Interview Between General Donovan and the Defendant Goering* – November 15, 1945 – Cornell University.

5. *Nuremberg's Voice of Doom*, pp.124–125.

6. *Memorandum* [written by Major Airey Neave] *to the General Secretary of the International Military Tribunal*, 24th October 1945 (National Archives) p.1.

7. *Nuremberg – A Personal Record of the Trial of Major Nazi War Criminals in 1945–6*, pp.219–222.

8. *Carinhall*, in the Schorfheide Forest north-east of Berlin, was Hermann Goering's country residence.

9. *Nuremberg – A Personal Record of the Trial of Major Nazi War Criminals in 1945–6*, pp.68–73 and 219–220.

10. *New York Times, Goering Selects Counsel*, 1 November 1945 p.4.

SECTION SIX

THE TRIALS

THE GREATEST TRIAL IN HISTORY – PART 1

'No half-century ever witnessed slaughter on such a scale, such cruelties and inhumanities.'[1]
MR JUSTICE JACKSON

AFTER DONOVAN'S: acrimonious premature departure, with the prosecution's continuing refusal to an execution by firing squad, and with the cyanide capsule safely in his possession, Goering made the Allies in general, and Jackson in particular, suffer for not going along with Donovan's recommendations.

Douglas Waller writes:

With the plea deal fallen through, Goering took the stand defiantly unrepentant and tried to rally the other defendants against the prosecution … His suit hanging limply from him, Goering, who was found guilty of 'crimes unique in their enormity', gave his judges a cynical look when the death sentence was read. He managed to cheat the hangman by swallowing a potassium cyanide capsule in his cell. He claimed to the end that Donovan was one prosecutor he could trust. As Donovan had warned, the tribunal and Jackson's prosecution were accused of dispensing victor's justice. But though the proceedings may have been flawed and Jackson's prosecution less than spectacular, the eleven ordered to the gallows and the rest who were sentenced to prison richly deserved the punishment they got.[2]

With or without Donovan's participation, Goering stuck to the script and throughout the trial he ran rings around Jackson and ultimately humiliated the justice further by dying a hero in the eyes of his people instead of as a common criminal as Jackson had planned.

The IMT opened on 20 November 1945. In his opening remarks Jackson's set out his intentions:[3]

The privilege of opening the first trial in history for crimes against the peace of the world imposes a grave responsibility. The wrongs which we seek to condemn and punish have been so calculated, so malignant, and so devastating, that civilization cannot tolerate their being ignored, because it cannot survive their being repeated. That four great nations, flushed with victory and stung with injury stay the hand of vengeance and voluntarily submit their captive enemies to the judgment of the law is one of the most significant tributes that Power has ever paid to Reason.

In the prisoners' dock sit twenty-odd broken men. Reproached by the humiliation of those they have led almost as bitterly as by the desolation of those they have attacked, their personal capacity for evil is forever past. It is hard now to perceive in these men as captives the power by which as Nazi leaders they once dominated much of the world and terrified most of it. Merely as individuals their fate is of little consequence to the world.

What makes this inquest significant is that these prisoners represent sinister influences that will lurk in the world long after their bodies have returned to dust. We will show them to be living symbols of racial hatreds, of terrorism and violence, and of the arrogance and cruelty of power. They are symbols of fierce nationalisms and of militarism, of intrigue and war-making which have embroiled Europe generation after generation, crushing its manhood, destroying its homes, and impoverishing its life. They have so identified themselves with the philosophies they conceived and with the forces they directed that any tenderness to them is a victory and an encouragement to all the evils which are attached to their names. Civilization can afford no compromise with the social forces which would gain renewed strength if we deal ambiguously or indecisively with the men in whom those forces now precariously survive.

Eight months later, on 26 July 1946, Justice Jackson said in his closing address[1]:

A glance over the dock will show that, despite quarrels among themselves, each defendant played a part which fitted in with every other, and that all advanced the common plan. It contradicts experience that men of such diverse backgrounds and talents should so forward each other's aims by coincidence.

The large and varied role of Goering was half militarist and half gangster. He stuck. He used his SA muscle-men to help bring the gang into power. In order to entrench that power he contrived to have the Reichstag burned, established the Gestapo, and created the concentration camps. He was equally adept at massacring opponents and at framing scandals to get rid of stubborn generals. He built up the Luftwaffe and hurled it at his defenseless neighbors. He was among the foremost in harrying the Jews out of the land. By mobilizing the total economic resources of Germany he made possible the waging of the war which he had taken a large part in planning. He was, next to Hitler, the man who tied the activities of all the defendants together in a common effort ...

Two World Wars have left a legacy of dead which number more than all the armies engaged in any way that made ancient or medieval history. No half-century ever witnessed slaughter on such a scale, such cruelties and inhumanities, such wholesale deportations of peoples into slavery, such annihilations of minorities ... It is against such a background that these defendants now ask this Tribunal to say that they are not guilty of planning, executing, or conspiring to commit this long list of crimes and wrongs. They stand before the record of this trial as blood-stained Gloucester stood by the body of his slain King. He begged of the widow, as they beg of you:

'Say I slew them not.' And the Queen replied,

'Then say they were not slain. But dead they are'[4]

'If you were to say of these men that they are not guilty, it would be as true to say there has been no war, there are no slain, there has been no crime'.

The opening and closing speeches of Justice Jackson were considered to be of the highest order, but his examination and cross-examination skills had, at times, proven to be, as Donovan had predicted, extremely weak. Jackson did however, to the satisfaction of the IMT, prove beyond reasonable doubt the guilt of all but three of those on trial.

CHAPTER TWENTY-EIGHT – NOTES & REFERENCES

1. Robert H. Jackson, *Closing Argument for Conviction of Nazi War Criminals*, (Robert H. Jackson Center).

2. *Wild Bill Donovan*, p.348.

3. Robert H. Jackson *Opening Arguments for Conviction of Nazi War Criminals*, (Robert H. Jackson Center).

4. William Shakespeare, *Richard III*, Act One, Scene Two.

THE GREATEST TRIAL IN HISTORY – PART 2

*'it was seen that Goering was the complete master of
Mr. Justice Jackson.'*[1]
MR JUSTICE BIRKETT

IN HIS COURTROOM DUAL WITH GOERING, Jackson was always seen to be second best, as Mr Justice Birkett, the British Alternate Judge at the IMT, later wrote[1]:

> The cross-examination had not proceeded more than ten minutes before it was seen that Goering was the complete master of Mr. Justice Jackson[1] ... He was overwhelmed by his documents [as Donovan had also predicted] and there was no chance of the lightning questions following upon some careless or damaging answer, no quick parry and thrust, no leading the witness on to the prepared pitfall, and above all no clear over-riding conception of the great issues which could have been put with simplicity and power ... The trial from now on is really outside the control of the Tribunal, and in the long months ahead the prestige of the trial will steadily diminish.

Despite Justice Birkett articulating a widely held view, and the catastrophic finale that Goering planned and carried out, the IMT is generally considered to have been a success. The trials established the principle that individuals, no matter how high their eminence or status, can be held responsible for atrocities under international law. The IMT also paved the way for the establishment of the International Criminal Court and human rights conventions. These principles have been the cornerstone of international justice ever since.

I do not intend to further discuss the proceedings of the IMT, other than where they are relevant to this narrative. However, may I remind readers, Plates 2–8 provide: illustrations of the courtroom layout; the participants and where they sat throughout the trial; brief details of each of the defendants; the charges those defendants faced; and the verdicts and sentences the court imposed upon each of them.

CHAPTER TWENTY-NINE – NOTES & REFERENCES

1. *The Anatomy of the Nuremberg Trials: A Personal Memoir*, Telford Taylor, p.341.

THE REICHSMARSCHALL & THE INTERPRETER

'At first the very idea of multilingual instantaneous interpretation was unthinkable.'[1]

PETER UIBERALL

WOLFE FRANK WAS NOT ONLY the star interpreter at Nuremberg, he was also the leading pioneer of the process that came to be known as 'simultaneous interpretation' – the instantaneous oral reproduction of speech from one language to another.

Peter Uiberall, the Chief German Interpreter at the trials described the process' origin in the following way: 'The system of simultaneous interpretation was crafted by trial and error in an attic room of the Palace of Justice' adding 'at first the very idea of multilingual instantaneous interpretation was unthinkable'[1].

The system, however. proved to be more successful than anyone had ever hoped and the US Museum of World War II acknowledges: 'The interpreters and translators were the unsung heroes at Nuremberg', and 'that without simultaneous interpretation the trials would have been unviable'.

This is true. Had it not been for the introduction of the simultaneous interpretation process every sentence spoken at the trials would have required translating consecutively into four languages. It is generally accepted that the system reduced the duration of the IMT alone by over three years and the Subsequent Proceedings[2] by even more.

Of the innovation and Frank's performance historians John and Ann Tusa record in their highly regarded account of the trial: 'The unanimous judgement on the simultaneous translation system was that it was a miracle like Pentecost. No one was ever unreasonable enough to expect all the translators to reach the standard of the ace of them all – Wolfe Frank ... whose use of German and English was noticeably better than that of most native speakers'[3].

To put Frank's contributions into context, he translated an estimated one third of the six million words spoken at the IMT, including nine of the twelve-thirteen hours Hermann Goering spent in the witness box.

Frank wrote: 'We interpreters were involved in the writing of history and our contribution was of the greatest importance. None of the judges understood German and everything said in that courtroom to them by the defendants and witnesses passed through the ears, brains and mouths of we interpreters'[4].

Some of Frank's most audacious bending of the rules concerned his encounters with Goering. On one occasion he received a reprimand for speaking out of turn with Hitler's deputy. Frank had somehow arranged for his Great Dane (Tiny) to be given a pass to all areas of the Palace of Justice except for the courtroom, and he records:

One day, when I stood near Goering in the courtroom, I heard him say to me out of the corner of his mouth 'I wish you'd feed me to that dog of yours instead of hanging me,' and I just had time to whisper back 'It won't work – he's fussy about his food' before a guard bore down on me to see if I had broken the rule and talked to an accused'.[5]

What at first appears to be an even more outrageous incident involving Goering occurred when Frank arranged for his then girlfriend, 'Captain Clare McCririck',[6] to fly to Nuremberg and sit in on a contrived interview, at the end of which Frank records:

'Herr Goering', I said. 'I have here a letter purportedly signed by General Koller. Would you please identify the signature?' and I handed the two bits of paper to him. He glanced at them.

'But I have already identified the signature on this letter,' he announced.

'Have you really?' I said in utter faked amazement, 'then the slip must have got lost. Please sign again on this one.'

He nodded and signed with much authority.

'Thank you, that will be all,' I declared, and rose.

So did Goering, he nodded briefly and headed for the door, preceded and followed by the two MPs. When he was level with Clare's chair, he suddenly stopped and turned to face her. 'Gnaediges Fraulein,' he said, 'no doubt I owe this little interlude to your presence in Nuremberg. I hope you have enjoyed it also.'

Then he bowed politely, turned and left for his cell. Clare had, indeed, met Goering and she had the interrogation slip with his autograph to prove it. He must have remembered this highly irregular performance of mine when he asked to be put on Tiny's menu.[5]

The two anecdotes of Wolfe Frank mentioned above are included to show the kind of relationship that existed between the interpreter and the Reichsmarschall. Frank admits to talking with Goering 'many times off the record'[7] and they clearly had an acceptable method of remaining civil and respectful to each other whilst, at times, conversing in a way that bordered on banter. Wolfe describes this, perhaps tongue in cheek, as being a 'palsy-walsy relationship between Hermann and me'[8].

Clare McCririck – A Brave, Secretive and Formidable Lady

There may be more to the incident involving 'Captain' McCririck (later Baroness Rendlesham) than is first apparent. *The London Gazette* of 6 November 1942[9] records she was commissioned as a second subaltern in the Auxiliary Territorial Service on 9 October 1942. However, this seems to have been a 'cover', for recently released records, now in the National Archives at Kew, show that Ms McCririck was in fact an intelligence agent with the Special Operations Executive (SOE)[6], the British equivalent of the OSS.

Frank does not indicate whether or not he was aware of Ms McCririck's role within the intelligence services, but there may be a suggestion he did in his use of 'Captain' – a rank not used in the ATS that was obtainable by ladies serving in SOE – a title notably held by Krystyna Skarbek, Nancy Wake and Margaret Paterson Archer, all of whom became well known SOE heroines.

(SOE had been set up by Winston Churchill in 1940 to conduct espionage, sabotage and reconnaissance in German-occupied Europe and to aid local resistance movements – including Room 900 of MI9 which, headed by Airey Neave, was dedicated to helping Allied prisoners of war escape and evade capture. The only British women permitted to have active combat roles during the Second World War, SOE women agents, like their male counterparts, demonstrated incredible courage and resourcefulness. They faced immense danger, with a high fatality rate, but their courage and actions were crucial to the Allied war effort. Donovan's OSS worked very closely with SOE agents behind enemy lines, especially leading up to and following the D-Day landings, and both organisations provided valuable evidence and assistance at the Nuremberg trials).

In view of Ms McCririck's active role as an SOE agent, one cannot help wondering, if there was a greater significance to the incident regarding the 'interrogation slip' signed by Goering that she took away with her. She clearly was a formidable lady of many talents, who like so many other brave colleagues, as far as I can ascertain, never revealed her involvement or spoke about her role as a secret agent.

Following the war Ms McCririck became editor of both *Vogue* and *Queen* magazines, where she was known to be a tough negotiator. Fashion photographer Helmut Newton said she was 'as thin as a rake and as hard as nails'. Following an acrimonious fall-out with the owner of *Queen*, during which it is said she threw her typewriter out of a window, she became the first manager of several well-known London boutiques including *Yves St. Laurent* and *Karl Lagerfeld*. She married Baron Rendlesham, with whom she had four children, and continued to write under the name Clare Rendlesham.

In 2012 Clare was portrayed in the BBC Four drama series *We'll Take Manhattan* by actress Helen McCrory. In a *Daily Mail* article about the series, the former SOE agent is described as having been 'the fire-breathing fashion editor who once staged a rock-starry tantrum by hurling her typewriter – eek! – out of the window. A dragon crossed with a diva'; and in a comparison with the actress playing her part, the article's author, Maureen Paton, writes – 'Husky drawl that could seduce a man at 30 paces? Check. Tongue as sharp as tailor's scissors? Check. Dramatic dark looks, dimples to die for and a highly individual sense of chic? Check, check, check.'

It is interesting to note that even in his private life, Frank seems to have been drawn to those involved in covert activities: pre-war it was the resistance movement; at Nuremberg it was people as diverse as Rudolf Diels, General Donovan and Airey Neave; there were his 'many off the record' meetings with Goering; during the Cold War he became an undercover correspondent for the *New York Herald Tribune*; and, besides Captain McCririck, there were other ladies in his life with secrets, most notably the third of his five wives, 'a woman of Eastern European origin' whom, it transpired, used a number of aliases and was thought to be a Russian spy.[10] (The possibility of Frank having been more closely involved with the intelligence agencies is considered at Appendix A).

CHAPTER THIRTY – NOTES & REFERENCES

1. *The Origins of Simultaneous Interpretation – The Nuremberg Trial*, Francesca Gaiba, Foreword.

2. Following the conclusion of the IMT, other Germans including politicians, industrialists, high ranking military personnel, physicians and jurists were arrested and brought before the courts to face war crimes charges in a series of twelve further hearings conducted by the US. Officially entitled, 'The Trials

of War Criminals before the Nuremberg Military Tribunals', these trials are more usually referred to as being the 'Subsequent Proceedings'. Telford Taylor was Chief Counsel of these trials and Wolfe Frank was Chief Interpreter.

3. *The Nuremberg Trial*, Ann Tusa and John Tusa, p.219.

4. *Nuremberg's Voice of Doom*, p.134.

5. ibid, p.148.

6. McCRIRICK, Clare Marion – born 23.10.1919. *Special Operations Executive: Personnel Files* (PF Series). Clare Marion McCRIRICK – born 23.10.1919. *Records of Special Operations Executive*. Date range: 01 January 1939 – 31 December 1946. Reference: HS 9/957/2. Subjects: Intelligence – National Archives.

7. *The Oregonian*, 23 September 1970.

8. *Nuremberg's Voice of Doom*, p.148.

9. *The London Gazette*, 6 November 1942, p.4866.

10. *Nuremberg's Voice of Doom*, p.181.

THE VOICE OF DOOM

'His guilt is unique in its enormity.'[1]
CHIEF JUSTICE GEOFFREY LAWRENCE

FROM THE VERY BEGINNING OF THE TRIALS, Wolfe Frank was a central figure in all stages of the IMT. He interpreted the Tribunal's opening remarks, was used more than any other interpreter, and then finally brought proceedings to a close by informing the defendants of their fate. It is true to say therefore that the first and last words the defendants heard at the trials were uttered by Frank.

On 30 September 1946, Frank, translating the words of the Tribunal's Chief Justice, Lord Geoffrey Lawrence, informed the Reichsmarschall that he had been found guilty on all counts: Conspiracy to Commit Crimes; Crimes Against Peace; War Crimes; and Crimes Against Humanity. Frank then continued to interpret the Chief Justice's summing up[1]:

There is nothing to be said in mitigation. For Goering was often, indeed almost always, the moving force, second only to his Leader. He was the leading war aggressor, both as political and as military leader; he was the director of the slave labor program and the creator of the oppressive program against the Jews and other races, at home and abroad. All these crimes he frankly admitted. On some specific cases there may be conflict in testimony, but in terms of the broad outline his own admissions are more than sufficiently wide to be conclusive of his guilt. His guilt is unique in its enormity.

The record discloses no excuses for this man.

Goering had not looked to excuse any of the charges levelled against him. He already knew what the verdicts and his fate would be. In his final statement, before the judgements were announced, he had defiantly issued one more rallying cry to the German People who, in spite of having lost the war, still held 'our Hermann' in high regard[2]:

I did not want a war, nor did I bring it about. I did everything to prevent it by negotiations. After it had broken out, I did everything to assure victory. Since the three greatest powers on earth, together with many other nations, were fighting against us, we finally succumbed to their tremendous superiority. I stand up for the things that I have done, but I deny most emphatically that my actions were dictated by the desire to subjugate foreign peoples by wars, to murder them, to rob them, or to enslave them, or to commit atrocities or crimes. The only motive which guided me was my ardent love for my people, its happiness, its freedom, and its life. And for this I call on the Almighty and my German people to witness.

The sentences

When Frank arrived at the Palace of Justice the following morning, 1 October, he recalls[3]: 'I was called out of the [interpreters] booth and told that in the afternoon I was to be the 'Voice of Doom' – translating to the defendants the sentences meted out by the International Military Tribunal'[3].

Frank describes his announcing of the death sentences that day as being the tensest hour of his life, but even this was not without incident. As he was about to inform Goering of his fate, the sound equipment cut out and Goering shrugged to indicate he could not hear what was being said. Once fixed Frank resumed and Goering gave him a thin smile and a thumbs-up, to indicate he could hear again – at the very moment Frank announced 'death by the rope'[3]. It was a moment frozen in time that haunted Frank for the rest of his life. Airey Neave, who was present in the courtroom at the time of this incident, records in his memoirs: 'It was one of the most macabre and shocking moments I have known'[4].

Assuming Frank was the witness Putzell indicates was present at the time the poison was transferred, was the thin smile Goering gave to the interpreter as he announced 'death by hanging' a dog whistle that only Frank, and perhaps Neave, would have understood?

Colonel Telford Taylor (Justice Jackson's Deputy) describes that moment in even more graphic detail[5]:

Tension in the court was very high; Biddle[6] wrote that he 'felt sick and miserable,' and I, who had done my best to convict the defendants, was glad indeed that I did not have to speak their fates. The session took only forty-five minutes, which meant less than two minutes per defendant. The spaces between seemed intolerable, but Lawrence spoke evenly and firmly, as did the interpreter, Wolfe Frank.

The elevator door opened, and Goering stepped out and put on the earphones. Lawrence started to speak, but at once Goering took them off and made motions to indicate the earphones were not working. It was the worst possible moment for what otherwise would have been trivial.

About those final moments, referring to the day (5 March 1933) Frank had witnessed what was probably the Third Reich's first act of violence, renowned *Times* columnist R. W. Cooper, who noticed Goering's 'little ironic smile' as he heard his sentence, wrote a most telling and poignant passage[7]:

Tod durch den Strang! – Death by the Rope! – The words came to them in German through the headphones as each prisoner was brought up alone into the vast emptiness of the dock ... they were uttered in translation by Captain Wolfe Frank, himself of German origin, who before departing from his country had watched the torchlight procession in Munich that hailed Hitler's coming to power. A strange turn of the wheel that he was now to utter the words that set the seal on Hitler's little day.

CHAPTER THIRTY-ONE – NOTES & REFERENCES

1. *Judgment of International Military Tribunal on Hermann Goering.* The Avalon Project.

2. *Closing Statement of Hermann Goering:* https://avalon.law.yale.edu/imt/suppb_part1_chap_03.asp

3. *Nuremberg's Voice of Doom,* p.153.

4. *Nuremberg – A Personal Record of the Trial of Major Nazi War Criminals in 1945–6,* p 312.

5. *The Anatomy of the Nuremberg Trials: A Personal Memoir,* p 598.

6. Mr Francis Biddle was the US Member of the International Military Tribunal.

7. *The Nuremberg Trial,* R. W. Cooper, p.271.

SECTION SEVEN

THE SUICIDE
AND
THE EXECUTIONS

'THEY WILL NOT HANG ME!

'after a pause, he repeated slowly, word for word,
"They will not hang me!"
HERMANN GOERING

ON 7 OCTOBER 1946 Hermann Goering saw his wife, Emmy, for the last time. In her book, *An der Seites meines Mannes (By My Husband's Side)*, Emmy records that during their final conversation, and just before their parting, Goering said to her 'Do not believe that I will hang. I will be given a silver bullet', to which an incredulous Emmy had enquired 'Do you really believe you will be shot?' Goering hesitated before concluding 'Of one thing you can be sure. They will not hang me!' then after a pause, he repeated slowly, word for word 'They will not hang me!'[1]

A few days after this meeting, Goering learned his final petition – to allow him to be executed by firing squad – had been denied.

The executions had been due to commence at midnight on 16 October with Goering leading the other ten condemned Nazis to the gallows that had been erected in the prison's gymnasium.

Throughout 15 October Goering had quizzed the prison's Protestant Chaplain, Henry Gerecke, for details of the timing of the executions. In answer to a question on this point posed by a reporter of the *St Louis Post-Dispatch* (printed on 17 October) Gerecke said 'all of the condemned men except Goering had the fixed idea in their minds that they would be put to death … on the morning of 16 October at the traditional hour of dawn … Whether as a result of secret information or just a hunch, Goering apparently suspected the hour would be earlier.'[2]

Dr Ludwig Pfluecker, the prison doctor and a reporter passed Goering's cell at 21.20 hours and were astonished to note that the Reichsmarschall appeared to be asleep with his hands, as demanded, outside the blanket which covered him. Ten minutes later the doctor returned accompanied by Lieutenant Arthur McLinden and gave Goering a sleeping pill which he swallowed as the two men looked on. Nothing unusual was noticed.

Goering, like all the condemned men, was watched twenty four-hours a day by prison guards posted outside his cell door (see Plate 18). Private Gordon Bingham, who was on duty at the time of Dr Pfluecker's final visit, stated that after the doctor had given Goering the sleeping pill the two men shook hands and Pfluecker and McLinden left the cell, after which he, Bingham, locked the door and continued to watch Goering, who laid on his bed with his hands, once again, above the covers.

Private Harold Johnson relieved Private Bingham at 22.30 and stated that at that time Goering was 'laying on his back with his hands stretched out above the blanket'. Johnson then testified[3]:

He then lifted his left hand clenched, as if to shield his eyes from the light, then let it fall back down to his side above the covers. He lay perfectly motionless till about 2240 when he brought his hands across his chest with fingers laced and turned his head to the wall. He lay that way for about 2 or 3 minutes and then placed his hands back along his sides. That was at 2244 exactly, as I looked at my watch then to check the time. About two to three minutes later he seemed to stiffen and make a blowing, choking sound through his lips. I called the sergeant who was Corporal of the Relief immediately. He was on the second tier and came down as quickly as he could. I told him there was something wrong with Goering, so he took off to the prison office on the double. He came back a few seconds [sic] with Lt. Croner, the Prison Officer, and Chaplain Gerecke ... I opened the door ... I followed them in ... Goering's right hand was hanging down over the side of the bed, the Chaplain took hold of it as soon as he came in and took his pulse and said 'Good Lord, this man is dead'. All this took place within the space of 1 or 2 minutes. I would place it about 2246 to 2248. I never at any time saw him put anything in his mouth or move his hands near his mouth. I saw no suspicious action at any time. No one entered his cell or gave him anything except as I have already stated.

Dr Pfluecker returned to find Goering dying and after confirming he had taken a sleeping pill every night, Pfluecker then stated in his testimony:

I saw the envelope in one hand. I told the Chaplain to look at the envelope that I found. He took the envelope and felt it and saw there was a cartridge case in it and 2 or 3 pieces of paper. I did not take the paper out. I tried to open the cartridge shell. There was nothing in it ... It must have contained the poison ... I asked the American doctor [who had arrived – Lieutenant Charles Roska] to please look at his mouth because if the powder had been in the phial, maybe some of the pieces of glass would still be there. I remember the story of Himmler. He took one small phial of poison and it was over with. I knew that most of the Nazis had phials of poison.[3]

Roska immediately recognised the distinctive odour of cyanide and found numerous pieces of glass on the tongue. Based on his examination of Goering's body and what he had been told by private Johnson, Roska's opinion was 'that death was due to cyanide poisoning.'[3]
Colonel Telford Taylor later recorded in his 1993 book:

In a few moments Goering was pronounced dead. There were glass fragments in his mouth, and it was apparent that Goering had smashed in his jaws and swallowed a cyanide capsule. He left a small envelope containing a few notes, one of which was addressed to Colonel Andrus. To this day there has been no official statement or public proof of the means by which Goering obtained the cyanide capsule.[4]

CHAPTER THIRTY-TWO – NOTES & REFERENCES

1. *The Mystery of Hermann Goering's Suicide*, p.152 (referencing an extract from Emmy Goering's book *An der Seites meines Mannes (By My Husband's Side)* p.308.

2. ibid, p.48.

3. *Report of Board of Proceedings in Case of Hermann Goering (Suicide) October 1946*, Exhibit "U".

4. *The Anatomy of the Nuremberg Trials: A Personal Memoir*, p.609.

CONCEALING THE POISON?

*'If Goering had his own teeth, why was he
talking like a toothless person?'*
WOLFE FRANK

AT THIS POINT, I return to the capsule-in-the-mouth first
mentioned in Chapter Twenty-Seven. To fully explain Frank's
assertions regarding this incident I take up the narrative from where I
left off, and, for the benefit of continuity, reproduce here the last
paragraph of that chapter. Wolfe Frank's words, as he wrote them,
are interspersed with my comments *printed in italic*.

Some time after Goering's suicide, I was relating the story of my
Sunday visit to his cell to a friend, Tom Ready [sic, should be
Reedy] of Associated Press[1]. Tom stared at me in amazement for
a long time and then exploded 'You stupid ****,' he screamed.
'Didn't you know Goering had perfect teeth?' It took some time
to sink in. If Goering had his own teeth, why was he talking like a
toothless person? My God, I thought, because he was concealing
something in his mouth …but more about that later.

*The 'later' referred to was Frank's subsequent comments in another
chapter of* Nuremberg's Voice of Doom *chronicling events following
Goering's suicide[2] – the relevant extract follows, but the question here
is – how would Reedy, a newspaperman, know about Goering's dental
health, and to such an extent as to be able to make such an authoritative
statement off-the-cuff?*

How Goering had managed to kill himself has been the subject
of conjecture and discussions ever since. It has not been resolved.
I think Tom Ready [Reedy], sometime afterwards, at the Press
Camp at Schloss Stein[3], supplied the first step of my own
reasoning when, before the beginning of the trial, I called on
Goering at his prison cell, I observed that he had failed to insert
his dentures. However, as Ready [Reedy] quite rightly said,
'Goering didn't need to wear dentures and his slurred speech
was a fake.'

Frank is not so emphatic or specific here, indicating only that the incident occurred 'before the beginning of the trial (which started on 20 November 1945).'

Two poison capsules had previously been found amongst Goering's possessions – one in the hollowed-out pages of a book and one in a tin of coffee. Such places of hiding were absurdly poor for a man of Goering's intelligence. Rather, I feel, he wanted those capsules found. To some extent, this would have dulled the minds of further searchers and it might produce the subconscious conclusion that two is all he could have had.

It seems from the above cross-references, and those discussed in Chapter Twenty-Seven, that Frank may have merged different meetings into one, either by accident or by design – and there is good reason to suspect the latter – as I will explain a little later.

Corroboration

At a late date in my researches, I found the solid corroboration for Frank's assertions on this important point that I had been looking for. Following Airey Neave's assassination in 1979, his volumes of papers were placed in the House of Lords Record Office by his widow, Baroness Airey. These papers, along with the whole of Parliamentary Archives, are, as I write, in the process of being transferred to National Archives. The considerable collection consists of constituency papers, subject files and personal papers and includes files relating to Neave's posts as Opposition Spokesman on Northern Ireland Affairs, and Head of the Private Office of the Leader of the Opposition.

By chance, within this extensive collection, I discovered the existence of a manilla folder that contained just two papers, both of which are of relevance to these matters and, to the best of my knowledge, have never been seen or discussed previously in the public domain. After much involvement and valued help from staff at both Parliamentary Archives and National Archives, I was able to obtain copies of both papers. One I will deal with a little later. The other is confirmation of what Frank wrote about the capsule-in-the-mouth incident.

Entitled *The Suicide of Goering by Airey Neave, M.P.*,[10] the document can be considered an accurate record of what is already known and accepted concerning events leading up to the suicide, the subsequent investigation by The Board of Officers, the Control Council's conclusions and Neave's direct involvements with Goering. The fact that Neave uses the designation 'M.P.' dates the document's creation as being sometime between 1953 (when he became a Member of Parliament) and 1979 (when he was assassinated).

Within the document Neave also refers to the capsule-in-the-mouth, and the similarity between his and Frank's recollections of this incident during their first encounter with Goering on 19 October 1945 – which they both say did not register with them until after the suicide a year later – is quite extraordinary. Neave wrote:

When I entered the cell of the fallen Reichsmarschall on October, 18th, 1945, he was asleep. He awoke suddenly, and his huge body rose unsteadily from the bed. It seemed to me that his long mouth twitched in a curious fashion. He looked like a man discovered without his false teeth. I did not realise then that he had good natural teeth and the strange movement of his lips seemed of no importance. When I heard of his death, I wondered if what I had seen was a clue to a great mystery. Had I surprised him with his secret means of suicide? Was he hiding a small glass phial in a gap between his teeth as Heinrich Himmler had done in May of the same year.

As a reminder Frank's references state:

On that dark, rainy Sunday afternoon I came very close to making history – and I missed my chance! As the door of Goering's cell was noisily unlocked, the former Reichsmarshall rose from his cot where he had, obviously, been napping. Feeling rather nervous, I told him why I was there ... I also noted that he was not using his dentures. He was lisping in the manner typical of the temporarily toothless ... He was, it seems, concealing something in his mouth and because I had not seen his medical history sheet, I fell for the trick ... If Goering had his own teeth, why was he talking like a toothless person? My God, I thought, because he was concealing something in his mouth

In Neave's document, he discusses the possible involvements of some of the 'usual suspects' and previously held theories, but he does not offer up any clues as to how or when Goering obtained the poison. No doubt speaking from his own experiences as a prisoner-of-war escapee and as one of Britain's top spymasters, he does say:

When all the possibilities have been exhausted, there remains the simpler solution that Goering had kept the poison all the time.

Those who have been prisoners or have guarded them will know how difficult it is to prevent a determined man from concealing some treasured object. If he is intent on suicide or escape he will display the greatest ingenuity. His thoughts are concentrated on the protection of his precious instrument from his gaolers. In Goering's case, the sentence of hanging, considered a disgrace in military circles, provided a strong motive.

Neave then states:

The Commission, probably, came to the right conclusion, when they declared their findings. They found that Goering had hidden the poison either in or on his body. Perhaps he had swallowed it from time to time and allowed it to pass through him. Yet we still do not know for certain how or when he obtained it.

In his book, *Nuremberg*, Major Neave describes in detail Goering's appearance and demeanour, including the tenor of his voice,[4] at the time he and Frank first met the Reichsmarschall, but he makes no reference to the possibility of Goering hiding something in his mouth. In his unpublished record *The Suicide of Goering*[10] however he does emphasise that point, suggesting the same as Frank does and in very similar wording. If, however, that had happened, as they both suggest, it would have rung alarm bells with Colonel Andrus who – as Neave confirms in both his memoirs and the memorandum he produced for the judges – was present in the cell throughout the encounter. Andrus had watched Goering like a hawk for many months. He knew everything there was to know about the Reichsmarschall – including his traits, demeanour and physical conditions. He would have been on high alert, watching out for the slightest indication of anything being unusual. The colonel would have immediately known therefore that Goering did not wear dentures, would have spotted any deviation from his normal speech pattern and would have raised an alarm.

The incident could not therefore, in my opinion, have occurred at Frank's and Neave's first meetings with Goering in October 1945, but it might have happened at Frank's last – in October 1946 – and here I refer to details, reproduced as I received them in correspondence from Frank's former wife, who in response to my enquiry, replied:

About the cyanide capsule, I remember Wolfe telling me that nobody knew where the capsule had come from and it could only be assumed that Goering had kept it hidden on his person all the time [Here Frank is repeating the conclusion of the official enquiry]. When Wolfe went to interview him in his cell unannounced shortly before he was to be executed, Goering mumbled and pretended that some serious dental problem or toothache prevented him from articulating properly. After his suicide, Wolfe established with the resident dentist, that no such problem had existed and therefore concluded that Goering already had the capsule in his mouth ready to bite on it, which he did moments later. This is what he told me. Whether it's true or not is anybody's guess.

Wolfe's wife also confirmed this information to me in a second response:

The only thing I know about Goering at Nuremberg that is not already documented and published many times over is the little anecdote I wrote down for you in my last email. As I said, this is what Wolfe told me (and others), but whether it is actually true or not is another question. You are welcome to include it, but perhaps with this caveat.

So, we have several versions of the timing of this incident: the one told to Wolfe's wife (and others) that states it happened on the night of the suicide, and the two Frank mentions that happened during the preparations a year earlier, which is almost identical to Major Neave's account. At his meetings with friends, including Charlotte (see Chapter Two), that occurred late in his life, Frank went further and confessed he had been a witness to the transfer of the capsule.

In Frank's manuscript there are three separate drafts covering these details. They all say roughly the same thing, but it is clear he had had second, or even third thoughts, on exactly what should be included and how it should be presented. Tantalisingly, there is a crucial page missing and he has added a hand-written sheet that states 'pages 202 to page 244 [which includes the relevant section] separate chapter – Not for the record'. (Charlotte, who acted as Frank's PA in his final years, undertook manuscript typing duties, and while she could not be specific, she confirmed some of the replacement pages were of the kind she remembered typing. Under Frank's direction, Charlotte also destroyed many documents). I shall return to the capsule-in-the-mouth a little later in the narrative.

There is however a good deal more than is first apparent with regards to Frank's conversations about the incident with Tom Reedy and, after he indicates a desire to be present for the executions, Frank's sudden decision to leave The Palace of Justice immediately after Goering's suicide and before the other defendants had been hanged. His record on these matters is as follows:[5]

The Executions

The events during the night of the executions are a matter of record. I, myself, couldn't stay away. That the hangings would take place during that night was certain since the time between the sentencing and execution, set at fifteen days by the rules governing the trial, had elapsed. Midnight on 16 October 1946 was it.

The setting was exactly as a film director would have wanted – a little moonlight, clouds racing across the sky, a night almost without sound. The Press Corps was there, of course, in full strength [including and especially Tom Reedy] and, as their papers were being checked by the Military Police, everybody it seemed was talking in a whisper.

Eleven lives were to be taken that night, as the result of a gigantic effort to examine a record of crime, of murder, of inhuman brutality that has no parallel in history. We had, all of us who were at the Palace of Justice in Nuremberg on that night, attended this examination and, I feel sure, we wanted to see that final act of justice carried out.

I cannot imagine that any one of us felt the tiniest spark of compassion for the men who were now to die for their crimes. However, I also felt that we all would be glad when at last this horrible chapter of history that we had helped to record was ended.

To cover the final act the authorities had ruled that two journalists from each of the Allied Powers were to be admitted to the hangings – one representative of the Press and one radio reporter.

The Americans had made clever use of this arrangement as they had somehow managed to obtain a ruling whereby those eight men – two Americans, two Brits, two Frenchmen and two Russians – were to be allowed out of the jail at 04.00 hours after the executions. This, of course, was early enough for the press in the United States but too late for Europe. It certainly wasn't cricket, but good American business sense.

Until 04.00 hours the prison was hermetically sealed off. At 01.00 hours I decided I had hung around the building long enough, and I headed for home. A US woman reporter, who shall remain nameless, was with me. At the exit she was stopped by an MP sergeant who obviously knew her well. 'Hey Jeannie,' he called as we walked by, 'Y'know what? Goering's just killed himself.'

'Ha, ha, funny joke,' Jeannie said, and walked on, heading for her couch and a nap. Had she taken the MP seriously and followed up his information she would have scooped the whole of the world's press by three or four hours, and she would have become world famous.

A second anecdote concerns Britain's most illustrious daily. It had two people on the spot that night, both of who were young, very ingenious and determined to give everybody else the slip. They hired a couple of Germans, equipped them with field glasses and had them climb to the top of a ruined building across the road from the Palace of Justice. By careful scouting they had discovered that from this lookout point their spies would be able to see the gangway, which had been constructed between the prison and the gymnasium, in the courtyard where the gallows had been erected. A gap had been left open at the top of the gangway, presumably to let in daylight.

Obviously, the condemned men would be walking to the gallows singly. Each would be preceded, and followed, by an MP wearing the white helmet of his uniform. The tops of these helmets ought to be visible to the two German lookouts, posted on top of the ruins across the road from the Courthouse – and, indeed, they were. First one helmet could be seen, glistening in the light of a naked light bulb or two in the gangway. Some ten feet behind, a second helmet could be discerned. This, clearly, was the procession of a death candidate being led to the gallows and a light signal, blinked to the two Englishman below, reported the passing of each such procession.

What the lofty observers could not, of course, have known was that the last of the eleven men was not walking, but was being carried on a stretcher, already dead. It was Hermann Goering who had just killed himself!

Thus, when eleven pairs of helmets, obviously with eleven death candidates between them, had passed, the story was filed with London, and there we read how Goering, the first man due for execution, had 'Walked, his head erect, face emotionless, to the gallows and his death.'

Was There More to Tom Reedy's Role?

There are further sequels to these events that raise a number of important questions about the extent of the relationship and conversations Frank had with his 'friend' Tom Reedy of Associated Press.

To emphasise this point and what, concerning the press corps in general and Reedy in particular, took place during the critical few hours following Goering's suicide, it is necessary to explain what happened in the press room that fateful night as the world's top foreign correspondents waited – for several hours – for news of the executions – all conscious of the deadline they had to meet and the presses that were standing by to print their stories.

Many correspondents, unable to curb their impatience, did not wait for either the official announcement, that was to be relayed to them by Colonel Andrus, or confirmations from those representatives of the world's press who had been permitted to witness the executions.

Many reporters embarrassed both themselves and their publications by filing stories indicating Goering had, as Frank's anecdote above suggested, led the procession to the gallows, and that he had been the first of the condemned men to be hanged. Under pressure from their publishers, most of the other representatives followed suit. There were two journalists however who held back – Tom Reedy and his fellow AP reporter G. K. Hodenfield who said later 'Reedy and I were catching hell from New York … how come we didn't know what everyone else seemed to know? We could have followed the herd. Our sources indicated that it was all over.' Reedy, however, was adamant no story could be submitted until they were certain all the war criminals had been executed. Hodenfield thought his 'short and happy career with AP was over' as, entirely due to Reedy's advice, he held back from filing his report.

At 06.00 hours, an ashen faced Colonel Andrus, entered the press room and announced that Goering had not been hanged but had committed suicide. There was a moment of stunned silence as the majority of the world's press realised the blunder they had made. The silence was only broken by Reedy, who stood up and shouted, 'Yeahh, you smart-ass sons of bitches!' The correspondents then made a mad dash to the cable room in an attempt to correct their earlier reports.[6]

On his retirement in June 1977 a report in the *Sarasota Observer* said of Reedy 'During his career, he reported on the hanging [sic] at Nuremberg. He described the six hours he spent waiting to see if the executions were carried out as the worst six hours of his life.'

Recently the CIA released copies of minutes of events, recorded by the Agency's Assistant Director of Current Intelligence, that include the name of 'Tom Reedy (Associated Press) Feb. 56', along with other named correspondents. The record then goes on to say: 'In mid-September Harry Schwartz of the *New York Times* and Tom Reedy of the Associated Press were permitted to enter Poland. Reedy travelled extensively about Poland … In February Tom Reedy of Associated Press visited Prague and wrote a series of articles which appeared in the *Washington Post* and *Times Herald*.'

The CIA also released newspaper cuttings they had kept in their files that link Tom Reedy to the Agency, suggesting he was a CIA agent (these can be found online).

Under the heading 'U.S. HAD SPY RING IN SWEDEN, RED WRITER CHARGES', The *New York Times* cutting said:

MOSCOW, Oct 17 – The Soviet government newspaper *Izvestia* says the United States maintained an important intelligence network in Sweden employing American newspaper men and Soviet emigres.

A Soviet citizen who had lived in Sweden as an emigre charged in a signed article yesterday that he had been approached twice by members of the Central Intelligence Agency who tried to recruit him into the American spy ring.

He said a former bureau chief of the Associated Press in Stockholm, Thomas Reedy, had acted as an American agent there. Another Associated Press correspondent, Gustav Svensson, had been working under Reedy and later went on to the Soviet Union to work as an agent here, the article charged ... The article in *Izvestia* was signed by Arthur Haman, described as an Estonian-born scholar of linguistics ... In New York, Wes Gallagher, general manager of the Associated Press, said the story in *Izvestia* was untrue and that Haman's account seemed to be the product of an overripe imagination fed by an addiction to detective thrillers.

The *New York Daily News* ran the same story under the heading 'Reds say Newsmen Spy in Sweden' and printed exactly the same rebuttal, but the paper also stated: 'Moscow, Oct. 16 ...*Izvestia* said that Tom Reedy, the American AP bureau chief, was the leader of the ring and actually holds the rank of major in U.S. intelligence.'

A third newspaper cutting released by the CIA, from an unattributed publication, also ran the story under the heading 'U.S. Reporters Accused of Spying in Sweden' with, once again, the same, clearly syndicated response from AP, but then went on to say:

He [Haman] then mentioned Thomas A. Reedy, former chief of Scandinavian service for the AP ... Reedy is now assigned to AP's London Bureau ... Haman said he had been told 'Reedy made a proposal to Svensson to co-operate secretly with him.' He said the plan was to invite officials to visit Reedy's home where two employees of the U.S. Embassy could make contacts. 'It was supposed that acquaintances of Svensson would be drawn by the Americans into wild parties' and their conversations recorded. Haman said he asserted 'according to rumours, Reedy had the rank of major in the American Army.' [AP's Wes Gallagher, in the Agency's denial, added] 'Neither the Associated Press nor its employees have any connection with any department of the U.S. government. As far as can be ascertained, Arthur Haman worked briefly as a teleprinter operator for the Associated Press in 1957. Thomas Reedy at the time was chief of the bureau, concerned solely with the gathering of the news in Stockholm. He has not been in Stockholm since March 1960.'

The bottom line here is: press reports suggest Reedy may have led a spy ring and that he held the rank of major in US intelligence; the CIA kept a file on Reedy, reported on his movements and he is a named in copies of the Agency's minutes; Wolfe Frank spent the crucial hours of the suicide night with the world's press corps which included his 'friend' Tom Reedy, who did not follow the 'herd' that filed what we might now call 'fake news.'

More Questions than answers

These disclosures raise a number of important questions, including the following:

- Did Frank visit Goering in his cell just before he took his own life – as he told his wife and others he had and, if so, did he reveal the time of the executions to Goering, who had repeatedly been asking prison officers that question during the course of his final day?
- Why, after indicating he wanted to be present during the execution period, did Frank suddenly leave the Palace of Justice hours before any confirmations of the executions and soon after Goering's suicide?
- When exactly did Frank tell Tom Reedy about the capsule-in-the-mouth incident, and why did he muddy the waters by communicating different versions of the same incident?
- What made Reedy, almost alone it seems, hold back from reporting the executions of the Nazis, and counsel his AP colleague to do the same?

- Did Reedy already know more than the other correspondents, and if he did, did he get his information from Frank or the CIC (successor of the OSS and forerunner of the CIA)?
- Was Reedy connected to the CIC/OSS, as Frank had been, and then the CIA?
- Was Frank (who during the preparations worked directly with Donovan and Putzell), acting as interpreter, the colleague Putzell indicates was present when he 'handed' the cyanide to Goering?
- Assuming he was, why did Putzell and Frank leave it so late in their lives to reveal their involvements?

Not that Frank had any sympathy for Goering or the others on trial. In his memoirs he expresses his frustrations during the period prior to him moving to Nuremberg 'none of this brought Goering any nearer the gallows'[7]. He also made it clear elsewhere in his manuscript that he had, in his own words, 'not the tiniest spark of compassion for the men who were to die for their crimes' and 'history was indeed written indelibly, justly and rightfully.'[8] He echoed these words, and those recorded by Douglas Waller (attributed to General Donovan) in a response he, Frank, later gave to a reporter 'Nobody who got <u>hanged</u> shouldn't have been'[9] – but what about he who committed suicide? – did Frank agree Goering should be allowed to die as a soldier? or was he, like Putzell, just following the orders of General Donovan?

Whatever the answers to these questions are, by the date of the suicide Goering had had the cyanide capsule in his possession for almost a year and he had managed, as the official investigation concluded (Chapter Thirty-Five) 'to retain the poison in his possession through his own cleverness and thoughtful planning.'

CHAPTER THIRTY THREE – NOTES & REFERENCES

1. Thomas A. Reedy was a distinguished journalist with 37 years' experience as a White House reporter. During his long career he also reported on the trials and hangings at Nuremberg and the dropping of the atomic bombs on Japan *Sarasota Observer*, 2 June 1977.

2. *Nuremberg's Voice of Doom*, pp.156.

3. During the Nuremberg Trials, reporters were housed in Schloss Faber-Castell in Stein.

4. *Nuremberg – A Personal Record of the Trial of Major Nazi War Criminals in 1945–6*, pp.68–73.

5. *Nuremberg's Voice of Doom* pp.157–158.

6. *The Mystery of Hermann Goering's Suicide,* pp.57–58.

7. *Nuremberg's Voice of Doom,* p.96.

8. ibid, p.154.

9. *The Oregonian,* 23 September 1970.

10. *The Suicide of Goering* by Airey Neave, M.P., – The Parliamentary Archives Reference for this document was 'Papers of Airey Middleton Sheffield Neave (1916–1979) GB-061 Catalogue Reference: AN/660' – this reference is likely to change once Parliamentary Archives are incorporated into National Archives.

CHAPTER THIRTY-FOUR

THE LAST SPOTLIGHT

'mysteries the shrunken fat man perhaps took to his grave'
THOMAS A. REEDY

BY HOLDING BACK FROM FILING their stories until the official announcement was made, Tom Reedy and his AP colleague had scooped much of the world's press. His syndicated reports began to appear in later editions of many newspapers on the day of the executions (16 October) including *The Washington Evening Star* in which, under the banner headline *'Goering Suicide Probed by Army As Bodies of 11 Nazi Chieftains Are Taken to Nameless Graves'*, Reedy eloquently expressed the drama that had unfolded in the Palace of Justice[1]:

Hermann Goering, who ended his life mysteriously in the agony of poison, and ten other top Nazis who died on a hangman's rope were taken to nameless graves on this bleak, cold morning in final expiation for the colossal crimes of Germany.

Grim and manacled, because in some unexplained fashion Goering had been able to escape the ignominy of the gallows, Joachim von Ribbentrop started the death marches and plunged to eternity at 1:14 a.m.

How Goering get [sic] the poison, kept it, and took it, were mysteries the shrunken fat man perhaps took to his grave ... The other ten died stoically, plunging into an enclosed trap that hid their death pangs from the eight newspaper correspondents and 30 other witnesses ... By his manner of dying, Goering flamboyant to the last, not only took the last spotlight away from his colleagues but created a breath taking mystery which had army officers laboring in an effort to determine how he got, concealed and took the poison.' ...

When the last body had been cut down, Col. B. C. Andrus, prison commandant, emerged with the first news to the world that Goering had taken his own life.

Found by a Sentinel
'Goering was not hanged' Col. Andrus announced, 'he committed suicide at 10:45 p.m. (4.45 p.m. EST yesterday) last night by taking cyanide of potassium.

'He was discovered at once by the sentinel who watched and heard him make an odd noise and twitch. The sentinel called the doctor and chaplain who were in the corridor and who found him dying. There were pieces of glass in his mouth and an odor of cyanide of potassium on his breath.'

Goering's hands did not go beneath the blankets and were not observed to go to his mouth. An investigation is now going on to learn how he could conceal the poison when he was subject to daily and rigorous searches, both of his clothes and of his person. The cyanide was contained in a small cartridge case similar to those found before on other Nazis and like the one found on him a year ago last May at Mondorf Prison. At that time it was hidden in a can of Nescafe.

Alongside Reedy's story in *The Washington Evening Star* was another article revealing more graphic details written by Kingsbury Smith, the reporter for the *International News Service* who had been selected by ballot to be the sole representative of the American press at the executions.

The doors of a small gymnasium in the Nuremberg Jail courtyard, through which the living had come, opened early this morning and a dead man came in – a grotesque, self-destroyed remnant of a man who had once been destined to rule Nazi Germany.

It was that of Hermann Wilhelm Goering, who committed suicide by taking poison a short while before he was to have led 10 of his henchmen to the gallows. And it was inevitably and inescapably a dramatic moment in the course of history ...

The chaplains were reading from their prayer books. Suddenly the doors opened and the body of what was once the great marshal of the Reich, chief of the Luftwaffe and bearer of a dozen other titles was brought in.

He had succeeded in wrecking plans of the Allied Control Council to have him lead the parade of condemned chieftains to death on the gallows ... The face of this 20th Century freebooting political racketeer was still contorted with the pain of his last agonising moments and his final gesture of defiance.

J. J. Heydecker, who was present throughout the IMT, and historian J. Leeb, in their book *The Nuremberg Trials*, in just one sentence express the universal shock that followed the announcing of the suicide[2]: 'The sensational event struck the whole world like a thunderbolt, eclipsing even the news of the actual executions.'

But perhaps the most appropriate words with which to conclude this chapter are those used by legendary *Times* correspondent R.W. Cooper in the postscript of his book *The Nuremberg Trial*[3]:

They were hanged at dead of night on October 16 – hanged that is, with the exception of Goering. He, mocking to the end, took cyanide of potassium in his cell as the hour approached and was dead by the time the doctors were called. The finding of the board of inquiry that he had it all the time fit in well enough with the little ironical smile that we saw in the dock. For a day he made sport of Nuremberg, above all of American security and its year of pin-pricks. But Goering is dead and the others with him.

It could hardly have been more sordid – the grimy prison gymnasium in which soldiers played their ball games, with its row of blazing lights, its three scaffolds, the ugly scrawled inscription on one of the walls 'V. D. walks the streets.' Hollywood to the end. And one after another the monstrous leaders of the Third Reich fell with the name of the Fatherland on their lips. Have we after all created a grotesque legend?

CHAPTER THIRTY-FOUR – NOTES & REFERENCES

1. *The Evening Star (Washington)* 16 October 1946, p.1.

2. *The Nuremberg Trials*, J. J. Heydecker & J. Leeb, p.355.

3. *The Nuremberg Trial*, R. W. Cooper, p.301.

THE BOARD OF OFFICERS

'All the hallmarks of a whitewash.'

LESS THAN AN HOUR after Goering had swallowed the poison, a three-man Board of Officers (The Board) had been appointed by the Quadripartite Commission of the Allied Control Council (ACC)[1] 'To investigate and report on the suicide of Hermann Goering, convicted war criminal.' The Board was charged with two specific tasks:

1. The Board will investigate all matters connected with the safeguarding of the major war criminals in the Nuremberg Jail, establish the manner by which Prisoner Goering obtained the poison with which he took his own life and fix any responsibility in connection therewith.
2. The Board will submit its report to the Allied Commission[2] for the Control of Major War Crimes.

The Board immediately conducted a thorough search of Goering's corpse and his cell and its contents, and they interrogated those guards and prison personnel who had come into contact with Goering during the previous fourteen days. They took away several items for analysis including the cartridge case that had contained the poison capsule. Three days later The Board returned and discovered another identical cartridge case with the poison capsule still inside hidden in a jar of Vaseline in 'a fitted bag belonging to Goering' located 'in the prison store room, to which Goering never had access.'

On 23 October The Board returned again and heard the testimonies of Colonel Andrus, his assistant, two doctors and the operations officer. These were the only officers interrogated. Remarkably similarly written statements were provided by thirty-four other prison personnel, including Jack Wheelis:

The Board's Report recorded:[3]

(1) During the period from the announcement of sentence on 1 October 1946 to the date of the suicide the poison could have been obtained from a member of the civilian prison staff, his lawyer, his wife, another prisoner, and, as for that

matter, any one of the members of the Armed Forces on duty in the prison.

(2) During the period from his apprehension on 7 May 1945 until 1 October 1946, the poison could have been obtained from sources so numerous and diverse that all these possibilities and probabilities cannot be covered.

(3) Goering could have had this poison in his possession when apprehended and by means, known only to him, retained it until used on the night of 15 October 1946.

After sifting through all the evidence, including four letters Goering had written shortly before his death, The Board concluded two weeks later that: Goering was 'a clever and unrepenting individual' who had the poison in his possession at the time of his apprehension; security regulations 'prevented procurement from either his wife or his lawyer;' the loyalty to American authority shown by civilian workers removed 'any shadow of suspicion from this category'; and 'Insofar as American or Allied personnel are concerned, it can be said without fear of contradiction that this category would have left no stone unturned to insure Goering met his fate on the gallows.

The Board also concluded that: Goering outwitted guards by his 'clever maneuvering [sic] of the suicide device'; 'Inasmuch as two such devices were actually found in Goering's baggage, it is logical to conclude that he was in possession of a third'; that he might have concealed the device in the toilet, his pipe or pouch; his alimentary tract, his rectum or elsewhere on his person; and that it could have been introduced into his mouth while he used the toilet (which was not in full view of the guards) or had his back to the guards – 'at any time between his evening meal and his demise.'

The conclusion of The Board was[3]:

Reasonable safeguards had been planned and executed for the prevention of suicide by any one of the condemned. The fact that Goering succeeded in committing suicide is attributed to his cunning and not to dereliction on the part of any individual or group of individuals connected with the administration of the prison in which he had been confined.

The 'Findings' of The Board were:[3]

1. That the small brass container containing the suicide poison was in the possession of Goering at the time he was taken into custody by the American Army.

2. That all reasonable safeguards were taken in the guarding of Goering, and that he was able to retain the poison in his possession through his own cleverness and thoughtful planning and that no individual or individuals connected with the prison be held responsible for the death by suicide of Hermann Goering.

The report was submitted to the four members of the Control Council who discussed and accepted it on 30 October 1946 – and that has remained the official position ever since.

The Board's 'Finding 2' is entirely correct as far as General Donovan, Lieutenant Putzell and Captain Frank were concerned. Goering had been able to 'retain the poison in his possession through his own cleverness and thoughtful planning' and they were never connected with the prison and were never questioned about these matters – nor was anyone else outside the prison.

'Finding 1' may also be correct in its entirety if Lieutenant Putzell returned to Goering one of the two capsules that had been found amongst his possessions when he was captured (to be more fully discussed later). In any case, whether it was one of his own or some other capsule the OSS had obtained from another source, the evidence suggests Goering had almost certainly had the capsule that killed him in his possession since the time of the preparations.

CHAPTER THIRTY-FIVE – NOTES & REFERENCES

1. The Allied Control Council (ACC) or Allied Control Commission or Allied Control Authority was the governing body of the Allied occupation zones in Germany after the end of the Second World War. It was established to oversee the occupation and demilitarization of Germany and Austria. The ACC was comprised of representatives from the United Kingdom, the United States, the Soviet Union, and France.

2. The Allied Control Commission was a unique arrangement that took over the government of Germany. Its task was to establish and direct strategy and policy for the whole of Germany through an Allied Control Council (ACC), based in Berlin, composed of the four Allied Commanders-in-Chief, who were also Military Governors of the geographical zones in which they exercised supreme authority.

3. *Report of Board of Proceedings in Case of Hermann Goering (Suicide) October 1946.*

THE SUICIDE NOTES

'I elect to die as the great Hannibal did'[1]
HERMANN GOERING

FROM THE TIME OF THE SUICIDE the Russians had suspected the Americans of having provided Goering with the means of taking his own life. They suspected too, like many others, that the report of The Board and its acceptance by the Control Council was part of a cover up – the Russian representative didn't even bother to attend the meeting at which the report was accepted. Air Chief Marshal Sir Sholto Douglas, the British member of the Quadripartite Commission of the Control Council, added weight to this belief some years later when, referring to The Board's report, he wrote[2]:

> On this occasion, because of what we were going to discuss, it was decided to restrict the number of those present to the numbers of each delegation who were most directly concerned ... just before the meeting I had received my copy of the report on the way in which Goering had committed suicide, along with copies of the last letter he wrote to his wife and a statement that could be regarded as his final testament.
>
> It was agreed at our meeting that all of the copies of these documents which were in existence should be gathered up, and that all of them, except one – which should be preserved in the archives of the Control Commission – should be destroyed. It was further agreed that no information should ever be made public about the contents of any of these documents, that nothing more need to be said by any of us, and that we should forever remain silent about what had already been said that day.

Despite what Sir Sholto Douglas says in his final sentence, in 1990 Colonel Telford Taylor requested, and was granted, sight of both The Board's report and the four letters found in Goering's hand at the time of his death. The letters were, of course, written in German and Taylor had them translated into English by students at Columbia Law School where he was a professor and where he taught law for over thirty years. (During the war he had worked alongside General

Donovan. At the IMT, Taylor was assistant to Justice Jackson, whom he succeeded as Chief Prosecutor for the Subsequent Proceedings).

One of the letters, in two parts, was addressed to the Allied Control Council, the others were to: Pastor Henry Gereke, the Protestant chaplain at the prison; his wife, Emmy; and Colonel Andrus the prison Commandant. Three of the letters were dated 11 October 1946 (the day that Goering learned his final appeal to the Control Council – that he be shot rather than hanged – had been refused) and one was undated. All four, hand-written, letters refer to this refusal and indicate this was why Goering had chosen to die 'like the great Hannibal.' The letters, translated, are as follows:[3]

Letter to the Control Council Part I – *written on the letter-heading: Der Reichsmarschal des Grossdeutschen Reiches (The Reichsmarschall of the Greater German Realms):*

> Would that I might be shot! However, executing the German Reichsmarschall by hanging cannot be countenanced. I cannot permit this for Germany's sake. Besides, I have no more obligation to subject myself to punishment from my enemies. Therefore I elect to die as the great Hannibal did' [signed] Hermann Goering.

Letter to the Control Council Part II: *(written on the same letter-heading):*

> I knew from the beginning that a death sentence would fall on me, Having viewed the trial as a purely political act of the victors, but for my peoples sake I wanted to stand trial and I expected that at least I would not be denied the death of a soldier. Before God, my people and my conscience I feel free from the reprehension that my enemies put on me [signed] Hermann Goering.

The letter to Pastor Gerecke:

> Forgive me, but I had to do it in this way for political reasons. I have prayed for a long time to God and feel I am acting correctly. Would that I might be shot. Please console my wife and tell her that mine was no ordinary suicide and that she should be certain that God will take me to his grace … God bless you, dear Pastor. Yours [signed] Hermann Goering.

Goering's letter to his wife Emmy is undated and at the top he asks Pastor Gereke to deliver it to her – Telford Taylor felt that parts of this letter should remain private, but that the following should be published – it is addressed to 'My heart's only love':

> Upon mature reflection and intimate prayer to God I decided to take my own life and not allow my enemies to execute me in that way. I would have consented anytime to be shot but the Reichsmarschall of Germany cannot be hanged. Furthermore the execution would be presented as a spectacle in the press, in the movies, etc. (for the newsreels I assume). Sensation is the main thing. But I wish to die peacefully without publicity … I take it a sign from God that through all the months of imprisonment he left me with the means to free me from earthly worry and that it was never discovered [signed] Hermann.

Telford Taylor expresses the view that; 'The last sentence, of course, is the one that bears most importantly on Goering's means of suicide.'

The Letter to Colonel Andrus:

> Since my imprisonment I have always kept the poison capsule on my person. I had three capsules when I was committed to prison in Mondorf. The first one I left in my clothing, so that it would be found in the search. The second I left under the coat-stand while undressing and took it again when I dressed. I hid this in Mondorf and here in the cell so well that, in spite of the frequent and very thorough searches, it could not be found. During the trial I kept it in my high riding boots. The third capsule is still in my toilet case in the round container of skin cream (hidden in the cream). I had two opportunities to take the capsule in Mondorf, had I needed it. No one in charge of the searches was at fault, since it was almost impossible to find the capsule. It would have been purely by chance [signed] Hermann Goering.
>
> [P.S.] Doctor Gilbert told me that the Control Council rejected the change in the manner of execution to death by firing squad[signed] Goering.'

Taylor does not question the Control Board's conclusions or that the only reason Goering took his own life was because of the insistence of him being hanged. He does however have a strong view on the letter addressed to Colonel Andrus. In his book, *The Anatomy of the Nuremberg Trials* – having analysed and scrutinised this letter in fine detail; knowing Goering, his character and thinking pattern so well; and having been involved in many stages of the interrogations and trial of the Reichsmarschall – Telford Taylor's learned opinion of the apparent and/or hidden meanings within this letter was that it was 'vaguely' written and whilst it absolved from fault anyone 'in charge of searches' it did not absolve anyone 'not charged, which was most people'. Taylor thought the purpose of the letter was to enable Goering to boast about how he had been able to outwit his gaolers, and to 'exonerate the guards and others from assisting in his suicide.' Taylor concludes his summarisation by suggesting Goering had nothing to lose by revealing how he had hidden the capsule '*unless* someone else was involved,' and that Goering would have 'done much better not to send the letter to Andrus and to leave the whole matter a mystery. Characteristically, though, he could not resist the temptation to crow.'[4]

CHAPTER THIRTY SIX – NOTES & REFERENCES

1. Hannibal, general of the Carthaginian army, lived in the second and third century B.C. He was born into a Carthaginian military family and made to swear hostility toward Rome. During the Second Punic War, Hannibal swept across southern Europe and through the Alps, consistently defeating the Roman army, but never taking the city itself. Rome counterattacked and he was forced to return to Carthage where he was defeated. In approximately 183 B.C., at Libyssa, near the Bosporus Straits, Hannibal took his own life by ingesting a vial of poison – biography.com/military-figures/hannibal

2. *The Anatomy of the Nuremberg Trials: A Personal Memoir*, pp.618–619.

3. ibid, pp.620–621.

4. ibid, pp 621–624.

THE SILVER BULLET

'A simple and immediate remedy for an intractable problem.'[1]

TO HERMANN GOERING 'DEATH BY THE ROPE' was the ultimate disgrace – it always had been, and for him it was never going to happen. When his former prodigy and relation by marriage Rudolf Diels, first Head of the Gestapo, was found to have been involved in the 20 July 1944 plot to assassinate Hitler[2], Goering had intervened to save his life – not because he didn't think he deserved to die but because, as Diels made clear to *Der Spiegel*[3], Goering had told him in disgust 'I do not want a hanged man in my clan!'

In Goering's own mind, and in the eyes of many Germans, he was a hero who deserved to die a hero's death – he made that clear in his suicide notes and there is no doubt he remained a hero to many of his fellow countrymen and women long after his death.

Regarding Goering's suicide letter to his wife, Telford Taylor, who had studied the original document and the event in detail (and referencing Sholto Douglas' records), indicated Emmy Goering had known about the suicide capsule since before 'October 11 1946.' Taylor also refers to a letter, dated 28 November 1975, written by Robert Kempner (his fellow Assistant US Prosecutor at Nuremberg) that stated Emmy Goering had told him 'a friend whose name she would not give, had passed the poison to her husband in Nuremberg.' Kempner went on to state Emmy had told him that when visiting Goering in prison, she used the code 'have you got the comb?' to make certain the capsule had not been discovered. She also confirmed Goering 'had not intended to use the poison unless his application to be shot was refused'. Taylor's assessment of these letters was that Emmy 'knew what was in her husband's mind, which suggests that her statement about a secret friend is probably correct.'[4]

About the Suicide Capsule

The suicide capsule that Goering used to kill himself was of a kind issued to all the top Nazis, and appears to have come from the same batch as those provided to Hitler and those confiscated from Bach-Zelewski when he was captured – who produced other identical capsules at a later date with serial numbers close to that used by Goering and who admitted to taking some into the prison at Nuremberg[5]. He also indicated that he received the ampoules from Arthur Nebe (see below) who was executed after the 20 July plot to kill Hitler[2].

Along with Justice Jackson and Telford Taylor, Bach-Zelewski, who turned what we now call King's Evidence, was also being dealt with by General Donovan at the same time as the General was making his plans with Goering – and Donovan was still being appraised on both matters as late as 26 November 1945 – in fact Donovan topped the list of those who were to be kept informed of the prosecution's intentions regarding Bach-Zelewski.[6]

Albert Widmann, an SS Officer and Chief German Chemist on the Nazi's euthanasia programme, made a statement in 1973 which includes the following:[7]

> On orders of our Department Chief Nebe, Reich Director of Criminal Investigation, Brigade General of Police and SS Gruppenfuehrer, self-destruction devices were developed and manufactured. They were intended for distribution to German agents. It might have been 1943 or 1944, when approximately 950 of these devices were ordered by the Reich Chancellery for distribution to the senior leadership ... Some 3,000 to 4,000 were made. We made the glass ampoules to fit the containers. The diameter was 9 mm, and the total length after annealing about 35 mm. The bottoms of the ampoules were flat ... As containers for the self-destructors, spend [sic] infantry rifle cartridges were fashioned into small cases. The cartridge cases were cut away on a lathe below the narrowing point. Their length came to about 41 cm. The 9 mm long caps were also made from cartridge cases. The caps were simply pushed down over the cases. The total length of the self-destructor therefore came to 46 mm, the diameter about 11 mm. It should be added that we probably received 1,000 empty ampoules from the Army Medical Centre, each at three different times. I do not [know] which lot went to the Reich Chancellery' [see Plate 23].

There are other references to batches of 5,000 and 4,000[8] identical 'capsules in cartridges' being distributed and one of 950 being given directly to Hitler's Berlin headquarters many of which the Fuehrer handed out during his last days in April 1945 – before possibly ingesting one, as the Russians have suggested, prior to him shooting himself. He personally gave two of this batch to aviator Hanna Reitsch shortly before the end. Reitsch was arrested on 10 October 1945 and interrogated until at least 16 November. During this period she surrendered one of the capsules Hitler had given her (the other was used by her fellow aviator and lover Robert von Greim) it was examined by US interrogators and its description matches that of the one used by Goering and those found to have been in the possession of other top Nazis including Heinrich Himmler and Erich Bach-Zelewski.

In a lengthy and detailed statement taken by Chief Interrogator Captain Robert E. Work[9] at US Air Division Headquarters in Austria on 16 November 1945, Reitsch gave a thorough appraisal of the situation at the Reich Chancellory during Hitler's final days, including details of the suicide capsules being handed out by Hitler and the Fuehrer's despair regarding Goering's treachery:

Reitsch then told her story ... [Hitler to Greim] 'Hermann Goering has betrayed and deserted both me and his Fatherland. Behind my back he has established connections with the enemy' ... there were tears in the Feuhrer's eyes as he told her of Goering's treachery ... With eyes hard and half-closed and in a voice unusually low he went on: 'I immediately had Goering arrested as a traitor to the Reich, took from his offices, and removed him from all organizations. That is why I have called you to me. I hereby declare you Goering's successor as Oberbofelhahaber [Supreme commander] der Luftwaffe. In the name of the German people I give you my hand...'

Later that first evening Hitler called Reitsch to him in his room ... in a very small voice he said 'Hanna, you belong to those who will die with me. Each of us has a vial of poison such as this' with which he handed her one for herself and one for Greim. 'I do not wish that one of us falls to the Russians alive, nor do I wish our bodies to be found by then. Each person is responsible for destroying his body so that nothing recognisable remains. Eva and I will have our bodies burned. You will devise your own method. Will you please so inform von Greim?' ... The next morning [27 April] ...she learned the identity of all those who were facing the end with Hitler ... [many named including: Goebbels, his wife and six children; Bormann; Eva Braun; et. al.] ... in the early hours of the 28 April [a 'Suicide Council' was called and] instructions were given as to the use of the suicide vials (Reitsch still had hers in her possession. It was examined by the interrogator and found to be a little brass capsule with removable top containing a fragile glass bottle filled with about half a teaspoonful of amber liquid. The bottle was to be broken between the teeth and the liquid quickly swallowed).'[9]

Reitsch and Greim were ordered out of the Chancellery on 30 April – to try and muster aircraft to evacuate those remaining – and both flew planes out of Berlin, later learning of Hitler's death, Greim committed suicide in Salzburg on 24th May [using the vial Hitler had provided].

Captain Work states in his report that it will be forwarded to the trials and 'Reitsch is one of the last, if not the very last person who got out of the shelter alive'. He also confirms 'It is the opinion of the interrogator that the above information is given with a sincere and conscientious effort to be truthful and exact.'

It is clear from what Reitsch says during her interrogation, that everyone in the Fuehrerbunker – which was situated under the garden of the Reich Chancellery (Hitler's headquarters) – was given a suicide capsule and they were expected to use it. Many did, such as the Goebbels family and Eva Braun, but many others didn't – including some who later turned up at the Nuremberg trials including Minister of State Erich Neumann, General Paul von Below, and Werner Lorenz who was Head of the Main Office for Ethnic Germans. There were others also present at the Suicide Council, who Reitsch doesn't name, such as clerical staff 'and various SS orderlies and messengers'. There can be little doubt therefore that at least some of these, and others who got out of the bunker alive, may have voluntarily surrendered their suicide capsules, as Reitsch had done, or were relieved of them during the thorough search they would have been given upon capture or surrender. It is fair to surmise that those devices would have come from the batch of 950 that Albert Widmann gave 'to the courier from the Reich Chancellery' and which he confirms were 'for distribution to the senior leadership.'

Regarding the comments Reitsch makes and Captain Work's records about the suicide capsules, in their book *Nazi Millionaires*, authors Kenneth A. Alford and Theodore P. Savas add: 'The Germans manufactured more than 5,000 of these thin glass cyanide ampules hidden inside rifle cartridges modified with a screw top.'[8]

CHAPTER THIRTY-SEVEN – NOTES & REFERENCES

1. Collins Dictionary – meaning of the term 'silver bullet'.

2. On 20 July 1944, a plot by senior German military officials to murder Adolf Hitler and take control of his government failed when a bomb planted in a

briefcase went off but did not kill the Nazi leader. Hundreds of people thought to be involved in the conspiracy were arrested and brought before the Nazi People's Court – around 200 were executed.

3. *Der Spiegel*, 5 December 1949.

4. *The Anatomy of the Nuremberg Trials: A Personal Memoir*, p.623.

5. *Der Spiegel* 2/59 and *Associated Press* report sent from Ansbach dated 2 April 1951.

6. Memorandum from Colonel Telford Taylor 26 November 1945 and an undated, hand-written response from General Donovan (US National Archives).

7. *The Secretary. Martin Bormann: The Man Who Manipulated Hitler*, p.365.

8. *Nazi Millionaires*, p.135.

9. *The Condemnation of Goering by Hanna Reitsch – Captain E. Work 16 November 1945* (US National Archives). Reitsch was a famous female German test pilot. She was the only woman to win the German Iron Cross. She is believed to be the last person to leave Hitler's air raid shelter alive. The report gives her first-hand account of the last days in Hitler's bunker.

THE FIRE BRIGADE COLONEL

'[Andrus] moved majestically into the court, impeccably garbed in his uniform and highly shellacked helmet.'[1]
JOHN STANTON

LONG BEFORE THE DISASTROUS EVENT of 15 November had occurred, the world's press had grown to dislike Colonel Burton C. Andrus, the Commandant of the prison at the Palace of Justice who, because of the pristine uniform and the shiny helmet he always wore, Goering had nicknamed the 'Fire Brigade Colonel.'[2]

Having repeatedly advised the authorities that what had happened to Dr Ley (see below) would not be repeated, Andrus, rather arrogantly, informed news correspondents that he had devised a suicide proof prison. Because of his then failure to prevent the suicide, Andrus became the focus of the Army's, the prosecutions, the media's and the public's fury – and the events of that night were to haunt the colonel for the rest of his life.

There was already great unrest amongst the press corps at being kept waiting for news of the executions when Colonel Andrus emerged at 06.00 hours on 16 October to announce, over seven hours after the event, that:[3]

> Goering was not hanged, he committed suicide at 10:45 p.m. last night by taking cyanide of potassium. He was discovered at once by the sentinel who watched and heard him make an odd noise and twitch. The sentinel called the doctor and chaplain who were in the corridor and who found him dying. There were pieces of glass in his mouth and an odor of cyanide of potassium on his breath.

The hostile news correspondents, most of whom had already sent erroneous reports indicating Goering had been the first to walk to the gallows, did not hold back on expressing their frustration and condemnation of Andrus. John Stanton in *TIME* articulated the widely held views of those who had knowledge of how the prison security had been managed, or not, by Colonel Andrus:[1]

Down Without Tears[1]

How did Hermann Goring kill himself? How did he manage, in the midst of defeat and humiliation, to become a hero and thus virtually to destroy the positive psychological effect of the Nürnberg trial? From Nürnberg, *TIME* Correspondent John Stanton cabled:

It happened because the Army had placed in charge of the prison a pompous, unimaginative, and thoroughly unlikable officer who wasn't up to his job. Colonel Burton C. Andrus loved that job. Every morning his plump little figure, looking like an inflated pouter pigeon, moved majestically into the court, impeccably garbed in his uniform and highly shellacked helmet. His bow to the judges as they entered was one of the sights of Nürnberg …

He had spent long hours with his staff planning every last detail of the prisoners' life. He arranged anti-suicide cells in which even the tables were designed to collapse under a man's weight. He posted 24-hour guards before each cell and insisted that the prisoners sleep with hands outside the blankets. He required prisoners to take exercise periods during which their cells were searched. He had designed interview booths in which prisoners and visitors could converse with one another without being able to touch hands. All seemed well, but Andrus forgot that a pattern had been set, and with men like Göring, just to see the pattern was to see ways to break it.

Wolfe Frank was even more contemptuous of Andrus' ability. In his memoirs he wrote[4]:

The non-hero of the story is Colonel Burton C. Andrus, Commandant of the Nuremberg prison. I had first seen him during a pre-trial press conference when he assured the members of the press that he had designed and organised a suicide-proof prison. Andrus was a fairly short, or short-seeming, man who looked every inch the professional, intellectually stunted officer. I remember him as being devoid of any sense of humour or imagination. His men, I was told, saw in him an intolerable disciplinarian. It is certainly true that he had them keep up their highly polished appearance all the way through the trial and they did their stuff persistently, standing behind the dock, wearing white gloves and white painted helmets, pouncing like trained seals upon a prisoner leaning forward in the dock to whisper to a colleague.

It was a pity that the Americans in order to avoid such incidents as, for instance, that of a guard addressing the President of the Court as, 'Hey, you,' when Sir 'Geoffrey Lawrence [the President of the IMT] had slipped through some control point without showing his pass, but, most of all, so that Colonel Andrus's dream of a suicide-proof jail could come true. As it was, there was Dr Ley, committing suicide by hanging himself with a towel, torn into strips, on the water pipe of the WC in his cell. There was also a witness who managed to jump from an upper landing of the jail. Then, as the grand finale, there was Goering's dramatically timed suicide.

Two poison capsules had previously been found amongst Goering's possessions – one in the hollowed-out pages of a book and one in a tin of coffee. Such places of hiding were absurdly poor for a man of Goering's intelligence. Rather, I feel, he wanted those capsules found. To some extent, this would have dulled the minds of further searchers and it might produce the subconscious conclusion that 'two is all he could have had.'

Andrus' announcement caused 'pandemonium' in the press room, after which it was said he 'slumped dejectedly, his customary panache completely gone.' He had done his best, but he quickly realised the enormity of his failing – as the prosecution team were swift to point out, Goering's final triumphal act had 'wiped out all the work of the Tribunal'[5].

There were those who never forgave or forgot Andrus' monumental failing, as Wolfe Frank describes: 'Could a professional jailer, a trained prison warden have prevented it? Probably, yes. At least, some members of the press corps at Nuremberg must have thought so. Every year they sent a cable to Andrus on the anniversary of Goering's suicide "fondly remembering" Andrus and his successful performance as Commandant of the Nuremberg War Crimes Jail.'[6]

CHAPTER THIRTY-EIGHT – NOTES & REFERENCES

1. *TIME: Down without Tears* John Stanton, 28 October 1946. https://time.com/archive/6606341/international-down-without-tears/

2. *Nuremberg – A Personal Record of the Trial of Major Nazi War Criminals in 1945–6*, p.69.

3. *The Mystery of Hermann Goering's Suicide*, p.56.

4. *Nuremberg's Voice of Doom*, pp.155–156.

5. *St. Louis Post-Dispatch*, 16 October 1946.

6. *Nuremberg's Voice of Doom*, p.156.

SECTION EIGHT

SUSPECTS, INTEGRITIES, EVIDENCE & CONCLUSIONS

DISCOUNTING THE USUAL SUSPECTS

'No explanation is very convincing; none is backed by any proof'[1]
ANN & JOHN TUSA

OVER THE YEARS, several theories, together with the names of a number of suspects, have been put forward suggesting how Hermann Goering might have obtained the cyanide capsule that enabled him to commit suicide on 15 October 1946, and who might have provided it to him.

Even respected historians however, who have meticulously poured over all the then known evidence, could often only come up with solutions that were 'possible' or at best 'probable'. Ann and John Tusa, who carefully studied this subject in depth as part of the research for their highly regarded book *The Nuremberg Trial*, sum up the thoughts of many with the conclusion – 'No explanation is very convincing; none is backed by any proof.'[1]

My great hope is that the explanations put forward in *GOERING'S SUICIDE: 'They Will Not Hang Me!'* will be found to be convincing, and that the evidence provided will be accepted as proof that, in obeying an instruction given to him by General William Donovan, it was Lieutenant Edwin Putzell who provided the suicide capsule to Goering, and that Captain Wolfe Frank, acting as interpreter, was, most probably, the witness to the event that Putzell mentions during the interview he gave to Petronella Wyatt – published in the *Spectator* on 1 February 2003 (see Chapter Forty-Two).

Before I go into the details of these matters further however, I think it best to very briefly elucidate at this stage why investigators and sceptics, such as myself and Mr and Mrs Tusa, found previous explanations unconvincing, and why I suggest other suspects should now be discounted.

Some of those who studied this event, without the benefit of the evidence now available, believed Goering might have had the poison with him when he was first taken to Nuremberg (Goering indicated as much in the suicide note he left for Colonel Andrus, and at least two similar capsules had been found amongst his belongings before the suicide and a further one after). Others, who have scrutinised these matters, think this to have been highly unlikely. The view of most historical investigators is that the capsule was passed to Goering within Nuremberg prison. The evidence revealed and discussed in the following chapters will, I hope, convince readers that this theory is correct. It also reveals the identities and the extent of the involvement of those who ordered and carried out the deed and those that may have assisted.

Chief amongst previous suspects had been:

1. Lieutenant Jack Wheelis – the US Army guard to whom Goering had given a gold watch, a pen and a cigarette case.
2. Private Herbert Lee Stivers (another guard) – who, in 2005, claimed he had, at the request of an attractive German woman named Mona, been persuaded to smuggle to Goering a fountain pen containing 'medicine.'
3. US Army psychiatrist Dr Douglas Kelley – who had spent some time interviewing Goering during the trial period and who later took his own life using a similar type of potassium cyanide to that Goering had used.
4. General Erich Bach-Zelewski – who claimed the capsule was hidden in a bar of soap he had handed to Goering as they passed each other in the prison corridor.

Herbert Lee Stiver's account, whilst being considered vaguely plausible by some, had always been treated with caution, and although Dr Kelley had the means at his disposal, he was always considered to be the least likely of all the previous prime suspects.

While US District Attorney, William Canfield, was undecided on Bach-Zelewski's story (see Chapter Seventeen) it has always been considered to be highly unlikely, not least because Goering and Bach-Zelewski would never have come into contact with each other – their cells were on two separate levels – but mostly because the two men despised each other with Goering calling Bach-Zelewski: 'A traitor … bastard … and the bloodiest murderer in this whole system.'[2]

Ann and John Tusa were entirely justified in showing their skepticism. There is, however, room to speculate, with some justification, that Lieutenant Wheelis, in particular, and Erich Bach-Zelewski to a far lesser extent, could have played a, albeit subsidiary, role in the chain of events that enabled the suicide.

In his 1984 book, *The Mystery of Hermann Goering's Suicide*, historian Ben Swearingen speculated that Wheelis, who had got on well with

Goering, may have allowed him to visit a prison storeroom (where his luggage was held) and retrieve the cyanide from his personal belongings. This would, however, have been a monumental breach of security which would have been hard for Wheelis to carry out, would have put him at grave risk, and would have required the collusion of other prison guards.

Mr Swearingen spent many years painstakingly researching and writing about this subject and he met with people who had been directly involved at Nuremberg or with their families. He left no, then known, stone unturned, and it is a great shame that he did not have the benefit of studying the evidence that came to light after his death. However, even though he thought Wheelis to be the prime suspect, there remained a nagging doubt in his mind. As Colonel Telford Taylor, who knew Sergeant Wheelis, wrote:[3]

I myself have a pretty clear recollection of 'Tex' Wheelis ... For present purposes, Wheelis (who died in 1954) is important because he had access to the prison baggage room and had formed a friendship with Goering ... When author Ben Swearingen visited Wheelis's widow in 1976, she showed him 'a solid gold Mont Blanc fountain pen with Goering's name inscribed on the cap, a large and elaborate Swiss wristwatch bearing his name in facsimile signature, a solid gold cigarette case, and a handsome pair of gloves' Mrs Wheelis stated that 'All these gifts ... were given to her husband for favors done on behalf of Frau Goering and her little daughter' ... Like his nine fellow guardians of the baggage room, Wheelis signed identical prepared oaths stating: 'I have had in my possession the key to the baggage room of the prison during the period 10 October 1946 to 15 October 1946 and can state positively that Göring received nothing from, nor had acces [sic] to, the baggage room during this period' ... This extraordinary limiting of the oath certainly was no credit to the Board of Officers ... Swearingen, despite the remarkable evidence he has amassed, makes no claim of positive proof that Wheelis aided Goering in procuring or keeping the cyanide. Neither do I, but I think it probable that if Goering had such assistance, it was provided by Tex Wheelis.

This record, by someone who was present throughout the IMT and knew Wheelis, the jail and the baggage room, is important. Josef Persico reached a similar conclusion, recording: 'The character of Wheelis appears capable of foolishness, but not of criminality.'[4] Taylor, Persico, and John and Ann Tusa were never convinced of the Wheelis theory, and even Ben Swearigen could not be certain. However, their thoughts that Wheelis might have, in some way, been implicated could well have been sound, for there is a possibility that, in a more supportive role, Wheelis did play a part in the overall scenario.

CHAPTER THIRTY-NINE – NOTES & REFERENCES

1. *The Nuremberg Trial*, Ann and John Tusa, p.484.

2. *Deutsche Welle (DW)* – Germany's international broadcaster – https://www.dw.com/en/daddy-was-a-man-of-honor-daughter-of-nazi-ss-officer-insists/a-51853837

3. *The Anatomy of the Nuremberg Trials: A Personal Memoir*, pp.623–624.

4. *Nuremberg: Infamy on Trial*, p.446.

SILENT WITNESS

'like-minded conspirators who could share secrets'[1]
GENERAL WILLIAM DONOVAN

I HAVE, WHEREVER APPROPRIATE, paid tribute to the work of Ben Swearingen (who sadly died in 1998) and the valuable information and records he has left behind, that are included in his book *The Mystery of Hermann Goering's Suicide*, (published in 1984, paperback version 1990). It truly is a testament to the hard work of a capable author, who dedicated so much time and effort seeking an answer to a question that has perplexed historians and the public alike since 1946. Swearingen's book has been read, and is held in high regard, by many who have since used it as a reliable reference source in their own investigations, including me. Now there is one further incident Swearingen has recorded that is immensely helpful in proving the point that General Donovan was the prime mover in the enabling of Goering's Suicide.

Although this further evidence came Swearingen's way after he had completed the first draft of his manuscript, and even though it didn't fit with his favoured conclusion, he still considered it to be something of importance that should be mentioned. That he included these details in his book, despite his preferences, is a great credit to him and of great help to this author.

Like other researchers, I was frustrated by the lack of any records of events surrounding the 'private meetings' General Donovan had had with Goering prior to the start of the IMT. Harry Shotwell's recorded interview[2] had provided evidence that showed he and five other guards had been delegated to take Goering to and from interrogations and instructed to take their orders from OSS/CIC 'Spooks', and that General Donovan, head of OSS/CIC, ordered guards to wait outside interview rooms so he could talk to Goering in private, also that the general was prepared to assist Goering in ending his life. Shotwell was one of six guards chosen for these duties, Wheelis was most likely another, leaving four others similarly placed. I always thought there must have been at least one or more of those four specially selected guards who had witnessed similar incidents to those described by Shotwell, or who had overheard discussions between the Reichsmarschall and the general to which they too may have been instructed: 'not to hear a single word uttered in this room.'

A chapter in Ben Swearingen's book provided that further confirmation, for which I had been looking. The author had asked a former (unnamed) 'Nuremberg prison official', who had already supplied information included in the book, to read a copy of Swearingen's first draft. 'I found his memory sharp, his knowledge of personalities and events of the trial firsthand, and I had come to respect his opinions' wrote Swearingen 'Nevertheless I was totally surprised and unprepared for the questions he raised during our visit.'[3]

Swearingen asked the former prison official 'if he felt I had made a fundamental error in my conclusions or had omitted a crucial part in my research'. Following a discussion the prison official, who was troubled by Swearingen's conclusion, stated: 'we need a "star," don't we? Take away that "star" and those trials are meaningless. Goering was the "star."' The prison official then said: 'Goering made a deal with Wild Bill Donovan.' A surprised Swearingen then asked, 'Do you mean that Donovan made a deal with Goering, a deal in which he would not hang if he cooperated during the trial?' – 'Yes, he might have' replied Swearingen's guest – 'I know that Donovan talked to Goering and after that Goering's whole attitude changed. I think you need to look into this.'

Swearingen did look into what the former prison official had said and his investigations led him to write: 'When Donovan left the cell, Goering began to prepare his defense. A "deal" had been struck.'

Swearingen then concluded:

Donovan's Departure from the Nuremberg scene was a heavy blow to Goering. Dr. Gilbert [prison psychologist] recorded in his diary that Goering felt he had lost 'a good bet.' Nevertheless, the disappointed Reichsmarschall went through with his part of the bargain, giving the trial the 'star' it needed.

So my guest had up to a point been correct. There had been a 'deal' struck between the two, after which Goering agreed to take part in the trial proceedings. But the 'deal' did not include any type of consideration of Goering's personal fate. In fact, after the two had reached agreement on Donovan's proposal, the OSS chief said quietly but firmly 'to the man of whom he was asking so much,' But Herr Goering, I cannot save your head!'[3]

Douglas Waller, who had the advantage of seeing far more evidence than Swearingen, was able to go much further in describing the agreement that had been reached between Donovan and Goering, who had always known he would be executed and had prepared himself for such an event – it was only the manner of his own demise that now interested the Reichsmarschall. Included earlier in this book (at Chapter Twenty-Six) are Waller's more detailed record of these events which are well worth repeating here for continuity and to prove the point[4]:

> There was no way Goering could escape death, Donovan told him in one of their meetings. But he could 'die like a man' after a full confession, Donovan said. The egotistical Goering, who knew the only question remaining was how he met his end, was intrigued with the idea of copping a plea and ratting on his comrades – if the price was right. Donovan was after what could be the world's most sensational plea bargain. Goering would accept full responsibility for the war crimes, which would dramatically shorten the trial, and would take the stand to sell out Doenitz and the other top Nazis under indictment with testimony on their complicity. In return, the Reichsmarschall would be executed as a soldier before a firing squad instead of suffering the humiliation of hanging as a common criminal. The scene in the courtroom with Donovan as the star prosecutor and Goering on the witness stand could be dramatic, the spy chief knew, if he could pull it off, which on November 6 was far from certain.

Not being in possession of all the details, Douglas Waller had uncovered, nor those included in the interview Lieutenant Putzell gave to Petronella Wyatt, Swearingen was unable to pursue further the lead given to him by the former prison official. He ended his chapter on the 'Donovan Connection' by saying:

> The board, I therefore concluded, was correct in its decision to ignore the Russian charge that the United States government was in some way involved in Goering's suicide. It was one of the few correct decisions the board made.'

Ben Swearingen was correct in his assessment of The Board and his belief that the US government was not involved. However, by not being in possession of the further and better particulars revealed by Douglas Waller and Petronella Wyatt, Swearingen was unable to reach a vital conclusion – the 'deal' wasn't something sanctioned, or even known about, by the US authorities, this was an agreement, an understanding, reached between 'two like-minded conspirators who could share secrets' – one of whom would do anything to be able to 'die like a man' and the other who, against the wishes of the Chief Prosecutor, 'went off reservation and began organizing his own prosecution strategy for the trial.'[5]

Had Ben Swearingen had sight of this evidence at the time he was writing his book, I feel sure he would have investigated further the lead provided to him by his former Nuremberg prison official source. I also feel certain that this would have caused him to reappraise his conclusion that it was probably Jack Wheelis who facilitated the suicide. However none of Ben's work is wasted, on the contrary, it has helped lead to where we are today, and like him, I do feel Wheelis may well have played a part in the overall scenario that saw two veterans, of the more honourable Great War, keep to an agreement they had made during one of the 'ten private meetings' they had during the preparations period of what many historian's refer to as being 'the last battle of the Second World War.'

CHAPTER FORTY – NOTES & REFERENCES

1. *Wild Bill Donovan*, p.342.

2. Recorded interview: *Harry Shotwell Recalls a Day with Nazi Hermann Goering and 'Wild Bill' Donovan:* https://omny.fm/shows/rep-audio-vault/harry-shotwell-recalls-a-day-with-nazi-hermann-goe

3. *The Mystery of Hermann Goering's Suicide*, pp.99–104.

4. *Wild Bill Donovan*, pp.342–343.

5. ibid, p.345.

INTEGRITY

'I felt I was like every other warm-blooded American, obligated to do what I could for my country.'[1]
EDWIN J. PUTZELL, Jr.

IN PRESENTING THE CASE THAT – (a) under the orders of General William Donovan, it was his protege, most trusted compatriot, right hand man, executive officer, constant companion and closest friend and confidante, Lieutenant Edwin Putzell, who passed to Hermann Goering the capsule of potassium cyanide that enabled the Reichsmarschall to end his own life; and (b) Captain Wolfe Frank, acting as interpreter, was most probably the witness Putzell refers to as being present at the time of the transfer – I have relied heavily upon the character, reputations and integrity of those involved, as well as the writings of renowned authors Douglas Waller and Petronella Wyatt and their respective publishers – Free Press (Simon & Schuster) and *The Spectator*. I once again sincerely thank them all for allowing me to use extracts from Mr Waller's Book *Wild Bill Donovan*, and the whole of the interview Ms Wyatt conducted with Edwin Putzell in 2003, just a few months before his death.

For the benefit of readers, I think it is only right that, before I reintroduce and analyse the crucial piece of substantive evidence (Ms Wyatt's article), I provide brief biographical notes of the key individuals involved, and say something about the authors and publishers I have mentioned.

General William Donovan was no ordinary General. Following his heroic service in the First World War he returned to Wall Street where he enhanced his reputation as a lawyer and prosecutor, and later held, for five years, the office of Assistant US Attorney General. Prior to the US entering the Second World War, President Franklin D. Roosevelt gave Donovan an increasing number of special assignments in Europe and asked him to set up the OSS, which was originally based at the White House. By the end of the war Donovan was the commander of 13,000 (perhaps many more) world-wide intelligence agents. Following victory in Europe he was appointed to be a special prosecutor at Nuremberg.

A law unto himself, answerable only to the president and the Joint Chiefs of Staff of America's armed forces, Donovan was described by the *New York Times* as being 'a combination of bold innovator and imprudent rule bender, which made him not only a remarkable wartime leader but also an extraordinary figure in American history'[2]. In his biography of Donovan, *Wild Bill Donovan – The Last Hero,* author Anthony Clive Brown describes the general as being 'monkish, intense, intricate …the devoted secret servant of the state …adored by his men. To Donovan they were "my league of gentleman."'[3]

A national hero, Donovan is the only person to have received all four of the US' highest awards: the Medal of Honor, the Distinguished Service Cross, the Distinguished Service Medal, and the National Security Medal. He was also awarded the Silver Star, Purple Heart and further decorations from other nations for his service during both world wars. President Eisenhower called Donovan the 'Last Hero' and today, over sixty years after his death, he is still held in the highest possible regard at the CIA who say he 'remains an inspiration to the men and women of the CIA. Although he never directed the agency that was based on his ideas and initially staffed by people he personally led, Major General William Donovan embodied the creativity, courage, and can-do spirit that are the hallmarks of the CIA. Its officers regard him as the founder of both their agency and the American intelligence profession.'[4]

After Nuremberg, Donovan returned to Wall Street and his highly successful law firm, but always remained available to postwar presidents who requested his advice on intelligence matters. In 1949 he became Chairman of the American Committee on United Europe, and in 1953 President Eisenhower appointed him U.S. Ambassador to Thailand. Many other countries conferred their highest honours upon General Donovan including the UK where he was appointed to be an Honorary Knight Commander of the Most Excellent Order of the British Empire (see Appendix B for a list of the major honours awarded to General Donovan).

Edwin 'Ned' Putzell, Jr. was no ordinary lieutenant. He was the OSS' executive officer throughout the agency's existence, in which capacity he advised world leaders. A man of outstanding stature, character and achievement, Putzell was also General Donovan's 'gatekeeper.'

Ned Putzell had joined Donovan in his Wall Street legal practice in the 1930s, where their offices were next to each. They had a 'father/ son' relationship and, at one time, Putzell lived with the Donovan family. When President Roosevelt asked Donovan to form the OSS, Putzell was at his side – he stayed there throughout the war and at

Nuremberg. From that first day, Donovan and Putzell built the OSS into the world's leading intelligence agency. In May 1986 at a 'Dinner for Former Members of the OSS,' President Ronald Reagan, on behalf of a grateful nation, thanked those who had been involved in the agency and singled out Putzell for special praise.[5]

Following the war, and briefly chronicling his involvements up to the time of his meeting with Petronella Wyatt in 2003, Edwin Putzell continued to dedicate his life to serving the USA and the communities in which he lived. He became a leading attorney (still advising presidents and congressmen) and company secretary, general counsel and vice president of Monsanto in St Louis, the city where he was also vice chairman of the Board of Police Commissioners, chairman of the St Louis Public TV Commission and president of the Social Planning Committee. He moved to Naples, California in 1979 where he became Mayor, Chairman of the Airport Authority, and where he served on many civic boards. He was awarded the Outstanding Citizen Award of Naples in 1995. (It seems too that Putzell never applied for any of the civic or community positions he held, many on a voluntary basis, but was always approached and persuaded by the authorities he served). A self-deprecating and honourable man, one of Putzell's greatest achievements was helping General Donovan introduce the US to the world of strategic intelligence, unorthodox warfare and sabotage about which he would only say he 'felt obliged to do whatever I could for my country.'[1]

Wolfe Frank, was no ordinary interpreter. Uncovered as an underground resistance worker who smuggled Jews and large amounts of money out of Nazi Germany, he fled to England in 1937, unable to speak the language. By the time of the Nuremberg trials he was a peerless interpreter. Dubbed the 'Voice of Doom' by the world's press following his announcing of the death sentences at Nuremberg, Frank was asked to handle all the big moments at the IMT including the judges opening remarks; closing statements; the decisions of the court; the announcing of punishments and sentences; and he spent nine hours translating, both ways, the marathon twelve-thirteen hour examination and cross-examination of Hermann Goering. As an interrogator he dealt with all the major war criminals including Goering, Hess, von Rippentrop, et al, and he drew confessions out of some that helped seal their fate. At the end of the Nuremberg trials, (which, for Frank, lasted over two years), the US Chief Counsel of War Crimes described him as possessing 'superlative scholarship and administrative assistance and intellectual integrity satisfactory alike to the bench, the defence, and the prosecution.'[6]

In 1949, backed by the *New York Herald Tribune* Frank risked his life again by returning to the country of his birth during the 'Cold War' period to make an 'undercover' survey and write a series of highly acclaimed articles regarding the main facets of post-war German life and viewpoints. During this mission he single-handedly tracked down and arrested the German general ranked 'fourth' on the Allies 'most wanted' list (and Himmler's choice to head the SS in Great Britain if Germany had won the war) – before personally taking and transcribing the Nazi's confession.

The high regard held for Wolfe Frank extended to those many people he met and/or interviewed on this mission, at all levels of society and the armed forces – see under 'Captain Wolfe Frank: B2', Chapter Forty-Three, a list of those he dealt with, as confirmed by Geoffrey Parsons Jr., Editor of the *New York Herald Tribune European Edition*, who said of Frank's *Hangover After Hitler* series of articles, in the 1949 Preface he wrote for the book that was to become, seventy years later, *The Undercover Nazi Hunter:*

> Every sentence, every term, every phrase, and even a great many hundreds of nouns and adjectives, had been checked on by more than one critical editorial mind, and not infrequently debated and argued with the patient Mr Frank and we were satisfied that we had done our job, discharged our responsibility, and played fair both with our own and all the other [syndicated] papers' reading public, and with Mr Frank.

There was no one better placed, more experienced, more skilled, more reliable, or more able, to fulfil a translating task of such enormous importance as the one hereunder discussion than Wolfe Frank – the finest of interpreters who was known to, and trusted by, General Donovan, Lieutenant Putzell and Reichsmarschall Hermann Goering.

Douglas Waller was a former correspondent for *Newsweek* and *Time* and reported on the CIA for six years. He also served for eight years on the staffs of Representative Edward Markey and Senator William Proxmire. He is the author of a number of best-selling books on these involvements and the critically acclaimed biographies of Donovan and General Billy Mitchell. For *Wild Bill Donovan,* (subtitled *The Spymaster Who Created the OSS and Modern American Espionage),* Waller drew on US and UK government documents and those of Donovan's relatives and friends, many of whom were interviewed along with the general's former colleagues and staff. Waller's exhaustively-researched biography benefited from a number of research grants which allowed him to spend many months wading through the voluminous collections of Donovan's papers held at: the US Army Military History Centre; Columbia University's Oral History Research Office; The Roosevelt Institute; The Truman Library; The Eisenhower Foundation; the archives of the authors of three previous Donovan biographies; declassified OSS records; the US National Archives; The Hoover Institute; Donovan's Nuremberg papers held at Cornell University Law Library (which extend to 150 volumes); and many other university and official record collections including those held in the UK at or by the National Archives at Kew, the Cabinet Office, the Foreign Office, the Churchill Archives Centre and the Prime Minister's Office.

Free Press is an imprint of Simon a Schuster (S&S). Considered to be one of the 'Big Five' English language publishers, S&S is the third largest publisher in the United States, publishing 2,000 titles annually under thirty-five imprints. At the time of producing *Wild Bill Donovan* (2011) Free Press was one of the best-known publishers of serious nonfiction. In 2012 it was merged with S&S with the parent company announcing: 'We plan to continue publishing thought leaders and other important cultural voices under the Free Press imprimatur, while also introducing many other Free Press authors, such as novelists and historians and business writers, to the flagship Simon & Schuster imprint.'

Petronella Wyatt is a well-known journalist, author, broadcaster, political commentator and streaming channel consultant. She is best known as a weekly columnist for the *Sunday Telegraph* and as a deputy editor of *The Spectator*. During her period at *The Spectator* (1996–2011), the magazine published many high-profile interviews Ms Wyatt had conducted with top political figures such as Margaret Thatcher, John Major, Denis Healey, Gordon Brown, Douglas Hurd and with celebrities such as Leonardo di Caprio.

The Spectator was founded in 1828. It is considered to be the oldest weekly magazine in the world, and the oldest general-interest magazine continuously in print. In 2020 it published its 10,000th edition. In its mission statement *The Spectator* states: 'Our writers have no party line; their only allegiance is to clarity of thought, elegance of expression and independence of opinion … We are a member of IPSO, the independent press regulator, and abide by the Editor's Code. We also uphold strict standards of accuracy.'

CHAPTER FORTY-ONE – NOTES & REFERENCES

1. *Edwin Putzell Interview* 12 March 2003 with Mary Jane Robinson (US Library of Congress).

2. *New York Times* book review of *Wild Bill Donovan.*

3. *Wild Bill Donovan – The Last Hero*, p.298.

4. CIA: *Profiles in Leadership* 1941–2023, p.12.

5. *Remarks at a Dinner for Former Members of the OSS*, President Ronald Reagan (The Reagan Presidential Library & Museum): https://www.reaganlibrary.gov/archives/speech/remarks-dinner-former-members-office-strategic-services).

6. Testimonial written in support of Wolfe Frank by Major General Telford Taylor, Chief Prosecutor of the Subsequent Proceedings at Nuremberg.

SUBSTANTIVE EVIDENCE

Evidence that directly supports a claim or proves a fact.
LEGAL DEFINITION

THE BEST WAY OF PRESENTING **the evidence in support of the revelations included in Edwin Putzell's interview – in a way that, I believe, is easiest to follow – is to once again reproduce Mr Wyatt's** *Spectator* **article of 1 February 2003, this time interspersed with, where necessary, my evidence, explanations, comments and references** *printed in italics.* **(I have underlined a few of my words to emphasise their importance).**

THE QUALITY OF MERCY
PETRONELLA WYATT

I am sitting on a cream sofa in the evening sunset of Florida. Next to me is the man who killed Hermann Goering — or rather helped him to kill himself. Some received wisdom says that Goering committed suicide without aid, but this is not the case, as I have just found out. When a young man of about 30, this person beside me gave the Reichmarshall the cyanide pill that saved him from having to undergo the ordeal of the gallows.

Petronella Wyatt's interview with Edwin Putzell was impromptu. The former Lieutenant had not pre-determined to make these revelations public and Ms Wyatt had stumbled upon him quite by chance. When she asked her questions, Putzell responded immediately, off the cuff, about events that had taken place almost sixty years earlier.

The name of this extraordinary man is Ned Putzell. Now eighty-nine, he has retired to Naples on the Gulf coast.

Where he had: been Mayor; Chairman of the Airport Authority; a member of numerous civic and community boards; awarded the Outstanding Citizen Award; and was considered to be a pillar of his community.

He is tanned, spare and has laser-bright brown-grey eyes. He is wearing a crisp, white shirt, chequered trousers and large spectacles.

It all began when my host mentioned to me casually that in the apartment upstairs lived the man who gave Goering a cyanide pill. At first I thought he was joshing. But here I am, sipping a Diet Coke and listening to this fantastic tale.

Other historians and investigative journalists who have studied Ms Wyatt's article and are aware of the known, undisputed facts regarding Goering's suicide, while accepting Putzell's admission as being plausible, have had difficulty in accepting it as being fact only because the poison is referred to as having been in the form of a 'pill' – rather than as the 'capsule', 'phial' or 'vial' that it was known to be. A typical example is that of respected historian Dr Mark Felton, who in his excellent documentary (well worth watching), opines 'The only problem with Putzell's story seems to be the description he gave of the cyanide pill was different to the crushed glass ampoule found in Goering's mouth.'[1]

There is a very simple answer to this. 'Suicide Pill' is an all-embracing term that was used by OSS officers, other military personnel and the media as a generic term. Because it is important to prove this point, I give a few examples of the term being used during the Second World War and still today – some even mention Goering:

The official US Government National Library of Medicine is still referring to the device that killed Goering in the following terms: 'The night before his scheduled death by hanging, Goering committed suicide via cyanide pill.'[15]

In June 2016 under the heading 'Hermann Goering's cyanide pill container offered in Munich,' Paul Fraser Collectibles, 'the world's largest privately owned dealer in rare collectibles' announced: 'The brass container Hermann Goering used to conceal the cyanide pill he took prior to his execution in 1946 is to sell in Munich. It forms part of the collection of John K Lattimer, who served as the general medical officer during the Nuremburg trials … The pill was one of three he carried with him. One was discovered by the guards before he could use it.'[16]

Helias Doundoulakis, a former OSS agent, in his book Trained to be an OSS Spy *records: 'If we were proven to be enemy agents, we would rather die by way of ingesting the so-called 'Q pill' that we carried with us (a small glass vial containing cyanide for a 'quick' death).'[2]*

In an interview he gave to **The Guardian** *on 3 October 2006, US Sergeant Clancy Sigal said: Sixty years ago, I was a sergeant in the American army of occupation in Germany. I was the only Jew in my unit … When the prosecution showed films of piled-up corpses at Auschwitz, Goering kept turning his head away, sometimes in my direction. I'm ashamed to say he stared me down, because I had never before felt myself in the presence of such unmitigated evil … On October 1 1946, the Allied judges handed down their sentences. Most of the accused were found guilty and sentenced to death. Goering swallowed a cyanide <u>pill</u> hours before he was to mount the gallows.'*[3]

Military Wiki, the World's largest, free, interactive online Military encyclopedia states: <u>'A suicide pill (also known as the cyanide pill, kill-pill, lethal pill, death-pill, or L-pill) is a pill, capsule, ampoule, or tablet</u> containing a fatally poisonous substance that one ingests deliberately in order to quickly achieve death through suicide. Military and espionage organizations have provided their agents in danger of being captured by the enemy with suicide <u>pills</u> and devices which can be used in order to avoid an imminent and far more unpleasant death (such as through torture), or to ensure that they cannot be interrogated and forced to disclose secret information … At the end of World War II, Hitler's companion Eva Braun and a number of leading Nazis, such as Heinrich Himmler, Hermann Göring, Philipp Bouhler and Martin Bormann died by suicide using lethal <u>pills</u> containing a solution of cyanide salts.'[4]

Suicide <u>Pill</u> is also still being used to describe the capsule Goering had, as is further instanced by the BBC on-line headline when reporting the Herbert Lee Stivers comments – 'Guard 'gave Goering suicide <u>pill</u>' and in the text it records, 'The Luftwaffe head left a suicide note claiming he had had the <u>pill</u> during his entire 11-month war crimes trial. An army investigation decided he must have hidden the <u>pill</u> on his body and in his cell.[5]

The Los Angeles Times when commenting upon another suggestion, wrote – 'Army Lt. Jack Wheelis, who had a key to the prison storeroom, had allowed Goering to visit the storage area shortly before his death to retrieve the poison <u>pill</u> from his luggage.'[6]

In another BBC on-line feature under the heading: 'Allied 'bandits' behind enemy lines' presenter Robert Hall states under the sub heading 'Suicide <u>pills</u>': 'So they were issued with cyanide capsules to use in any such event and Mr Piesch recalls the words of the mission commander.

"We were to pop the <u>pill</u> in our mouth, hold it in our cheek, and if it became necessary we were to bite down and take a deep breath – then goodbye Charlie," he said.[7]

Mr Putzell was born in Louisiana. He attended Harvard Law School and eventually ended up working for the law firm of a man called Donovan. This was no ordinary Donovan, but the great American hero of the first world war. Mr Putzell, leaning forward conspiratorially, told me that Donovan was a far greater soldier than MacArthur, the latter a name far better known to English ears.

During the 1914–18 war, Donovan was stationed in northern France, fighting in the trenches. MacArthur was leading the regiment next to him, geographically. When the Germans attacked, it is a little-known fact that MacArthur turned on his heels. Donovan, however, stood his ground, won and was awarded the Congressional Medal of Honour. Americans, it seems, do not appear to know of MacArthur's behaviour on this occasion.

'Through Donovan, I came to examine Goering during the preparations for the Nuremberg trials,' Putzell told me.

Edwin Putzell had been a lawyer all his life and in this sentence he is using precise legal terminology. '<u>Examination,</u> in law, is the interrogation of a witness by attorneys or by a judge' – Britannica.

'<u>Preparations</u>' refers to that period before the trial starts, two typical explanations of the term are as follows:

'The proper <u>preparation</u> of any case by an attorney. It includes witness interviews, knowing the facts and laws applicable to the case and having consultation with the client' – The Law Dictionary.

'Trial <u>preparation</u> refers to all of the activity carried out by legal professionals before they present their case in court. As part of the trial <u>preparation</u> process you could be involved in collating evidence, obtaining witness statements, identifying expert witnesses, ensuring witnesses will attend court, and drafting and reviewing legal documents. It also requires the development of robust legal arguments and discussing strategies for responding to the potential challenges you may be presented with during the trial itself' – University of Law.

In using those legal terms Putzell is pinpointing the period when he, Donovan, Frank and Neave '<u>examined</u>' Hermann Goering – that was from 3 October 1945 when Putzell and Donovan arrived in Nuremberg, until 20 November 1945 when the '<u>Preparations</u>' ended and the IMT began. The poison capsule would therefore have been passed to Goering between these two dates (Neave did not arrive until 18 October and

Donovan and Putzell left Nuremberg altogether on 30 November and had nothing further to do with the trial).

'A lot of high-ranking Americans believed his heart had not really been in the Nazi cause. Before Hitler killed himself, Goering was already giving vital information to us which I passed on to the president.'

This is an entirely correct statement, confirmed by Hitler himself. During her interrogation, German fighter pilot Hanna Reitsch stated that on 26 April 1945 Hitler had told her and her fellow aviator and lover Robert von Greim that Goering had 'deserted both me and his Fatherland. Behind my back he has established connections with the enemy' … there were 'tears in the Führer's eyes as he told her of Goering's treachery.'[8]

In the 'Second Part of the Political Testament' attached to his Will, signed and dated 29 April 1945 (the day before he committed suicide), Hitler confirms: 'Apart from the disloyalty against my person, Goering and Himmler have inflicted immeasurable damage upon the country and the entire people through secret negotiations with the enemy which they have made without my knowledge and against my will, and also through the attempt to invest themselves illegally with the power in the state.'[9]

Roosevelt had decided a while before that the United States required a proper espionage system. This was started by Donovan and became known as the OSS — the Office of Strategic Services. Donovan was chosen to be one of the co-prosecutors at Nuremberg and took Putzell with him as his aide. Other high-ranking Nazis on trial were Albert Speer, Ribbentrop, Alfred Rosenberg and Julius Streicher.

What was Goering like? I asked Putzell. 'Oh, he could be very charming indeed.' This was a view shared by Hartley Shawcross on the British side, who recollects that Goering repeatedly winked at him during examination. 'Then, again, he might have been acting,' Putzell continues.

'When I questioned Goering, the plan was to find out whether he had been a truly dedicated Nazi. I don't think he was, Hitler had suspected him of disloyalty and other Germans told us that Goering was not a strong supporter.'

The matter of Goering's 'disloyalty' is evidenced above. However, to be able to question Goering, gauge his reactions and be convinced of the Reichmarschall's position, Putzell would have required the services of an interpreter with exceptional skills and sufficient authority who could be implicitly trusted. Only one man fitted that description – Captain

Wolfe Frank – about whom legendary times correspondent R. W. Cooper wrote 'his voice and manner, the nuances of his vocabulary, the ability to convey the character of the person for whom he was translating were all outstanding'. To have been able to: make the judgement he did; and to endorse General Donovan's momentous decision and execute the transfer; Putzell would have needed to have been provided with those assurances, in the precise and unambiguous way that was Wolfe Frank's hallmark.

But he was condemned, nonetheless. I retorted. Putzell nods, his glasses sliding towards the middle of his aquiline and rather handsome nose.

'Yes, but Donovan secretly decided, with the agreement of the British contingent, to let him die by cyanide.'

Firstly, it is impossible to exaggerate the levels of admiration, respect, pride, loyalty and affection held for General Donovan, at home and abroad, at all levels of society – from those of the humblest of backgrounds who would risk their lives should he request it, to US Presidents who would stand to attention in his presence. As a graduate, in 1937, during the Great Depression, Edwin Putzell was offered five job opportunities with Wall Street law firms including Donovan's, about which he said in his audio interview for the US library of Congress: 'since he'd been a hero in this country and in my family's home since World War I, I chose to go there.' This was very much a partnership in many ways, with Donovan somewhat dependent on Putzell not only for 'enforcing his orders' but as one of the few people who could tell the General 'You can't do anything in the heat of the moment' and if necessary to wait 'until you have calmed down.'[14] (It is hard to believe there are many other examples of a relationship that allowed a Lieutenant to advise a General in such a way – and for such advice to be heeded).

Donovan's authority, however, was never questioned. If he made a decision, including a 'secret' one, any request that ensued would be carried out exactly as he had requested. Other than perhaps a nod of agreement from Putzell, he never sought confirmation – even from a higher source – indeed only General Eisenhower and President Truman fell into that category.

Secondly, it seems that Wolfe Frank and Airey Neave may well have been the 'British contingent' to which Putzell is referring.

In his memoirs Frank writes: 'There then followed a fascinating period when, <u>before the arrival of my colleagues</u> and the equipment from IBM [this arrived on 15 November], I was assigned to pre-trial interrogations of the defendants-to-be and the innumerable witnesses *whom teams of investigators had been rounding up on the orders of the prosecuting teams'*[10].

In his memoirs, Airey Neave, who had been sent ahead of the British prosecutors, writes: 'I tried to plan for the big occasion [serving the indictments on Goering, et. al. on 19 October] for <u>I had no one on my side to consult … I was the only Englishmen taking part in the event</u>' Later that day Neave records, perhaps with some relief: 'I sat next to Wolfe Frank a German from Munich, who had joined the British Army as a refugee from Hitler … He accompanied me on subsequent visits to the cells'[11].

'Goering had been very co-operative with us and he genuinely did seem deserving of some sort of mercy.'

Donovan had told Goering, that if he co-operated with the General's plan, 'In return, the Reichsmarschall would be executed as a soldier before a firing squad instead of suffering the humiliation of hanging as a common criminal.'[12]

How did they get hold of the cyanide? I was surprised by the answer. 'Everyone in active service in the OSS was given a cyanide pill in case they were captured by the Germans and tortured. So we had quite a few on us.'

The suicide capsule-in-a-cartridge-case that Putzell passed over to Goering was almost certainly one of the many identical German devices that had fallen into the hands of the OSS, and in particular from the batch of 950 Albert Widmann confirmed went to the Reich Chancellery 'for distribution to the senior leadership'. We know from Hanna Reitsch's testament that Hitler was handing out these capsules in the Chancellery in the days leading up to his suicide and that a 'Suicide Council' had been called to show all present how the devices should be used.

Goering had been present in the Chancellery on the occasion of Hitler's 56th birthday party – 20 April 1945 (ten days before the Fuehrer's demise) – and learned of Hitler's intended suicide two days later. Apart from Goering, other top Nazis who used the poison were Joseph Goebels and his wife and six children, Heinrich Himmler, Eva Braun and Martin Bormann. Others present at the party, who later appeared at Nuremberg, included Albert Speer and Karl Doenitz. Twenty-four captured Nazis were on trial at the IMT and over 1600 at the Subsequent Proceedings. Many would still have had the capsules on them when they were captured. The device that Putzell gave to

Goering could have been from any of these, or was perhaps the one surrendered by Hanna Reitsch, or one of those confiscated from Bach-Zelewski – who later produced others from the same batch as the one Goering used. (Bach-Zelewski also admitted taking some capsules into the prison at Nuremberg).

There can be no doubt therefore that the OSS had many identical capsules. It is even possible that Putzell returned to Goering one of the two capsules discovered earlier amongst his possessions. There is another aspect to this possibility that would be of interest to the Russians and others who feel there may have been a cover up, for it would have allowed the members of The Board and the Control Council, who met in such secrecy, to be able to honestly state, as they did in their findings: 'That the small brass container containing the suicide poison was in the possession of Goering at the time he was taken into custody by the American Army' – the statement is very specific and doesn't say, as one would have thought it might, that Goering had had it in his possession throughout!

Putzell and a colleague handed one tablet to Goering.

('Tablet' is Ms Wyatt's word). The main point here is that Putzell states he had a witness. Wolfe Frank disclosed to a small group of friends, shortly before he took his own life in 1988 – fifteen years before Putzell made his statement – that he had been witness to the transfer of the poison, and Frank must be considered to be the best placed person to have fulfilled such a task. He was working directly with Donovan and Putzell at that time and Putzell would have needed an interpreter he, Donovan and Goering could all implicitly trust.

How did he react? Putzell laughs gutturally. 'I think he was glad to have it. It was better than being hanged.' Much better as it turned out. Some of the hangings were botched horribly.

Putzell and his wife Dorothy, a pristine and smart blonde, now live in Naples permanently. Most English people believe that the west coast of Florida is quiet and uneventful, full of purblind retired bankers and brokers. Full of men and women whose reminiscences are solely about dosh. But this is not the case.

Consider my host: his division was one of the first into Hitler's house beneath the Eagle's Nest.

Frank used the Eagle's Nest as a retreat during the immediate post-war period and enthused about cooking meals on 'Hitler's stove.'[13]

Opposite me now sits the Führer's silver cigar box with the logo of the Third Reich on its lid. Then, in a drawer in the next room, there is an exquisite, lacquered box given to Hitler by the Emperor of Japan. These mementoes of the Second World War are unique. So is Mr Putzell.

Wolfe Frank was also involved in removing 'mementoes' from the Eagle's Nest together with 'Olympic ski-jump champion Freddy Stoll and Fritz Haegele' described by Frank as being 'Goering's valet' who was being 'employed by the US as a caretaker of the property'. Amongst the items the trio removed was Hitler's bathtub, about which Frank commented 'I have often soaked in it, and it was sheer luxury'[13]. (Stoll, who also knew Goering, was arrested by the CIC with the bath in his vehicle. He was, however, released again without charge following a representation by Frank to the CIC – the successor agency to the OSS that in Nuremberg was headed by Donovan and Putzell).

Editor: As a footnote to this chapter, I believe it is worth pointing out, Putzell's and Frank's stated involvements in the event that, perhaps in a small way, did change the course of history, have become public knowledge via similar routes. Frank, late in his life and perhaps at a time he was contemplating his own destiny, told a group of friends he had been present when Goering was given the cyanide that allowed him to end his life in a way that, to use Putzell's own words, 'was better than being hanged.' One of that group passed the information on to me, in the knowledge that, as a writer, I would be making it more widely known. In like fashion, Putzell, also during his final months, confided in a friend and neighbour. That neighbour in turn revealed the event to Ms Wyatt, a writer who Ned Putzell granted an interview well knowing that in doing so the secret he had kept for almost sixty years would be released into the public domain.

CHAPTER FORTY-TWO – NOTES & REFERENCES

1. *Hermann Göring's Mysterious Death,* Dr Mark Felton: https://www.youtube.com/watch?v=2IMhFW7539s

2. *Trained to be an OSS Spy,* Helias Doundoulakis, p.135.

3. *The Guardian,* 3 October 2006.

4. *Military Wikipedia:* https://military-history.fandom.com/wiki/Suicide_pill

5. BBC Online: http://news.bbc.co.uk/1/hi/world/americas/4247069.stm

6. *Los Angeles Times,* 7 February 2005.

7. BBC Online: http://news.bbc.co.uk/1/mobile/uk/8085383.stm

8. *The Condemnation of Goering by Hanna Reitsch – Captain E. Work 16 November 1945* (US National Archives).

9. *Will of Adolf Hitler* Eisenhower Library: https://www.eisenhowerlibrary.gov/sites/default/files/research/online-documents/holocaust/hitler-marriage-will-political-testament.pdf

10. *Nuremberg's Voice of Doom* p.123.

11. *Nuremberg – A Personal Record of the Trial of Major Nazi War Criminals in 1945–6, pp.56–61.*

12. *Wild Bill Donovan, p.343.*

13. Wolfe Frank's memoirs – see *Nuremberg's Voice of Doom,* p.174.

14. *Wild Bill Donovan, p.231.*

15. US National Library of Medicine, *"A Profound, Abiding Hatred": An Analysis of Hermann Goering's Alleged Morphine Addiction:* https://pmc.ncbi.nlm.nih.gov/articles/PMC10144812/

16. https://www.paulfrasercollectibles.com/blogs/medals-militaria/hermann-goerings-cyanide-pill-container-offered-in-munich?srsltid=AfmBOopB6am0Abymi1ulRSEGb3bqPnwnVDY6oJYWPKc-j0yXo_LbgF5c

RECAP & CONCLUSIONS

*'A new perspective on one of the 20th century's most enduring and
frustrating unsolved mysteries'*
PAUL HOOLEY

HAVING CLOSELY STUDIED: every sentence uttered by Edwin Putzell in the interview he gave to Ms Wyatt – and found solid evidence to support each point he made; and having looked carefully into his background, character and standing – I believe the former Executive Officer of the OSS was a man of great probity and that he answered every question Ms Wyatt put to him truthfully, factually and with integrity. I am convinced, therefore, that, following a 'request' from General William Donovan, Lieutenant Putzell did provide Hermann Goering with the cyanide capsule he used to end his life on 15 October 1946. In reaching that conclusion I hope I have provided enough evidence in support of my belief, and that this will be accepted as being the definitive answer to the mystery of how the architect of 'The Final Solution', (and originator of the euphemism), obtained the cyanide capsule that enabled him to cheat the hangman.

I have highlighted the word 'request' above because General Donovan had a way of issuing the most serious and dangerous of orders in the friendliest of ways – as Carlton Coon, another OSS secret agent hand-picked by the general, was to recall when asked about the make-up of Donovan's 'league of gentleman': '[we were] gentleman volunteers on our honor. We were never under orders. We were always asked, "Would you like to … (e.g., get yourself killed)?" To which we always said "yes" … I never took an oath for the COI or the OSS.'[1] Edwin Putzell also confirmed Donovan was the sort of leader who was 'unwilling to ask anyone to take a risk that he himself would not take.'[2]

On 12 March 2003, a few weeks after his interview with Ms Wyatt, Edwin Puzzle gave an oral testimony to Mary Jane Robinson for the US Library of Congress. This recording is well worth a listen, not just for the fascinating details it reveals about the OSS and the Second World War, but also to show the warmth, integrity, sincerity and the sharpness of mind Putzell still possessed, even at the age of eighty-nine. The interview also shows how close he was to William Donovan and the affection he felt for his mentor: 'he was an incredible guy. He is the only one in my limited experience who had both physical and intellectual daring in one person ... No, I didn't feel closer [to Donovan than to his father]. I felt a different relationship. A very warm and a very affectionate one. He was blue-eyed and had typical Irish personality and he wooed everybody, male and female. And my affection for him was there ... there was a sort of a father/son relationship which I will always treasure.'[3]

Unlike others who 'confessed' to passing the poison to Goering – Herbert Lee Stivers, a US Army guard who perhaps sought fame or fortune, and General Bach-Zelewski who thought he could do another 'deal' with the prosecuting authorities in the hope of a lighter sentence – Edwin Putzell had nothing to gain, and he sought no reward or recognition for revealing what he did about the suicide capsule. Putzell was a quiet, unassuming, modest man of impeccable standing and character who, among his many OSS duties had advised world leaders including presidents Roosevelt and Truman, Andrei Gromyko (Russia's US ambassador) and Prime Minister Winston Churchill. Throughout his life, Putzell was highly regarded by all who knew him, whether that be in his roles as a top attorney, champion of worthy causes or as Executive Officer of the OSS – the current job description of which seems to have changed very little from the duties so admirably fulfilled by Putzell during the Second World War:

> In the US Army, Executive Officer duties include acting as the commander's second-in-command to handle administrative and logistical details, which allows the commander to focus on tactical operations. Key responsibilities include managing staff and personnel, overseeing logistics and supply, and ensuring training readiness and property accountability. The Executive Officer also serves as the commander's representative, implementing policy, and advising on plans, acts as the commander's representative for daily operations, manages the commander's schedule, and often serves as the acting commander in their absence.

There are two examples I mention here to illustrate: Edwin Putzell's kindness, modesty and reluctance to take credit or in any way seek to put himself forward; and the regard in which he was held at all levels of society – from presidents to members of his community. Firstly, the lieutenant was, on one occasion, standing over President Roosevelt as he read 'a for your eyes only' document, when FDR broke off to express his high regard for the key fob on Putzell's watch chain, it had been awarded to the lieutenant by the Phi Beta Kappa ('Love of learning is the guide of life') Society – the US' most prestigious and best known academic honor society. The president casually expressed his admiration for those who had received the award. In his interview with Mary Jane Robinson (MJR) Putzell relates what happened next: 'So I wrote to [The College of] William and Mary where they founded it and recommended he [the president] be given an honorary. And you'll see that early photographs during his era he had a gold chain with nothing on it. But once he got it, it was hanging right here'. MJR then asks: 'did he ever know what you'd done?' to which Putzell replied 'No. And no need to, you know'[3].

The second illustration of Putzell's high standing and wide appeal concerns the time he was 'Encouraged by residents to run for Mayor of Naples, he admitted openly that he had never been in or was inspired to get involved in public affairs', but he would stand if it was the wish of the community and no one opposed him. As an indication of the affection and esteem in which he was held, Putzell *was* unopposed, yet a staggering 73 percent of the electorate turned out to cast their vote for him – and he became the first person to hold the office of City Mayor for a four-year period.[46]

I find it inconceivable therefore, that a man who had lived such a distinguished, trustworthy and exemplary life as Edwin Putzell would, shortly before his death, 'invent' the statements he gave to Ms Wyatt, or in any way attach any kind of falsehood to the name of the man he most admired – his dear and close friend, colleague, superior officer, life-long hero and mentor General William Donovan – of whom biographer Anthony Cave Brown said, regarding the relationship he had with his OSS colleagues, 'More than in World War I, he was adored by his men.'[1]

Like Minded Conspirators

William Donovan and Robert Jackson had known each other from long before the establishment of the IMT and the appointment of Jackson as Chief Prosecutor and Donovan as his special assistant. Both men were leading New York attorneys. They had been political rivals before the war – Jackson was a democrat, Donovan a republican – and both men had been considered presidential prospects by their respective parties.

Despite President Truman having doubts about the future of the OSS, the pairing of Jackson and Donovan as US prosecutors at the IMT at first seemed to be a perfect match, and their early relationship at Nuremberg was cordial and constructive. Jackson was starting with no evidence, no witnesses and no venue for what was to become the world's greatest trial – as he said in his *Retrospect* 'very little real evidence was in our possession, the overwhelming mass of documents being still undiscovered and their existence largely unsuspected ... we did not even know whether a court-house that could house such a trial was still standing in Germany, or if so, where it was to be found.'[4]

Donovan immediately came to Jackson's aid. He provided funds for the prosecution to get started, found and recommended the Palace of Justice at Nuremberg as the venue for the trials, and he offered Jackson the full resources of the OSS, telling the Chief Prosecutor he 'knew who was "the captain of the team" and "he would play wherever" the Justice could use him. Donovan didn't really mean that. He intended to play a star role in the trials'. Over the next six months, 172 of Donovan's officers/agents joined Jackson's team and Donovan provided vast amounts of evidence and opened doors for the Justice in British and European governments and General Eisenhower's command. 'Donovan soon became Jackson's most trusted emissary, with the OSS insinuated into every aspect of the justice's operation.'[5]

As the trial date grew ever closer, however, Jackson came to realise that his and Donovan's strategies for conducting the prosecution were quite different and that they were on a collision course. Already stung by Truman's decision to close down the OSS on 30 September 1945, Donovan had returned to Nuremberg three days later intent on putting into place his plan to persuade Hermann Goering to accept responsibility for all Nazi war crimes and to implicate the other defendants. In return Goering would be allowed to die more honourably than by the 'death by the rope' method Jackson had in mind – and would strenuously argue for throughout the IMT.

Over the following eight weeks Donovan and Goering had 'ten private meetings' during which time Donovan had offered the Reichsmarschall a way of avoiding hanging. The critical meeting between the two had occurred on 6 November, and Douglas Waller's record is well worth repeating here:

Like a skilled intelligence operative, Donovan eventually convinced Goering they were both like-minded conspirators who could share secrets ... There was no way Goering could escape death, Donovan told him in one of their meetings. But he could 'die like a man' after a full confession, Donovan said. The egotistical Goering, who knew the only question remaining was how he met his end, was intrigued with the idea of copping a plea and ratting on his comrades – if the price was right. Donovan was after what could be the world's most sensational plea bargain. Goering would accept full responsibility for the war crimes, which would dramatically shorten the trial, and would take the stand to sell out Doenitz and the other top Nazis under indictment with testimony on their complicity. In return, the Reichsmarschall would be executed as a soldier before a firing squad instead of suffering the humiliation of hanging as a common criminal. The scene in the courtroom with Donovan as the star prosecutor and Goering on the witness stand could be dramatic, the spy chief knew, if he could pull it off, which on November 6 was far from certain.[6]

This was all Goering had asked for. His whole attitude changed and he began to co-operate immediately as Ben Swearingen's former prison official source[7] and Goering's lawyer's memo of 15 November (referring to a meeting that had taken place three days earlier) had confirmed.[8]

That memo indicated Goering had promised to give 'truthful answers, in writing, to any questions which might be put to him by General Donovan' – this was to be the script of the performances Goering and Donovan would give at the trial, which both men saw as being the highlight of the IMT.

On receiving a report of the 12 October meeting, and learning that Goering was prepared to meet only with Donovan, Jackson realised exactly what the general was planning and that he and Donovan were pursuing two entirely different strategies on how the Nazi defendants in general, and Goering in particular, would be dealt with in the witness box … and he wasn't having that!

'Star' is a word used by Douglas Waller, Ben Swearingen and the latter's former prison official source. Both Donovan and Jackson saw themselves fulfilling that role, but in sidelining Donovan and pursuing his own prosecution plan, Jackson was going head-to-head with the eventual 'star' of the show, Hermann Goering.

Goering claimed to the end that Donovan was the one prosecutor he could trust, but he could not have afforded to rely purely upon a verbal agreement. The Reichsmarschall would have wanted insurance and would have insisted that, in return for his compliance, he be provided with a guaranteed alternative means of avoiding the rope if, for any reason, the Tribunal did not honour Donovan's commitment or if the general was no longer around (which is exactly what happened).

Once the IMT had commenced, Goering followed the script he had agreed with Donovan, with two major changes.

Firstly, as Wolfe Frank intimated, Goering had his bewildered attorney, Stahmer, take Donovan's place and ask the list of questions he and Donovan had worked out, plus others that suited his objective – including questions that Donovan would not have permitted. Over twelve hours in the dock (nine of which were interpreted by Frank), Goering delivered a defence of his actions and a denial of guilt for war crimes and crimes against humanity. His whole performance was intended to show his followers he was still the hero they thought he was, and that he had only ever acted with the best intentions, his only motives being 'an ardent love for my people, its happiness, its freedom, and its life.'

Secondly, with Donovan long gone (disgusted with Jackson's treatment of him and the justice's lack of courtroom, directional and structural abilities) – and with the poison capsule safely in his possession, Goering had no need, or reason, to comply with the second part of his agreement with Donovan – that required him to: accept full responsibility for the Nazi war crimes and atrocities; and 'take to the stand to sell out Donitz and the other top Nazis under indictment with testimony on their complicity.'[9]

As Putzell stated in his revelations to Ms Wyatt: 'Donovan secretly decided, with the agreement of the British contingent, to let him die by cyanide' and 'Goering had been very co-operative with us and he genuinely did seem deserving of some sort of mercy.'

(There was another aspect to these matters. Donovan's word was his bond. He and Goering were veterans of the more honourable Great War – and there is an example of Goering himself showing mercy during a First World War aerial dogfight, referred to by Airey Neave: 'The Danish pilot Captain Krause-Jensen, who flew for the French, describes how his machine-gun had jammed during a dogfight with Goering. He beat his fist against the useless weapon in desperation. When Goering saw this, he banked his machine, saluted and flew off'. In relating this incident, Neave was quick to point out 'He [Goering] did not carry his chivalry into peacetime politics. He was one of the cruelest political criminals of all time').[10]

Clearly Donovan's motives for providing the cyanide were to: give Goering the insurance/incentive/reward he would have demanded for going along with Donovan's plan, and honour a commitment he had made to 'a like minded conspirator' that allowed Goering to avoid 'death by the rope'. The result would, Donovan hoped: provide a dramatic courtroom scene with him as the 'star' prosecutor; prove his methods were superior to Jackson's; deny Jackson the triumph he sought of seeing the Reichsmarschall 'hang like a common criminal';

evince to those involved in disbanding the OSS that they had been wrong to do so; and, above all, show to Truman the true value of the OSS, its structure and operatives, and convince the president of the need to retain the agency (or its successor), with him as its head.

Donovan was also very much against indicting the whole of the Nazi High Command, pointing out that if Germany had won the war, on Jackson's thinking it would have made him, Donovan, a war criminal simply because he was in command of men who might have committed a war crime. 'Hang a general because he committed a crime, Donovan said, not because he was a general.'[59] Jackson's reply was that 'he was going ahead with the prosecution of the High Command anyway.' Yet one more issue between the two prosecutors, again refused by Jackson, concerned Hjalmar Schacht, the Nazi Minister of Economics, with whom Donovan was also prepared to offer a plea bargain.

The day after a final confrontation between the two men, Jackson told Donovan he was dispensing with his services. 'Wild Bill had been fired'. Donovan did not go quietly. He told the US Judge, Francis Biddle, that Jackson was 'a poor manager and that the prosecution office was a shambles' and that he no longer wanted 'to be part of this fiasco.'[59] Donovan said much the same in his final letter to Jackson of 27 November 1945. (Once again, the general was ultimately proven to be right on these matters. The IMT found the Nazi High Command not guilty and Schacht was acquitted).

To protect and justify his position, Jackson sent a dossier to President Truman with a covering letter saying he found Donovan 'would not work in second place with anybody'. Truman backed Jackson and felt 'he was right to be rid of the bad apple.'[11]

In his letter to Donovan of 26 November 1946 Jackson wrote: 'You and I appear to have developed certain fundamental differences in viewpoint about this case. Time alone will tell which of us is right, but there can be no doubt that the case cannot follow both of our lines ... In short, I do not think we can afford to negotiate with any of these defendants or their counsel for testimony ... To use one of them ourselves will create the impression that there was some kind of bargain about his testimony, opening the door to that defendant to plead for leniency on the ground he was "helpful" and may give a background for claims that promises were made to that effect.'[12]

Jackson was being less than honest with this statement, for, on the very day he sent the letter to Donovan, the general received a memorandum from Jackson's deputy, Telford Taylor[13], indicating the prosecution was prepared to go along with such an arrangement in the case of Bach-Zelewski who, despite his responsibility for numerous war crimes and crimes against humanity, did not stand trial at the IMT, and instead appeared as a witness for the prosecution:

> On Jan. 7, 1946, General [then Colonel] Telford Taylor called to the stand SS Obergruppenfuehrer [General] Erich von dem Bach-Zelewski. He testified that at the beginning of the war he was a Higher SS and Police Leader in the central section of the campaign against the Soviet Union. 'My principal task was fighting partisans.' He stated that 'the principal task of the Einsatzgruppen [SS Task Force] was the annihilation of the Jews, Gypsies and political commissars.' At the end of 1942, he became the Chief of Anti-Partisan Combat Units for the entire Eastern Front. He confirmed that orders were issued by the highest authorities that German soldiers committing excesses were not to be punished in the military courts.[14]

Donovan replied to Jackson's letter of 26 November the following day, and concluded by suggesting Jackson was not up to the job:[15]

> It is true that I have frequently told you squarely and honestly that
>
> (1) the case needed centralized administrative control.
> (2) that there was a lack of intellectual direction.
> (3) that it was not handled as an entity.
> (4) that because it was a lawsuit plus something else it needed an affirmative human aspect with German as well as foreign witnesses.
>
> I never knew that there was ever disagreement on these points.
> As I told you several weeks ago I am leaving within a few days.
> Time will not be concerned with our opinions – right or wrong.

That last sentence was in response to the re-emphasised final comment in Jackson's letter: 'I repeat that time may prove you right and me wrong. I do not claim any great wisdom in so novel and complex a matter. I only have responsibility.'

Three days later, on 30 November, Donovan and Putzell left the IMT and had nothing further to do with the trial. Donovan had seen the writing on the wall much earlier, and that had persuaded him to state 'I told you several weeks ago I am leaving within a few days'. This would fit in with the most likely time Putzell passed the poison to Goering as being between the 6 November, when Donovan had had the crucial meeting with Goering, and 12 November (referred to in Stahmer's memo of the 15 November) when it is clear the Reichsmarschall's whole attitude had changed and he was cooperating fully with Donovan's plan. The unusual conditions at play on 6 November were described in exactly the same way by Wolfe Frank, recalling the day he said he later realised Goering was concealing something in his mouth.

'Time' isn't entirely clear who was right or wrong. Jackson's opening and closing statements at the IMT were of the highest order and are still considered to be amongst the finest examples of courtroom oratory, but his examination and cross-examination of the defendants in general, and Goering in particular, was weak, as Airey Neave, who witnessed it all, records:

> Soon Jackson was overwhelmed by his documents and in his resonant voice, Goering offered to help him … Goering was in the driving seat. He had immense knowledge and was a master of the detail of captured documents … After the first day, Jackson was said to be 'beside himself' and 'distraught' … Soon there was an atmosphere of panic in the American camp. Jackson had completely lost his nerve … I was appalled to see that Jackson was near to tears … Goering smiled his wide, triumphant smile and looked directly at me as if to say, 'What do you think of that?' Then he swaggered back to the dock as if he were still the Reichsmarschall.[55]

At the end of the day, however, Jackson did succeed in proving nineteen of the twenty-four Nazi war criminals were guilty as charged and he ensured that twelve of them, including Hermann Goering, were sentenced to death by hanging. It had however taken him ten months to do so, and instead of getting the Reichsmarschall to acknowledge his role in the atrocities at an early stage, as Donovan would have done, the prosecution was forced to laboriously go through, and prove, every point – not only with Goering, but also with all the other defendants.

Donovan, on the other hand, was right about Jackson's limitations in the courtroom. British Alternate Judge Norman Birkett later wrote, 'The cross-examination had not proceeded more than ten minutes before it was seen that Goering was the complete master of Mr. Justice Jackson'[16]. Telford Taylor also said that his boss 'paid dearly for his tactical blunder, in both public prestige and his own discontent.' Donovan's approach would have achieved the same results in a fraction of the time and would have seen Goering accepting responsibility, implicating and condemning the other war criminals at an early stage and avoiding the disaster of the suicide and the horrendous condemnations that followed. The only real difference between the two heavyweight lawyers' objectives were that Donovan would have been seen as the 'star' and Goering's sentence would have allowed him to die by firing squad rather than by the rope.

Was Wolfe Frank the Witness?

Throughout both the IMT and the Subsequent Proceedings, Wolfe Frank was the 'star' interpreter at Nuremberg, gaining accolades from every quarter, as this selection confirms:

His Superior's View 'Wolfe Frank's performance was most excellent and, indeed, may be described as brilliant ...he is an outstanding expert in not only simultaneous interpretation, but in the selection and training of interpreters for this very difficult work.' *Brigadier General Telford Taylor, US Chief of Counsel for War Crimes (in a testimonial).*

A Judges View 'Wolfe Frank, Ace Interpreter at the Nuremberg International War Crimes Trials, and so far as I am concerned the whole world round.' *Judge Michael Musmanno, one of the Presiding Judges at Nuremberg (on a signed photo – See Plate 13).*

A Prosecutor's View 'Frank's translations were delicious. He had a great command of the English Language. I used to go to the courtroom sometimes in the afternoon just to listen to him. *Henry T. King Jr., a US prosecutor at Nuremberg: The Nuremberg Context Through the Eyes of the Participant.*

A Colleague's View 'Frank was the best. He could interpret just as deftly from German to English as the other way around, and was able to keep up with any speaker, no matter how fast.' *Lieutenant Colonel Peter Uiberall (Chief German Translator at the IMT) Origins of Simultaneous Interpretation.*

A Newspaper's View 'Wolfe Frank, ex-German and ex-British officer, as chief interpreter for two years at the Nuremberg trials materially contributed to the practical success of those enormously difficult procedures. He won the unreserved tributes of the American and British jurists.' *New York Herald Tribune*

A Reporter's View 'By common accord Captain Wolfe Frank, translating from German into English, who came to Nuremberg in British uniform and returned as a civilian, was the ace of them all.' *R.W. Cooper, correspondent of The Times and author of The Nuremberg Trial (1947).*

Historians' Views 'No one was ever unreasonable enough to expect all the translators to reach the standard of the ace of them all – Wolfe Frank ... his use of German and English was noticeably better than that of most native speakers. His voice and manner, the nuances of his vocabulary, the ability to convey the character of the person for whom he was translating were all outstanding.' *John and Ann Tusa, The Nuremberg Trial.*

On 1 October 1946: Ten months and six million translated words after the IMT had commenced and Donovan and Putzell had left Nuremberg, Wolfe Frank 'the ace of them all' acquired the epithet 'The Voice of Doom' as he spoke the final words that brought down the curtain on the Third Reich, announcing to the Nazi war criminals the sentences imposed upon them. Hermann Goering was the first to learn that his punishment would be 'death by the rope'. The thin smile he gave Frank at that point may have been a dog whistle that only Frank, and possibly Neave and even Wheelis – would have understood.

This would mean Frank, assuming he was Putzell's 'colleague' and the witness to his actions, and Goering had kept the cyanide capsule a secret for almost a year. This length of time would allow for some of the theories explaining the possible hiding places of the capsule, for Frank and Goering had nothing but contempt for Colonel Andrus' ability to find the item under the regime the commandant had implemented. Goering insolently referred to Andrus as the 'Fire Brigade Colonel'[54] because of the shiny lacquered helmet he wore and Frank is even more cutting in his final comments on these events:

Let us return to the somewhat simple-minded Colonel Andrus. He certainly instituted searches and controls of the prisoners. It went something like this: Every Monday: search blankets. Every Tuesday: look under the seats of the toilets in the cells. Wednesday: windowsills. Thursday: the prisoner's mouths. Friday: the rectum; and so on and so forth. The odds in favour of the brilliant mind of a Goering versus such military non-ingenuity must have been enormous. Goering had no other aim or purpose than to outwit his jailers. He succeeded.[17]

Major Neave states in his book: 'after his [Goering's] plea to be shot had been refused [lastly on 13 October 1946], he bit the phial of potassium cyanide [on 15 October], which he had <u>long concealed,</u> and died'[18]. Neave was a lawyer who chose his words carefully. He is not speculating with this comment, he is making a statement, suggesting (perhaps as a member of the 'British contingent') that he *knew* Goering had <u>'long concealed'</u> the cyanide and that it had not been made available to him, as some have suggested, shortly before his death. There is another comment from Major Neave indicating he knew more than he was able, or prepared, to disclose: 'In Fleet Street, twelve months exactly since the day of the indictment, I read the news of Goering's suicide in the *Evening Standard*. I could scarcely repress a laugh. <u>The old rascal had got away with it.</u>'[19]

In making a 'deal' with Goering, General Donovan had lived up to his reputation of being 'a bold innovator and imprudent rule bender' (*New York Times*). He could not share the knowledge of his 'deal' with other US prosecutors – and it is known he ordered guards to wait outside interrogation rooms during his interrogations of Goering. He and/or Putzell did however need an interpreter, and Frank was the perfect candidate. Putzell confirms Donovan had 'the agreement of the British contingent' – and Frank and Neave, who had arrived in Nuremberg ahead of their colleagues, seem to have been the 'British contingent' – to give Goering cyanide, and in Frank they had the finest interpreter, (much needed to deal with any delicate 'unrecorded' matters to ensure there were no misunderstandings), a British Army Captain, who could be relied upon to keep secrets and who, like Donovan, was 'a bold innovator and imprudent rule bender.'

The general and the interpreter were kindred spirits, and they had history. Donovan had sanctioned Frank's request to allow Rudolf Diels, the former head of the Gestapo, to stay with him in British Army quarters rather than in jail with the rest of the Nazis, and when Jackson had Diels arrested for non-cooperation with his prosecution team, it was Donovan who, at Frank's behest, had Diels released – and then allowed him to live with his former mistress as Frank had also requested. With regards to this arrangement Frank commented 'This was, of course, monumentally irregular and pleased me enormously since breaking rules was, and still is, one of my favourite pastimes'[20]. Frank also confirmed: 'Donovan had been involved in some intelligence activities in Berlin [pre-US involvement in the Second World War] where Diels had met him when he was in the Ministry of the Interior and before he became a head of Gestapo.'[20]

(As a consequence of his relationship with Donovan, Jackson's team were never convinced of Diels' reliability and in the trials they used his evidence sparingly, however he was called upon as a witness by both the prosecution and Goering, to whom he was related through marriage).

The IMT lasted ten months – a year including the two month Preparations. During this time Frank and Goering came to know each other very well. Frank had easier access to Goering than most and, it seems, could see the prisoner whenever he pleased – even for the flimsiest of reasons and his own devious purposes (such as to impress a girlfriend by letting her sit in on a contrived interrogation).

In his memoirs Frank makes detailed comments on Goering's Suicide yet he points the finger of suspicion at no one and ridicules only the prison commandant, a man he clearly did not like, for not finding the capsule. He also indicates that he and Goering knew the daily search routine of cells and prisoners off by heart and in detail.

It is quite clear that Frank thought justice had been done at Nuremberg and that along with the other war criminals Goering deserved to die – and here a choice of words he used in an interview he gave to a journalist years later is interesting[21] – 'Nobody who got <u>hanged</u> shouldn't have been'. However it is also most likely he: (a) agreed with Donovan/Putzell's intentions; (b) thought Goering's wish to be allowed to 'die as a soldier' should have been granted; and (c) was a witness to the facilitating of that wish – as he said he was – certainly those who knew Frank well in his final days and had discussed these events with him then, and amongst themselves after his demise, had thought so!

Bravest of the Brave

There is no doubt either that Donovan, Putzell, Frank and Neave were amongst the bravest of their countries' armed forces. Unique, talented, intelligent, resourceful individuals driven by an overwhelming sense of duty and honour, they brought all these characteristics into play whilst making courageous stands against the enemy.

Of the action during the First World War, which earned Donovan the Medal of Honor, his alma mater, Columbia College, records:

At the Second Battle of the Marne, he [Donovan] went into combat wearing his decorations and insignia, as if daring the Germans to target him. 'They can't hit me and they won't hit you!' he shouted. Though shot in the knee, attacked by gas and showered with the shreds of three of his men, he threatened to court-martial anyone who tried to get him off the field.[66]

American author and historian Evan Thomas (who was granted historical access to classified CIA files) in a 2011 edition of *Vanity Fair* profile on General Donovan, entitled *Spymaster General*, observed: 'Donovan's exploits are utterly improbable but by now well documented in declassified wartime records that portray a brave, noble, headlong, gleeful, sometimes outrageous pursuit of action and skullduggery.' Thomas gives an excellent example of that description, and Donovan's own references to suicide pills, as follows:[22]

> On June 7, 1944 – D-day Plus One – General William J. Donovan ... landed on Utah Beach in Normandy. His presence in the combat zone had been strictly forbidden by his superiors in Washington, in order to protect the spymaster and his secrets from being captured. Donovan, characteristically, ignored the order ... On Utah Beach, Donovan and his commander of covert operations in Europe, Colonel David K. E. Bruce ... Advancing toward a hedgerow, the two O.S.S. officers suddenly ran into German machine-gun fire. Flattened on the ground, Donovan turned to Bruce and said, 'David, we mustn't be captured. We know too much.' Bruce mechanically answered, 'Yes, sir.' Donovan then inquired, 'Have you the pill?' Bruce confessed that he was not carrying the death pellet concocted by the O.S.S.'s scientific adviser, Stanley Lovell. 'Never mind,' replied Donovan. 'I have two of them.' [then realising he too had forgotten the cyanide capsules Donovan continued] ... if we are about to be captured, I'll shoot you first. After all, I am your commanding officer.

Wherever Donovan went, and whatever Donovan did during the Second World War, Edwin Putzell was, more often than not, by his side. So often the lieutenant matched his friend and superior officer, stride for stride, and the affection and loyalty was very much a two way affair, as Putzell indicated: 'I was in Rome in June of '44, I know that, because, you know, I got jaundice, and Donovan flew me back, nursed me personally, in the DC 4 we had all the way back to Washington from Rome.'[61]

Amongst the most audacious schemes the duo dreamt up was the 1943 planned abduction of Adolf Hitler – whilst the Fuehrer was aboard a yacht at sea. 'We were going to surface by submarine and board the damn thing and kidnap Hitler' Putzell told the *Naples Daily*

News 'it was well thought out. We'd even rehearsed the damn thing ... President Franklin Delano Roosevelt foiled the plan because he thought it might set a precedent for kidnapping future heads of state'. Putzell was reluctant to say more about the detail of his work but he did say: 'I could tell you stories about being in a haystack scared to death, carrying a cyanide <u>pill</u>'.[62] (We know from former OSS agent Helias Doundoulakis that '[OSS] Agents were issued a <u>"Q" pill</u> which was a glass vial, filled with cyanide ... enough for a "quick" death).'

Wolfe Frank's exploits were, at times, no less daring: before the war when he was a resistance worker involved in smuggling endangered Jews and large amounts of money out of Nazi Germany; during the war in the Pioneer Corps and as a second lieutenant in the Royal Northumberland Fusiliers; and during the 'Cold War', when he went undercover to write his acclaimed series of articles for the *New York Herald Tribune* under the series title *'Hangover After Hitler.'* Whilst on this assignment, with the help of Rudolf Diels, he single-handedly captured and interrogated the Nazi general, ranked fourth on the Allies 'most wanted' list, who had been earmarked to head the SS in Great Britain.

The *NYHT* was well aware of the dangers Wolfe Frank faced on this assignment, as this this unsympathetic exchange of memos between executives C. Patrick Thompson and Bruel Weare clearly indicates:[67]

[Thompson]: He [Frank] might not come back; but that would be his and our bad luck. He wants insurance against death or accident.

[Weir]: I frankly do not believe we should go into the business of insuring his life. That's his lookout. If he wants to do something safe he'd better forget the newspaper business.

In Airey Neave, General Donovan knew he had an ally who matched him in every way – a brave war hero, a trained lawyer, a fearless prosecutor, a chief spymaster and an officer prepared to take a risk for the right cause, as his biographer, Paul Routledge, indicated, Neave was 'adventurous and unconventional' in his approach to warfare and that his units were referred to as being 'irregulars.' Routledge summed his character up by suggesting 'Neave' was an officer in an invading army and had to obey orders, but there was a freelance feel to his military activities.'

Neave had remained with Room 900 for the rest of the war and his main responsibilities included: supporting underground escape organizations in occupied Europe, with equipment, agents, and money;

and assisting downed Allied airmen and other military personnel evade and escape capture by the Germans. (Following the war he returned to the legal profession and became an MP, but he also remained undercover with MI6).

Service, Fairness, Compassion and Understanding

Besides their bravery, Donovan, Putzell, Frank and Neave possessed other admirable qualities, amongst the foremost of which was their unshakeable commitment to service, fairness, loyalty, kindness and compassion. My narrative thus far may have already demonstrated this, however as further evidence of these characteristics I give the following examples:

General William Donovan, in spite of the irretrievable breakdown in his relationship with Jackson, nonetheless came to the justice's rescue during one further, rather poignant, last meeting between the two men that highlighted: the vulnerability of Jackson, who had overall responsibility for running the IMT; the overriding authority, grace and compassion of General Donovan, the man whose services the Justice had decided were no longer required; and the painful personal side of their disagreement.

Shortly before Donovan left Nuremberg, a difficult moment had arisen for Jackson when a guard, who knew who the justice was but who, following the orders of Secretary General Mitchell, barred him from leaving the courtroom, of which he was in charge, until it was adjourned. What followed is recorded by Josef Persico, sourcing Robert Jackson's own oral history (held at Columbia University): 'Jackson reddened' [and was pondering what to do next when]: 'He heard a firm, quiet voice over his shoulder "I outrank General Mitchell and I say open the door". Jackson turned to see Wild Bill Donovan. The guard quickly complied, and the two men stepped out. They greeted each other awkwardly. After this purely ceremonial appearance, Donovan would be flying home. Jackson wished it had turned out better between them.'[60]

In that moment Jackson will have been shocked to realise, in addition to the 170 plus loyal Donovan lawyers he had on the prosecution team, in reality he commanded less respect and authority than the general. Donovan would have known this, and it is to his credit that, rather than capitalise on his position of strength with an in-fight or a power struggle – that would have benefited no one – he left Jackson to show the world that, in the courtroom at least, and unlike the General, he was no match for Hermann Goering.

Lieutenant Edwin Putzell, as late as 2001, and at the age of eighty-eight, was still showing tact and understanding. When asked by a journalist to comment on a delicate diplomatic matter suggesting that: 'OSS operatives in occupied France continually complained that members of the fabled "La Resistance" were often merely bandits who stole their equipment and held their agents for ransom'. Putzell's typically measured response was: 'Regardless of the country or the era, you don't change human beings very much, or their instincts ... Their basic drives, good and bad, are always there.'[62]

On another occasion, when Putzell was asked to comment on General Donovan's relationship with Justice Jackson he wouldn't take sides, all he would say was: 'It wasn't a very good one ... Everything about them was different personality-wise and Donovan's theory of how to handle the trial and Jackson's were totally different ... He had some attitudes towards Goering and a bunch of them that Jackson and he didn't agree on ... there was a fundamental philosophical difference. That's why Donovan pulled out.'[75]

Major Airey Neave, who had suffered so much under the Nazis, often stood up for the war criminals during the proceedings whenever he felt the law wasn't being followed to the letter, or if he felt the slightest element of unfairness was creeping into the tribunal. This sometimes involved him confronting the judges and arguing the defendants case. On this point he later wrote: 'I now spoke on behalf of the top Nazis, my former captors. This extraordinary reversal of fortune was not lost upon the judges as they considered my pleas.'[74]

Captain Wolfe Frank, bent over backwards to ensure that everything communicated to and by the defendants was conveyed exactly in the tone and manner in which it was said. Of the 'off the record' meetings he had with Goering, Frank wrote: 'at no time during the entire trial was there a complaint, or even a challenge, directed at the interpreters.'[63]

Frank ensured that politeness and courtesy were at all times extended to everyone involved in the trial including the defendants. Albert Speer, Minister of Armament and War Production in Nazi Germany requested, and was granted, a private audience with Frank, he wrote in his memoirs *Inside the Third Reich:* 'In the courtroom, however, we encountered only hostile faces, icy dogmas.' Then, no doubt with Frank in mind, he continued: 'The only exception was the interpreters' booth. From there I might expect a friendly nod.'

This kind of commitment to preciseness and cordiality seemed to get under the skin of some of the judges, with Mr Justice Birkett writing of the interpreting collective: 'Touchy, vain, unaccountable, puffed up with self-importance of the most explosive kind, inexplicably egotistical, and as a rule violent opponents of soap and sunlight.'[64] These comments could not have extended to Wolfe Frank whose appearance and deportment were universally admired. He was always professional, disciplined and immaculately turned out, be that in Army uniform or, following his mid trial transfer to the Foreign Office, his Savile Row suits – an incident that raised eyebrows as Frank recorded: 'My twenty-one "clients" in the dock looked up with interest when I appeared in a new suit. There were even some barely concealed grins. Schacht, who sat nearest to the English booth, slowly nodded approval.'[65]

Summary of My Thoughts

It is a fact that Lieutenant Edwin Putzell, a man of the highest standing and integrity, openly admitted that it was he who passed cyanide to Hermann Goering on the instructions of his Commanding Officer and mentor, spymaster General William Donovan, Head of the world's largest, most successful, most clandestine cloak-and-dagger agency who was 'a law unto himself' (Donovan may have been officially classified as being subordinate to the Joint Chiefs of the US armed forces, but in reality he answered to no one. Putzell was answerable only to Donovan. Neave and Frank could be 'mavericks' for the good of a worthy cause. All four were interrogating Goering during the preparations – i.e. up to 20 November 1945).

Putzell also admitted he carried out the transfer of the poison 'with the agreement of the British contingent' in the presence of a 'colleague' – and clearly, for a duty of this magnitude and importance, he would have required the services of an interpreter. Wolfe Frank was the ace interpreter at Nuremberg, who had been 'assigned' to interrogations during the preparations and (fifteen years prior to Putzell's revelations) he admitted to friends that he had witnessed the transfer of the poison to Goering. He was a 'colleague', trusted implicitly by Donovan, Putzell and Goering, who delighted in 'monumentally irregular' activities and 'breaking the rules'. He was also the man most capable of translating to all parties exactly what was being said – in German or English, in the precise and unambiguous manner that was his hallmark.

Donovan and Putzell were *THE* leading practitioners of the 'dark arts of espionage' who instructed the 'Q' of US covert operations, and counted the 'M' of MI5 and the creator of James Bond amongst their closest allies and advisers. The OSS' existence and reputation was built, and operated throughout, on their leadership and subtle skills of subterfuge, including sleight of hand – to them negotiating through, and with, those involved in their world-wide network of allied, foreign, enemy and even 'double' agents, and surreptitiously passing on items (including poison capsules) in ingenious and undetectable ways, was routine.

Facilitating an assisted suicide in a 'home environment' would have been one of the spymaster duos easier tasks, especially when, other than Putzell's 'colleague', there were no other witnesses and the person they intended to outwit – Colonel Andrus – was considered to be a man of limited ability who had already 'lost two' prisoners, who had taken their own lives while under his supervision in the 'suicide proof' jail he had so proudly introduced to the world.

General Donovan was not only the most senior military officer at the IMT, he had his agents in every corner of the proceedings (172 officially, many more unofficially), and at every level of administration at Nuremberg, in Washington, throughout the Allied armed forces and in the wider world. It is not beyond the realms of possibility that he could have, in some way, influenced the subsequent investigation, its terms of reference, its membership, and who was, and more importantly, who was not investigated. One thing is certain. Donovan was 'adored' by those who served under him. They knew whatever they were asked to do was sanctioned by their nation's most decorated war hero and was adjudged by him to be for the good of their country. They knew also: they would not, under any circumstances, be abandoned by the commanding officer who would never 'ask anyone to take a risk that he himself would not take'; and the general would, at all times be looking after their welfare and best interests. As Charles Pinck, President of the OSS Society, stated: 'In an organization whose personnel volunteered for the most dangerous missions of World War II, one can only imagine the powerful effect that Donovan's example had on those who served under his command. Donovan made it clear that he was willing to risk his life, not just the lives of others.'[2]

The people most involved with the interrogation of Goering during the 'Preparations' were: (a) Donovan – who had had ten unrecorded 'private meetings' with the Reichsmarschall and had agreed a 'deal' with him; (b) Putzell who confessed to having given Goering the cyanide that killed him; (c) Frank who admitted to meeting Goering 'many times off the record' and being a witness to the transfer of the poison; and (d) Neave, the MI9 secret agent, who along with Wolfe Frank, appear to have been the 'British contingent' in Nuremberg at that time. Goering respected them all, and they, in turn, had a (perhaps grudging) respect for the way the Reichsmarschall had 'provided valuable information to the Allies' and had conducted himself during the trial. Neave records: 'His enemies acknowledged his courage ... Murderer he might have been, but he was a brave bastard too.'[56]

As with Harry Shotwell, perhaps Ned Putzell took the unexpected opportunity presented by Ms Wyatt's unscheduled visit and questioning – in the last months of his life, and after almost sixty years of keeping a monumental secret – to simply set the record straight while he still had time to do so. Perhaps also, to protect others, this was a story that could only be told by the last survivor of an extraordinary incident that had shocked the world in 1945.

Wolfe Frank may well have been thinking the same when he decided to make his revelation to friends late in his life. The Official Secrets Act would have prevented him from ever openly mentioning any such matters in which he might have been involved, and to have fallen foul of authorities in 1945/6 could have put his British Citizenship application at risk (it was not granted until October 1948). He would also have been bound by the US version of the Official Secrets Act, as well as Donovan's OSS/CIC code. He would have known too, that anyone associated with assisting Goering achieve his objective could be charged with any or all of the following: (a) being involved, or knowing about, an act that prevented the decision, sentence and punishment of the IMT from being implemented; (b) sabotage; (c) aiding a foreign convicted mass murderer avoid the punishment imposed by the court; (d) assisting a suicide; and (e) betrayal or even treason. Frank was in a very vulnerable position – Donovan and Putzell had returned to the US almost a year earlier, and Major Neave had left Nuremberg well before the time of the suicide.

Frank was therefore very much on his own. He was, however, a meticulous planner and forward thinker so often able to manoeuvre his way out of difficult situations. Throughout his life he considered all the consequences well in advance (right up to and including his own suicide), and he planned accordingly – including the provisions of escape routes and 'get out of jail cards' if necessary. In writing about the crucial moment he says he realized Goering was concealing something in his mouth Frank may, in mentioning this to his journalist 'friend' (Tom Reedy of Associated Press), have been preparing the basis of an acceptable 'cover' story – one that would stand up to scrutiny should he ever be placed in a position where he was asked to account for any observations he may have noticed on a day when he might have acted as the interpreter at a crucial meeting that had taken place between Putzell and Goering.

Frank may also have been laying the basis of a thread of a much wider, meticulously planned, scenario, for Major Neave's almost identical account of this incident raises the possibility of it being part of a 'cover story' put in place to add weight, if ever it was needed, to the suggestion Goering had had the poison with him when he arrived in Nuremberg. Britain's two leading interrogators, at that time, being prepared to state they 'later realised Goering was concealing something in his mouth, the very first time they came into contact with him prior to the start of the IMT', would be a huge endorsement of any Donovan-led strategy to get the Control Board to conclude: Goering had the poison on him all the time; no one attached to the prison was to blame; and no one unconnected with the prison should ever come under suspicion.

(As an example of Frank's planning for all eventualities, before he commenced his 1949 'undercover' Cold War project as a reporter for the *New York Herald Tribune* the editor recorded: 'It was first cleared with the Allied Military Authorities in Western Germany. Though they are in no way responsible for his findings, his survey was made with their foreknowledge[23]' and, as Frank states in his memoirs – through the personal involvement of General Huebner, Acting Military Governor of the American Zone – 'an off-the-record arrangement was made whereby I had a contact in the US Army through which I could get myself fished out of any German prison').[24]

As it was, and as perhaps Donovan/Putzell had hoped and planned, The Board of Officers, under the direction of the Allied Control Council, confined its investigations entirely to the prison block and any guards and other prison personnel who had come into contact with Goering in the fourteen days prior to the suicide. During its search of the prison, The Board discovered another 'similar' cartridge case with the poison capsule still inside hidden in a jar of Vaseline in 'a fitted bag' belonging to Goering located 'in the prison store room, to which Goering never had access'[25]. Goering had directed The Board's attention to the location of this further device in his suicide note to Colonel Andrus (see below): 'The third capsule is still in my toilet case in the round container of skin cream (hidden in the cream).'

It is important to remind readers of The Board's 'Conclusion' and 'Findings' – Once again, The Board's words are interspersed with my comments and/or explanations *printed in italics*.

The Conclusion of The Board was:[25]

Reasonable safeguards had been planned and executed for the prevention of suicide by any one of the condemned. The fact that Goering succeeded in committing suicide is attributed to his cunning and not to dereliction on the part of any individual or group of individuals connected with the administration of the prison in which he had been confined.

Leaving aside the question of 'whitewash', Goering himself could have written this conclusion, in fact he practically did in the suicide note he left for Colonel Andrus:

'Since my imprisonment I have always kept the poison capsule on my person. I had three capsules when I was committed to prison in Mondorf. The first one I left in my clothing, so that it would be found in the search. The second I left under the coat-stand while undressing and took it again when I dressed. I hid this in Mondorf and here in the cell so well that, in spite of the frequent and very thorough searches, it could not be found. During the trial I kept it in my high riding boots. The third capsule is still in my toilet case in the round container of skin cream (hidden in the cream). I had two opportunities to take the capsule in Mondorf, had I needed it. No one in charge of the searches was at fault, since it was almost impossible to find the capsule. It would have been purely by chance [signed] Hermann Goering.

[P.S.] Doctor Gilbert told me that the Control Council rejected the change in the manner of execution to death by firing squad[signed] Goering'.

The Board's 'Findings', were:[25]

1. That the small brass container containing the suicide poison was in the possession of Goering at the time he was taken into custody by the American Army.

This statement may be correct in its entirety if Lieutenant Putzell returned to Goering one of the two capsules that had been found amongst his possessions when he was captured. In any case, whether it was one of his own or some other capsule the OSS had obtained (discussed earlier) from another other source, Putzell's revelations confirm Goering had only had the capsule that killed him in his possession since the time of the preparations (i.e. not before 3 October 1945 and not later than 20 November – he had been taken prisoner in May).

2. That all reasonable safeguards were taken in the guarding of Goering, and that he was able to retain the poison in his possession through his own cleverness and thoughtful planning and that no individual or individuals connected

with the prison be held responsible for the death by suicide of Hermann Goering'.

The Board's Finding is entirely correct as far as General Donovan, Lieutenant Putzell and Captain Frank were concerned. Goering had been able to 'retain the poison in his possession through his own cleverness and thoughtful planning' for almost a year and they were never 'connected with the prison' and were, therefore, never questioned about these matters – nor was anyone else outside the prison.

The report was submitted to the four members of the Control Council, who discussed and accepted it on 30 October 1946. It has remained the official position ever since.

So What about Wheelis?

Before Edwin Putzell's admissions, the prime suspect for aiding Goering's suicide had been US Army guard Jack 'Tex' Wheelis. There is accepted evidence that he was very friendly with Goering who had given him several gifts.

In his book *Nuremberg – Infamy on Trial* Joseph Persico records: 'He [Goering] needed not antagonists but friends, like Tex Wheelis. He had already given Wheelis a handsome watch. Within the next few days, he managed to have a gold cigarette case extracted from his luggage in the baggage room, and he gave it to the lieutenant.[26]

Persico also records:

Tex Wheelis was a controversial man whose brash camaraderie split people between admirers and detractors. He and Goering got along famously. Recently, Wheelis had had his picture taken with Goering who inscribed it 'to the great Texas hunter'. One night at the Grand, Wheelis had shown a handsome silver watch to his friends. He turned it over and revealed the engraved signature of Hermann Goering. Goering had given it to him as a gift, he boasted.[27]

(This is the watch that Ben Swearingen, amongst other mementoes, had purchased from Wheelis' widow).[28]

Brigadier General Eugene Phillips, who knew Wheelis well at Nuremberg, recalled him as being 'a gregarious and skilled raconteur who was always surrounded by an eager coterie of friends anxious to hear his stories – whether of his military experiences, his contacts with Hermann Goering, or amusing regional anecdotes'

Another officer, Colonel Gerald R. Wilson, held a different view and told Swearingen he remembered Wheelis as being an 'opportunist' and that 'after Goering killed himself, there was much talk among the Nuremberg officer's about Wheelis's close relationship with the former Reichsmarschall.' The talk intensified after Wheelis was 'suddenly gone' from the Nuremberg scene. 'I didn't see him again for a month' Colonel Wilson said. 'No one knew where Wheelis had gone nor the reason for his departure, but his absence added fuel to the fire of controversy that surrounded him'. Repeated attempts by Wilson to discuss the matter with senior officers were cut short and he was told not to raise the matter again.

While Lieutenant Putzell's admissions make clear it was not Wheelis who handed Goering the cyanide capsule, there is room to believe that he could well have played a role in both the incident itself and a possible diversion that followed.

Wheelis might have been the officer guarding Goering at the time of the Putzell transfer and he may have been persuaded/instructed/ ordered to wait outside or look the other way whilst Putzell/Frank had a quiet word with the Reichsmarschall in his cell – or in the interrogation room used by Donovan – where it is known (from Harry Shotwell's testimony) the general forcefully ordered guards 'not to hear a single word uttered in this room'– (Donovan may have asked his agents 'if they'd like to get killed' in the friendliest of ways, however he was also capable of making hardened war heroes run for the toilet after he had given them a dressing down, as Sergeant Shotwell ruefully recalled in his recorded interview).

There is however another, far more subtle, way Wheelis could have played a part in the suicide plot, that, it seems, has not occurred to others who have studied these matters – and this could be the reason why, during the year he had the capsule in his possession, the Reichsmarschall gave Wheelis so many mementoes.

I pose the following questions and then give answers as to why I feel such a scenario was more than plausible.

Was it possible that Jack Wheelis, like Harry Shotwell, was placed in a similar situation when: 'in October 1945 'out of the blue 'I and five other guards were ordered to go with two OSS Spooks ... I was told I was to follow the orders of these two men from now on?'

Was Wheelis: one of those 'five other guards'? Whether he was or not, on any occasion he accompanied Goering: did he hear something he was told 'not to hear'?; was he 'asked' to play a more prominent part in a clandestine operation?; and could that involvement be, not to pass to Goering a poison capsule taken from his 'toilet case' located in the baggage room of which he was in charge and had the key, but instead to take <u>into</u> that area, and place in Goering's toilet case, a jar of Vaseline with another capsule hidden in it?

Such a 'request' would have been: far easier to carry out and would allow Goering to be able, in his suicide note to Colonel Andrus, to draw attention to the capsule in the Vaseline jar – to convince The Board that 'No one in charge of the searches was at fault' and that he had had both capsules with him all the time – which is what The Board concluded and the Control Council accepted.[29]

Few historians and military researchers believe the thorough searches of Goering and his belongings that took place in Mondorf and Nuremberg would have missed the capsule in so obvious a place as the Vaseline jar and many more, including Ben Swearingen, believe The Board's findings and report were a 'whitewash.'

Some may consider such suggestions as I have outlined above to be fanciful and such possibilities to be far-fetched. On the surface that may appear so. However, I ask sceptics to consider the following:

General Donovan and Lieutenant Putzell were the world's leading espionage agents. In an interview he gave to *historynet* Douglas Waller spells out Donovan's ethos: 'Initially he recruited peers, friends on Wall Street [and people] from prominent families. He wanted to recruit [people] with upstanding character and said he "could teach them the dark arts of espionage when they came in." he also recruited people who already knew the dark arts – people from seamier backgrounds'[31]. Donovan also brought in people like Stanley Lovell who Donovan referred to as being his 'Professor Moriarty' (thought to be the inspiration for 'Q' in the James Bond books[32]). On appointment the general informed the chemist 'I need every subtle device and every underhanded trick to use against the Germans and the Japanese – You will have to invent all of them, Lovell, because you're going to be my man.'[33]

OSS Society President, Charles Pinck, in an article he wrote for *Small Wars Journal*, explained in more detail: the 'Donovan spirit'; the extent of the general's recruitment regime and autonomy; and his positive encouragement of those connected with the OSS to, if necessary, ignore conventional channels and to go way above their pay grades :[68]

The Office of Strategic Services (OSS) – the World War II predecessor to the C.I.A., the U.S. Special Operations Command, and the State Department's Bureau of Intelligence and Research –

was renowned for its innovation, experimentation, and risk-taking. CIA Director and OSS veteran William Casey described its ethos perfectly: 'You didn't wait six months for a feasibility study to prove that an idea could work. You gambled that it might work. You didn't tie up the organization with red tape designed mostly to cover somebody's rear end. You took the initiative and the responsibility. You went around end, you went over somebody's head if you had to. But you acted. That's what drove the regular military and the State Department chair-warmers crazy about the OSS.'

An OSS veteran said the OSS was 'the greatest collection of people in the history of the world.' They included Nobel laureate Ralph Bunche; Hollywood director John Ford; architect Eero Saarinen; the 'French Chef' Julia Child; actors Sterling Hayden and Marlene Dietrich; Virginia Hall, the only American woman who received the Distinguished Service Cross in World War II; Supreme Court Justice Arthur Goldberg; Jay Kilby, who invented the integrated circuit; and Col. William Eddy – the 'Lawrence of America,' to name just a few.

Its founder, the legendary General William 'Wild Bill' Donovan – the only American to receive our Nation's four highest decorations whom President Roosevelt called his 'secret legs' – welcomed seemingly outlandish ideas because he said you never knew where a good one might come from. Ambassador David Bruce, who served as one of General Donovan's closest deputies, said 'woe to the officer who turned down a project because, on its face, it seemed ridiculous or at least unusual.' Bruce said that Donovan's imagination was 'unlimited. Ideas were his plaything. Excitement made him snort like a race horse.'

Every aspect of every operation initiated and undertaken by Donovan and Putzell would have been planned and carried out with OSS military precision – Neave was their British counterpart and Frank was of the same ilk – and in this matter the spymasters intended to carry out one of their most audacious of 'tasks' that was destined to stun the world. They would have left nothing to chance, either during the transfer or afterwards. The whole operation would have been planned with exactitude, including a sub-plot that would divert attention away from anyone outside the Nuremberg prison. It must be remembered too that Donovan had 13,000 men under his command by the end of the war, 9,000 of whom were military personnel – men who operated undercover, and most often unknown to each other, who were active within every country, at every level of society and the armed forces – it is more than possible that the general called on the skills of some members of his 'league of gentleman' who 'adored' him to complete the 'task' without them knowing who else might have been involved. Perhaps he influenced, even verbally drafted, Goering's suicide note to Colonel Andrus to create the conditions that led The Board to 'discover' the second suicide capsule and to confine the investigation entirely and narrowly to those working within the prison who might have come into contact with Goering during the last two weeks of his life.

Certainly, that is what happened. Those who may have known something never spoke out. Donovan, 'the last hero', – like his counterpart Elliott Ness over at the FBI – was untouchable. Neave's endorsement of Frank's possible 'cover' story, and vice versa, has only recently come to light. Wheelis never revealed anything, and Shotwell and Frank only made their admissions in the final months of their lives. Likewise, Edwin Putzell kept this mission, among so many others in which he had been involved, secret from the world until shortly before he died – no doubt believing that as 'the last man standing' it was his duty to reveal what had really happened almost sixty years earlier during the Preparation period of the world's greatest trial.

OSS Manual

In 1944 General Donovan issued a 'Top Secret' manual for the guidance of those assigned to the OSS, permanently, or for a specific operation (this publication was probably written by Putzell who was drafting Donovan's speeches as early as 1937 and as late as 1946).[69] Entitled *Secret Intelligence Field Manual – Strategic Services (Provisional)*[34], the publication emphasised: 'In view of its highly secret nature, this manual will be given a very limited distribution'. Amongst its directives it gives the following explanations that would have applied to any personnel working with OSS – permanently or for a specific 'mission'. If they were involved, Wolfe Frank and Jack Wheelis would have fallen into this category – Wheelis was a serving soldier, and Frank was also on the US Army payroll and, during October/November 1945, had been 'assigned to pre-trial interrogations'. The clauses in the manual that would have applied to both men in the areas hereunder review, are as follows (once again my comments/clarifications are *printed in italics*):

- FIELD – all areas outside of the of the United States in which Strategic Services activities take place.

Nuremberg certainly fitted this description.

- MISSION – a statement of purpose set forth in a special program for the accomplishment of a given objective.

- TASK – a detailed operation, usually planned in the field, which contributes toward the accomplishment of a mission.

Frank's 'task' would have been to act as interpreter, and Wheelis', as suggested above.

- SUB-AGENT – an individual not a regular member of OSS who is employed and directed by an agent in the field. Sub-agents may be paid or they may be volunteers.

Neither Frank nor Wheelis were regular members of OSS, although Wheelis, like Harry Shotwell, may have been instructed to take his orders from OSS 'Spooks.'

- SI [Secret Intelligence] personnel are recruited from civilians or from the armed forces of the United States and its Allies. Military personnel of the United States armed forces may be assigned to OSS within authorized allotment and detailed SI activities.

Both Frank and Wheelis fell into this category.

- COVER – an open status, assumed or bona fide, which serves to conceal the secret activities of an operative or agent.

The regular duties of both Frank and Wheelis, as interpreter and guard respectively, would have served as their 'open status' – the perfect cover for concealing any 'secret activities'.

- The qualifications for SI personnel vary according to the requirements of the assignment. Members of OSS, Washington, or Field Base staffs are selected for integrity, intelligence, initiative, and for special qualifications fitting them for a particular job.

Frank and Wheelis had all these special qualifications for specific 'tasks' essential for successfully concluding the 'mission.'

- Undercover field operatives are, if possible, selected with specific cover jobs in view. Unless they can conform thoroughly to a reasonable cover, they cannot be used. Natural resourcefulness, energy, a broad general background, familiarity with the area, language fluency, patience, discretion, and judgment are important attributes. The operative should be able handle men, mix easily, judge character so as to be able to deal with agents. Unqualified loyalty to the United States and unqualified sympathy with the vigorous prosecution of the war by all methods are essential.

Both men lived up to all these requirements.

- In the event of capture by the enemy, a secret intelligence operative or agent should stick by his cover story and deny all charges. Despite the seriousness of his own position, he should not fail to protect to the end the security of the organisation of which he is a member.

Although not dealing with 'an enemy' this rule would apply in these particular circumstances. Wheelis stuck rigidly to his story, which was accepted by The Board and the Control Council, and to the end of his life never divulged any information he may have known about the suicide.

As in other tight situations in his life, such as when he was an underground resistance worker or working undercover during the Cold War, Frank would have had a pre-planned, highly believable, cover story. The same would have been true in such a situation as is here under consideration. In this case the capsule-in-the-mouth incident may well have been part of a cover story he and Neave may have intended to bring into play if needed.

- Wherever possible, agents should be recruited whose motives for working against the enemy are patriotic rather than financial. Remuneration should be regarded as a reward rather than as an inducement to render services. Many individuals, particularly in enemy-occupied territory, will serve as agents out of reasons of Patriotism.

Frank's patriotism has never been doubted and his performance at Nuremberg was considered to be one of the major contributing factors to the success of the trials and in achieving the convictions of the Nazi war criminals.

Wheelis was a true United States patriot. In 1984, author Ben Swearingen travelled to the former Lieutenant's home town of Mart, Texas and located Lieutenant Wheelis' grave in the local cemetery. 'I read the simple, yet proud, inscription on his gray [sic] marble marker –"Capt. Jack G. Wheelis" – and saw the crossed rifles of the U. S. Army Infantry carved into the stone' wrote Swearingen. The author also noted 'Beside the marker – and probably placed there on the fourth of July by the local veterans group – was a small faded American flag on a stick. The flag was listing precariously, and I instinctively righted it.'[35]

There is also a section in the manual dealing with the 'Evaluation of information':

(a) Information is evaluated both as to the reliability of the source and as to the truth, credibility, or probability of the information itself. The following rating scale is used in evaluating the source:

    A – Completely reliable
    B – Usually reliable
    C – Fairly reliable
    D – Not usually reliable
    E – Unreliable
    F – Untried

(b) The following rating scale is used in evaluating the truth, credibility, or probability of the information.

    1 – Report confirmed by other sources
    2 – Probably true
    3 – Possibly true
    4 – Doubtful
    5 – Improbable
    0 – Truth cannot be judged

Evaluation of Information

By applying these scales to the involvements of those who: were, say they were, or may have been present on the occasion a cyanide capsule was passed to the Reichsmarschall, the following results emerge:

Lieutenant Edwin Putzell: A1 or A2

In 1937, whilst still studying at Harvard, Lieutenant Putzell began drafting speeches for General Donovan. In 2002, shortly before the interview he gave to Ms Wyatt, and at the age of eighty-nine, he became the first recipient of the Greater Naples Leadership Award, given for 'moulding the geography of the city as well as the careers of future local leaders'. Throughout the intervening years, it appears he never once put himself forward for any position, but was approached and persuaded to accept the many roles he filled with such distinction – be that in the military, in business, the judiciary, industry, public office or as a champion of voluntary causes. Without exception, my researches have shown, Putzell was ever considered to be a man of impeccable honesty to whom others, at all levels of society from presidents to neighbours, trustingly turned for advice, guidance and representation.

Enough sources have shown that General Donovan had made a 'deal' with Hermann Goering that, in return for accepting full responsibility for the Nazi war crimes and implicating his fellow defendants, Donovan would ensure the Reichsmarschall would not be hanged as a common criminal. When Justice Jackson made it clear he was not prepared to agree to such a scheme; denied Donovan further access to Goering; and then turned down Goering's requests to be shot, Putzell states (in the interview he gave to Ms Wyatt): 'Donovan secretly decided, with the agreement of the British contingent, to let him die by cyanide'. Ms Wyatt then records: 'Putzell and a colleague handed one tablet to Goering'.

I repeat, I find it inconceivable, that a man of such integrity and standing as Edwin Putzell would, shortly before his death, 'invent' the statements he gave to Ms Wyatt in 2003 or in any way attach any kind of falsehood to the name of General Donovan, the man he most admired in a partnership he described as being: 'like father-and-son … a relationship which I will always treasure.'

For these reasons, as well as: the praise he attracted in all the positions of trust and responsibility he occupied throughout his life, I do not doubt the integrity of his admissions in the interview he gave to Ms Wyatt a few months before he died. I have no hesitation in rating 'the truth, credibility, or probability' of the 'source' and the 'information' as being 'A' – Completely reliable'. Because of this, my instincts lead me to believe '1' to be the rating for 'evaluating the truth, credibility, or probability of the information'. The only reason I hesitate between '1' and '2' is because the top rating requires that the 'Report' be 'confirmed by other sources'. If one accepts Wolfe Frank's admission as being the 'other source', and there were people who were convinced, then the rating for Lieutenant Putzell and the information he provided has to be 'A1!'

Captain Wolfe Frank: B2

Wolfe Frank, the ace interpreter at Nuremberg, was also held in high estimation by all who knew and worked with him. His fairness and dedication to duty greatly impressed all who were involved with him, or witnessed his performances, at the Nuremberg trials – perhaps best summed up by The Office of Chief Counsel for War Crimes: 'Wolfe Frank … superlative scholarship and administrative assistance … and intellectual integrity …satisfactory alike to the bench, the defence and the prosecution.'

Frank's reputation as an interpreter had preceded him, and it was General Eisenhower's personal interpreter and Head of Translations, Colonel Leon Dostert, who personally interviewed and immediately seconded Frank on to the USA team. Frank said of his interview:

> During our first meeting Dostert grilled me for two hours about my background, education, topical subjects, hobbies, contacts, references and my Army career. When we finished, he requested (ordered would have been more accurate) my transfer from Turrell's minions [BWCE] to his own staff [US Army]. The CO was upset. Here was the worst officer he had, getting the best job. He even put up some resistance and got himself into everybody's bad books[36].

Frank was a man of his word, who all concerned, including the Nazi war criminals, could trust. As in the cases of Edwin Putzell and Harry Shotwell, Frank never owned up to being present when suicide was discussed with Goering – until his last months. Frank ended his own life soon after in March 1988 – fifteen years before Putzell made his revelations, which included a 'colleague' being present on the occasion, 'with the agreement of the British contingent', that he had carried out General Donovan's instructions 'to let him [Goering] die by cyanide.'

Frank, who had arrived in Nuremberg by early October, was a 'colleague' of Putzell's who stated 'before the arrival of my colleagues [fellow interpreters] and the arrival of the equipment from IBM [15 November 1945] I was assigned to pre-trial [the preparation period] interrogations of the defendants to be'. Donovan and Putzell arrived 3 October and left on 30 November and they conducted their interrogations of Goering during the 'preparations' which ended on 20 November when the IMT began. (Airey Neave arrived ahead of other British prosecutors on 17 October and began his interrogations of Goering, along with Frank, the following day).

The unique set of circumstances that occurred on 6 November, as described by Donovan and recorded in *Wild Bill Donovan* on the occasion the General and Goering finalised the details of the 'deal' they made were:

> A large military detail mingled outside the interrogation room [on 6 November]. Rumors had circulated in Nuremberg that Nazi diehards still at large were hatching a plot to spring Goering from jail, he was under heavy guard.[37]

Wild Bill Donovan was first published in 2011. Sometime between 1950 and the early 1980s (not published until 2018), Wolfe Frank in his memoirs (that had languished in an attic for over twenty-five years) had described, in almost identical terms, the conditions that prevailed on the day he interviewed Goering and realised later that the Reichsmarschall had been concealing something in his mouth.

> Shortly after I had my first encounter with Hermann Goering. Intelligence reports had reached the security people in Nuremberg that all over Germany an unusual number of railway tickets were being purchased for Nuremberg. Unfounded rumours suggested that plans were afoot to kidnap Goering from jail. Security precautions in the courthouse had been dramatically increased and an order had been issued excluding him from the daily exercise period prisoners were allowed in the courtyard of the building.[38]

There can be no doubt that Frank is also describing the unique events that took place on 6 November. Goering's counsel Dr Stahmer's memo of 15 November confirms Goering had already started cooperating with Donovan's requests – and had been doing so since at least 12 November. Ben Swearingen's prison officer source, in suggesting Donovan was behind the transfer, also confirmed: 'Goering made a deal with Wild Bill Donovan … I know that Donovan talked to Goering and after that Goering's whole attitude changed' – these are statements suggesting the (unnamed for protection) prison officer, perhaps like Harry Shotwell, had been present when the 'deal' was done and had noticed the changed attitude of cooperation in Goering that ensued. This narrows the likely date when the transfer was made down to being on or after 6 November, and before the meeting Stahmer attended on 12 November.

Frank and Donovan were of similar character, and they lived up to their reputations of being brave, noble, gleeful and outrageous when they arranged for Rudolf Diels, the first head of the Gestapo, to be accommodated as a 'house guest' in Frank's quarters, instead of locked up in the prison at the Palace of Justice with the other Nazi war criminals. Frank was a man, Donovan and Putzell knew, who was not only as brave as they were, but one who delighted in being involved in 'monumentally irregular' practices which, he said, 'pleased me enormously since breaking rules was, and still is, one of my favourite pastimes.' This derring-do spirit was entirely in line with the Donovan ethos, as Charles Pinck, President of the OSS Society (whose father, Daniel C. Pinck, served under the general) described in his article *Remembering The Last Hero:*[2] 'Donovan frequently told OSS personnel that they "could not succeed without taking chances" or engaging in what he termed "calculated recklessness." An ideal OSS candidate was described as a "PhD who could win a bar fight".'

Clearly the rules were broken in a monumentally irregular way when the cyanide was passed to Goering, an event Frank told a handful of friends he had witnessed. His record above, with its identical description to that of General Donovan's, confirms he was with Goering the same day as the general (6 November 1945). The only thing wrong with Frank's statement is that he says this was his first meeting with Goering, which it wasn't, for Major Neave's records clearly show he and Frank had been meeting with the Reichsmarschall since 18/19 October.

One can only guess as to why this has occurred: perhaps a gap of up to forty years between the event and him writing the record had dimmed Frank's memory, and he had merged two meetings into one; or perhaps, and this is much more likely, he was following Donovan's directive to OSS operatives 'assigned under special programs to field activities' – that was: 'to stick by his cover story and deny all charges.'

This would have been nothing out of the ordinary for Frank who was already a master of such tactics and adopted them many times throughout his life in England, Germany, elsewhere in Europe and the USA – with astonishing success and almost always without suspicion. This is perfectly described by Frank himself in his outline to the editor-in-chief of the *New York Herald Tribune* prior to his six-month undercover assignment in Germany during the Cold War period:[57]

Dear Mr Parsons ...Since talking to you in Paris I have, of course, given the matter considerable thought. The most serious problem would appear to be that once I am in Germany and have become a member of the German population I will have to account for my prolonged absence from that country. It would be no good posing as a returned prisoner of war. This would simply multiply the number of people who might find me out by the number of other ex-prisoners of war who were imprisoned under similar circumstances. In other words it would require a complete knowledge of units, locations, names of officers and so on and so forth, which it would take months to acquire.

To cut a long story short I propose to appear as a young man who, early in 1939, was sent to Switzerland with Tuberculosis. He went to Davos, a place known to all Germans, was still there requiring treatment when war broke out and who, being somewhat opposed to the Nazi Regime, had decided not to follow the call to arms of his Fatherland, but to stay on in Switzerland. When his lungs got better he took a job in a sports shop, and during the summer he worked as a keeper of the local tennis courts. In 1949 he got himself into trouble through doing a bit of black marketeering and the Swiss chucked him out of the country.

Having friends in Davos I shall be able to substantiate this tale with some testimonials and it has the advantage that I know conditions there so well that I could not be caught out by any questions. There will also, of course, be the necessary doctor's certificate showing that I was sent there in 1939.

I have also been able to arrange for a perfectly genuine set of German papers belonging to a friend of mine who is at present in England and who will let me have the use of his German documents – which he will report lost if necessary.

Furthermore, as there is a great deal of unemployment in Germany at this stage, I have seen to it that I will not lose too much time in obtaining work once I get there.

During our conversation you asked me for some proof of my integrity and for some evidence that I could write. I have therefore discussed the scheme with Sir David Maxwell Fyfe [later the Earl of Kilmuir, who was Britain's Deputy Chief Prosecutor at the IMT] and asked him to give me a reference. He suggested that this would hardly be a case of a 'To whom it may Concern' letter, and he suggested that I should write him a letter to which he would reply. Copies of my letter to Sir David and his answer are enclosed.

I adopted the same procedure with Mr Tim Holland Bennett (head of casting at BBC Television) who was formerly a commentator with BBC Radio Newsreel and as such reported on the Nuremberg Trials. He later arranged for me to work for Newsreel as a Special Correspondent. His answer to my letter (which is similar to the one I sent to Sir David) is also enclosed.

Should you require an American reference then I would suggest General Telford Taylor who may, as you said, impress your New York office. I do not know Taylor's address at the moment, but would obtain it quickly for you should you so require.'

To complete the picture of Frank's abilities to convincingly appear to be someone else with an entirely different character and life story, the *NYHT* announced his safe return and his remarkable series of articles in the following terms:[58]

The European Edition of the *New York Herald Tribune* announces the publication, beginning Monday, of a series of articles, entitled *Hangover After Hitler* by Wolfe Frank.

The writer of the articles, which deal with many of the major aspects of post-war Germany, was born in Germany and lived there until he was twenty-four years old, when he escaped arrest by the Gestapo by fleeing to Switzerland. He served in the British Army as an officer during the recent war and later became chief interpreter at the Nuremberg war-crimes trials.

From June until October of this year Mr Frank lived again as a German, worked as a German in many parts of the Western Zones and talked to Germans as a fellow German. As a result, he emerged with 50,000 words of notes on what Germans are saying when they are talking among themselves and not to impress Military Government officials or Western Allied correspondents. These notes form the basis of his series.

His fifteen [eventually sixteen] articles cover many important topics, including de-Nazification, anti-Semitism, sex and morals, entertainment, politics and the tremendous German refugee problem.

He uncloaked a 'wanted' SS (Elite Guard) officer who was working under an assumed name for the Western Allies and visited Landsberg prison as a 'relative' of a Nazi sentenced to death. He worked in the Volkswagen plant, and played the part of a refugee in a refugee camp …

He worked as a German alongside Germans in Ruhr factories, on the Hamburg docks, in Berlin and elsewhere. Some of his investigations were aided by top German state officials; others, knowingly or unknowingly, by such persons as ex-SS members, Hitler's former masseur, Emmi [sic] Goering's former major-domo and chauffeur, Dr Schacht, armament industrialists, factory managers, foremen and workmen, prostitutes, Berlin entertainers, an SS general in hiding, black marketeers, housewives, lawyers, school-masters, university professors, parsons, food officials, refugee camp commanders, a former Gestapo chief, editors and writers, Jew survivors, customs officials, policemen, refugees in various camps, etc.

Quite simply, therefore, there were few men more capable of creating a false impression and having a convincing cover story, as well as a 'get-out-of-jail card', than Wolfe Frank. He would have revelled in being involved in the Donovan/Putzell/ Goering deception, all of whom would have known that the British Army captain would unfailingly live up to the OSS' requirement: 'Despite the seriousness of his own position, he should not fail to protect to the end the security of the organisation of which he is a member.' That organisation only had one master – General William 'Wild Bill' Donovan, who author Rick Atkinson described as being 'an extraordinary figure in 20th century American history, a man beyond the power of fiction to invent' – a description that could also be applied to Wolfe Frank.

Taking all the above into consideration, as well as the (accidental or deliberate) anomaly of the 'capsule-in-the mouth' incident, and having studied the man so closely, I rate Frank as being 'B' – 'Usually reliable'; and his admission as being '2' – 'Probably true'!

Airey Neave: A2
Frank and Neave arrived at Nuremberg, as their memoirs state, ahead of their language and legal colleagues respectively. They were dealing directly with Goering alongside Donovan and Putzell and had been 'assigned to pretrial interrogations.' They must surely therefore have been the 'British contingent' to whom Putzell refers to as being in agreement with the intended course of action. Having studied the characters of both men, it is clear to me they would be prepared to go along with such an arrangement if they thought it was the correct thing to do and believed it to be for the good of the cause.

The involvements of Frank at Nuremberg went far beyond the remit of an 'interpreter'. (The possibility of him having played a bigger role in one of the British or US intelligence services is discussed at Appendix A). However, Frank was not afraid to go armed into enemy territory. During his *NYHT* mission (described above) he single-handedly tracked down, arrested, interrogated and took the 'Confession' of the 'missing' Nazi general on the Allies 'most wanted' list. The general gave up without a fight, but in his record Frank indicates how far he was prepared to go if necessary: 'His face whitened and his hands shook as he dropped into a chair. I had been prepared for quite a different reaction and felt a little silly about the small automatic I had handy in my jacket pocket.'[39]

Airey Neave was of similar character, and here, I introduce the second document, that I referred to earlier. This was filed in a manilla folder – within the Neave archive currently being transferred from Parliamentary Archives to National Archives – alongside the only other item in the folder – Neave's unpublished account of Goering's suicide.

The document is entitled *Cognac for Judas. A Short Story By Airey Neave.* It is only four pages long (1,000 words) and was produced on the same typewriter as his record of Goering's suicide.[72]

The story, written in the first person, is centred on the Rue Babylone and Rue Vaneau in Paris, and describes the clandestine movements of 'Captain Louis' a Second World War double agent who had infiltrated the underground resistance movement that provided downed RAF and American airmen with escape routes back to Britain via France, Spain and Gibraltar. The theme is based on the narrator recounting to himself, in a contemptuous and gloating fashion, his own treacherous actions that have seen him, for financial reward, repeatedly betray the trust of resistance member colleagues and escapees by informing on them and leading them into traps that resulted in arrests by the Gestapo, imprisonment within concentration camps, and disappearances without trace. Revelling in his role as a Judas, Captain Louis recounts how it had all started when he led an unsuspecting RAF squadron leader, named Tom, dressed as a priest, into a trap that led to his arrest.

The story continues with Louis, on his way to a rendezvous in a cafe, realising he is being watched and followed by 'Roland ... the great agent from England I had come to meet.' Louis hopes Roland will provide him with information that will enable him to 'penetrate the whole escape organisation.' The two men enter the cafe separately and Louis is shown to a table by 'the patron, a fat bustling creature ... I despised the patron, in any case he was working for the British. I smiled at him contemptuously.' Noticing 'the white flower in my button-hole, my recognition signal' and having 'carried out the farce of exchanging passwords' Roland sits at Louis' table and confirms he has brought a large amount of money for the traitor, and they are to set up a 'new group' (see Appendix I). The two men buy each other glasses of cognac and Louis, to his annoyance, is called to the telephone and told there are two 'parcels' for collection 'at Gaston's place at eight.'

Preoccupied by the puzzling phone call, Louis returns to the table and drains his glass, then, as the story concludes: 'Roland smiled and fury seized me as a blinding light flashed in my eyes and a violent pain shot through my whole body so that I fell forward choking. I tried to reach for my gun, but my arms would not function. Dimly I saw Roland rise and walk towards the door as the fat proprietor bent over me and sneered, 'What, the cognac too strong for you, Judas?'

In real life, as head of Room 900, Airey Neave, a 'great agent from England,' dealt with this very kind of situation. He was personally responsible for the British involvement in 'escape lines' including the 'Comet Line,'[73] a major Resistance escape network headed by a courageous 24-year-old Belgian woman Andrée de Jongh (codename Dédée and known also as the Little Cyclone) and her father Frederic (codename Paul). Backed financially by MI9, Comet organised escape lines for downed RAF and US airmen and others from Belgium and Paris to neutral Spain via the Pyrenees. Comet's Paris headquarters were situated at 37 Rue Babylone, and Frederic's property on Rue Vaneau was a Comet safe house and where forged papers and identity cards were produced. Over 800 Allied servicemen, including 337 air crew, were led to safety via the Comet Line, often by Andrée herself. It is said that 'the airman she rescued were often moved to tears by her courage.'

Comet was infiltrated by Nazi agents and hundreds of 'helpers' were betrayed to the Gestapo or, more particularly, to Hermann Goering's Luftwaffe branch of the Secret Police 'who regarded escape organisations as their special province.' Among those betrayed were Andrée and Frederic de Jongh. Frederic was executed in March 1944 and Andrée spent the rest of the war in concentration camps. An estimated 3,000 'helpers' were involved in the Comet Line – over 700 were arrested and 290 were shot or died in prison.[73]

In 1954, Airey Neave sat down with Andrée De Jongh – who had by then been made a countess in Belgium and awarded the George Medal by Britain, the Medal of Freedom by the US and the Légion d'honneur by France – and they produced a book that is a record of Andrée's and her comrades,' as well as Room 900's and escapees,' involvements in the Comet Line. Entitled *Little Cyclone: The Girl Who Started the Comet Line*, the book mentions much that went on at 37 Rue Babylone and in Frederic's house on Rue Vaneau, and in another parallel with his short story, Neave also refers to an RAF officer named Tom, who had posed as a priest in his attempt to make his escape.[73]

A Belgian traitor who went under the alias Jean Masson was responsible for over 100 arrests of Comet Line members and Allied airmen. As part of an MI9 entrapment plan Masson was promised a large amount of money to 'set up the Belgian camp for Allied Airmen, which he would have pocketed and then turned the airmen in.' Masson had been identified by another brave Comet Line member, Michelle Dumon (codename Michou), who had discovered his identity, followed him to a cafe, and reported back to MI9, who sent a French Resistance agent to kill him. A man was assassinated, but it wasn't Masson 'The wrong man – whoever he was – had been liquidated.'[76] (see Appendix I for further details of Comet Line).

In *Cognac for Judas*, Neave, is clearly writing about his own experiences of the clandestine world in which he operated and his personal knowledge of the Comet Line operation in Paris, where escapees, ready to be led to safety, were referred to as being 'parcels' for collection and the 'new group' was no doubt a reference to one of the camps for downed Allied airmen Neave and Comet Line were setting up in forest areas behind enemy lines. Neave may have referred to the work as being 'a short story' but in truth he was probably recounting an event of which he was aware, or in which he had even been involved – for as Roger Bolton, a television producer who knew him and produced a documentary on his assassination, indicated – Neave was a moral man willing to do things that immoral people were not: 'If necessary, he took the gun out and there were difficult things to be done but for the most honourable of reasons.'[40]

A second Judas, Englishman Harold Cole, who Neave decribed as being 'amongst the most selfish and callous traitors who ever served the enemy in time of war' was shot dead by French police in a room above Billy's Bar in Paris. He had betrayed over 150 resistance workers to the German secret police before, following the Allied invasion, escaping dressed as a German officer. Pursued by Neave, Cole continued betraying many more escaping airmen and resistance workers before, once the war was lost, switching sides again. Adopting the title 'Captain Mason', he joined CIC as an intelligence agent where he then informed on many of his former Nazi employers. With unwitting help from one of his mistresses, Cole was uncovered by MI9 and arrested by French intelligence agents. He escaped wearing a US Army captain's jacket and hid in Billy's Bar for several weeks before the final shoot-out in which he was killed.[76]

About the demise of a third major traitor, Airey Neave would only say: 'Of the end of Roger Leneveu [or Le Neveu, also known as Roger Le Legionnaire] … there is little information … He was liquidated by the marquis [French resistance fighters] at the liberation of France [1944].'[76] Another report states 'Le Neveu went on to penetrate lines in Brittany and escape routes into Spain until June 1944 but was "dealt with" appropriately by the French Resistance after the Liberation of France.'[81] The character of 'Captain Louis', the narrator in *Cognac for Judas*, was perhaps based on one, or a composite, of these traitors.

(In the *OSS Secret Intelligence Field Manual*, General Donovan – whose OSS was working alongside Neave's MI9 and the SOE in occupied France and Belgium – described Resistance Groups such as Comet Line as being: 'Individuals associated together in enemy-held territory to injure the enemy by any or all means short of military operations, e.g., by sabotage, espionage, non-cooperation').

Wolfe Frank's war did not end on VE Day in 1945. He was deeply involved in the last great battle of the Second World War – the IMT – then the Subsequent Proceedings, then finally in capturing a 'missing' Nazi war criminal in 1949. General Donovan's war continued with his involvement in the Subsequent Proceedings – as a prosecutor seeking justice for the deaths and ill treatment of so many of his OSS agents.

In like fashion, Airey Neave's war continued long after the guns had fallen silent, as his biographer, Paul Routledge, wrote: 'He was a public servant who never really stopped being a secret agent.'[41]

One can only speculate, of course, what Neave's motive was in writing *Cognac for Judas* – and whether it was based on real events he had personally witnessed. However, like Donovan, Neave was driven by a need to seek justice for those who had suffered, as he had, the tortures of a concentration camp, been betrayed by traitors, and had not been amongst the 3,000 Allied aircrews successfully brought back from behind enemy lines – brave servicemen and others, including members of the Comet Line, for whom Neave felt personally responsible.[70]

In his book *Saturday at M.I.9* Neave wrote:

I returned to Germany by the same route from Emmerich on the Rhine that I had followed as a half-starved prisoner in 1940. At first it was as a prosecutor and collector of evidence against the Krupp armament firm at Essen. I was deeply embittered against the Nazis, not on my own account, but for those who had died for the escape organisations … Hitler and Goering attached importance to smashing the escape lines. They realised the importance of hundreds of trained airmen slipping through their hands. This accounted for the employment of the Secret Police of the Luftwaffe, of which Goering was the Commander in Chief. The brutality displayed by their secret police to those who helped Allied airman was a disgrace to an otherwise honourable Air Force.[76]

Neave also wrote 'Goering realised the existence of secret escape organisations for recovery of R.A.F. pilots and crews. He must have known its value to the Allied air forces. He gave orders it was to be crushed,'[77] and 'Goering was intent upon revenge for the escape of so many Allied airman, and smarting under the defeats inflicted on his Air Force.'[78]

As head of Room 900 of MI9, and besides the escape routes aspects, Neave's work also involved exposing and pursuing those British, French and Belgian double-agents and collaborators who had betrayed airmen and Resistance members to the Gestapo or the Luftwaffe Secret Police.

I feel therefore that *Cognac for Judas* is almost certainly an allegorical account of true events that happened on Neave's watch, with the moral perhaps being that the act of betrayal is so heinous it forfeits a traitor's right to live. Goering betrayed Hitler by feeding information to the Allies (including that which Putzell passed on to President Truman). He was also present when, following the most audacious break out by seventy-six RAF officers from Stalag Luft III prisoner-of-war camp (featured in the film *The Great Escape*), Hitler ordered the deaths of all who were recaptured. Goering, who was commander of Stalag Luft III, persuaded Hitler to kill less. This resulted in fifty RAF officers being shot 'whilst trying to escape' – still a horrendous crime, but Goering's intervention did save 23 lives. These executions were illegal under the Geneva Convention and a betrayal of their rights as prisoners of war. Of the seventy-six who escaped, seventy-three were recaptured. Of the three who made it to safety, one, Flight Lieutenant Bram van der Stok, MBE, a Dutch pilot of 41 Squadron RAF, did so with the help of an escape line.[79] The Great Escape took place on 24 March 1944 and van der Stok arrived back in the UK on 11 July where he was debriefed by MI9 and other intelligence agencies.[80]

Cognac for Judas was the only other document Neave filed alongside his account of Goering's suicide. Linking the two documents might have been Neave's way of feeling he had personally had a hand in seeing justice meted out to the man whose fate was sealed on the very issues described in the story and the murders of the fifty RAF officers – as Neave explained in his memoirs.

The trial was not going well. Goering had got the better of Justice Jackson, who was in despair, near to tears and said to be 'beside himself' and 'distraught'. Judge Justice Birkett noted: 'The great battle was lost, and once lost there may be partial but never complete recovery.' Neave too could not have been more anxious. He saw the trial, including his own input regarding lost airmen and resistance workers, as being at a crossroads. Goering, he wrote, was able to put forward 'a plausible case on almost every aspect.'

It was Britain's Deputy Chief Prosecutor, Sir David Maxwell-Fyfe, who came to the prosecution's rescue when he took over from Jackson, as Neave, with great relief, recorded:[71]

> Sir Maxwell-Fyfe rose to cross-examine and he pressed Goering about his knowledge of the murder of the fifty RAF officers after their escape. Goering immediately looked frightened and ashamed. Soon, with clenched fists and red with anger, he denied he or Field Marshall Milch knew anything about it. For many in the courtroom the affair of the 'Great Escape' sounded the death knell for Goering. Outside the courtroom, at the lunch interval, I said to Maxwell-Fyfe: 'You've got him.' He smiled at me and said, 'I know how you must feel.'

If the above wasn't enough, there are three other possible reasons why Neave, assuming he was a member of the 'British contingent', might have agreed to Goering being given the poison. Firstly, as one of the British prosecutors, he may have thought, in return for accepting responsibility for all Nazi war crimes and providing evidence against the other war criminals, Donovan's decision was the best and most expedient method of achieving the justice they all sought – with Goering's acceptance of all charges ensuring death penalties would be imposed. Secondly, as a lawyer, Neave would have known only too well that, at the preparations stage (when the poison was transferred), without admissions of guilt there was no certainty of the death penalty being imposed, and that Goering might be given a life sentence (which is what happened to Rudolf Hess who spent over forty years in Spandau Prison, twenty of them as the sole inmate, before committing suicide). Neave knew Goering, as a proud soldier, would choose to die a martyr in like fashion to 'the Great Hannibal' rather than be hanged or condemned to languish in Spandau for forty years as a common criminal and as an example to the German people – who still saw him as a hero. Thirdly, Neave may have been persuaded, as Putzell was, that Goering was deserving of some mercy (for the treachery he had shown to Hitler, the information he provided that Putzell passed on to the President and for saving the lives of 23 RAF officers), or being granted a more honourable way of ending his life.

These possibilities make the title and theme of *Cognac for Judas* seem so apt, and this may have been the reason Neave chose to write the 'story' and file it alongside his account of Goering's suicide.

(I looked on-line to see if I could find any other reference to the title Neave had given to his story. There was only one – an electronic opinion from A.I. While I do not place reliance on A.I., in this instance I was interested to note it had trawled the internet and concluded: 'The specific phrase "Cognac for Judas" does not appear in any common religious texts or well-known literature. However, it is a phrase that likely refers to a symbolic offering or a gesture of kindness or appeasement towards a traitor, given that Judas is a biblical figure known for betraying Jesus, and cognac is a fine spirit).

Based on all I know and have read about Airey Neave, and taking into account his experiences as a prisoner of war, head of one of the intelligence departments, mastermind of escape plans, saviour of so many stranded airmen, a practicing lawyer and a Member of Parliament, I rate him, as a person, as being 'A' – Completely reliable; and the likelihood of him being part of the 'British contingent' who agreed with the Donovan/Putzell proposal as being '2' – Probably true.

I raised my initial mark from '3' – Possibly true – when I discovered Neave's linked and unpublished record of Goering's suicide and *Cognac for Judas* and re-read his remarks on learning of Goering's demise: 'I could scarcely repress a laugh. <u>The old rascal had got away with it,</u>' and 'he bit the phial of potassium cyanide, which he had <u>long concealed</u>, and died.'[42] Neave was a lawyer and here, in October 1946, he is making two precise statements, not suppositions, that only someone who *knew* Goering had 'got away' with a daring plot and had 'long concealed' (since November 1945) the capsule, could make.

(Assuming the capsule-in-the-mouth was part of their 'cover stories', the near identical records of Frank and Neave regarding this incident would have led General Donovan to assess the men and their statements as being A1. The general would have known both were 'completely reliable' and that the information provided was, in every way, a perfect cover – both men had bona fide reasons for interrogating Goering and their references to the poison capsule would have fitted perfectly with Donovan's OSS Manual directive that 'The most effective cover is that which is as near truth as possible'.[34] Importantly, the two distinct records in themselves fulfil Donovan's requirement for him to have be able give the top rating of '1' – that is, that the 'Report [be] confirmed by other sources'[34]).

Lieutenant Jack Wheelis: C3

Jack Wheelis had become property officer in charge of the baggage area where the war criminals' confiscated possessions were stored. It has been alleged, without any evidence, that Wheelis enabled Goering to visit the room shortly before 15 October to retrieve a cyanide capsule hidden among the Reichmarschall's personal effects that had been confiscated by the US Army. Although some historians and writers, including Ben Swearingen, have thought this possible, many more have always viewed this with skepticism – the prisoners were on twenty-four-hour suicide watch (see Plate 18) that would not have allowed for such a visit to have gone unnoticed, unrecorded or unconsidered by the investigating Board of Officers.

Regarding the report of The Board, Swearingen, who studied the documentation more thoroughly than most, concluded 'my research had convinced me the board's explanation of how Goering retained and concealed the poison was "so full of holes" that I found it impossible to accept.'[43]

The statement Wheelis gave to The Board (repeated below) was, along with all the others, accepted by The Board and The Allied Control Council.

Portraits painted of Wheelis describe him variously as being a 'hail-fellow-well-met' type; a 'gregarious and a skilled raconteur'; 'an easy going guy who made friends everywhere'; without 'social distinctions'; and someone it was considered would not accept a bribe from Goering in return for the poison.

Others were not so certain of his motives, suggesting he: 'was a very unconventional character'; 'arrogant and an opportunist'; had a 'split personality;' and that his friendship with Goering was 'unprincipled.'

There is no doubt Wheelis and Goering were on very friendly terms, and the fact the lieutenant had accepted a number of gifts from the Reichsmarschall, which he openly bragged about, gave rise to the belief in some quarters that he had somehow aided the suicide.

Wheelis was author Ben Swearingen's choice as being the man who passed the poison to Goering, however Swearingen had sadly died long before Lieutenant Putzell's revelations (2003) and Douglas Waller's researches (2011) had been published. He never therefore had the opportunity of investigating the option I now put forward for consideration – that Wheelis may have played a supporting role in a much bigger plot hatched by the US' two top spymasters. All the work Swearingen put into his researches is, however, a valuable contribution to this theory.

I do believe Wheelis knew more than he was ever prepared to admit and that he could well have been any, or all, of the following: one of the six guards who Harry Shotwell confirmed 'were ordered to go with two OSS "Spooks"' and told 'to follow the orders of these two men from now on'; the guard on duty when Donovan had one of his 'ten private meetings' with Goering and obeyed an order 'not to hear a single word uttered in this room'; recruited by the general or Lieutenant Putzell as 'an individual not a regular member of OSS who is employed and directed by an agent in the field for a single OSS [/CIC] assignment'; one of the secret intelligence personnel 'recruited from civilians or from the armed forces of the United States and its Allies' for a specific mission.'

Wheelis had all the qualifications for such a role – perceived 'integrity, intelligence, initiative … Natural resourcefulness, energy, a broad general background, familiarity with the area … patience, discretion, and judgment … able to handle men, mix easily, judge character', and someone 'selected with specific cover jobs in view' who had 'Unqualified loyalty to the United States and unqualified sympathy with the vigorous prosecution of the war by all methods.'

A lieutenant so involved could have been instructed 'In the event of capture …a secret intelligence operative or agent should stick by his cover story and deny all charges. Despite the seriousness of his own position, he should not fail to protect to the end the security of the organisation of which he is a member.'

One can see that working undercover directly for the US' most decorated war hero on a secret assignment of great significance would appeal to a man like Wheelis. Especially so if that mission allowed a war criminal, with whom he had become friends, to die a more honourable death than the one Justice Jackson had advocated and was determined to see carried out.

He could have just 'not heard' details of the 'deal' struck between Donovan and Goering – as he followed orders and, at all times, remained within 'five paces' of the prisoner. He may have simply looked the other way, or waited outside the interrogation room, while the sleight of hand artist carried out the deed. Or he might have placed a jar of Vaseline containing a suicide capsule into a wash bag that was stored in a baggage room of which he was in charge and had the key.

Any one of those possibilities would have allowed Wheelis – with hand on heart, a clear conscience and without fear of contradiction – to swear and sign an Affidavit (written for him using identical wording to that that appeared on the statements of nine other guards) – 'I have had in my possession the key to the baggage room of the prison during the period 10 October 1946 to 15 October 1946 and can state positively that Goering received nothing from, nor had access to the baggage room during this period.'[44]

Whatever Wheelis knew, he steadfastly refused to discuss. He died of a heart attack in 1954, and never admitted to having any involvement in the incident. If he had been grilled, he would, no doubt, have protected: 'to the end the security of the organisation of which he is [was] a member' – albeit for a: 'single OSS assignment.'

Although Ben Swearingen, clearly believed Wheelis had played a significant role, even he could only say that Wheelis had died 'taking with him the definitive answer to the riddle of Goering's suicide', and the former lieutenant's son, Judge James Wheelis, was only able to add: 'I believe that my father thoroughly enjoyed the cloud of mystery which swirled around him as a result of all the rumours.'[45]

My assessment is that I think Wheelis probably did know something and that it may well have been as I have suggested. However, he, and any others involved, have taken that knowledge with them to the grave. The highest rating I feel I can give Wheelis therefore is 'C' – Fairly reliable – as a source, and '3'– Possibly true, as far as 'credibility' of my suggestions are concerned.

Last Words

Hermann Goering's vision of how he thought the German people would judge him was:

> 'I am determined to go down in German history as a great man … If I cannot convince the court, I shall at least convince the German people that all I did was done for the Greater German Reich. In fifty or sixty years there will be statues of Hermann Goering all over German', he paused and then added 'Little statues maybe, but one in every home.'[47]

Wolfe Frank's view, perhaps offering some mitigating circumstances in defence of anyone who might have been involved in giving Goering the means to kill himself – if of course any were needed, was:

> 'Whether he had the eventual capsule that killed him all the time or whether it was smuggled into the jail for him seems to me to be of secondary importance. It should have been found in either

case, and the job was bungled. It certainly changed the record, but I don't think the history of the world was changed greatly.'[48]

I have yet to discover any defining comments attributable to **General Donovan** on the suicide or the cyanide capsule, but **Lieutenant Putzell's** were: 'I think he was glad to have it. It was better than being hanged!'[49]

Airey Neave had returned to London to start practice as a barrister. He was in Fleet Street exactly twelve months after he had served the indictment on the Reichsmarschall when: 'I read of Goering's suicide in the *Evening Standard*. I could scarcely repress a laugh. The old rascal had got away with it.'[50]

Robert Jackson, within hours of the suicide, released a statement in which he said:

> 'Hermann Goering's suicide was "as anti climatic as a burlesque after a Wagnerian overture" and destroyed his opportunity to become a "German Martyr Hero" ... "His end betrayed the weakness of his whole life – cunning and crafty, always outwitting somebody, bullying and cowardly" ... "The gallows offered him the most effective platform from which to impress his sympathisers with the depth of his conviction and his selflessness for the cause ... but he lacked the character."[51]

Few people agreed with Jackson, certainly the world's press didn't. *Time* magazine on 28 October 1946 printed correspondent John Stanton's assessment, cabled from Nuremberg, it typically, and oh so eloquently, summed up the general feelings in Germany, the US and elsewhere on 16 October 1946:[52]

> Teutonic Drums. On the day after the executions, bowed Nürnberg suddenly straightened up. Men with glistening eyes stopped for excited talks with one another. Little knots gathered before the Haupt-bahnhof. Germans who had avoided the eyes of Americans the night before now looked at them frankly with derisive smiles. Johannes Breit, ex-Wehrmacht major, said: 'His was a noble deed.' A little old man shrilled: 'It is Scapa Flow over again; you cannot take what is ours!' You heard over & over again from passers-by on the streets: 'Unser Hermann' (Our Herman).
>
> The general reaction was: 'He put one over on you.' The rich old Göring legend was back: Göring was really a jovial, pleasant man, and a clever one to boot. He just loved the good things in

life, with a greedy appetite Germans can appreciate. He was courageous (after all, he had been a fighter ace). He was clever (did he not dominate the trials?). He had obeyed every rule, had been watched day & night, had boasted he wouldn't hang, and na, siehst du, he didn't.

The old Teutonic drums were beating strong in the sunlight. There were no German tears, no German regrets or shame. On the contrary, the Germans now had the feeling of triumph which they had lacked so long. Göring's one sharp, breath-taking act wiped away ten months of painstaking work.

The final words, and the right of reply, in this narrative, belong to the one and only Reichsmarschall of the Greater German Realms – the man who lost a war but won its last battle – these words, which must have haunted Robert Jackson for the rest of his life, are indisputable:

'THEY WILL NOT HANG ME!'[53]

CHAPTER FORTY-THREE – NOTES & REFERENCES

1. *Wild Bill Donovan – The Last Hero*, p.298.

2. *Remembering the Last Hero*, Charles Pinck, President of the OSS Society: https://www.thecrimson.com/article/2011/4/21/war-oss-donovan-world/

3. Edwin Putzell Interview 12 March 2003 with Mary Jane Robinson (US Library of Congress).

4. *Nuremberg in Retrospect*, Robert Jackson (American Law Journal, October 1949).

5. *Wild Bill Donovan*, pp.324–325.

6. ibid, pp.341–343.

7. *The Mystery of Hermann Goering's Suicide*, p.101.

8. *Memo from Dr Stahmer* [Goering's Lawyer] 15 November 1945 (US National Archives).

9. *Wild Bill Donovan*, pp.342–343.

10. *Nuremberg – A Personal Record of the Trial of Major Nazi War Criminals in 1945–6*, p.66.

11. *Wild Bill Donovan*, p.347.

12. *Letter from Robert Jackson to William Donovan, 26 November 1945*, Harry S. Truman Library & Museum.

13. *Memorandum from Colonel Telford Taylor to General Donovan and others, 26 November 1945*, Cornell University Library.

14. Robert H. Jackson Centre – Bach-Zelewski II, 7 January 1946.

15. *Letter from William Donovan to Robert Jackson, 27 November 1945*, Harry S. Truman Library & Museum.

16. *The Anatomy of the Nuremberg Trials: A Personal Memoir*, p.341.

17. *Nuremberg's Voice of Doom*, pp.156.

18. *Nuremberg – A Personal Record of the Trial of Major Nazi War Criminals in 1945–6*, p.312.

19. ibid, p.314.

20. *Nuremberg's Voice of Doom*, p.107.

21. *The Oregonian*, 23 September 1970.

22. *Vanity Fair – Spymaster General*, 3 March 2011.

23. *The Undercover Nazi Hunter*, p.60.

24. ibid, p.2.

25. *Report of Board of Proceedings in Case of Hermann Goering (Suicide) October 1946.*

26. *Nuremberg: Infamy on Trial*, p.299.

27. ibid, p.253.

28. *The Mystery of Hermann Goering's Suicide*, p.116.

29. *Report of Board of Proceedings in Case of Hermann Goering (Suicide) October 1946.*

30. *The Mystery of Hermann Goering's Suicide*, p.217.

31. Douglas Waller: www.historynet.com/interview-with-wild-bill-donovan-biographer-douglas-waller/

32. Stanley Lovell is thought to be the inspiration for 'Q' in the James Bond books – Bond's creator Ian Fleming: knew Donovan and Putzell and advised them when originally setting up the OSS; worked with Neave at MI6 and MI9; and was at Nuremberg in November 1945 to watch Frank in action – features of all four can readily be seen in the James Bond character.

33. *The OSS Combat Manual* by James Loriega (Lulu.com 2019) – and other publications.

34. *Secret Intelligence Field Manual – Strategic Services (Provisional)*, Office of Strategic Services, 22 March 1944.

35. *The Mystery of Hermann Goering's Suicide*, p.216.

36. *Nuremberg's Voice of Doom*, p.122.

37. *Wild Bill Donovan*, Douglas Waller, p.342.

38. *Nuremberg's Voice of Doom*, p.124.

39. *The Undercover Nazi Hunter*, p.159.

40. *Public Servant, Secret Agent*, p 15.

41. Ibid, p.10.

42. *Nuremberg – A Personal Record of the Trial of Major Nazi War Criminals in 1945–6*, pp.312–314

43. *The Mystery of Hermann Goering's Suicide*, p.167.

44. *Report of Board of Proceedings in Case of Hermann Goering (Suicide) October 1946.*

45. *The Mystery of Hermann Goering's Suicide*, p.217.

46. *He Wore Many Hats*, Lila Zuck, City of Naples: www.naplescentennial.com/untold-stories/he-wore-many-hats/

47. *The Reich Marshal: A Biography of Hermann Goering*, p.397.

48. *Nuremberg's Voice of Doom*, p.156.

49. Lieutenant Putzell's admissions to Petronella Wyatt in her article that appeared in the 1 February 2003 edition of *The Spectator* p.48.

50. *Nuremberg – A Personal Record of the Trial of Major Nazi War Criminals in 1945–6*, p.314.

51. *The Westbury Democrat*, 16 October 1945, p 1.

52. *Time – Down Without Tears*, John Stanton, 28 October 1946.

53. *The Mystery of Hermann Goering's Suicide*, p.152 (referencing an extract from Emmy Goering's book *An der Seites meines Mannes (By My Husband's Side)* p.308.

54. *Nuremberg – A Personal Record of the Trial of Major Nazi War Criminals in 1945–6*, p.69.

55. ibid, p.258–260.

56. ibid, pp.256–257.

57. *The Undercover Nazi Hunter*, pp.5–6.

58. ibid, pp.53–55.

59. *Nuremberg: Infamy on Trial* pp.120–121.

60. ibid, p.134.

61. Georgetown University, *OSS Oral History Project: Interview with Edwin Putzell*, 11 April 1997, transcript, p.59.

62. Comments made to correspondent Mark Fritz that appeared in *The Boston Globe*, 19 November 2001.

63. *Nuremberg's Voice of Doom*, p.135.

64. *Nuremberg – A Personal Record of the Trial of Major Nazi War Criminals in 1945–6*, p 241.

65. *Nuremberg's Voice of Doom*, p.141.

66. Columbia College Web Site: https://www.college.columbia.edu/cct/issue/summer20/article/swashbuckling-lawyer-who-was-ultimate-spy

67. *The Undercover Nazi Hunter*, pp. 17 and 20.

68. *Small Wars Journal:* https://smallwarsjournal.com/2022/03/05/glorious-ukrainian-resistance/

69. Georgetown University, *OSS Oral History Project: Interview with Edwin Putzell*, 11 April 1997, transcript, pp. 1 and 79.

70. *Public Servant, Secret Agent*, p.156.

71. *Nuremberg – A Personal Record of the Trial of Major Nazi War Criminals in 1945–6*, pp.258–261.

72. *Cognac for Judas, a Short Story* by Airey Neave, M.P., and a paper entitled *Goering's Suicide* – The Parliamentary Archives Reference for these documents was 'Papers of Airey Middleton Sheffield Neave (1916–1979) GB-061 Catalogue Reference: AN/660' – this reference may well change once Parliamentary Archives are incorporated into National Archives.

73. See Appendix I

74. *Nuremberg – A Personal Record of the Trial of Major Nazi War Criminals in 1945–6*, pp.228–229.

75. Georgetown University, *OSS Oral History Project: Interview with Edwin Putzell*, 11 April 1997, transcript, pp.78–79.

76. *Saturday at M.I.9 – The Traitors*, pp.303–317.

77. *Saturday at M.I.9*, pp.133–134.

78. ibid, p.171.

79. *79 RAF Evaders*, pp.155–156.

80. *Account of Escape of F/Lt. Bram van der Stok, M.I.9/S/P.G. (G) 2032*, National Archives.

81. Fanny Rodocanachi & Christopher Long: https://www.christopherlong.co.uk/per/rodocanachigeorge.html

SECTION NINE

LIVES REMEMBERED ...

William Donovan in 1924, US Attorney for the Western District of New York.

Wolfe Frank in the early 1980s, whilst working as an interpreter at the EU.

Edwin Putzell, during his term of office as Mayor of Naples, Florida (1986–90).

Airey Neave in July 1946, at the International Military Tribunal.

CHAPTER FORTY-FOUR

LIVES REMEMBERED

*The definitive solution to 'a riddle wrapped in a
mystery inside an enigma'*
WINSTON CHURCHILL

A GROUP OF NO MORE THAN SIX MEN, bound by secrecy, came together at the Palace of Justice in Nuremberg in the autumn of 1945 and there was executed what illusionists might term as being: an act of monumental subterfuge and audacity, carried out by masters of deception, who artfully manipulated perceptions and, with the aid of smoke and mirrors, created a breathtaking feat that defied logic and belief – a feat so brilliantly accomplished it could not be fathomed, even by seasoned historical investigators, until the last survivor of the group explained what had really happened, shortly before his death, almost sixty years after the event. So good was the deception that the inquisitive seeking an answer to the 'riddle, wrapped in a mystery inside an enigma' ever looked at the wrong people, in the wrong place, at the wrong time. This led, understandably, to wrong conclusions being drawn – which is exactly what the world's most accomplished spymasters had intended.

The solution to how Hermann Goering had obtained the cyanide capsule that enabled him to commit suicide, and wreck the Allied Control Council's plans for a 'show-piece' hanging, was only solved following the admissions of two of that group of men, many years apart, during the final months of their lives, and the bringing together of the records and stories of: the most notorious of all Nazi war criminals; America's top spymaster; the prodigy he taught 'the dark arts of espionage'; the Chief Prosecutor at the IMT; the first escapee from Colditz Castle; the man the world's media dubbed 'The Voice of Doom'; and one or two others who were, or may have been, part of the most sensational of events at 'history's greatest trial'.

So what happened to those men following the provision of the cyanide capsule to Hermann Goering in the autumn of 1945 and after the Reichsmarschall of Nazi Germany had used it on 15 October 1946?

GENERAL WILLIAM DONOVAN

*'I doubt whether any one person contributed more to the ultimate
victory of the Allies than Bill Donovan.'*
THE EARL MOUNTBATTEN OF BURMA

WILLIAM JOSEPH 'WILD BILL' DONOVAN, accompanied by his faithful lieutenant, left Nuremberg on 30 November 1945. He had nothing further to do with the IMT, although his many allies on the prosecution team at Nuremberg 'continued to feed him inside information on the mistakes Justice Jackson was making throughout the ten-month trial.'[1]

The General resumed his role as head of the successful Wall Street law firm Donovan, Leisure, Newton & Irvine, and he returned to Nuremberg for the Subsequent Proceedings where he served as special assistant to Telford Taylor, who had succeeded Robert Jackson as Chief Counsel. During those trials he had the personal satisfaction of seeing Nazi leaders responsible for the torture and murder of OSS agents brought to justice. He also carried on with his involvements in politics, the armed forces and intelligence activities – where he often continued to ruffle feathers from the president down. However, in 1947 President Truman approved plans for the CIA along the lines Donovan had proposed. Today the Agency continues to pay tribute to its roots and gives due credit where due credit is due:

> Donovan remains an inspiration to the men and women of the CIA. Although he never directed the agency that was based on his ideas and initially staffed in large part by people he personally led, Major General William Donovan embodied the creativity, courage, and can-do spirit that are the hallmarks of the CIA. Its officers regard him as the founder of both their agency and the American intelligence profession.[2]

Donovan went on to hold a number of official offices in the US and Europe and in 1953 was appointed US Ambassador to Thailand. In 1957 he began to suffer from dementia and was eventually hospitalized where, in true Donovan fashion, 'He imagined he saw the Red Army coming over the 59th Street Bridge, into Manhattan, and in one memorable last mission, fled the hospital, wandering down the street in his pyjamas.' Shortly before his death in 1959 [8 February] aged 76 he was visited in hospital by President Eisenhower. 'The president visibly stiffened and stood erect in the presence of a man who had shown such bravery under fire. Donovan was, Eisenhower told a friend, "the last hero."'[3]

William Donovan was a graduate of both Columbia College and Columbia Law School, whose Alumni refer to him as being 'the ace of agents — architect of covert operations, recruiter of undercover assets, manipulator of disinformation, gatherer of priceless intelligence, perpetrator of psychological warfare, the all-seeing man in the shadows'. Ten years after his death friends and associates of the general commissioned a memorial as a tribute to 'Wild Bill' – which is sited on the 'sky bridge' over New York's Amsterdam Avenue near to Columbia University (see Plate 24). The bronze statue weighs 842 pounds and stands over 14 feet tall. It is the work of Dutch sculptor Kees Verkade and depicts two tightrope walkers, one balancing upon the shoulders of the other. Verkade said he 'wanted to display the courage and controlled daring of General Donovan'. It could of course also portray Donovan and Putzell – the derring-do of the 'brave, noble, headlong, gleeful' general and the steadying influence and balanced approach of his trusted lieutenant – each dependent upon the other to get out of any tight spot they found themselves in while doing 'all they could for their Country.'

William Donovan is considered to be the founding father of the CIA and another bronze statue of him stands in the lobby of its headquarters in Langley Virginia (see Plate 24). The OSS Society, founded by Donovan in 1947, presents an award in his name to: 'someone who has exemplified the distinguishing features that characterized General Donovan's lifetime of public service to the United of States of America as a citizen and a soldier' – notable recipients include: presidents Eisenhower, Reagan and George H. Bush; Prime Minister Margaret Thatcher; and the Earl Mountbatten of Burma who, on collecting his award in 1966, paid Donovan perhaps his ultimate accolade: 'William Donovan wasn't just a great American. He was a great international citizen, a man of enormous courage, leadership, and vision. I doubt whether any one person contributed more to the ultimate victory of the Allies than Bill Donovan.'[4] (See Appendix E for details of the OSS Society).

General William 'Wild Bill' Donovan is buried at Arlington National Cemetery, Virginia and remains the only holder of the top four highest awards of the United States: The Medal of Honor, the Distinguished

Service Cross, the Distinguished Service Medal and the National Security Medal (For a more complete list of General Donovan's Awards see Appendix B).

In early 1923, some four thousand veterans had crowded into the armory of the U.S. Army, 165th Infantry, 42d Division to see General Donovan receive the Medal of Honor – awarded for his heroic acts at Landres-et-Saint-Georges during the First World War (see 'Bravest of the Brave' Chapter Twenty Three). His biographer, Douglas Waller, records what happened next – it is an illustration as to why Donovan, throughout his life, was 'adored' by all who served under him and it is a fitting way to end these brief biographical notes: 'he pivoted on his heel and called the regiment to attention. He unsnapped the ribbon from his neck and presented the medal to his unit "it doesn't belong to me" he said quietly." It belongs "to the boys who are not here, the boys who are resting under the white crosses in France or in the cemeteries of New York, also to the boys who were lucky enough to come through." He left the medal with the armory.'[5]

CHAPTER FORTY-FIVE – NOTES & REFERENCES

1. *Wild Bill Donovan*, Douglas Waller, p 348.

2. CIA, *Profiles in Leadership:* https://www.cia.gov/resources/csi/static/4789eee9 e734cd7409eed3d133929b36/Profiles-in-Leadership-Updated-July-2023.pdf

3. *Vanity Fair – Spymaster General*, Evan Thomas, 3 March 2011.

4. The OSS society: osssociety.org/pdfs/donovan2007.pdf

5. *Wild Bill Donovan*, Douglas Waller, p 35.

EDWIN J. 'NED' PUTZELL, JR.

'I would much rather have men ask why I have no statue,
than why I have one'
CATO THE ELDER

EARL MOUNTBATTEN OF BURMA'S STATEMENT: 'I doubt whether any one person contributed more to the ultimate victory of the Allies than Bill Donovan', along with many other similarly expressed acclamations, does not give recognition to the important, perhaps crucial, role Edwin Putzell played in bringing about such accolades that, along with Putzell himself, followed General Donovan all over the world. In film industry terms, whilst Donovan would have had few rivals for the best actor award, Ned Putzell would surely have picked up the Oscar for Best Supporting Actor – a role that so often in real life, as well as in motion pictures, quietly matches, enhances and makes possible the 'star' performance.

In real life however there are no statues for lieutenants, yet wherever the general went and whatever he did during the war and at Nuremberg, he was accompanied by his protege, confidante, sounding board, sometimes adviser and faithful friend Ned Putzell. At the very moment President Roosevelt asked Donovan to form the OSS in 1942, Putzell was at his side. At the very moment the agency ceased to exist (30 September 1945) Putzell was at his side (helping the general to surreptitiously copy all the agency's records). Throughout all the campaigns of the Second World War in which Donovan was involved and enhanced his legendary status, Putzell was at his side. When Donovan flew to Nuremberg on 3 October 1945, Putzell was at his side, and when Donovan quit the trials and flew home on 30 November, Putzell was at his side … and there their partnership, but not their friendship, was to come to an end as Putzell was confronted by the stark realities of a world outside espionage.

Having, throughout the US' involvement in the Second World War, served as General Donovan's Executive Officer within the Office of Strategic Services, and then at the Nuremberg trials, Lieutenant Edwin J. 'Ned' Putzell, Jr. returned to the US in November 1945 and was given an ultimatum by his wife, as he explained in an interview he gave in 1997 to Tim Naftali for the OSS Oral History Project at Georgetown University:

> At the end of the war, my wife said to me: 'Look, the war is over now and you either have got to decide between Donovan and his life-style or having a family and a more normal life-style.' And, you know, she had lived through the war not knowing where I was or what I was doing, I couldn't blame her[1] … the thing that got her was, first, she didn't know where I was and she was concerned for my physical safety. Second, we had a daughter at that point, she was born in '42'.[2]

While pondering his future, Putzell had agreed to travel to Hollywood to assist legendary film producer/director John Ford in putting together documentaries that would be shown at Nuremberg. (Donovan had recruited Ford to set up the OSS Field Photographic Branch [OSSFPB] and he played a significant role in gathering film evidence of Nazi war crimes for use in the trials. This footage became crucial evidence in convicting the Nazis. Ford brought with him over 300 writers, directors, cameramen and other technicians and made over 100 short films about the OSS and naval activities, including *Undercover* and *How to Operate Behind Enemy Lines*. He also made training films for OSS agents such as *Training Group* and *The Mole*, both of which, like *Undercover*, are now declassified and in the public domain – see Appendices C & D for further details of the significant role Ford played during the war and at the IMT, and a list of the films the OSSFPB produced).

Another OSS agent, wealthy banker and businessman Charlie Cheston, arranged for Putzell to break his journeys to and from Hollywood to stay for a few days at the home, in St Louis, of Edward Queeney Chairman of petro-chemical giant Monsanto, of which Cheston was also a director. Having taken an immediate liking to Putzell, and having made due enquiries regarding his background, character, talents and abilities, out of the blue, Queeney offered him the position of assistant company treasurer. Putzell's protests that he was a lawyer not a finance man were waived aside and he was told the checks already made led Queeney to believe, that once in the company, he would be moved into a role more suited to his legal leanings. Putzell accepted the offer and was soon promoted, eventually becoming a director, a vice president, chief counsel and company secretary.[3]

While at Monsanto, Putzell, became a spokesman for both his company and the atomic energy industry, setting out a vision, not only for the development of nuclear power in the US, but also in many other nations, including the UK. In a speech he gave to the Fifth Annual Summer Institute of Atomic Energy, held at the University of Michigan Law School in June 1952, Putzell indicated that Monsanto had, since September 1946 (nine months after he had joined the company), at its own cost, been involved in investigating the feasibility of producing electric power from nuclear energy and was now discussing, with the Atomic Energy Commission, the possibility of constructing a pilot plant. Putzell also said:

> Look at England. It is now almost too costly for her to produce electric power from coal mined within her boundaries. At Ruabon, North Wales, Monsanto has a chemical plant, and immediately adjacent to it is a government-owned coal mine. Some of the shafts of that mine are beneath our plant. However, on many occasions since the war, that plant has had to purchase coal in the United States and ship it to England. It was cheaper to purchase the coal in New York, ship it to London and transship it to Ruabon than to purchase the coal from the mine next door. How great, then, must be the range of possible benefits to the British economy, of power produced from atomic energy.

Putzell, whose electrical engineer father 'built most of the first electric plants in the south', was not making a political point with this statement – that was not his style. Rather, he was emphasising the economic, ecological and defence benefits of nuclear power for the US, the UK and their allies, and advocating for nuclear power plants to be built in a new post-war world that: needed to satisfy an ever increasing demand for cheaper, cleaner energy; was, in some regions, running out of expensive-to-mine fossil fuels; and needed plutonium for defence purposes. (A year after Putzell delivered this address, the British government gave the 'go-ahead' for the construction of the world's first commercial nuclear power station at Calder Hall in Cumbria. Shortly after the announcement, in August 1953, work began on the site and just over three years later, on 17 October 1956, the station was officially opened by Queen Elizabeth II).

Within a few months of joining Monsanto, in December 1945, yet another great honour had been extended to the former OSS Executive Officer when he was invited to become a director of Westminster College. Of this appointment, he said: 'I ended up in St. Louis after the war and I was invited on the board, became vice chairman ... I was involved with the [Winston Churchill] Iron Curtain speech in Westminster College' (It was during this speech on 5 March 1946 that Churchill uttered his famous words 'From Stettin in the Baltic, to Trieste in the Adriatic, an **iron curtain** has descended across the continent.' [Purely by coincidence, this speech, that warned of a new threat from Russia and ushered in the Cold War, was made on the thirteenth anniversary of the birth of the Third Reich]. During the course of this address, Churchill also included another of his, now famous, phrases when he highlighted the existence of 'a **special relationship** between the British Commonwealth and Empire and the United States').

Churchill was introduced by no less a person than President Truman, who travelled 'a thousand miles' especially for the occasion. Putzell had advised both men during the war, but refused to take personal credit for arranging the event, simply saying 'I didn't personally organise it, I was part of a group'. Perhaps still smarting from the president's decision to close the OSS, General Donovan turned down Putzell's invitation to attend on this occasion, but he did accept a request from his former Executive Officer (who was still drafting some of the general's speeches) to address the college at a later date.[4]

Following his years with Monsanto, Putzell moved back into the legal profession, becoming senior partner at Coburn, Croft & Putzell, a leading corporate law firm that by the time of Putzell's retirement proudly displayed over seventy attorneys on its letter-heading. During his years in St Louis Putzell was also vice chairman of the St. Louis County Board of Police Commissioners, president of the St. Louis Social Planning Council, chairman of the St. Louis Public TV Commission, and a board member of both the Manufacturers Bank & Trust Co and St Luke's Hospital. He was also involved in numerous voluntary causes, including the Child Welfare League of America, of which he was a vice president – an organisation whose current website declares it to be 'an association of more than 1,100 public and private nonprofit agencies that assist over 3.5 million abused and neglected children and their families each year'.

Upon retirement in 1979, Ned Putzell moved to Naples in Florida. Here he was persuaded to take on the role of Chairman of the Naples Airport Authority, in which capacity he was responsible for the building of the airport's passenger terminal. He spent four years as a volunteer with Collier County Conservancy (an organisation dedicated to protecting Florida's water, land and wildlife), before becoming the Conservancy's President and Chief Executive and later Chairman of the Board. Following this work, Putzell took on the Interim Chairmanship of Princetown-Boston Airlines and was the recipient of the *Naples Daily News* Outstanding Citizen Award and the Greater Naples Leadership Award where 'Through his influence and counsel, Ned helped mold [sic] the geography of the city as well as the careers of future local leaders.'[5]

In 1986 he was encouraged by residents to stand for the office of Mayor of Naples – and he became the first person to hold the office for a four-year period. In the years following his mayoralty, he sat on the boards of Moorings Park Hospice, the Chamber of Commerce and the Community Foundation.

Ned Putzell was held in the highest possible regard by all who knew him, whether that be in his role as a top attorney, Executive Officer of the OSS, or any of the many roles he fulfilled with such distinction in St Louis and Florida. Throughout his long and distinguished life, he was ever considered to be a man of great integrity. Among his many war time duties he advised world leaders including presidents Roosevelt and Truman, Andrei Gromyko (Russia's US ambassador) and Prime Minister Winston Churchill. Yet this quiet, unassuming, modest man preferred not to seek the limelight and always played down his achievements. This was never better illustrated than in a recorded interview he gave to Mary Jane Robinson for the US Library of Congress shortly before he died. In answer to a question the interviewer posed about his achievements, he answered simply: 'I'm so grateful. I can't tell you. I literally truly am. I don't attribute that to my doing it. It just happened.'

Legacy

Because of the shadowy world in which it operated, details of many of the OSS' and its agents' involvements during the Second World War are still only now coming to light. President Ronald Reagan predicted this would be the case when in 1986 at a dinner for OSS veterans, during which he named both Donovan and Putzell, the President said: '[I can't] think of any group whose accomplishments and devotion to country makes them more worthy of accolades and praise. And yet it's precisely that praise and those accolades that you decided to forgo when you chose a twilight war, a secret profession, a profession where praise and thanks can only come from history and not from your contemporaries'. The President was right, it is only in the decades that followed the agency's demise that the full extent of the OSS' achievements and value are being uncovered, understood and brought to the attention of the wider public. Amongst the most telling of latter day tributes that I have come across, is the one delivered by the Hon Jack H. McDonald of Michigan, when addressing Congress on

8 June 1971 (which also mentioned Donovan and Putzell): 'the D-day offensive would not have been successful without the Office of Strategic Services, nor would millions of Jews be alive today were it not for the countless acts of heroism by OSS agents that will doubtless go untold.' Millions of Jews alive today because of the OSS – what a wonderful legacy to leave behind and attach to the names of all who served in an agency that, in just four years, had grown from an idea and an office in the White House basement and had, throughout its existence, remained under the leadership and control of its sole director General Donovan and his executive officer Lieutenant Putzell.

In typical style, and with many of his commitments and achievements still not widely known, Ned Putzell passed away quietly on 23 December 2003 and was buried at sea without fuss. His name, amongst many others, appears on a plaque at the Trinity-By-The-Cove Episcopal Church Cemetery, Naples, Florida. The plaque simply records the years of his birth (1913) and death (2003) and the name by which he always preferred to be known – Edwin J. 'Ned' Putzell. As far as I know, no other memorial and, other than what is recorded in this work, no consolidated record exists to mark the lifetime of service given by this thoroughly decent human being – this may in part be due to the fact that, as with CIA agents of today, he subscribed to the first rule of the 'intelligence community': never reveal more than is absolutely necessary to as few people as possible. Hopefully this book will draw more attention to his 'devotion to country' and others will now think him worthy of the 'accolades and praise' he, in my opinion, so richly deserves.

While writing this last chapter of Ned Putzell's life, I was reminded of a beautifully crafted and eloquent poem written by Sir John Betjeman called *The Hon. Sec.* In this work, the poet describes the passing of a dear friend whom he greatly misses. The poem so accurately describes how, throughout his life, Putzell quietly went about every task he was set without seeking praise or recognition, and with his many accomplishments and contributions not being acknowledged or fully realised until it was too late. Astonishingly the name the great poet chose to use in this poem is 'Ned'! There is therefore no more fitting way to end this biographical sketch than to include the last two verses of Sir John's poem, which are reproduced here with the permission of the copyright holders, Hodder & Stoughton, to whom I extend my grateful thanks.

The Times would never have the space
For Ned's discreet achievements;
The public prints are not the place
For intimate bereavements.

A gentle guest, a willing host,
Affection deeply planted –
It's strange that those we miss the most
Are those we take for granted.

CHAPTER FORTY-SIX – NOTES & REFERENCES

1. Georgetown University, *OSS Oral History Project: Interview with Edwin Putzell*, 11 April 1997, transcript, p.67.

2. ibid.

3. ibid, pp.80–83, *Monsanto Annual Report*, 1970 and *Steel* magazine, 31 December 1948, p.48.

4. Georgetown University, *OSS Oral History Project*, op. cit. pp.80–83.

5. The Distinguished Leadership Award is presented to a Greater Naples Leadership member who 'outstandingly exemplifies the mission of our [the] organization – to provide proven leaders with a unique opportunity to learn firsthand about the issues and needs in Collier County and to encourage the use of their skills individually and collectively in bettering the community. https://www.gnlwebsite.org/gnl-distinguished-leadership-award/

6. *Bulletin of the Atomic Scientists*, Volume 8, Number 8, November, 1952, pp.275–277.

WOLFE FRANK

'A wrongfully forgotten hero of the twentieth century.'
TOM GARNER[1]

WOLFE FRANK STAYED ON AT NUREMBERG after the IMT and was appointed Chief Interpreter of the 'Subsequent Proceedings' – the twelve further trials the USA conducted to hear the war crimes committed by other Nazi war criminals, many of whom were no less evil than those convicted at the IMT. In total almost 500 cases were tried at the Subsequent Proceedings involving over 1,600 defendants of which 1,400 were found guilty.

After all he had experienced prior to and during the Second World War, Frank then endured twenty-eight months of emotional anguish at Nuremberg by being exposed daily to the utter degradation of fellow human beings, and of witnessing the abominations and depravation that had taken place in Nazi concentration camps. He then had the unenviable task of processing it all and explaining it in another language. One can only marvel at his ability to have been able to cope with such burdens. Yet his final comments also reveal his suffering, and it is little wonder he left the trials with the parting words 'I had heard enough about atrocities, mass murder, war crimes, extermination camps and genocide'[2].

In 1949 the former resistance worker risked his life again by going undercover in occupied Germany during the 'Cold War.' Having been set the task of finding out what had happened to over two thousand war criminals who had disappeared without trace, Frank, with the help of Rudolf Diels, single-handedly tracked down and arrested Waldemar Wappenhans, the SS General then ranked 'fourth' on the allies 'most wanted' list, before personally taking and transcribing his 'Confession', of which only two copies were ever produced – one was handed in to the Admiralty with the Nazi general, and can no longer be found, the other copy remained hidden for 65 years in Frank's archive.

Convinced the SS general was not guilty of the crimes the Russians had charged him with Frank, once again seemingly exceeding his authority, spoke in Wappenhans' favour and guided him on the presentation of his 'confession'. This resulted in the former SS general receiving a short prison sentence as opposed to the death penalty sought by the Russians. Eternally grateful to Frank, Wappenhans added a final clause to his confession that read: 'I have faced death often and even sought it once – but it was God's will that I should live to fill other tasks. I would have hanged most certainly, as have many of my comrades, without reasonable justice, if I had been made a prisoner in 1945'[3].

Frank's personal war against the Nazis had therefore lasted from 5 March 1933, when he witnessed the first atrocity on the first day of the Third Reich, until that day in December 1949 when he handed the German general over to the Admiralty.

In a packed lifetime Frank was also at various times an engineer, a financial advisor, racing driver, theatre impresario, broadcaster, journalist, salesman, businessman, restaurateur, skier and property developer. Finally, in his later years, he returned to the role for which he had become famous – he joined the EU as an interpreter, where the process of simultaneous interpretation that he had pioneered, perfected and in which he had trained those who followed him, had become the norm.

Like Edwin Putzell, I do not believe Frank was given the credit he deserved. Britain's two judges at Nuremberg, Geoffrey Lawrence and Norman Birkett, and two leading prosecutors, Hartley Shawcross and David Maxwell Fyfe, were all raised to the peerage. Frank's contributions however seem to have been overlooked, for he received no recognition. Yet he had matched, word for word, everything their lordships and everyone else had said and heard at the trials – from the most vulnerable of traumatised survivors of the Holocaust to the most arrogant of war criminals who had created it – only Frank had done it in two languages at once and conveyed it all in a unique way, never previously attempted, that enabled every listener to fully and immediately understand the depth of victims' suffering and the unbelievable cruelty of the perpetrators.

In summing him up, I would say Wolfe Frank was a unique character of extreme contrasts. On the one hand he spent a lifetime in the fast lane thoroughly enjoying himself – even during the most difficult of times. It cannot be denied that he was a maverick who took liberties, a playboy, a risk taker, and he was an opportunist who liked nothing more than a challenge – even if that meant him risking his life.

His other side however showed him to be a man of immense courage, charm, good manners, honour and ability. His handling of the translations and interrogations at Nuremberg sets him apart from all other interpreters of his time, perhaps of all time. He was asked to undertake the toughest of assignments imaginable and he was perhaps the only man in the world who could have so satisfied all concerned.

When I asked Mike Dilliway, the beneficiary of Wolfe's archive, to sum up Frank's character, he rather movingly replied: 'He was a superb cook, great company and a wonderful raconteur. The stories of his early life, his escape from Nazi Germany, Nuremberg and his undercover operation never ceased to enthrall me, and the other things that impressed me and left a lasting impression were his intelligence, his immaculate appearance on all occasions, his bearing, his good manners, his fellowship, his charm and his sincerity. He was a dear friend whom to this day I miss very much.'

On one of his last visits to Brussels Wolfe must have mentioned his illness and his changed circumstances to others, for amongst his papers I found the kind of letter few men will ever be fortunate enough to receive:

'It doesn't matter whether or not you remember who I am,' wrote an anonymous admirer (or former lover?) 'this is not fan mail. I am only telling you something many other people have thought …you are still totally recognizable as one of the most attractive men I have ever seen. When I first met you, some ten years ago, I was struck by your very special air, that of an exceptionally charming man. What you had then you still have now, and I daresay you will keep it about you through whatever illness and age do to you. I hope you enjoy it even half as much as those who meet you do.'[4]

Illness eventually made it impossible for Frank to continue travelling to the EU in Belgium, at the same time his fifth marriage broke down and he then lost his savings through a bad investment. He was obliged to move out of his home into sheltered housing and needed to accept State benefits. On 10 March 1988, reflecting on his situation, upon what he had once had and knowing what he had lost forever, this proud man visited Mike Dilliway at his vehicle repair shop and asked if he could borrow a roll of masking tape. When Mike asked him what he wanted it for Wolfe simply replied: 'If anyone asks I'm going to be doing some decorating.' It was the last thing said between the two friends. Wolfe returned to his home, prepared himself to look his immaculate best, dressed himself in his finest clothes and went to his favourite local restaurant, The Old Ship Inn at Mere – which abutted his former Malt House home – and he indulged himself in their finest cuisine which he washed down with a bottle of vintage champagne before getting into his car and driving off into the night.

The following day Mike Dilliway was visited by Wiltshire Police and, as the local recovery service, he was asked to go to a farm track just off the Mere By-pass and remove a car in which the body of a man had been discovered. The driver had died, Mike was told, from carbon monoxide fumes he had inhaled while in a vehicle that had a hose pipe attached and its windows sealed with masking tape. Mike did not need to ask the number of the vehicle or the name of the deceased.

Wolfe Frank was, without doubt, a major contributing factor in the success of 'the greatest trial in history,' yet until the discovery and publication of his memoirs he had become 'a wrongfully forgotten hero of the twentieth century' – and of the Nuremberg Trials. In 2021 this was partially rectified when a plaque honouring his services and achievements at the IMT, awarded by Salisbury Civic Society, was erected on the facia of his former home – The Malt House in Mere, Wiltshire (see Plate 24).

An estimated 400 million radio listeners had tuned in to hear Wolfe Frank's performance as the 'Voice of Doom' as he read, to the convicted war criminals, the sentences imposed upon them by the IMT. In his final days, however, he had become somewhat reclusive and just a handful of friends attended his funeral service at Salisbury. Later his former wife took his ashes to Davos, a favourite spot where he had once lived, and they were interned in the plot in which his mother had been buried. May they rest in peace.

(The full story of Wolfe Frank's life and involvements can be found in my books: *Nuremberg's Voice of Doom* and *The Undercover Nazi Hunter* – see Appendix G for further details).

CHAPTER FORTY-SEVEN – NOTES & REFERENCES

1. Tom Garner, Features Editor, *History of War.*

2. *Nuremberg's Voice of Doom,* p. xviii.

3. *The Undercover Nazi Hunter* pp.162–163.

4. *Nuremberg's Voice of Doom,* pp.188–189.

AIREY NEAVE

'he became conspicuously inconspicuous'[1]
PAUL ROUTLEDGE

DAVID CORNWELL, BETTER KNOWN as John Le Carré, said in an interview 'I feebly protested that I was a writer who had once happened to be a spy rather than a spy who had turned to writing, the broad message I got back was, forget it: once a spy, always a spy.'[2] This was very true of Airey Neave, as author Paul Routledge makes clear in the title of his biography of Neave – *Public Servant, Secret Agent*[1]. About the man, and in introducing his book, Routledge wrote:

Neave's sensational escape and his equally sensational death are the extent of most people's knowledge and appreciation of one of Britain's most mysterious public figures. The two events, separated by thirty-five years are crucially linked: Neave joined a division of MI6 following his wartime bravery to advise other would-be escapees. He was also active in establishing the Gladio network [a clandestine 'stay-behind' army linked to NATO] with SOE. Soon after the war, and after working as a prosecutor at the Nurenburg trials, he successfully entered Parliament as Conservative MP for Abingdon, where he sat until his death. Overlooked by Macmillan and Heath for high office, ostensibly on health grounds, Neave pursued a public life of a very unusual kind: he became conspicuously inconspicuous, operating almost entirely outside the public gaze. During the early 1970s Neave was in contact with anti-Wilson plotters and by 1974 he was calling for Edward Heath's resignation too, seeing weakness in the Tory leader's capitulation to the miners. Thatcher was his crusading angel and he ran a brilliant leadership campaign, fooling more experienced candidates into complacency and securing Thatcher's triumph. She offered him any job in her Cabinet in return. Inexplicably to most he chose Northern Ireland and had prepared the most confrontational and explicitly belligerent strategy ever seen there. A matter of weeks before Thatcher's General Election victory began eighteen years of Conservative government, Neave's extraordinary life of intrigue and scheming was ended by a plot he had not foreseen[1].

The Right Honourable Lieutenant Colonel Airey Middleton Sheffield Neave, DSO, OBE, MC, TD, was killed on 30 March 1979 when the car he was driving exploded as he drove out of the car park at the Palace of Westminster. He was 63 years of age. The Irish National Liberation Army (INLA) later claimed responsibility for the assassination.

Airey Neave had been the mastermind behind Margaret Thatcher's success in becoming leader of the Conservative Party. If he had lived a few weeks longer, he would have seen her become Britain's first female prime minister on 4 May 1979. Less than two weeks after her victory Mrs Thatcher delivered the eulogy at Airey Neave's Memorial Service which was held at St Martin-in-the-Fields, Trafalgar Square. In her address the prime minister said[3]:

Airey Neave was my very dear and deeply trusted friend. When we were in Opposition, he was head of my Private Office, a Member of the Shadow Cabinet and our Spokesman on Northern Ireland. Had he lived, he would have been a Member of the Cabinet.

But just after 3 o'clock in the afternoon following the day the General Election was announced, Airey, who had come through all manner of personal trials in the war; who held the Distinguished Service Order, the Military Cross and the French Croix de Guerre; whose escape from Colditz, the prison which the Germans claimed was escape-proof, had become a legend in his lifetime; who played a prominent part at the Nuremberg trials – Airey the quiet, Airey the soft-spoken, was murdered by a terrorist's bomb.

… In the Autumn of last year, Airey's study of the Nuremberg trials was published. In her foreword, Rebecca West wrote of Airey: 'It is, I think, against his principles to care much about danger, but he would do all he could to spare the rest of us unnecessary risk'.

Words written with astonishing insight.

In the final chapter, Airey reflected on the meaning of the Nuremberg experience which had a lasting influence on his life, and the great struggle of good against evil, freedom against tyranny, that the war embodied.

'Before our eyes', he wrote, 'the problems of race and terrorism are a frightening reminder of Hitler's example. Those who use terror to gain their political ends are the heirs of his Revolution of Destruction however much they may claim to represent opposing doctrines'.

It is deeply poignant to recall those words today. But I want to recall something else Airey wrote at the time that his book was published. He gave me a copy, with this inscription:

'Remembering that tyranny has many sides and freedom but one.'

If it is possible for a single sentence to sum up a man, that sums up Airey Neave. Certainly none could serve better as his epitaph.

The words of Prime Minister Margaret Thatcher and author Paul Routledge say so much about the man and the extraordinary life of Airey Neave. Following his death, his memory was saluted at every level of government, the military and society, including the following which are recorded in Hansard under *Lords tributes to Airey Neave 2 April 1979*:

The kindest of men, his own courage knew no limits – *Lord Chancellor, Lord Elwyn-Jones.*

No man of this age ever served his country with greater fortitude and determination – *Lord Maybray-King.*

The kindest and most dedicated [of] people. Courteous, gentle, charming, almost shy, Airey Neave's façade masked a brilliant and meticulous mind – *Earl Ferrersone.*

No one was less flamboyant, less demonstrative than Airey Neave. In a profession noted for assertiveness and display, he kept to the shadows, as if for ever playing the part he had created for himself in MI9 – *Lord Lexden (formerly Alistair Cooke).*

In one more hand-written tribute Prime Minister Margaret Thatcher wrote:

He was one of freedom's warriors. No one knew of the great man he was, except those nearest to him. He was staunch, brave, true, strong: but he was very gentle and kind and loyal. It's a rare combination of qualities.

Airey Neave is buried in the churchyard extension of St Margaret of Antioch, Hinton Waldrist, near Farringdon, Oxfordshire. There is: a stained glass window dedicated to his memory at St Mary the Virgin Church, Fryerning, Ingatestone, Essex, that includes a portrayal of Colditz; a wooden shield bearing his arms and name above the door facing the Speaker's chair in the House of Commons; and memorials to him at the National Memorial Arboretum, Merton College, Oxford (his alma Mater) and elsewhere. In 1979 a trust was set up in his name, the objectives of which are: 'to support and promote research that contributes in a practical way to the struggle against international terrorist activity' (see Appendix F).

(Author: During the 1970s, I worked with a number of prominent people, whose opinions I valued, who had been personally associated with Airey Neave, and I can say that it seemed none knew him but to admire him, none named him but in praise).

CHAPTER FORTY-EIGHT – NOTES & REFERENCES

1. *Public Servant, Secret Agent* is the title of a biography of Airey Neave written by Paul Routledge.

2. Interview given to National Post entitled: *Once a spy, always a spy': An excerpt from John le Carré's The Pigeon Tunnel: Stories From My Life.*

3. *Speech at Airey Neave's Memorial Service,* Margaret Thatcher Foundation: www.margaretthatcher.org/document/104085

JUSTICE ROBERT H. JACKSON

'He kept the ancient landmarks and built the new'[1]

JUSTICE ROBERT JACKSON ACHIEVED WHAT he had set out to do at Nuremberg, but it came at a high price. He had made a number of serious miscalculations including overestimating his own skills of examination and cross-examination, underestimating the craftiness and abilities of Hermann Goering and falling out with America's 'last hero' General Donovan – who was proven to be right about Jackson's limitations in the courtroom.

Jackson's biggest error was to believe he could restrict Goering to 'yes' or 'no' answers which he hoped would lead the Reichsmarschall into condemning himself and the whole of the Nazi philosophy. The judges decided, however, that Goering should be given leeway to answer questions at length. The ruling undermined Jackson's strategy and his performance deteriorated from them on. He often lost his temper and was reprimanded for doing so. Jackson knew also that Donovan was being kept informed of his failings and he must have realised the general would have achieved the same results in a fraction of the time.

British Alternate Judge Norman Birkett later wrote, 'The cross-examination had not proceeded more than ten minutes before it was seen that Goering was the complete master of Mr. Justice Jackson'[2]. Telford Taylor also said that his boss 'paid dearly for his tactical blunder, in both public prestige and his own discontent.'[3]

On 7 October 1946, a week after the judgements had been passed and Wolfe Frank had informed the war criminals of their fate, Justice Jackson submitted his final report and letter of resignation to President Truman, in which he said[4]:

The International Military Tribunal sitting at Nurnberg, Germany on 30 September and 1 October, 1946 rendered judgment in the first international criminal assizes in history. It found 19 of the 22 defendants guilty on one or more of the counts of the Indictment, and acquitted 3. It sentenced 12 to death by hanging, 3 to imprisonment for life, and the four others to terms of 10 to 20 years imprisonment.

The Tribunal also declared 4 Nazi organizations to have been criminal in character. These are: The Leadership Corps of the Nazi Party; Die Schutzstaffeln, known as the SS; Die Sicherheitsdienst, known as the SD; and Die Geheimstaatspolizie, known as the Gestapo, or Secret State Police.

Jackson conclude his letter to the President, by stating:

> I hereby resign my commission as your representative and Chief of Counsel for the United States. In its execution I have had the help of many able men and women, too many to mention individually, who have made personal sacrifice to carry on a work in which they earnestly believed. I also want to express deep personal appreciation for this opportunity to do what I believe to be a constructive work for the peace of the world and for the better protection of persecuted peoples. It was, perhaps, the greatest opportunity ever presented to an American lawyer. In pursuit of it many mistakes have been made and many inadequacies must be confessed. I am consoled by the fact that in proceedings of this novelty, errors and missteps may also be instructive to the future.

Jackson's final two sentences were, perhaps, a nod in the direction of General Donovan and it says a lot for the man that he was able to include such remarks. President Truman's official letter of reply[5] was less than fulsome, and there were two reasons for that.

Firstly, a number of sources kept the president fully informed of Jackson's differences with Donovan and the justice's weaknesses and failings, as well as his strengths and achievements.

Secondly, at the same time as he was falling out with Donovan, Jackson also became involved in a public spat with a fellow Supreme Court Judge Hugo Black. Jackson suggested Black had failed to declare an interest in a case and implied President Truman was susceptible to Black's influence.

These issues cost Jackson dearly, for they led Truman to believe Jackson's personal and professional conflicts made him unsuitable for the role of Chief Justice of the United States, the highest-ranking position in the US federal judiciary – a job Jackson coveted and felt he should have been given – believing he was the best qualified Justice to fulfil the role and that there was an understanding he would be appointed to the position as a reward for his service at Nuremberg.

While Truman's letter therefore commended Jackson's 'prodigious' effort at Nuremberg, due to the bad blood that the justice's actions had created, the response lacked the personal warmth and full support expected of a president to his high-profile appointee.

What Jackson did not know of course when he submitted his resignation, was Donovan had, during the preparation period a year earlier, instructed Lieutenant Putzell to provide Goering with cyanide, and that eight days after he had submitted his letter, the Reichsmarschall would use that poison to end his own life and avoid the 'death by hanging' that Jackson had worked so hard to achieve. President Truman's acceptance is dated 17 October 1946 – a day after the suicide was announced.

Following the IMT, Jackson resumed his position as an Associate Justice of the Supreme Court of the United States. Prior to Nuremberg he had also been the 57th US Attorney General and the 24th US Solicitor General – he remains the only person to have held all three offices. In 1947 President Truman awarded him the Medal of Merit.

Among all his many successes and high offices, Jackson regarded his participation in the Nuremberg Trials as the crowning achievement of his career.

Robert Houghwout Jackson suffered three heart attacks in 1954 and died on 9 October aged sixty-two. He had two funeral services. The first was held at Washington's National Cathedral on 12 October. Following this, family and friends journeyed with the coffin by overnight train to New York for the second service at St Luke's Episcopal Church. All eight of the other Supreme Court judges, including Hugo Black, attended this service. He was later laid to rest in Maple Grove Cemetery, Frewsburg, New York, near to where he used to live. His memorial includes the epitaph: 'He kept the ancient landmarks and built the new.'

The Robert H. Jackson Centre in Jamestown, New York houses an extensive collection of his papers and photographs, including those from Nuremberg, and statues were erected of him at the centre and outside Chautauqua-Jamestown Airport.

In 2011 a new US district court was opened in Buffalo and named the Robert H. Jackson United States Courthouse – ironically the only other name considered for the courthouse was that of William Donovan.

CHAPTER FORTY-NINE – NOTES & REFERENCES

1. *Encyclopedia of War Crimes and Genocide* Leslie Alan Horvitz; Christopher Catherwood (Infobase Publishing), p.251.

2. *The Anatomy of the Nuremberg Trials: A Personal Memoir*, p.341.

3. ibid, p.343.

4. *Justice Jackson's Final Report to the President Concerning the Nuremberg War Crimes,* Temple Quarterly (1946–7) p.338.

5. *Letter to Justice Jackson Upon the Conclusion of His Duties With the Nurnberg Tribunal.* 17 October 1946: Harry S. Truman Library & Museum: https://www.trumanlibrary.gov/library/public-papers/233/letter-justice-jackson-upon-conclusion-his-duties-nurnberg-tribunal

THE OTHERS

'The laws of war are not a one way street'[1]

BRIGADIER GENERAL TELFORD TAYLOR

Following the IMT, Telford Taylor was promoted to the rank of brigadier general and appointed Chief Counsel of War Crimes for the Subsequent Proceedings – the twelve further trials the USA conducted to hear the war crimes committed by other Nazi war criminals. The first task Taylor undertook in this role was to appoint Wolfe Frank to be Chief Interpreter. Amongst his decorations he was awarded the Army Distinguished Service Medal. At the end of the Subsequent Proceedings, Taylor suggested: 'The laws of war are not a one way street'[1], an oft-repeated view that would be the subject of many of his future lectures and the last words of his final book (see below).

In 1949, with the trials completed, Taylor worked in private practice and became well known, and well respected, as a lawyer who stood up for civil liberties. He wrote a number of books including *Sword and Swastika: Generals and Nazis in the Third Reich*, *Munich: The Price of Peace* (which won the National Book Critics Circle Award), and *The Anatomy of the Nuremberg Trials*, which he completed in his mid-eighties.

He became Professor of Law at Columbia Law School, where he taught for over thirty years, and was a visiting professor at both Harvard and Yale. An accomplished musician who played piano and clarinet, Taylor also became well versed in sports law and in resolving disputes for the US National Basketball Association.

Brigadier General Telford Taylor died in New York, aged ninety, on 23 May 1998, after suffering a stroke. He is buried at Morningside Cemetery in Gaylordsville, Connecticut. In his *New York Times* obituary, fellow professor Jonathan Bush said: 'He'll be remembered as a chief Nuremberg prosecutor, but also more as a giant of American liberalism and a man of integrity.' *The Columbia Journal of Transitional Law (Vol. 7, 1999)* described him as being a 'gifted author, lawyer, prosecutor, professor, sportsman, musician, composer and visionary, [who] will best be remembered as a far-sighted and courageous champion of universal human rights.'

COLONEL BURTON ANDRUS

Telford Taylor painted a vivid portrait of how Colonel Burton C. Andrus had appeared to the war criminals: 'Most of the defendants, as holders of high positions, detested the colonel, who addressed them like a martinet drill sergeant. Goering … railed at him, but Andrus, regardless of past rank, treated all the inmates alike. He could be vastly irritating, but he did his best to be fair.'[2]

Ben Swearingen had the opportunity of meeting Andrus' son (also named Burton C.) who allowed the author to go through his father's papers. Swearingen concluded that Andrus 'dutifully shouldered the blame for Goering's suicide.'[3]

Soon after the events of 15 October 1946, Andrus returned to the United States where, following a period as executive officer of the Army Service Unit, he attended the Strategic Intelligence School, before being appointed military attaché to Israel a position he held until the end of 1949. He was then assigned to the same role in Brazil until April 1952 when he retired from the U.S. Army.

Following retirement, Andrus moved to Tacoma, Washington where he studied at the College (now University) of Puget Sound and where he earned a Bachelor of Arts degree in Business Administration in 1955 and a master's degree a year later. He was asked to stay on at the college as a professor. He published two books: *I Was the Nuremberg Jailer* and *The Infamous of Nuremberg*. He has been portrayed in several dramatisations including the 2025 film *Nuremberg* where his role was played by actor and director John Slattery.

Colonel Andrus was awarded the Legion of Merit 'For exceptionally meritorious conduct in the performance of outstanding services to the Government of the United States as Commanding Officer, 96th Bomb Wing, during the period from 1 March 1959 to 31 May 1961.'[4] and the Distinguished Flying Cross (DFC) whilst a Major with the 783rd Bombardment Squadron, 465th Bombardment Group, U.S. Army Air Forces. His other military decorations include The Bronze Star, Order of Leopold with palm, Croix de Guerre with palm (Belgium), Order of the Oak Wreath Crown (Luxembourg), and the Military Medal (Brazil)[5].

Colonel Burton C. Andrus died on 1 February 1977 and is buried at Fort Worden Military Cemetery, Port Townsend, Jefferson County, Washington

CAPTAIN JACK WHEELIS

Immediately after The Board's report of Goering's suicide had been accepted by the Control Council, Jack Wheelis disappeared for a few weeks. Colonel Gerald R. Wilson, one of Wheelis' superior officers, was interviewed by Ben Swearingen. He told the author he remembered Wheelis as being an 'opportunist' and that 'after Goering killed himself, there was much talk among the Nuremberg officer's about Wheelis's close relationship with the former Reichsmarschall. The talk intensified after Wheelis was 'suddenly gone' from the Nuremberg scene. 'I didn't see him again for a month', Colonel Wilson said. 'No one knew where Wheelis had gone nor the reason for his departure, but his absence added fuel to the fire of controversy that surrounded him.'[6]

Details about Jack Wheelis' involvements post Nuremberg are sketchy, but it is known he never admitted being involved in any event concerning Goering's suicide. His family believed he did not pass the poison to Goering, and his son, Justice James Wheelis, when interviewed by Ben Swearingen could only say, 'I believe that my father thoroughly enjoyed the cloud of mystery which swirled around him as a result of all the rumours.'[7]

Jack Wheelis was subsequently promoted to the rank of captain, and he served in Korea before returning to the United States. Tragically, just eight years after Goering's suicide, he died in a Fort Hood hospital of heart disease. He was forty-one years of age and had served a total of seventeen years and eight months in the US Army. He is buried at Mart Cemetery, McLennan County, Texas.

SERGEANT HARRY SHOTWELL

Sergeant Harry Shotwell never knew why 'out of the blue' he and five other Nuremberg prison guards were singled out and instructed to take their future orders from General Donovan's OSS/CIC, where he was assigned to provide special escort duties for Hermann Goering, including those times he was having 'private meetings' with the general. Shotwell was just as mystified as to why, following the occasion Donovan had ordered him 'not to hear a single word' said during an interrogation of Goering, he was, just three days before the start of the IMT, unceremoniously taken off that special assignment.

On returning to the United States, after Nuremberg, Harry Shotwell married and began a career with Republic Steel in Canton, firstly in the mechanical and electrical department and then as a crane driver. His association with the company lasted for thirty-four years. He wrote stories of his war time experiences as a machine gunner where he had been awarded a Bronze Star and a Purple Heart following his heroism at the Battle of the Bulge (16 December 1944–16 January 1945) – the last major German offensive on the Western Front during the Second World War

A devoted family man, his marriage to Laberta Dallas lasted sixty-nine years. Shortly before he died he gave several interviews, including the important audio recording in which he explained his encounter with General Donovan[8], and his final comment to *Alliance Review* reporter Thomas Clapper, was a quote of First World War fighter ace Eddie Rickenbacker – it is a fitting tribute to attach to the name of the war hero who was Harry Shotwell: 'Courage is doing what you are afraid to do. There can be no courage unless you're scared'. He showed that courage as a soldier and when he stood up to General 'Wild Bill' Donovan.

Sergeant Harry Glennwood Shotwell – of the 1st Infantry Division, 1st Battalion, 26th Regiment, Able Company, 4th Platoon – died on 1 April 2018 aged ninety-three and was buried with full military honours at the East Lawn Cemetery in Minerva, Ohio.

CHAPTER FIFTY – NOTES & REFERENCES

1. *The Anatomy of the Nuremberg Trials: A Personal Memoir*, p.641.

2. ibid, p.230.

3. *The Mystery of Hermann Goering's Suicide,* pp.194–195.

4. *Traces of War:* https://www.tracesofwar.com/persons/112304/Andrus-Burton-Curtis.htm

5. Friends of the Air Force Academy Library: www.usafalibrary.com/collections_pages/andrus_collection.html

6. *The Mystery of Hermann Goering's Suicide,* pp.166.

7. ibid, pp.217.

8. *Harry Shotwell Recalls a Day with Nazi Hermann Goering and "Wild Bill" Donovan* – Recorded interview: https://omny.fm/shows/rep-audio-vault/harry-shotwell-recalls-a-day-with-nazi-hermann-goe

SECTION TEN

...AND BEST FORGOTTEN

END OF THE ROAD

'The evil that men do lives after them'[1]
WILLIAM SHAKESPEARE

The Remains of Hermann Goering:

The body of Hermann Goering was photographed, naked and clothed. Having succeeded in wrecking the plans of Chief Prosecutor Robert Jackson and the Allied Control Council, Goering's body was brought into the gymnasium at Nuremberg prison and laid with those of the other ten war criminals who had died on the gallows. Of that moment Kingsbury Smith, representing the Combined American Press, wrote: 'The face of this 20th Century freebooting political racketeer was still contorted with the pain of his last agonising moments and his final gesture of defiance.'[2]

There have been a number of versions of what happened next, all are very similar apart from minor details about the closely guarded locations. Author Anthony Read's account in his book *The Devil's Disciples* is considered as good a description as any[3]:

Goering's body was added to the others as they were photographed, wrapped in mattress covers, sealed in coffins then driven off in army trucks with a military escort to a crematorium in Munich, which had been told to expect the bodies of fourteen American soldiers. The coffins were opened for inspection by American, British, French and Soviet officials, before being loaded in the cremation ovens. That same evening, a container holding all the ashes was driven away into the Bavarian countryside, in the rain. It stopped in a quiet lane about an hour later, and the ashes were poured into a muddy ditch. Goering, like the other disciples, had come to the end of the road.

Time magazine, in its edition of 28 October 1946, summed up the mood of the victors and the vanquished on the day of the suicide and the executions:

The wind had blown through the night and swept away the clouds. The morning which the eleven did not see dawned clear and brilliant over Nürnberg, but it held neither cheer nor reassurance for the victors. They had permitted new doubts of Nürnberg's justice to arise even out of this last, relatively simple business of hanging ten men by the neck. And they had given Germany a sense of victory when they permitted Hermann Goering to die not as they willed but as he willed.'[4]

Contrary to Goerings belief that: 'In fifty or sixty years there will be statues of Hermann Goering all over Germany,'[5] there are no shrines to his evil memory.

Erich von dem Bach-Zelewski

Justice Robert Jackson in his fall-out with Donovan had told the general in the letter that ended their relationship: 'I do not think we can afford to negotiate with any of these defendants ... To use one of them ourselves will create the impression that there was some kind of bargain about his testimony ... we will have no negotiations on such matters, either with defendants.'[6] However that is exactly what the prosecution, through Jackson and Telford Taylor, proceeded to do with Bach -Zelewski, who Goering denounced as a 'swine', a 'skunk', and 'the bloodiest murderer in the whole damn set up ...selling his soul to save his stinking neck.'[7]

Telford Taylor also dismissed the suggestion that Bach-Zelewski handed the suicide capsule to Goering saying 'no one gave him [Bach-Zelewski] credence, especially since the two men loathed each other'.

As the Second World War ended Bach-Zelewski went into hiding but was arrested in August 1945 attempting to flee Germany. However, in return for his testimony against Goering and the other war criminals, he was never prosecuted at Nuremberg. He justified his position on the Holocaust in the following terms: 'If, for years, for decades, the doctrine is preached that the Slav race is an inferior race and that the Jews are not even human beings, then an explosion of this sort is inevitable.'[8]

Bach-Zelewski was held in prison and appeared in the Subsequent Proceedings. He was later released from prison and worked as a night watchman. In March 1951, he was condemned by a Munich de-Nazification court to ten years house arrest. In 1961, following a further arrest, he was sentenced to four and a half years in prison for ordering the murder of an SS officer. A year later, he received a second sentence because of more murders in the 1930s. This time, he was sentenced to life imprisonment. He was indicted again in 1962, for the murder of six communists in 1933. He was tried before a jury in Nuremberg and was sentenced to life imprisonment.[9]

SS Obergruppenführer Erich Julius Eberhard von Zelewski died in prison on 8 March 1972 and was buried at Landkreis Roth in Bavaria.

Rudolf Diels – The Jury is Still Out

Rudolf Diels was an SS Officer and the first head of the Gestapo, however, even though he was related to Goering by marriage, he was considered to be too lenient, and was relieved of his Gestapo post by Heinrich Himmler (head of the SS) who appointed Reinhard Heydrich in his place. (Himmler and Heydrich were two of the darkest figures within the Nazi regime).

In an affidavit he gave on 31 October 1945 Diels condemned the Gestapo and explained: how he had been appointed its head in 1933; the duties he was ordered to carry out; how and why after failing to carry out Hitler's orders he had felt obliged to resign from office; and the atrocities that were carried out by the Gestapo following his resignation[10]:

As for the deprivation of freedom, there was no legal reasons for protective custody orders after 1934, which had still been the case before that date, since from 1934 on the power of the totalitarian state was so stabilized that the arrest of a person for his own protection was only an excuse for arbitrary arrest – without court verdict and without legal measures for him. The terroristic measures, which led to the development of the pure force system and punishment to an increasing degree each critical remark and each impulse of freedom with the concentration camp, took on more and more arbitrary and cruel forms. The Gestapo became the regime of force. Fear of it ruled everybody, especially because of the tortures connected with the arrests. From the events which caused me to tend my resignation I recognized that the Gestapo was developing as the willing executor not only of Hitler's orders but also of his wishes. Hitler ordered me to the Obersalzberg [Hitler's retreat in Berchtesgaden] in January 1934 and told me in the presence of Goering that some 'traitors' had to disappear. From his words I had to infer the order to remove Strasser (Gregor), Schleicher, and other persons. Since I had not done anything to execute this order about a week [sic], Goering informed me that he would accept my resignation, which had already been tendered earlier, and that he wanted to subject the

Prussian police to Himmler and Heyrdich. The above named persons and many others were killed on 30 June 1934.

The declaration was taken by Major G. Stephens, Jr. of US Infantry, on behalf of the Offices of the US Chief of Counsel [Robert Jackson] who confirmed: 'Before me appeared on 31st October 1945 the undersigned trustworthy personality, Mr Rudolf DIELS, whom I know personally and who declared under oath that he had the opportunity to write and to read carefully the two previous pages signed by him and that the contents and facts are true and without mistakes.'

Diels had been implicated in the 20 July 1944 plot to assassinate Adolf Hitler. He was sentenced to death but was saved by Goering who said, 'he did not want a hanged man in his family'. Diels was sent to the Eastern Front instead, from where he escaped and surrendered to the Allies. Wolfe Frank took responsibility for Diels and backed by General Donovan, who had known Diels prior to the war, made good use of the former Gestapo head's 'encyclopaedic' memory during the preparation period for the IMT. Diels refused to implicate living Nazis by name, but he did not 'claim ignorance of the horrors of the time, only the impossibility for anyone to swim against the monstrous tide.'[11] At the IMT he testified for both the prosecution and for Goering. He was imprisoned for two years. On his release he served on the government of Lower Saxony and then in the Ministry of the Interior until his retirement in 1953.

In 1949 Wolfe Frank returned to Germany to write his *Hangover After Hitler* series of articles for the *New York Herald Tribune*. Having been set the task of finding out what had happened to the 2,000 'missing' Nazi war criminals on the Allies 'most wanted' list, Frank contacted Rudolf Diels who – partly in return for all Frank had done for him, and partly to 'get even' with a former Nazi general against whom he held a grudge – provided the information that enabled Frank to arrest, detain and take the 'Confession' of Waldemar Wappenhans. Frank honoured a promise he made to Wappenhans not to identify the general by name in his article for the *NYHT*. Diels however revealed Wappenhans true identity in an interview he gave to *Der Spiegel*.

Diels died on 18 November 1957 when his rifle accidentally discharged whilst he was out hunting. There may be no more to his demise than that. However, Diels was the son of a farmer, a veteran of two world wars, the former head of the Gestapo and, as confirmed by Frank,'a keen hunter and an excellent shot'. This raises the question as to how a man who had been around firearms his whole life 'accidentally shot himself with a hunting gun'.

Wappenhans had a long memory and his confession indicates he was a man who found it difficult to forgive and forget. In this context, and bearing in mind it was Diels who had revealed the true identity of the former SS-Gruppenfuehrer – and then made it publicly known through *Der Spiegel* – that Wapppenhans' comment in his private, previously unseen, letter to Wolfe Frank raises a more chilling possibility: 'As I've told you already', he wrote, 'I cannot understand at all why Herr Deils [sic] and Herr Wendt told Mr Augstein from *Der Spiegel* about my case. It was definitely not in their interest to do so'.[12]

(KlausWallbaum in his book on Diels – *Der Überläufer* (The Turncoat) – seems to agree there may be more to the officially recorded verdict. In his on-line introduction he records: 'He [Diels] died in 1957 supposedly after a hunting accident, but many, including Erik Larson, author of *In the Garden of Beasts* question this, as does this writer').

Rudolf Diels is buried in a family plot at Berghausen, Rhein-Lahn-Kreis, Rheinland-Pfalz, Germany.[13]

CHAPTER FIFTY-ONE – NOTES & REFERENCES

1. *Julius Caesar, William Shakespeare.*

2. *The Washington Evening Star*, Kingsbury Smith, Representing the Combined American Press, 16 October 1946.

3. *The Devil's Disciples*, Anthony Read, (W. W. Norton & Company, 2003), p.923.

4. *Time* magazine in its 28 October 1946 – *'Night Without Dawn.'*

5. *The Reich Marshal: A Biography of Hermann Goering*, p.397.

6. *Letter from Robert Jackson to William Donovan, 26 November 1945* Harry S. Truman Library & Museum.

7. *The Anatomy of the Nuremberg Trials: A Personal Memoir*, p.259.

8. ibid, p 260.

9. Holocaust Historical Society: www.holocausthistoricalsociety.org.uk/contents/germanbiographies/erichvondembachzelewski.html

10. *IMT Nuremberg Archives*, Stamford University H-3338.

11. *Nuremberg's Voice of Doom*, p.108.

12. Personal handwritten letter in Wolfe Frank's archive.

13. www.findagrave.com/memorial/117919130/rudolph-diels

SECTION ELEVEN

APPENDICES

WAS WOLFE FRANK CONNECTED TO AN INTELLIGENCE AGENCY?

*'Since real spies are so good, you never really
know what actual spying is.'*
RICHARD C. ARMITAGE

(I first included this Appendix in *The Undercover Nazi Hunter* – see Appendix G. However, as its content is so relevant to the subjects covered in this work, I felt it should also be included here. Other details are taken from Frank's life story included in *Nuremberg's Voice of Doom* (see Appendix G). Some of this information is part of the main text of this book. It is included again here for the sake of continuity and to assist readers).

TO SUGGEST WOLFE FRANK CONJURES UP images of the Scarlet Pimpernel or James Bond is not to exaggerate the lifestyle, charisma and appeal of this twentieth century adventurer. In the years leading up to the Second World War, Frank gave the impression of being little more than a pleasure-seeking philanderer with a somewhat cavalier attitude who managed to regularly take refreshment in the presence of Adolf Hitler without ever giving the Nazi salute[1]. However, this persona camouflaged the true character of a man who, in reality, was involved in an underground resistance movement, centred on those who met at the Carlton Tearooms in Munich, and who was risking his life smuggling Jews and large amounts of money out of Germany.

Likewise, during his pre-war years in England as an escapee, and his transition into a businessman, and then a British Army captain – as well as during his undercover operation for the *NYHT* – Frank could have passed as the model for Ian Fleming's archetypal hero (and Fleming had seen Frank in action at Nuremberg). An astonishingly handsome man irresistible to women, he was suave, chivalrous, cultured, charming, a gifted raconteur, a gambler, a risk taker, highly intelligent and a unique linguist who spoke five languages. He was also an intrepid adventurer who was prepared to risk his life for his adopted country or a worthy cause, and he could move flawlessly between all levels of society, never looking out of place in whatever role he adopted – he was as convincing as a German nobleman, an English aristocrat, or a British Army officer, as he was as a squaddie, a factory hand, a farmer, a schools' inspector, a Bavarian coal miner or a refugee – all roles he successfully fulfilled, without detection.

As a peerless translator, interpreter and interrogator he was one of the stars of 'history's greatest trials', and as an undercover investigative journalist for the *NHHT* he undertook a unique and dangerous challenge that delved deeply into some of post-war Germany's most pressing issues. These included the refugee crisis, anti-Semitism, de-Nazification, morality, nationalism, black marketeering and, most importantly, Germany's widespread willingness to protect the whereabouts and identities of wanted Nazi war criminals.

While it is clear that Frank's enterprise was to a great extent being supported, directed and financed by the *NYHT*, was it possible he was also in some way involved with one or other of the British or US Military Intelligence services?

There are a number of clues and circumstantial evidence contained in Frank's memoirs, archives and in other evidence to suggest that he could have been.

Firstly, there was his pre-war friendship and associations with Major Humphrey Sykes[2] whom Frank first met in the Italian Alpine resort of Sestriere in February 1937. Frank was on holiday with his then fiancée Baroness Maditta von Skrbensky and he had explained to Sykes that because of his Jewish ancestry it was impossible for him and Maditta to marry in Germany or another Axis-aligned country. In spite of having only just met them Sykes offered to arrange for Wolfe and Maditta to be married from his home on the British Army base at Tidworth in Wiltshire. The offer was accepted and the marriage took place at Andover Register Office in April.

After a brief honeymoon in Tidworth the newlyweds returned to Germany where Wolfe was tipped off, by a friend in the Gestapo, that he was to be arrested the following morning and interned in Dachau concentration camp.With little money and few clothes he fled from Germany, leaving behind his bride of six days – whom he did not see again for almost ten years.

Frank suggests in his memoirs that it may have been Maditta's father, Baron von Skrbensky, who had reported him and his non-Arian background to the authorities, stating that the Baron 'belonged to the "Herrenclub" in Berlin – a sort-of political, social, sinister assembly of nobles, industrialists and political grey eminences of Germany who were of considerable importance to Hitler.' Frank also indicates that his involvement with the underground group may have come to the attention of the Nazis. He may therefore have been under surveillance, and his meeting with a British Army major in Italy, at a sensitive time, and his subsequent marriage in England and stay at an officer's home on a British Army base may also have heightened suspicions.

Frank managed to escape in the nick of time, just before the Gestapo arrived to arrest him in the early hours of the following morning. He fled to Switzerland where Humphrey Sykes sent money for his passage to England and then allowed him to live at his family home. After a short period of integration, during which Frank learned the language, Sykes appointed him to be CEO of several companies and introduced him to many acquaintances in society, the theatre, to friends at Scotland Yard and members of both houses of Parliament. Sykes also arranged for Frank to work with a development scheme in Cape Canaveral, and advised him how to completely disassociate himself from his former homeland to become 'a stateless person'.

Internment

At the outbreak of war, Frank, along with all other German and Austrian refugees, was arrested and interned as an 'enemy alien'. However, he and Sykes engaged with a number of parliamentary members and camp officials, including Sir Timothy Eden, brother of the then Secretary of State for War, Sir Anthony Eden (later Prime Minister). This led to Frank's release, which in turn led to him being allowed to join the British Army where he gained a commission and rose to the rank of captain.

Sykes may, of course, have just taken a fraternal or comradely interest in Frank or he may simply have acted as a Good Samaritan. However, following Frank's death, Sykes, by then retired, travelled down from Scotland especially to go through Frank's papers, some of which were very sensitive documents that Frank should not have had. Mike Dilliway, the beneficiary of Wolfe's estate, was careful not to let Sykes see Frank's memoirs, but the former army major did leave with a number of other files, at least some of which, no doubt, pertained to the army, Nuremberg and Frank's undercover operation for the *NYHT*. Among all the many documents retained in Frank's archives, and apart from what he has written in his memoirs and a single photograph (see plate 10), there is not one record of his years of service in the British Army. Frank was a hoarder, yet there is no trace of his army records, any medals, awards or achievements. There were no discharge papers; identification, medical or grade cards; service record; pay book; certificate of transfer to reserve; or any other document connecting him to his years of service in the British Army, or indeed anything that linked Frank to Humphrey Sykes[2].

Leaving aside Sykes' desire to get hold of documents that may have caused him concern, any official or unofficial association Frank may have had with Military Intelligence is also likely to have extended to his undercover operation for the *New York Herald Tribune* – the resultant information clearly being of as much value to the intelligence services as it was to Frank and the *NYHT*.

Such an arrangement, if one existed, and the way it was conducted would therefore have benefitted all concerned. If Frank was captured and interrogated, especially by the Russians, MI could have distanced themselves from any involvement by pointing out Frank was simply working as a journalist – which he was. The *NYHT* in turn could claim that they only had an arms-length agreement to print anything Frank, as a freelance, might put their way. Frank on the other hand was, in reality: being financed and supported by one of Europe's top newspapers; acting with the knowledge of the Allied Military Forces; able to get into places it would be difficult to penetrate without the cooperation of senior intelligence and military personnel; and, importantly, had a 'get out of jail card' if ever he was caught (which he never was).

Among the most compelling evidence to consider in this context is the following:

- The degree of subterfuge involved in Frank's cover story (see Chapter Forty-Three), his assuming of another German's identity and the involvement of the former French Resistance workers who prepared his forged documents.
- The readiness of Sir David Maxwell-Fyfe[3], (soon to become Home Secretary and then Lord High Chancellor) to support Frank's undercover proposal.
- The *NYHT's* belief that Frank's life could be at risk on the mission and that 'he might not come back'.
- The fact that prior to commencement, Geoffrey Parsons Jr., the *NYHT's* European Editor, discussed the project with, and had the support of, Senator Foster Dulles the Republican nominee for president the previous year, who later became the 52nd United States Secretary of State (and whose brother Allen became Director of the CIA after having served under General Donovan at the OSS and smoothed the way for Germany's surrender in Italy). At their meeting on this matter Foster Dulles indicated 'no American correspondent could get underneath

the surface' and Parsons affirmed Frank had 'the highest recommendations from top British and American officials'.

- Prior to the final go-ahead, Parsons had flown to Heidelberg to get the whole project cleared personally by General Clarence Huebner, the Military Governor of the American Zone in Germany, to get the General's assurance that Frank would be 'bailed out of jail' if he got caught. Parsons had also received approval from General Lucius Clay, the senior US Army officer responsible for the administration of occupied Germany after the war.
- The relative ease with which Frank gained access to: refugee camps, high ranking politicians, bankers, industrialists, economists, government ministers, judges, lawyers, black marketeers, former SS officers and their families, and a prisoner on death row.
- The help he received from British Intelligence officers. He had discussed every aspect of his proposed investigation with the British Military Governor and other high ranking British and US officers, all of whom went out of their way to assist him in his mission. Whether or not he was 'licenced to kill', Frank was armed during his period in Germany.
- Perhaps the most compelling evidence that Frank may have had some connection to MI, however, was the level of authority he seemed to have been given or assumed which gave him access to military and intelligence personnel and records. This allowed him the freedom to negotiate the terms of a high-ranking SS officer's surrender and then decide what should be done with him, who he should be turned over to, what he did and did not include in his testimony and what would happen to him following his arrest. Quite simply, it seems, Frank alone had the power to decide whether Wappenhans lived or died.
- In a further development, and following the publication in 2018 of *Nuremberg's Voice of Doom*, Charlotte (not her real name) came forward and attested that, late in his life, Wolfe had asked for her assistance in destroying a quantity of documents and photographs from his past. Charlotte duly provided that help and further confirmed that, following Frank's death, she had, late at night, been interviewed at length by a 'police officer' and that, soon after, Frank's home had been broken into and searched by a person, or persons, unknown. There is no Police record of either the interview or the break in, posing the question, 'which branch of the Police or intelligence services

had visited Charlotte and dealt with the break in?' Whilst Charlotte, under Frank's direction and employ, assisted him to destroy evidence, and was subjected to the 'interrogation', she also received unwanted visits from the media. For these reasons she now wishes to remain anonymous. I can confirm, however, that she is a highly respected citizen of uprightness and integrity and a reliable witness who, in my presence, signed a statement confirming what she told me to be a true record and an eyewitness account of events of which she had personal first-hand knowledge.

APPENDIX A – NOTES & REFERENCES

1. In his memoirs Frank records 'Whenever the Fuehrer was in Munich and had some time on his hands, he would arrive at the Carlton [Tea Rooms] for coffee after his presumably vegetarian lunch. His arrival was signalled by a quickly gathering crowd outside and the shouts of 'Heil Hitler'. I would get up as rapidly and as inconspicuously as possible and disappear into the washroom. The other guests would rise upon Hitler's entry and would stand, facing his route of progress, with their arms raised until he had sat down. His party was usually small, perhaps four to six people and would invariably include his adjutant, Brückner, with whom I sometimes played tennis. Once Hitler had sat down at his table in the left corner of the second of the Carlton's two rooms, I would return to my seat. This I usually managed to choose in such a way that I could also pretend to miss his departure which was always over very quickly since he left the place with fast long strides before anyone had time to get up and 'Heil' him. Thus, during my three years of visiting the Carlton, unlike all the other guests, I never once gave the Hitler salute as the Fuehrer went by'.

2. Humphrey Hugh Sykes was born in 1907. He was the son of Major Herbert Rushton Sykes and Hon. Constance Harriet Georgina Skeffington. He married, firstly, Grizel Sophie, daughter of AirVice-Marshal Sir Norman Duckworth Kerr MacEwen, in 1936 – from whom he was divorced in 1948. He married, secondly, Muriel Hooper, daughter of Colonel John Charles Hooper, in 1958. He was educated at Rugby School and gained the rank of Major in the service of the 9th Lancers. He died in 1991 after having travelled from Scotland to the home of Mike Dilliway in Mere in search of Wolfe Frank's manuscript and other documents.

3. Sir David Maxwell Fyfe (1900–1967) was a Member of Parliament, lawyer and judge who variously held the offices of Solicitor General, Attorney General, Home Secretary and Lord High Chancellor. He later became the Earl of Kilmuir. At Nuremberg he was Britain's Deputy Chief Prosecutor and his cross- examination of Hermann Goering, which was translated by Wolfe Frank, is regarded as having been one of the most noted in history.

A LIST OF MAJOR HONOURS AWARDED TO GENERAL WILLIAM J. DONOVAN[1]

'Time will not dim the glory of their deeds.'
GENERAL OF THE ARMIES JOHN J. PERSHING

US Medals and Awards

Medal of Honor
Distinguished Service Cross
Distinguished Service Medal with 2 Bronze Oak Leaf Clusters
National Security Medal
Silver Star Medal
Purple Heart with Bronze Oak Leaf Cluster
Mexican Border Service Medal
World War I Victory Medal with 5 Battle Clasps
Occupation of Germany World War I Medal
American Defense Service Medal
American Campaign Medal
Asiatic-Pacific Campaign Medal with Arrowhead and 2 Bronze
   Service Stars
European-African-Middle Eastern Campaign Medal with Arrowhead,
   2 Silver and 2 Bronze Service Stars
World War II Victory Medal
Army of Occupation Medal with "Germany" Clasp
Armed Forces Reserve Medal with 1 Ten-Year Hourglass Device

Foreign Awards

Légion d'honneur (France) (World War I)
Commandeur de la Légion d'honneur (France) (World War II)
Croix de guerre with Palm and Silver Star (France) (World War I)
Honorary Knight Commander of the Most Excellent Order of the
   British Empire
Papal Lateran Cross (Vatican) (Italian: Croce Lateranese)
Knight Grand Cross of the Order of St. Sylvester (Vatican)

Order of the Crown (Italy)
Croce di Guerra (Italy)
Commander's Cross with Star of the Order of Polonia Restituta (Poland)
Grand Officer of the Order of Léopold of Belgium with Palm
Czechoslovakian War Cross (1939)
Grand Officer of the Order of Orange Nassau (Netherlands)
Grand Cross of the Royal Norwegian Order of St. Olav (Norway)
Knight Grand Cross (First Class) The Most Exalted Order of the White
   Elephant (Thailand)

APPENDIX TWO – NOTES & REFERENCES

1. Military Hall of Honor: https://militaryhallofhonor.com/honoree-record.
   php?id=70

JOHN FORD

'The Poet With a Camera'.
GENERAL WILLIAM DONOVAN

BORN JOHN MARTIN FEENEY, JOHN FORD (1894–1973) is regarded as being one of the most important and influential filmmakers of the 'Golden Age' of Hollywood. In a career lasting more than fifty years, he directed over 130 films between 1917 and 1970 and received a record four Academy Awards for Best Director for *The Informer* (1935), *The Grapes of Wrath* (1941), *How Green Was My Valley* (1942), and *The Quiet Man* (1952).

Seeing the vital need for photographic evidence of the Second World War and the atrocities being committed by the Axis Powers, General Donovan created the 'OSS Field Photographic Branch' (OSSFPB) and, wanting the very best, he recruited John Ford in 1941 and appointed him to be head of the unit. Ford brought with him over thirty of Hollywood's finest writers, directors, editors and cameramen and over 300 other technicians.

John Ford's OSSFPB went on to make over 100 short films about the OSS and naval activities including *Undercover* and *How to Operate Behind Enemy Lines*. He also made training films for OSS agents such as *Training Group* and *The Mole*, both of which, like *Undercover*, are now declassified and in the public domain (an extensive list of the unit's productions is shown at Appendix D).

Ford took one of the leading roles in *Undercover* and was an active participant as a director and as a cameraman throughout the war. He was promoted to the rank of Naval Reserve Commander in 1941 and later, at the Battle of Midway, despite being wounded he refused to leave his post and continued filming. For this he was awarded a purple heart. He used his film, with voice overs, and turned it into *The Battle of Midway*, a film that won him an Academy Award for Best Documentary in 1943. The following year he won a similar award for *December 7th*, (the attack on Pearl Harbor) establishing an unprecedented and never-equalled run of four-in-a-row Oscars – he had received Best Director Oscars for *The Grapes of Wrath* (1941) and *How Green Was My Valley* (1942).

One of the last films made by OSFFPB was *That Justice Be Done*, a ten-minute documentary compilation of newsreels and captured German films. Glimpses of massacred and desecrated bodies are shown as part of the acts committed by the Nazis during their reign of terror.

Schulberg Productions, who restored some of Ford's work in 2009, explained how the use of OSSFPB compilations, even after General Donovan had left Nuremberg, provided Robert Jackson with much film and photographic evidence that helped the justice to convict the war criminals:

> During preparation for the trial, Jackson made the bold and historic decision to use film and photo evidence to convict the Nazis. But these films had to be found. General William ("Wild Bill") Donovan proposed that his OSS Field Photographic Branch, headed by movie director John Ford, be given the job … just in time for the start of the trial, they found vital evidence, which, in close collaboration with Jackson's staff of lawyers, they edited into a 4-hour film for the courtroom called *The Nazi Plan*, which documented the party's rise to power. Jackson also presented their 1-hour compilation, *Nazi Concentration Camps*, shot by U.S. and British liberators, which shocked the courtroom when it was shown on November 29, 1945.[1]

It was, no doubt, this evidence with which Edwin Putzell, following his departure from Nuremberg, was helping John Ford compile.

For his heroic actions in the Battle of Midway, Ford was awarded the Legion of Merit with Combat 'V' (a decoration awarded for combat valor or heroism). The citation, as recorded by the *Bureau of Naval Personnel Information Bulletin No. 361 (March 1947)*, reads as follows:

> The President of the United States of America takes pleasure in presenting the Legion of Merit with Combat "V" to Captain John Ford, United States Navy, for exceptionally meritorious conduct in the performance of outstanding services to the Government of the United States as Chief of the Field Photographic Branch, Office of Strategic Services, from September 1941 to September 1945. Voluntarily recruiting and organizing approximately three hundred technicians as a Naval photographic group, Captain Ford greatly aided in establishing the photographic branch of the Office of Strategic Services and, exercising close and careful supervision of the numerous branch projects, developed valuable new equipment which is now in use by the United States Army

Signal Corps. Energetic and resourceful, he worked tirelessly toward the preparation and direction of the secret motion picture and still photographic reports and ably directed the initiation and execution of a program of secret intelligence photography. Participating in the Battle of Midway, the Tokyo Raid, North African Invasion, and the Invasion of the Norman Coast, Captain Ford controlled all seagoing photography of United Nations operations in these major battles, rendering this vital service under extremely difficult and dangerous combat conditions. Assigned the mission of observing and obtaining a photographic record of the impending enemy naval attack at Midway, Captain Ford courageously took station on top of the Midway Island power plant, where he remained a clear target as the enemy waged a savage, unexpected and continuous air attack and, although wounded early in the action, succeeded in delivering by telephone a running, verbal report of the battle, thereby aiding the Commanding Officer in the disposition and use of the defending American forces throughout the action. By his brilliant service in a highly specialized field, Captain Ford contributed materially to the successful prosecution of the war. (Captain Ford is authorized to wear the Combat 'V'.)

General Donovan pinned the Legion of Merit on the 'poet with a camera' in September 1945 and Ford was promoted to captain in the Naval Reserve. On his retirement in 1951 he was further promoted to the rank of rear admiral and, in 1973, shortly before his death, President Richard Nixon awarded him the Presidential Medal of Freedom. At his funeral service, Ford's coffin was, movingly, draped with the tattered US flag that had been hoisted by the Marines during the Battle of Midway and his memorial stone includes the final honour bestowed upon him – the title 'Admiral John Ford.'[2]

APPENDIX C – NOTES & REFERENCES

1. Schulberg Productions, *Nuremberg: Its Lesson for Today*: www.nuremberg film.org/old/press/Nuremberg_Theatrical_Press_Kit.pdf

2. US Naval Institute and other sources.

FILMS PRODUCED BY JOHN FORD OSS FIELD PHOTOGRAPHIC BRANCH: 1941 – 1945[1]

'What is done, is done: Spend not the time in tears,
but seek for justice'.
JOHN FORD

Sex Hygiene, (Director; 30-minute training film).
Iceland; 11 minutes.
Canal Report
Doolittle Raid: Ships in Task Force (unedited)
Task Force at Sea: On Way to Doolittle's Tokyo Raid (unedited)
Doolittle Raid: Flyers Take Off from USS Enterprise & USS Hornet (unedited)
The Battle of Midway;[2] 18 minutes.
The Battle of Midway (outtakes)
USS Yorktown (CV-5), in Battle of Midway
Torpedo Squadron, (Director; documentary short for the United States Navy);
    8 minutes.
Pearl Harbor (Damage)
USS Kearny (aka Damage Repair of the WWII Destroyer); 4 minutes.
North African Invasion; 302 minutes.
December 7th;[3] (two versions); 82 minutes and 20 minutes.
At the Front in North Africa; (John Ford appears); 41 minutes.
War Department Report; 46 minutes.
German Manpower; 22 minutes.
German Airpower; 20 minutes.
OSS Camera Report: China, Burma, India; 17 minutes.
Inside Tibet; 39 minutes.
Preview of Assam; 9 minutes.
Homenaje a Mexico (Mexico National Celebration); 10 minutes.
Maneuver Report No. 1; 24 minutes.
Victory in Burma
We Sail at Midnight, (Director, Documentary short for the United States Navy).
How to Operate Behind Enemy Lines, (Director, Actor; Ford training film for
    OSS; filmed in Burma).
Show Business at War, (Actor; Ford is shown with the OSS in this documentary
    short).
Burial of Air Crash Victims; 4 minutes.

We Sail at Midnight; (Maritime Commission); 10 minutes.
Personnel Inspection of Field Photographic Brank; 6 minutes.
Marshal Tito's Wartime Headquarters; 4 minutes.
King George Inspects USS Augusta, LST, LCI, and LCTs at Portland, England
Normandy Invasion; (Navy/Coast Guard/Field Photo/Allied governments).
Manuel Quezon: In Memoriam; (John Ford also appears); 18 minutes.
German Reprisals: Destruction in Greece; 53 minutes.
Japanese Surrender [Burma]; 9 minutes.
A Report on OSS Morale Operations in Italy; 10 minutes.
Campbell Missile; 10 minutes.
Cayuga Mission (outtakes); 11 minutes.
Mission to Giessen; 7 minutes.
Evacuation of Prisoner of War; 3 minutes.
A Report on Airborne Rockets Prepared by the Joint Committee on New Weapons
    and Equipment of the Joint Chiefs of Staff.
That Justice Be Done; (on the Nuremberg Nazi War Crimes Trials); 10 minutes.
Nazi Supreme Court Trial of the Anti-Hitler Plot, Sept. 1944-Jan. 1945; 44 minutes.
Nazi Concentration Camps; (compilation shown at the Nuremberg Trials, largely
    photographed by U.S. Army Lieutenant George Stevens); 59 minutes.
The Nazi Plan; (compilation shown at the Nuremberg Trials, assembled by
    Stevens and Budd Schulberg).
Nuremberg; record of the Nuremberg Trials, (filmed and assembled by Ray
    Kellogg, Pare Lorentz, and Stuart Schulberg); 76 minutes.
Blind Bombing; 14 minutes.
Body Search; 19 minutes.
Brazilian Material OSS Unit No. 17
Burma Butterflies; 9 minutes.
Burma, Kachin Guerrilla Camp; 9 minutes.
Burmese Troops; 9 minutes.
Chinese Commandos; 10 minutes.
Crete; 30 minutes.
The E 2-Man Fol-Boat; 8 minutes.
The 8-Man Fol-Boat; 6 minutes.
Farish Report; 11 minutes.
Fate Conoscenza Colnemico: Uniformi Tedesche e Distintivi; (Italian sound track);
    14 minutes.
Galahad Forces; 20 minutes.
Ground to Air Transfer; 11 minutes.
House Search; 27 minutes.
Iconography; 30 minutes.
Japanese Background Study Program: Natural Resources of Japan: Part 2; 22 minutes.
Japanese Behavior; 50 minutes.
Joan and Eleanor; 18 minutes.
Kachin State, Burma; 11 minutes.
Kachin State, Burma, During World War II; 7 minutes.

Kachin State, Burma; 10 minutes.
Meet the Enemy (Germany); 40 minutes.
Morale Operations Field Report No. 1; 46 minutes.
Nassau Training Report; 10 minutes.
Nylon Rubber Boat; 16 minutes.
Office of Strategic Services Operations, Burma; 8 minutes.
OSS Activities in Burma During World War II; 8 minutes.
OSS Activities in Burma During World War II (a different film from the title listed above).
OSS Basic Military Training; 25 minutes.
OSS Training in Middle East; 10 minutes.
Pridi Phanomyong Meets Office of Strategic Services Officers; 2 minutes.
Project Eagle; 16 minutes.
Project Gunn; 21 minutes.
P.W.E. and M.O.—Cairo; 16 minutes.
Rescued Flyers; 4 minutes.
Seabees; 44 minutes.
S.I. in Action; 14 minutes.
Suspended Runway; 22 minutes.
This Is Japan; 12 minutes.
Undercover; 80 minutes.
Unfinished Report; 17 minutes.
Using the Lambertson Unit; 8 minutes.

APPENDIX D – NOTES & REFERENCES

1. As listed by John Ford Filmography: www.johnfordfilms.com/filmography

2. John Ford Director, Co-cinematographer, Editor, Producer War Activities Committee; starring Donald Crisp, Henry Fonda; received the 1943 Academy Award for Best Documentary Feature; Ford personally shot much of the footage during the actual Battle of Midway.

3. Co-directed with Gregg Toland; documentary short for the United States Navy; co-directed by Lieutenant Gregg Toland, USNR; received the 1944 Academy Award for Documentary Short Subject.

THE OSS SOCITY

'At its core, the OSS Society will always be about the values and achievements of the OSS and its founder, Gen. William Donovan.'
CHARLES PINCK, PRESIDENT OF THE OSS SOCIETY

THE OSS SOCIETY HONOURS the historic accomplishments of the Office of Strategic Services (OSS) during the Second World War: the first organised effort by the United States to implement a centralised system of strategic intelligence and the predecessor to the Central Intelligence Agency, the U.S. Special Operations Command, and the State Department's Bureau of Intelligence and Research. It educates the public about the importance of U.S. strategic intelligence and special operations to the preservation of freedom.

The OSS Society was founded in 1947 by General William Donovan as the Veterans of OSS (VOSS). It was based in New York City for fifty years. In 1997, it became The OSS Society and moved to Washington, D.C. The first William J. Donovan Award was presented to Allen Dulles in 1961. Amongst those to have received the award are: Presidents George H.W. Bush, Dwight Eisenhower, and Ronald Reagan; British Prime Minister Margaret Thatcher; The Earl Mountbatten of Burma; CIA Directors William Burns, William Casey, William Colby, Allen Dulles, Robert Gates, Gina Haspel, Richard Helms, Leon Panetta, Gen. David Petraeus, George Tenet, and Judge William Webster; and former SOCOM Commanders Admirals Eric Olson and William McRaven.

It also presents eight other awards: the Peter Ortiz Award, which is presented to an active duty member of the U.S. Special Operations Command; the Hugh Montgomery Award, which is named in honour the OSS Society's former chairman and presented to a retired officer from the Central Intelligence Agency's Directorate of Operations; the John Waller Award recognises achievement in OSS scholarship; the Distinguished Service Award, which is presented to OSS veterans and other individuals who have made significant contributions to its operations or legacy; the Virginia Hall Award that recognises the contributions made by women to the U.S. intelligence and special operations communities; the Victor Hugo Award that is presented to a member of U.S Special Forces; the Stanley Lovell Award that recognises contributions made by private industry to U.S. national security; and the Jack Taylor Award that is presented to a U.S. Navy SEAL.

The OSS Society is working to build the National Museum of Intelligence and Special Operations to honour Americans who have served at the 'tip of the spear' and inspire future generations to serve their country. It was the sponsoring organisation for the OSS Congressional Gold Medal Act that was signed into law by President Obama on 14 December 2016. It led a successful effort to save the OSS and first CIA headquarters on Navy Hill in Washington, D.C., from being demolished as part of a redevelopment of this site and have these buildings added to the National Register of Historic Places. The OSS Society installed a memorial at Arlington National Cemetery honouring OSS personnel killed and missing in action.

Membership in The OSS Society is available to OSS veterans, their descendants, members Of the U.S. intelligence, special operations and national security communities, and citizens of the U.S. and other nations who have a serious interest in the OSS.

To learn more about The OSS Society visit: *osssociety.org*

THE AIREY NEAVE TRUST

*'Remembering that tyranny has many sides and freedom but one.'**
AIREY NEAVE

THE AIREY NEAVE TRUST was established in memory of Airey Neave, DSO, OBE, MC, TD (1916–1979), British lawyer, soldier, and politician whose life and work was cut short by terrorism. The objective of the Airey Neave Trust is to support and promote research that contributes in a practical way to the struggle against international terrorist activity.

Research Fellowships: The Trust invites Fellows of established university departments to submit applications for Airey Neave Trust Research Fellowships on any topic which falls within the definition of helping to protect and/or enhance personal freedom under the rule of democratic law, either national or international.

Favourable consideration will be given to publications designed to make a discernible impact and to contribute in a practical way to the struggle against international terrorist activity.

The Airey Neave Book Prize is awarded to the work of non-fiction which the judging panel considers to have made the most significant, original, relevant, and practically valuable contribution to the understanding of terrorism.

For further information, please contact the Trust: <u>aireyneavetrust@gmail.com</u>
Website: https://www.aireyneavetrust.org.uk

* Airey Neave's inscription on the copy of his book *Nuremberg – A Personal Record of the Trial of Major Nazi War Criminals in 1945–6*, that he gave to Margaret Thatcher. In the eulogy she delivered at Airey Neave's Memorial Service, Prime Minister Thatcher's opening words were: 'Airey Neave was my very dear and deeply trusted friend' and, of the inscription in the book, she said: 'If it is possible for a single sentence to sum up a man, that sums up Airey Neave. Certainly none could serve better as his epitaph.'

PREQUEL/SEQUEL

Completing the Wolfe Frank Story

NUREMBERG'S VOICE OF DOOM

Based upon his memoirs, *Nuremberg's Voice of Doom* is the life story of Wolfe Frank – who has been variously described as being a refugee, resistance worker, soldier, playboy, Nazi hunter and wrongfully forgotten hero – as compiled, edited and expanded upon by Paul Hooley. The book includes a unique record of what happened at 'the greatest trial in history' as seen through the eyes of a man who bore witness to the whole proceedings. It includes important historical information never previously revealed and details of Frank's personal encounters, inside and outside the courtroom, with all the war criminals, particularly Hermann Goering. It is also an absorbing and fascinating life story of one of the 20th century's most charismatic and colourful characters.

'Wolfe Frank's extraordinary memoirs give a fresh insight into how Hitler's henchmen faced the hangman's noose – and how the handsome playboy mixed his harrowing work with pleasure … In the book Paul Hooley's well-researched notes are printed in a different typeface but they brilliantly fill in the blank spaces and bring order to the intriguing narrative of Wolfe's incredible life.' **James Murray**, *Daily Express*

'*Nuremberg's Voice of Doom* vividly brings to life the character of Wolfe Frank: refugee, soldier, playboy, Nazi hunter and Chief Interpreter at the Nuremberg Trials. Historian Paul Hooley has done a magnificent job compiling Frank's papers to create a startling posthumous autobiography of the man who literally pronounced judgement on some of the most evil men in history. Readers will be astonished at the sheer charisma of Wolfe Frank whose sparkling personality leaps off the page in a historically important war memoir like no other. A must read to uncover a complex but wrongfully forgotten hero of the 20th Century.' **Tom Garner**, *Features Editor: History of War Magazine*

'A fascinating new book *Nuremberg's Voice of Doom*, the autobiography of Wolfe Frank, chief interpreter at the Nuremberg Trials, edited by Paul Hooley, looks at the man who was so instrumental in the trials and possibly the only person to get the most intricate details of all that went on – it is a truly remarkable story – you really don't want to miss what this book has to say'. ***Phil Dave***, *Jewish Views*

'A fabulous book about one of those people that seem too big for everyday life. This is an important book, a page-turner, a book that moves at fast pace, full of adventure, historical detail, and with a protagonist that even the most skilled fiction writers would struggle to improve on. Read it and recommend it. I'm sure you will. I am surprised nobody has picked up on Wolfe Frank as a subject for a movie, or even better a TV series, I'm sure if you read it you'll be casting the movie in your head'. ***Olga Nunez Miret***, *Goodreads*

Dear Mr Hooley, I was given your book recently as an early Christmas present, by a friend. I have just read it, and feel moved to make contact, to congratulate you on a fabulous read, and a superb piece of historical education, combined with great humour. I could hardly put it down! Well done on giving this truly amazing man the recognition that he deserves, albeit after his life. Thank you for your accomplishment, 'from a box, in the attic'. I salute you!' ***John Pentreath***

'I have finished the book in almost one sitting and wanted to let you know how much I enjoyed learning about the life of Wolfgang Frank. An amazing tale that I'm sure no one in our family knew about in such detail. Fascinating information about an incredible man. Such an important story to tell.' ***Peter Goyert*** *(a descendant of Wolfe Frank's half sister)*

'I loved the book and the way it was written. I read it over a period of four days and found it to be thoroughly interesting … a style that ends a chapter with the reader wanting to know more and for that reason it was hard to put down. I shall read it again and have bought copies for my sons and two other friends.' ***Graham Fuller***

'Editor Paul Hooley has taken the original copy and married it to extensive notes creating a readable account with the ups and downs of a novel … this story and book provide a clear look at another should-never-be-forgotten chapter of civilization's modern history … It makes a cracking read … I recommend buying it!' ***John Koenig***

'I can tell you this – it was wonderful. I read it on the day I bought it, taking me about fifteen hours. I couldn't put it down because it was so interesting and well written. I am so looking forward to – *Undercover Nazi Hunter*.' **John Carthy**

THE UNDERCOVER NAZI HUNTER

The Undercover Nazi Hunter is Paul Hooley's sequel to *Nuremberg's Voice of Doom* and *GOERING'S SUICIDE: 'They Will Not Hang Me!'* In the months following his service at Nuremberg, Frank became increasingly alarmed at the misinformation coming out of Germany so in 1949, backed by the *New York Herald Tribune,* he risked his life again by returning to the country of his birth during the Cold War period to make an 'undercover' survey of the main facets of post-war German life and viewpoints. During this enterprise he worked as a German alongside Germans in factories, on the docks, in a refugee camp and elsewhere. Equipped with false papers he sought objective answers to many questions including: the refugee crisis; anti-Semitism; morality, de-Nazification; religion; and nationalism. While on this mission he single-handedly tracked down and arrested Waldemar Wappenhans, the German General ranked 'fourth' on the Allies 'most wanted' list (and Himmler's choice to head the SS in Great Britain) – before personally taking and transcribing the Nazi's Confession – which is included, for the first time in any language, within the book – and handing him over to the authorities.

'This remarkable book by Wolfe Frank, chief interpreter at the Nuremberg war crimes trials, has two main characters that both deserve more attention: Wolfe Frank himself and the SS general that was supposed to lead the British section of the Waffen-SS. Thanks to the editor of *The Undercover Nazi Hunter*, Paul Hooley, a vivid and often surprising picture of Wolfe Frank emerges … His path to Nuremberg, from playboy to German refugee to British Army volunteer, is one of those most incredible but true stories of WWII. The amount of work that the editor has invested in researching Frank's whole career is impressive and the result is also a vast painting of post-war Germany with many insights'. **Lars Gyllenhaal,** *Author, film researcher & member of the Swedish Military History Commission.*

'Historian Paul Hooley has written two books about Wolfe Frank who was Chief Interpreter at the Nuremberg Trials and announced the sentences of the court to the Nazi War Criminals. Based on Frank's memoirs and some remarkable historical sleuthing *Nuremberg's Voice of Doom* and *The Undercover Nazi Hunter* are the expanded memoirs of a quite extraordinary character who was involved in incredibly dangerous stuff bringing Nazis to justice. They are a fascinating couple of books and these stories were almost lost to history – check them out and enjoy!' **Dan Snow**, *Historian and Broadcaster*

'This book with its two distinct parts gives a valuable insight and record of the life in post war Germany and of a senior military man who tried to do his duty within all the complications and constraints of Hitler's Germany ... With short chapters and snappy writing this book is an easy read. The story is an unusual one, well told flowing at a pace'. **Robert Bartlett CBE**, *Historian*

'Following his service at Nuremberg he [Frank] returned to Germany, undercover, to write a series of articles for the *New York Herald and Tribune* ... Fortuitously he discovered the whereabouts and arrested SS General Waldemar Wappenhans, listed fourth on the allies wanted list. He transcribed the SS General's confession and this, together with his articles for the *New York Herald Tribune*, provides the reader with a fresh look at a nation in defeat'. **Richard Gough**, *Military Author and Historian*

'*The Undercover Nazi Hunter* continues Wolfe's story as he goes back to Germany post war to assess the situation on the ground for the Americans and whilst he is there bring more Nazi war criminals to justice. I like to consider myself as a bit of a History buff but had never heard of Wolfe Frank. His story is incredible and he really is one of the unsung heroes of the Second World War. One whose story everyone should hear'. **Chris Sartin**, *Waterstones*

'Review Breakdown: Readability 93%; Historical Accuracy 93%, Historical Value 93%; Details 93%. The result of Wolfe Frank's research and undercover work is a great book and exposes how the German everyman perceived the world post World War II ... The Allies were fortunate to have this man serving in this role. He set the gold standard for investigating war crimes and handling enemy prisoners of war for interrogation purposes.' **Christopher (Moon) Mullins, MA, BA**, *Reviewer for ARGunners*

'For anyone interested in the Nuremberg trial, and understanding how the Germans tried to claw their way out of their recent horrors of their Nazi past, this book is invaluable'. **Dr Adrian Greaves,** *The Anglo-Zulu War Historical Society*

'Paul Hooley is to be congratulated on bringing to the reader a masterful rending of this part of the multi faceted life of Wolfe Frank'. **Martin Willoughby,** *The Wessex Branch of the Western Front Association*

Both books are published by Frontline Books, an imprint of Pen & Sword Books Ltd

COURTROOM 600

Teaching the Lessons of Nuremberg

COURTROOM 600 is both a virtual museum and an educational resource built around the legacy of the Nuremberg Trials. Through story-based learning, it brings history to life for students, educators, and the general public.

Online audiences can explore a 300-image gallery of rare artefacts and curated photographs from the first Nuremberg Trial (IMT), offering an immersive glimpse behind the scenes of history in the making.

For educators, *Courtroom 600* provides a suite of experiential resources designed for a variety of secondary social studies classes. Learners can investigate the causes and consequences of WWII in Europe by working directly with Nuremberg primary source documents. They can also explore how Nazi racial ideology — not economic grievances — was the driving force behind the war, and that genocide was part of Hitler's war aims from the outset. Four modules are structured around the Nuremberg indictments: Conspiracy, Crimes Against Peace, War Crimes, and Crimes Against Humanity. Each is designed with narrative podcasts, curated photos, teacher training podcasts, and flexible activities adaptable to a wide range of educational settings.

In the years ahead, *Courtroom 600* will grow beyond its current offerings, introducing interactive experiences, travelling exhibits, and new media projects. All are designed to connect Nuremberg's enduring lessons to the world students live in today – and to preserve its legacy for generations yet to come.

For further information visit: *Courtroom600.org*

THE COMET LINE

Resistance members who risked their lives to spirit
Allied servicemen to freedom

THE COMET LINE was a major resistance organisation escape network pioneered by a twenty-four-year-old Belgian woman, Andrée de Jongh (codename Dédée) and her father Frederic (codename Paul). Backed financially by MI9 and working directly with Airey Neave, Comet organised escape lines (now referred to as being 'Freedom Trails') for downed RAF and US airmen and others.

Comet's Paris headquarters were situated on Rue Babylone, and Frederic's property on Rue Vaneau was a Comet safe house (the two roads are the setting for Neave's short 'story' *Cognac for Judas*). It is estimated over 800 Allied servicemen were led to safety, often by Andrée, from Belgium and France into neutral Spain where the escapees were handed over to MI9's Michael Cresswell (codename Monday).

An estimated 3,000 'helpers' assisted the Comet Line. Over 700 were arrested and 290 were shot or died in prison. In the spring of 1944, with the Allied invasion of France looming, Airey Neave and Comet Line began gathering Allied airmen into forest camps where they could await the Allied armies. Neave arranged airdrops of 'tents, medicines, clothes and food to supplement provisions bought locally' and he recalled, 'The diet was surprisingly generous for a clandestine camp surviving virtually under the noses of the Nazis.'

Comet Line was infiltrated by German agents and hundreds of 'helpers' were betrayed to the German secret police including Andrée and Frederic de Jongh. Frederic was executed in March 1944. Andrée was sent to a Ravensbück, and then Mauthausen concentration camps – if the Nazis had realised who she was, she too would have been executed. Liberated by the Allies, and in a dreadful condition, she somehow made her way to Paris, arriving at the MI9 office, in the middle of the night, still wearing her concentration camp dress. She was received by Donald Darling (codename Sunday) who took over central control from Airey Neave (codename Saturday), once Neave began following the Allied invasion – his specific tasks then being to liberate and rescue those airmen stranded in forest camps and thank the many heroes of the escape lines.

Andrée died aged ninety in 2007. Among the many awards she received for her bravery were the US Medal of Freedom, the George

Medal and the Légion d'honneur. (Much more information can be found about Comet Line, Andrée and Frederic and their associations with MI9 in Airey Neave's books *Little Cyclone* and *Saturday at M.I.9*, and in *Public Servant, Secret Agent*, the biography of Neave written by Paul Routledge).

In France some Nazi collaborators were poisoned, and it is believed over 10,000 were executed after legal proceedings or extrajudicially. Chief amongst the infiltrating traitors of the Comet Line were Jacques Desoubrie, alias Pierre Boulain, alias Jean Masson; Harold Cole also known as Captain Mason; and Roger Leneveu (or Le Neveu), who was also known as Roger Le Legionnaire. These three were responsible for hundreds of arrests, and all three lived up to the evil portrait of a traitor painted by Airey Neave in *Cognac for Judas*.

Lenevue was 'liquidated' by the Resistance in 1944, and Cole was killed in a shoot-out with French police. Masson was unmasked by another of Comet Line's most courageous young ladies, Michelle Dumon, also known as Lily Dumont (codename Michou). She was just five feet tall and although in her early twenties looked only fifteen. France being considered too dangerous for her, Michou was persuaded by Michael Creswell to move to Britain in June 1944 where she worked closely with Airey Neave and MI9. Soon after she met and married Pierre Ugeux, a French major working for SOE.

Michou having proven Masson to be the traitor, MI9 asked the Resistance group French Forces of the Interior (FFI) to track him down and kill him. Although MI9 was later informed Masson had been eliminated he was later seen, and it was assumed the FFI had assassinated the wrong person.

Michou returned to Paris to help locate MI9 agents and missing airmen in the autumn of 1944, and the following year she picked out Pierre Boulain/Jean Masson/Jacques Desoubrie from photographs she was shown by US Intelligence, who told her he was working for the US in Nuremberg. Following Michou's identification, Masson was arrested and tried 'for having participated in the capture and assassination of members of the resistance and for sending Allied military to their deaths in violation of the Geneva Convention.' He was convicted, sentenced to death and executed by firing squad. His last words were, 'Heil Hitler.'

For her bravery and for her saving the lives of so many Allied servicemen, Michelle Dumon – Michou – was awarded: the George Medal and the US Medal of Freedom with Gold Palm. She and Pierre Ugeux lived in France and had four children. She died, aged ninety-six, in 2017.

SECTION TWELVE

END MATTER

ACKNOWLEDGEMENTS

M Y ORIGINAL INTENTION was to see this book published in 2024, but tragedy struck when my beloved wife, of almost sixty years, died suddenly soon after I had started work on this project. Dealing with the period of grief that followed was compounded by my never having cooked a meal in my life, or attended to any of the other domestic duties.

To cut a long story short, it took me many months to overcome my loss, learn new skills and find a way of carrying out the many daily tasks that require attention in order to survive. This left no time for writing. My burden was further exacerbated by the knowledge that I alone held the answer to one of the 20th century's most enduring and frustrating unsolved mysteries that needed to be shared with a wider audience.

My dear son Simon came up with the solution to my dilemma by offering to come and stay with me for three months, to relieve me of the chores that were taking up so much of my time – and that is what he did. Then, for the following period, he and my other son Ben, took it in turns to carry on that arrangement for a further week each month until my researches and the manuscript were complete. I can honestly say therefore that without their help this book would not have been produced. They both know how much their efforts are appreciated, but I am pleased to have this opportunity of bringing the importance of the roles they played to the attention of others.

In like fashion, I extend my appreciation to my publishers, Frontline/ Pen & Sword Books, and in particular to commissioning editor Martin Mace, for their patience and understanding of my situation and for the encouragement and assistance provided to me at every stage of this work.

Elsewhere, I have recorded my gratitude to Petronella Wyatt and *The Spectator* for giving me permission to include the article Ms Wyatt wrote following her interview with Edwin Putzell in 2003. The information contained in Ms Wyatt's feature, alongside that provided by 'Charlotte', to whom I also extend my grateful thanks, proved to be the catalyst for this project. As in my case with Charlotte, the opportunity of interviewing Mr Putzell had presented itself to Ms Wyatt unexpectedly. These encounters proved to be serendipity moments, for us both, and they led to all that followed in this work. In similar fashion I record once again my gratitude to Douglas Waller and Free Press for allowing me to use extracts from Mr Waller's meticulously researched book *Wild Bill Donovan*. These inclusions are of paramount importance, for they substantiate and add much further evidence to my own research and narrative.

I also extend grateful thanks to the following citizens and authorities of the City of Naples, Florida: Mayor Teresa Heitmann; Executive Office Coordinator Sandra Fazzino; and historian and author Lila Zuck and JohnTellischak of Naples History Society who both spent many hours searching for documents, and providing information, concerning Mayor Putzell's life and achievements.

Others who have made valued contributions, been helpful following my enquiries, or have given permissions to use extracts or illustrations include: the staff of The National Archives, Kew; US National Archives and Records Administration; William Neave and the Airey Neave Trust; Charles Pinck and the OSS Society; the Central Intelligence Agency Office of Public Affairs; the staff of Parliamentary Archives; Eileen Barroso (photographer), Jennifer Pellerito and Jocelyn Wilk of Columbia University Archives; Laurie Pasler and Courtroom 600; and Simon Hooley, for his work on some of the graphics.

I also take this opportunity to pay tribute to those authors whose works are listed in the Bibliography, and to Sir Tim Berners-Lee and his colleagues for inventing the World Wide Web and for making the 'Internet' available to all free of charge – an act of monumental generosity that has benefitted mankind in general and every computer user in particular, especially historians and researchers at every level. Credit must also be given to the countless experts and amateur enthusiasts who so willingly share their knowledge via the information super-highway. Without this technology and the wealth of resources it has made available to us all, books such as this would have been more difficult to produce and would be far less substantial in content.

I apologise unreservedly for any names I have inadvertently omitted from these acknowledgements, or for not giving proper credit in any instances where it has not been possible to verify authorship or ownership – if any such instances are found and brought to my attention, I will ensure appropriate permissions are sought and that any future editions of this book are amended accordingly.

Finally, but of paramount importance, this book is both a tribute to, and a further acknowledgement of, the history defining roles played throughout the Second World War and at Nuremberg by General William Donovan, Lieutenant Edwin Putzell, Major Airey Neave and

Captain Wolfe Frank – four of freedom's greatest champions, who came together by chance in the autumn of 1945 during the preparations for the trial of the major Nazi war criminals. During that eight-week period they interrogated Hermann Goering – 'the man who tied the activities of all the defendants together in a common effort.' The overriding mission of all four, on behalf of humanity, was to see the war criminals in general, and Goering in particular, answer for all the atrocities carried out by the Nazis during their reign of terror. Those officers, three of them attorneys and prosecutors, also had personal reasons for ensuring justice, guilt and punishments were rightly, but fairly, attributed and administered through due legal process. In Donovan's and Putzell's case it was on behalf of their OSS colleagues who had been tortured and murdered; for Neave it was for the Allied aircrews and resistance line agents and 'helpers' who had met with similar fates; and for Frank it was for the family, friends and all who had 'disappeared' into 'the fog and night' or who had suffered in concentration camps.

It has been an honour and a privilege for me to have researched and written this record of the journeys, the lives, the involvements and the achievements of four such unique, dedicated, courageous, charismatic and patriotic seekers of justice – the likes of which we may never see again.

Paul Hooley, MBE, JP

BIBLIOGRAPHY

BOOKS

Alford, Kenneth A.; Savas, Theodore P., *Nazi Millionaires*, (Casemate 2007)

Brown, Anthony Cave, *Wild Bill Donovan – The Last Hero*, (Times Books 1982)

Cooper, R.W., *The Nuremberg Trial, (Penguin Books 1947)*

Danczuk, Simon; Smith, Daniel, *Scandal at Dolphin Square*, (The History Press, 2022)

Doundoulakis, Helias, *Trained to be an OSS Spy*, (Xlibris 2014)

Frank, Wolfe; Hooley, Paul, *Nuremberg's Voice of Doom*, (Frontline/Pen & Sword Books 2018)

Frank, Wolfe; Hooley, Paul, *The Undercover Nazi Hunter*, (Frontline/Pen & Sword Books 2019)

Gaiba, Francesca, *The Origins of Simultaneous Interpretation – The Nuremberg Trial*, (University Ottawa Press 1998)

Heydecker, J. J.; Leeb, J., *The Nuremberg Trials*, (William Heinemann Ltd 1962)

Hooley, Paul, *One Foot in the Grave: In Search of My Grandfather*, (Paul Hooley 2006)

Horvitz, Leslie Alan; Catherwood, Christopher, *Encyclopaedia of War Crimes and Genocide* (Infobase Publishing)

Lang, Jochan von, *The Secretary. Martin Bormann: The Man Who Manipulated Hitler* (Random House 1979)

Loriega, James, *The OSS Combat Manual* (Lulu.com 2019)

Mosley, Leonard, *The Reich Marshal: A Biography of Hermann Goering*, (Dell Publishing Co., Inc 1974)

Neave, Airey, Nuremberg: *A Personal Record of the Trial of Major Nazi War Criminals in 1945–6*, (Hodder & Stoughton 1978)

Neave, Airey, *Little Cyclone: The Girl Who Started the Comet Line*, (Biteback Publishing 2013)

Neave, Airey, *Saturday at M.I.9*, (Coronet Books – Hodder & Stoughton, 1971)

Persico, Joseph E., *Nuremberg – Infamy on Trial*, (Penguin Books 1994)

Clutton-Brock, Oliver, RAF Evaders (Grub Street Publishing 2009)

Routledge, Paul, *Public Servant, Secret Agent –The Elusive Life and Violent Death of Airey Neave*, (4th Estate 2002)

Read, Anthony, *The Devil's Disciples*, (W. W. Norton & Company 2003)

Secret Intelligence Field Manual – Strategic Services (Provisional), (Office of Strategic Services, 22 March 1944)

Shakespeare, William, *Richard III*, Act One, Scene Two

Speer, Albert, *Inside the Third Reich: Memoirs*, (Orion Books 1970)

Stansfield, Turner, *Burn Before Reading: Presidents, CIA Directors, and Secret Intelligence*, (Hatchett UK)

Swearingen, Ben E., *The Mystery of Hermann Goering's Suicide*, (Robert Hale 1990)

Taylor, Telford, *The Anatomy of the Nuremberg Trials: A Personal Memoir*, (Skyhorse Publishing 2013)

Tusa, Ann and John, *The Nuremberg Trial*, (Skyhorse Publishing 2010)

Wallace, Robert, *Spycraft* (Penguin/Random House)

Waller, Douglas, *Wild Bill Donovan*, (Free Press 2011)

OTHER PUBLICATIONS & ON-LINE SOURCES

Any websites shown were active and available at the time of going to press.

Airey Neave Trust: https://www.aireyneavetrust.org.uk

Alliance Review, The, Minerva, Harry Shotwell interview given to Thomas Clapper, 26 January 2018: https://eu.the-review.com/story/news/2018/01/26/world-war-ii-veteran-harry/15364896007/

Avalon Project, The – *Judgment of International Military Tribunal on Hermann Goering: biography.com/military-figures/hannibal*

American Bar Journal, October 1949

Boston Globe, The, 19 November 2001

Bureau of Naval Personnel, *Information Bulletin No. 361* (March 1947)

Canton Repository, recorded interview: *Harry Shotwell Recalls a Day with Nazi Hermann Goering and "Wild Bill" Donovan:* https://omny.fm/shows/rep-audio-vault/harry-shotwell-recalls-a-day-with-nazi-hermann-goe

BBC On-line Biography – biography.com/military-figures/hannibal

BBC Online: http://news.bbc.co.uk/1/hi/world/americas/4247069.stm

BBC Online: http://news.bbc.co.uk/1/mobile/uk/8085383.stm

Bibliography of Adolf Hitler: f https://en.wikipedia.org/wiki/Bibliography_of_Adolf_Hitler

Boston Globe, The, 19 November 2001

Bulletin of the Atomic Scientists, Volume 8, Number 8, November, 1952

CIA: *Profiles in Leadership 1941–2023*

Columbia College Web Site: https://www.college.columbia.edu/cct/issue/summer20/article/swashbuckling-lawyer-who-was-ultimate-spy

Columbia University Oral History Research Office, *The Reminiscences of Robert H. Jackson, 1955.*

Columbia University Web Site: https://c250.columbia.edu/c250_celebrates/remarkable_columbians/telford_taylor.html

Cornell University Library – *Memorandum from Colonel Telford Taylor to General Donovan and others*, 26 November 1945

Cornell University Library – *Memorandum of Interview Between General Donovan and the Defendant Goering*, November 15, 1945

Council on Foreign Relations: https://www.cfr.org/about

Council on Foreign Relations Membership: https://tomjefferson1976.wordpress.com/2013/08/07/council-on-foreign-relations-membership-chart/

Courtroom 600: https://courtroom600.org/ (see also Appendix H)

Defense Media Network: https://www.defensemedianetwork.com/stories/the-oss-society-keepers-of-gen-donovans-flame/

Der Spiegel, 2/59

Der Spiegel, 5 December 1949

Deutsche Welle (DW) – Germany's international broadcaster – https://www.dw.com/en/daddy-was-a-man-of-honor-daughter-of-nazi-ss-officer-insists/a-51853837

Dorset Echo, The

Eisenhower Library, *Will of Adolf Hitler*: https://www.eisenhowerlibrary.gov/sites/default/files/research/online-documents/holocaust/hitler-marriage-will-political-testament.pdf

Evening Star, The (Washington), 16 October 1946

Felton, Mark, *Hermann Göring's Mysterious Death* – https://www.youtube.com/watch?v=2IMhFW7539s

Freeman, R. Austin, *The Art of the Detective Story*: http://gaslight-lit.s3-website.ca-central-1.amazonaws.com/gaslight/detcritF.htm

Friends of the Air Force Academy Library: www.usafalibrary.com/collections_pages/andrus_collection.html

Gazette, The

Georgetown University, OSS Oral History Project: *Tim Naftali Interview with Edwin Putzell*, 11 April 1997

Goering, Hermann, *Closing Statement at the IMT*: https://avalon.law.yale.edu/imt/suppb_part1_chap_03.asp

Greater Naples Leadership: https://www.gnlwebsite.org/gnl-distinguished-leadership-award/

Guardian, The, 3 October 2006

Hansard – 20 August 1940

Hansard – Lords Tributes to Airey Neave, 2 April 1979

Harry S. Truman Library & Museum, *Letter from Robert Jackson to William Donovan*, 26 November 1945

Harry S. Truman Library & Museum, *Letter from William Donovan to Robert Jackson*, 27 November 1945

Harvard Law Today: https://today.law.harvard.edu/in-memoriam-summer-2004-bulletin/

Harvard Crimson, The: https://www.thecrimson.com/article/2011/4/21/war-oss-donovan-world/

History Link (Andrus): https://www.historylink.org/File/11046

Holocaust Historical Society: www.holocausthistoricalsociety.org.uk/contents/germanbiographies/erichvondembachzelewski.html

IMT Nuremberg Archives, Stamford University H-3338

Independent, The, 25 May 1988: https://www.independent.co.uk/news/obituaries/obituary-telford-taylor-1157311.html

Jackson, Robert H., *Closing Arguments for Conviction of Nazi War Criminals*, (Robert H. Jackson Center, December 26, 1946, *Temple Law Quarterly*)

Jackson, Robert H., *Nuremberg in Retrospect, American Bar Journal*, October 1949

Jackson, Robert H., *Opening Arguments for Conviction of Nazi War Criminals*, (Robert H. Jackson Center)

Jackson, Robert, The Reminiscences of, Columbia University Oral History Research Office, 1955

John Ford Filmography: www.johnfordfilms.com/filmography

Justice Jackson's Story, transcript of tape recording taken by Harlan B. Phillips, Oral History Research Office, Columbia University, New York, N.Y., 1952–1953

King, Henry T., Jr., *The Nuremberg Context Through the Eyes of the Participant – Military Law Review*, 1995.

King, Henry T. Jr., *Robert H Jackson and the Triumph of Justice at Nuremberg*

London Gazette, The, 6 November 1942 (page 4866)

Los Angeles Times, 7 February 2005

Los Angeles Times, The

Margaret Thatcher Foundation – *Speech at Airey Neave's Memorial Service:* www.margaretthatcher.org/document/104085

Military Hall of Honor: https://militaryhallofhonor.com/honoree-record.php?id=70

Military Wikipedia: https://military-history.fandom.com/wiki/Suicide_pill

Monsanto Annual Report, 1970

Naftali, Tim, *Edwin Putzell Interview*, OSS Oral History History Project, Georgetown University, 11 April 1997

Naples Daily News, 25 December 2003

Naples NP Business Comments – Business Currents, Greater Naples Chamber of Commerce May 2007

Nation Magazine

National Archives (UK)

National Park Service: https://www.nps.gov/articles/a-wartime-organization-for-unconventional-warfare.htm

Neave, Airey, *Cognac for Judas** (National Archives)

Neave, Airey, *Goering's Suicide** (National Archives)

Neave, Airey, *Memorandum to the General Secretary of the International Military Tribunal*, 24th October 1945 (National Archives)

New York Times, The – Goering Selects Counsel, 1 November 1945

New York Herald Tribune

Oregonian, The, 23 September 1970

OSS Society, The: osssociety.org

OSS Society, The: osssociety.org/pdfs/donovan2007.pdf

Paul Fraser Collectibles: https://www.paulfrasercollectibles.com/blogs/medals-militaria/hermann-goerings-cyanide-pill-container-offered-in-munich?srsltid=AfmBOopB6am0Abymi1ulRSEGb3bqPnwnVDY6oJYW PKc-j0yXo_LbgF5c

Peerage, The

Pinck, Charles, (President of the OSS Society), *Remembering the Last Hero:* https://www.thecrimson.com/article/2011/4/21/war-oss-donovan-world/

Pinck, Charles, *Small Wars Journal:* https://smallwarsjournal.com/2022/03/05/glorious-ukrainian-resistance/

Reagan, President Ronald: *Remarks at a Dinner for Former Members of the OSS:* https://www.reaganlibrary.gov/archives/speech/remarks-dinner-former-members-office-strategic-services)

Reagan Presidential Library & Museum, The

Report of Board of Proceedings in Case of Hermann Goering (Suicide), October 1946

Robert H. Jackson Centre, *Bach-Zelewski II,* 7 January 1946.

Royal Fleet Auxiliary Association, The

Sarasota Observer, The, 2 June 1977

Shotwell, Harry, Recorded Interview: *Harry Shotwell Recalls a Day with Nazi Hermann Goering and "Wild Bill" Donovan* – https://omny.fm/shows/rep-audio-vault/harry-shotwell-recalls-a-day-with-nazi-hermann-goe

Schulberg Productions, *Nuremberg: Its Lesson for Today:* www.nurembergfilm.org/old/press/Nuremberg_Theatrical_Press_Kit.pdf

Small Wars Journal: https://smallwarsjournal.com/2022/03/05/glorious-ukrainian-resistance/

Special Operations Executive: Personnel Files (PF Series, (UK) National Archives

Spectator, The, 1 February 2003

Steel magazine, 31 December 1948

St. Louis Post-Dispatch, The, 16 October 1946

Taylor, Colonel Telford, *Memorandum to General Donovan and others,* 26 November 1945, Cornell University Library

Taylor, Major General Telford, *Testimonial written in support of Wolfe Frank*

Temple Quarterly (1946–7): Justice Jackson's Final Report to the President Concerning the Nuremberg War Crimes

Time, 28 October 1946 – *Down Without Tears:* https://time.com/archive/6606341/international-down-without-tears/

Time, 29 October 1945 – *The Defendants:* https://time.com/archive/6772741/germany-the-defendants/

Traces of War: https://www.tracesofwar.com/persons/112304/Andrus-Burton-Curtis.htm

Trial of the Major War Criminals before the International Military Tribunal. Volume II, Robert H. Jackson Center

US Army Official Web Site

US Holocaust Museum (film): *Telford Taylor During Justice Case*

US Holocaust Memorial Museum

US Library of Congress, Edwin J. Putzell, Jr., Interview 12 March 2003 with Mary Jane Robinson: https://memory.loc.gov/diglib/vhp-stories/loc.natlib.afc2001001.08441/

US National Archives – *Memo from 'Dr Stahmer [Goering's Lawyer]* 15 November 1945

US National Archives, *OSS Project: General Donovan's Files*

US National Library of Medicine, *"A Profound, Abiding Hatred": An Analysis of Hermann Goering's Alleged Morphine Addiction:* https://pmc.ncbi.nlm.nih.gov/articles/PMC10144812/

US National Park Service: https://www.nps.gov/articles/a-wartime-organization-for-unconventional-warfare.htm

US Naval Institute

US Senate, *Congressional Record,* 8 June 1971, p 18802

US Senate, *Congressional Record,* 16 June 1953, p 404

Vanity Fair, 3 March 2011, *Spymaster General: The adventures of Wild Bill Donovan and the 'Oh So Social' O.S.S.,* Evan Thomas

Variety, 7 September 1977, p 80

Vinciguerra, Thomas, *The Swashbuckling Lawyer Who Was the Ultimate Spy,* Columbia University: https://www.college.columbia.edu/cct/issue/summer20

Waller, Douglas: www.historynet.com/interview-with-wild-bill-donovan-biographer-douglas-waller/

Washington Evening Star, The, 2nd April 1951

Westbury Democrat, The, 16 October 1945

Work, Captain E., The *Condemnation of Goering by Hanna Reitsch – 16 November 1945* (US National Archives)

Zuck, Lila, *He Wore Many Hats,* City of Naples: www.naplescentennial.com/untold-stories/he-wore-many-hats/

* These two documents were, at the time of going to press, in the process of being transferred from Parliamentary Archives to National Archives. The Parliamentary Archives Reference for both documents was 'Papers of Airey Middleton Sheffield Neave (1916–1979) GB-061 Catalogue Reference: AN/660' – this reference is likely to change once Parliamentary Archives are incorporated into National Archives.

INDEX

ABOUT THE AUTHOR

Paul Hooley was born and educated in Surrey. He founded a design and printing company that grew to be ranked amongst the industry's top 1 percent. He has also been a director of a building society, a private hospital and companies involved in advertising, publishing, entertainment, finance, building, transport, property and engineering.

He retired from business in 1990, since when he has devoted much of his time to studying, writing and lecturing on a wide range of historical and military subjects.

A former town and district councillor, he was Mayor of Bedford in 1978. Among other involvements he has been a magistrate, a tax commissioner, a governor of many LEA and private schools and a prison visitor.

Until her sad passing in 2023, he had been married to Helen (née Richardson) for almost sixty years. He has three children and now lives in Dorset. He was appointed to be a Member of the Most Excellent Order of the British Empire (MBE) in 2003.

Weather Forecast

Sunny, mild; highest in low 70s this afternoon. Clear, warmer tonight; lowest about 47. Tomorrow mostly sunny, mild.

Temperatures today—High, 68, at 1:16 p.m.; low, 43, at 6:36 a.m. Yesterday—High, 68, at 1:28 p.m.; low, 42, at 6:24 a.m.

Full Report on Page A-15.

Late New York Markets, Page A-23.

The Eve

WITH SUNDAY

94th YEAR. No. 37,419   Phone NA. 5000.   WASHINGTON, D. C., WEDNESDAY

Goering Suicide Probed by Army
As Bodies of 11 Nazi Chieftain
Are Taken to Nameless Grave

Ribbentrop Is First In Machine-Like March to Gallows

By Thomas A. Reedy
Associated Press Foreign Correspondent

NUERNBERG, Oct. 16.—Hermann Goering, who ended his life mysteriously in the agony of poison, and 10 other top Nazis who died on a hangman's rope were taken to nameless graves on this bleak, cold morning in final expiation for the colossal crimes of Germany.

Grim and manacled because in some unexplained fashion Goering had been able to escape the ignominy of the gallows, Joachim von Ribbentrop started the death march and plunged to eternity at 1:16 a.m. (7:14 p.m., Tuesday, EST).

Arthur Seyss-Inquart was dead at 2:57 a.m., just an hour and 43 minutes after the once dapper German Foreign Minister had pulled taut the 13 coils of the noose placed by M/Sergt. John C. Wood of the United States Army.

Two Scaffolds Used.

The eight others climbed the 13 black steps one by one, dying alternately on a twin gallows set up to speed the grisly task ordered by the International Military Tribunal of the United States, Russia, Great Britain and France.

Goering, even by his death less than two hours before the execution, did not escape the shadow of the gallows.

While Seyss-Inquart and Col. Gen. Jodl still were twitching with the last faint sparks of life, the body of Goering was brought in on a stretcher and placed between the gallowses in symbolic execution.

In death, he had robbed his 10 fellows of another 10 minutes of life, for it took about that time for each to expire and Goering was to have been the first.

No Statement by Rosenberg.

The 10 others died stoically, plunging into an inclosed trap that hid their death pangs from the eight newspaper correspondents and 30 other witnesses. None collapsed. All but Alfred Rosenberg made brief statements, the main theme of which were "Long live Germany." Most endeavored to show bravery.

Hitler's Top Aide Gulps Poison As He Waits to Mount Gallows

Corpse Is Laid Between Two Scaffolds in Execution Room After Revival Efforts Fail

By Kingsbury Smith
Representing the Combined American Press

NUERNBERG, Oct. 16.—The doors of a small gymnasium in the Nuernberg Jail courtyard through which the living had come, opened early this morning and a dead man came in—a grotesque, self-destroyed remnant of a man who once had been destined to rule Nazi Germany.

It was that of Hermann Wilhelm Goering, who committed suicide by taking poison a short while before he was to have led 10 of his henchmen to the gallows.

And it was inevitably and inescapably a dramatic moment in the course of history.

The execution chamber and a handful of witnesses were waiting for Col. Gen. Alfred Jodl and Arthur Seyss-Inquart, the last of the Nazi prisoners to be pronounced dead at the bottom end of their tightly stretched hang-ropes.

Two Army chaplains stood half turned toward the gallows and the black canvas curtain at the far end of the room, behind which rested the remains of eight other political and military chieftains of the most terrible despotism the world has witnessed since mediaeval times.

The chaplains were reading from their prayer books.

Suddenly the doors opened and the body of what was once the great marshal of the Reich, chief of the Luftwaffe and bearer of a dozen other titles was brought in.

He had succeeded in wrecking plans of the Allied Control Council to have him lead the parade of condemned Nazi chieftains to death on the gallows.

But the Council's representatives were determined that Goering at least would take his place as a dead man beneath the shadow of the scaffold.

Guards carrying the stretcher that bore his body set it down between the first and second gallows.

Goering's big bare feet stuck out from under the bottom end of an ordinary khaki-colored United States Army blanket. One blue silk-pajamaed arm was hanging over the side.

The colonel in charge of the proceedings ordered the blanket removed so that witnesses and Allied correspondents could see that Goering was definitely dead. The Army did not want any legend to develop that Goering had managed to escape.

As the blanket came off it revealed Goering clad in black silk pajamas with a blue jacket shirt over them, and this was soaking wet, apparently the result of efforts by prison doctors to revive him.

The face of this 20th Century freebooting political racketeer was still contorted with the pain of his last agonizing moments and his final gesture of defiance.

They covered him up quickly and this Nazi war lord, who like a character out of the days of the Borgias had wallowed in blood and beauty, passed behind a canvas curtain into the black pages of history that mark the end of the Hitler era.

Joachim von Ribbentrop took

(See SMITH, Page A-4.)

Chaplain Believe He Carried Poison After His Captu

By the Associated Press

NUERNBERG, Oct. 16.—Prison Chaplain H. F. Gerecke said today he believed that Hermann Goering had carried the poison with which he committed suicide at the 11th hour last night, from the time he was captured.

The St. Louis churchman talked to Goering every day for four months. The former reich marshal died in an agonized suicide less than two hours before the 10 other top Nazis.

The puzzle was: How did Goering, guarded night and day for a year and a half and repeatedly searched, get the poison—and from whom?

To give an official answer to this question an anonymous investigating board of three was appointed today—headed by a "disinterested" United States Army officer, Richard McConnell of Army public relations said.

Col. McConnell said no arrests had been made and none were contemplated immediately.

Trained in Concealing Poison

The chaplain's theory was backed by members of the prison security detail, who said senior officers had been trained in concealing deadly poison.

The fact remained, however, that the principal war criminal had been searched 100 times in the Nuernberg jail and had, in

Mrs. Goering Denies Smuggling Poison To Husband in Jail

By the Associated Press

NEW YORK, Oct. 16.—Emmy Goering broke down and sobbed today when she was told her husband, Hermann Goering, cheated the gallows by swallowing poison, Ed Haaker of NBC said in a Nuernberg broadcast.

Mr. Haaker said Mrs. Goering denied she had smuggled the deadly capsule to her husband during her last visit to the prison.

Byrnes, Flying Home, Plans Radio Report On Parley Friday

Secretary and Wife Leave

Hurley and Chavez Spearhead Bitter New Mexico Campaign

Close Race Shapes Up

ing Star

An Associated Press Newspaper

OBER 16, 1946—FIFTY-TWO PAGES. ★★★ City Home Delivery, Daily and Sunday 90c a Month. When 5 Sundays, $1.00 **5 CENTS**

Hey Diddle Diddle . . . !

CattleHit$35.25; Records Broken In Wild Market

Flood of Livestock Fails to Satisfy Demand for Meat

By the Associated Press

Livestock traders smashed the highest cattle prices on record to smithereens in Chicago today in one of the wildest sessions the stockyards ever saw. They forced hog prices up to the new record established yesterday and indicated yesterday's record price on lambs would be well broken before the day's trading ended.

From all over the Nation came reports of much higher receipts of livestock than were anticipated overnight. Despite the increasing flood of truck-borne herds to terminal markets the demand was still much greater than the supply.

In consequence fed steers at Chicago hit $35.25 a hundred pounds, far above the $30.25 record set August 30. Hogs again sold at $27.50, the new peak reached yesterday, although later sales weakened to around $26 as buyers could not find facilities to move out their purchases. Lambs were being held for higher than the best bid price of $26.50, compared with the record set yesterday at $25.

Large Run in Cincinnati.

In Cincinnati a total of 6,500 hogs hit the market—the largest run since last January 1, when 7,000 were recorded.

Early bids indicated the top price would fall below yesterday's. Top prices in the early rounds reached $25.

Cattle prices were firm, with an early top of $25.50, showing a 50-cent increase over yesterday.

In Kansas City, producers sent cattle and hogs to market in such volume early today that police were called to direct traffic in the livestock district and trucks jammed streets. The same situation existed in Omaha.

The first day after the lifting of controls saw the Nation generally still on short meat rations and prices—where supplies had reached the retail markets—substantially above OPA ceilings.

Trucks Choke Highways.

Highways leading to Kansas City from all directions were choked with trucks loaded with livestock.

Unloading was delayed by a shortage of help at the stockyards where a gateman estimated 9,000 to 12,000 cattle and 3,000 hogs had been received before dawn. Policeman Foster Thornhill reported that at one time trucks were lined up for 15 blocks.

R Support Added Women Rally to rage Plebiscite

rs. Talmadge Voices ferendum Approval Flag Ceremony

men are swinging to support of the election day plebiscite for District suffrage, with ise of turning out a tremenfeminine vote on Novem-

st group to urge Washington to go to the ballot boxes National Society of Daughof the American Revolution, housands of members throughe United States.

Julius Y. Talmadge, presineral of the DAR, voiced her ral of the referendum in a tic ceremony as she accepted American Flag for Memorial ental Hall.

District Poultry Prices Drop 2-6 Cents as Meat Is Expected

Decline in Costs of Cheese, Butter and Eggs Also Seen When More Beef Arrives in City

Poultry prices dropped 2 to 6 cents a pound today, going counter to the soaring prices for red meat.

Wholesale poultry dealers say people are fed up with poultry, and the hope of getting beef and other red meats has led them to turn their backs on the poultry counters.

Meanwhile, officials of packing house branches here say the dribble of red meat which has been reaching the District should turn into a fairly good trickle by the end of the week. This opinion was supported by Joseph B. Danzansky, counsel for the meat division of the Merchants and Manufacturers Association.

Concerning poultry prices, the Agriculture Department's market report today said roasting, frying and broiling chickens sold at 53 to 55 cents a pound today. Yesterday the price was 58 to 61 cents. Stewing

salers pays for dressed poultry. He gets 1 to 3 cents more from the retailer and the retailer gets an additional 7 or 8 cents a pound.

One wholesaler said he was staying out of the poultry market entirely in the belief the market will continue to drop. Some dealers predicted a decrease of as much as 20 cents a pound on some poultry grades within the next month if red meat arrives in good supply.

One poultry house spokesman said he expected eggs to sell much lower in a week or two. The present retail price is as much as 89 cents a dozen. Today's Agriculture Department's market report, however, noted little change in price and said the egg market was steady and firm.

Slackening in the demand for poultry market will benefit the egg supply. Laying flocks have been depleted by the sale of hens in the